Turncoats &True Believers

Turncoats & True Believers

The Dynamics

of Political Belief

and Disillusionment

Ted Goertzel

Prometheus Books • Buffalo, New York

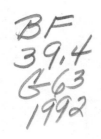

96 95 94 93 92   5 4 3 2 1

Goertzel, Ted George.
     Turncoats and true believers : the dynamics of political belief and disillusionment / Ted Goertzel.
          p.   cm.
     Includes bibliographical references and index.
     ISBN 0-87975-755-8 (acid-free paper)
     1. Psychology—Biographical methods. 2. Ideology—Psychological aspects. 3. Alienation (Social psychology). 4. Political psychology. I. Title.
BF39.4.G63   1992
320'.01'9—dc20   92–11253
                                                              CIP

Printed in the United States of America on acid-free paper.

For my parents,
whose devotion to reconciling commitment and skepticism
inspired this book.

Contents

Foreword

By Dennis Wrong

Loss of belief in political and social ideologies has been a common phenomenon in the twentieth century. This loss has often been metaphorically —or not so metaphorically—expressed in religious language: *The God That Failed, The Naked God,* and *Witness* are all titles of well-known books describing their authors' experiences of disillusionment. The disillusioned have been called "apostates" and "heretics," which are clearly labels of theological origin, but also "turncoats"—Ted Goertzel's chosen label—and "renegades," terms drawn from military and political conflict. Politics directly implies conflict, the effort to impose a policy or program upon the world against the opposition of those with rival programs; religion does not (or at least need not), although proselytizing religions have often made use of military metaphors—"soldiers of the Cross," "the Church Militant," "Jihad," and the like. Still, religious faith need not in itself imply active struggle with nonbelievers. Secular political ideologies, in contrast, emphatically do. This suggests an important difference in what is involved in *loss of belief,* despite the undeniable similarities between religious and political allegiance.

We need to explore the forms and origins of political faith and apostasy, and Ted Goertzel's book is an important contribution to this task. His concept of *ideological scripts* makes a valauable beginning, and, further, he suggests their psychoanalytic underpinnings. The range of twentieth-century movements that Goertzel covers, through numerous biographies of twentieth-century prophets, revolutionaries, true believers, and skeptics, while illustrating his scripts is truly impressive.

The story of his own political journey, interwoven with that of his friend Al Szymanski, lends a focus to the book, which is particularly vivid

and poignant in light of Szymanski's eventual suicide. As a fellow academic
sociologist I had met and seen them in action, disapprovingly on the whole,
at the various conventions of the American Sociological Association that
figure in Goertzel's account.

Goertzel's candor in telling his story imposes a similar obligation, I
believe, on the author of a foreword to his book, an obligation to make
clear just where one is "coming from" politically. My father was an official
of the Canadian foreign service, skeptical of any and all ideologies, an
adherent to the rather hard-headed *realpolitik* approach to international
relations, which tends to be the occupational credo of the professional
diplomat, a credo that is lucidly articulated in the early books of George
Kennan (for whom I once worked as a research assistant in Princeton).
My father was neither a hawk nor a dove in terms of Goertzel's scripts,
more probably a skeptic, but in his early twenties he was a junior officer
in the British Army and saw action on the Somme, where his older brother
and a first cousin to whom he was very close had been killed a few weeks
earlier. This experience undoubtedly led him a decade later to give up
an academic career for the foreign service in the vain hope of avoiding
another world war, assuring that Hitler would be defeated when that war
came about, and then avoiding, in relation to Stalin and the Soviet Union,
the disastrous diplomacy that had preceded the Second World War. My
father's attitude toward these momentous events certainly shaped my own
far more than I would ever have admitted during my teens and twenties.
I also recall my mother's intense indignation over the Munich agreement,
concerning which my father was obliged to maintain a discreet silence.
I am closer to Goertzel, who acknowledges the influence of his father's
skepticism, than to Szymanski, who remained an all-out rebel against his
father.

I decided I was a socialist when I was a teenage boarder at an elite
prep school as a result of reading books and pamphlets by such British
authors as Laski, Wells, Strachey, and Cole. I went on to read at least
the best-known texts of Marx, Engels, Lenin, and Trotsky. I was converted
intellectually, but I was also in conscious rebellion against the philistine
athleticism of my prep-school environment and nostalgic for the
"progressive" International School created by League of Nations officials
for their children, which I had attended in Geneva during my early teens.
Come to think of it, one of the French students at that school became
a leader of the French Communist Party; three of the Spanish students
were sons of the President of the Spanish Republic, its Foreign Minister,
and its Ambassador to London, one of them later becoming a leader in
exile of the Spanish Communist Party during the Franco years; the German
students, children of prosperous Jews sent to school in Geneva to get

them out of Nazi Germany, included the niece of a famous left-wing novelist; and my closest American friends were the sons of New York and Hollywood Jewish businessmen and professionals, one of them the younger brother of a promising novelist who was an active early Communist in the movie colony, another the grandson of one of the founders of the American Socialist Party. Clearly, I had lived in a predominantly left-wing political environment and undoubtedly had absorbed a good deal from it by osmosis before I ever became consciously interested in politics.

Wartime Canada was perhaps not the most promising place for radical political activism, and I certainly never centered my life around it to anything like the degree that Goertzel and Szymanski did in the sixties. I did, while a student at the University of Toronto, actively campaign for the Canadian socialist party (CCF), ancestor of the present New Democratic Party, which began to make headway during the war. In my senior year, I was president of the campus CCF club. A commitment to the "left" and to socialism was certainly an important part of my identity. Accordingly, I did not go to the arts college attended by nearly all of my prep-school classmates, but enrolled in the largest arts college, which was the university's public and nondenominational college with a student body that was one-third Jewish, from whose ranks most of my friends were drawn. I sacrificed my declared principles to the extent of joining a fraternity to which friends from prep school belonged. In my third year, however, I resigned along with two others in protest against the refusal to admit a black student from the Caribbean who had already undergone the grueling initiation hazing. (One highly visible alumnus allegedly objected, "You'll be pledging Jews next!") Also, in majoring in sociology, I had deliberately chosen a disreputable field, vaguely associated with socialism, that was particularly attractive to Jewish students.

In my senior year, during the last few months of the war, I became strongly anti-Communist, largely as a result of reading Arthur Koestler and *Partisan Review* and more directly because of the efforts of the Canadian Communists either to join the CCF in a new popular front or to undermine the party, which had high hopes in the brave new postwar world. This turned out to be a most consequential political choice, for when I went to graduate school at Columbia in the autumn after the end of the war, I instantly gravitated to the circles of anti-Stalinist left intellectuals. New York City was one of the very few places where the anti-Stalinist left was a real presence, though not by any means, as is sometimes anachronistically contended today, the dominating influence on the cultural and intellectual life of the city. Nor, for that matter, is it the case that all or even most of the anti-Communist liberal-left intellectuals became neoconservatives in the 1970s. Slightly under half of them did, the rest remaining somewhere on what the British call "the broad left," though never abandoning their anti-Communism or their qualified support for the Cold War. This was more or less my position for nearly forty years. It in no way ruled out opposition to many American Cold War policies, especially in the Third World, most notably to the Vietnam War, which, however, I always regarded as a mistake based on misjudgment rather than, according to the sixties protestors, an imperialistic crime. Although I knew where the neoconservatives were "coming from," I never forgot that the Cold War was initiated on our side by liberals and social democrats or that NATO was first proposed by Ernest Bevin and received strong initial support from the top Canadian foreign policy makers, including my father. I remained to the end an unregenerate "Cold War liberal," a term that was, I believe, coined with pejorative intent by my teacher C. Wright Mills.

Biographies of "turncoats and true believers" raise the question of who is the most or least likely to abandon a political faith, those who were born into it or those who embraced it in revolt against their background. Ted Goertzel was actually a third-generation "Red diaper baby," no less! Al Szymanski, on the other hand, was a rebel against his Polish Catholic working-class origins. Although I regarded my conversion to a politics of the left as rebellion against my upper-middle-class Anglo-Canadian background, my views on the Cold War were heavily influenced by my father's "presence at the creation"—as Dean Acheson titled his memoirs—as Canadian Ambassador to the United States during the Truman administration and my own experience as a research assistant to George Kennan, made possible through parental contacts. Goertzel's eventual rejection of radicalism was influenced by his father, he concedes, even though he came to it originally by inheritance, as it were.

On the whole I think that being born into the faith is more likely to ensure lifelong undeviating commitment to it. Turncoats who have rejected parental beliefs can always find their way back, though the psychological difficulty in conceding that "maybe papa and mama were right" is not to be underestimated. It may be that rebels, whether rebelling against a conventional conservative or radical background, are often more explosive, outspoken, and even flamboyant in their rebellion than those who are born to their political allegiances. Szymanski might be a case in point.

The collapse of Communism is one recent event that gives Goertzel's book a special timeliness. His closing remarks on the uncertain future of left ideologies are as cogent as any I have seen on the subject. They also highlight the difference between religious and political faiths, to revert in closing to my opening remarks. In contrast to religious commitment, socialism was a product of the Enlightenment representing a new and supposedly more rational way of organizing society—subject, therefore, to empirical test. Even if the Soviet Union was never the most propitious place in which to make the test, the fact that economic failure is primarily what did it in simply cannot be dodged by reducing socialism to a collection of lofty timeless ideals. These developments are what give Goertzel's inherently interesting book a special pathos and urgency.

Dennis Wrong
New York University

Acknowledgments

My most reliable and helpful support came from my wife Lillian Goertzel and my son, Benjamin Goertzel. Both took the time to read several drafts of each chapter and were honest enough to tell me when my biases were too blatant or when they detected gaps or flaws in the logic of the argument. Monica Deppen also read several of the chapters and offered many useful suggestions, particularly with regard to Bertrand Russell. Professor Jon Van Til at Rutgers-Camden gave me useful comments on the development of ideological scripts over the life cycle.

Paul Elovitz and the members of the Psychohistory Forum in New York City gave me constructive feedback on several parts of the book as well as a supportive reference group and many ideas about psychohistory in general. I also presented several parts of this project as papers at meetings of the International Psychohistorical Association and benefited greatly from their comments and their supportive tolerance of my sometimes dissenting role. Glen Wolfner, in particular, took the time to respond to several chapters. My ideas about the anti-Iraqi war movement were constructively received at a meeting of the International Society for Political Psychology in Helsinki, Finland. Ralph White and many of the other members proved remarkably open to ideas that challenged their basic assumptions.

My parents, Victor and Mildred Goertzel, provided much of the inspiration for the book as well as helpful feedback on the chapter drafts. The chapter on Linus Pauling is based largely on their research. I am also indebted to their friends Elise and Kenneth Boulding for criticism of the chapter on the doves, especially the material on Kenneth.

The chapter on Castro and Cuba was written during a National Endowment for the Humanities summer seminar led by Edward Friedman of the University of Wisconsin. In addition to criticizing the chapter, Friedman and the seminar participants provided many ideas on the psychology of leadership and the crisis of Leninism. I particularly benefited from the interchange with the participants who were defending Marxism from the assault of history.

My cousin Allen Hunter gave me some very useful suggestions on the first chapter. He also gave me some useful leads on the holocaust deniers.

An earlier version of the first chapter benefited greatly from a seminar in personal essay writing taught by Lisa Zeidner at Rutgers, Camden. I must thank her and the students in the seminar for helping me to break out of the straitjacket of turgid academic prose. Al Szymanski's mother, Verna, was kind enough to read the first chapter and to share her recollections of Al's childhood.

George Dolph gave me a useful orientation to the Libertarian movement and its relationship to the New Left. Albert Silverman gave me a similar orientation to the history of defectors from the Stalinist left. David Horowitz and the staff of the National Forum Foundation gave me a useful opportunity to meet a number of turncoats from the New Left, including Philip A. Luce.

Special thanks must go to the staff of the Rutgers-Camden library who have kept at the forefront of the information age with state-of-the-art electronic access to books and articles from university libraries across the nation. Elizabeth Hart of the library staff was always ready to get materials quickly and efficiently, as well as providing moral support with cheerful e-mail messages.

Also, I wish to thank Jeanne O'Day of Prometheus Books for a meticulous job of copy editing the manuscript, and especially for her suggestions and encouragement regarding the concluding chapter.

Chapter One

Confessions of a Turncoat and Remembrance of a True Believer

Every man, wherever he goes, is encompassed by a cloud of comforting convictions, which move with him like flies on a summer day.

—Bertrand Russell, *Sceptical Essays*

This book is about people whose convictions are not always comforting. Sometimes they turn vicious, stinging with a venom of anger and hatred. Sometimes they buzz around annoyingly, reminding the believer of doubts he would rather forget. Sometimes they fly further and further afield until he is caught without their comforting presence at a time of need. Sometimes new convictions spar piquedly with the old until he throws up his hands in disgust, hoping to drive them all away.

The inquiring reader will want to know what happened to the author's own cloud of convictions. I offer this chapter as a personal prologue in which I give my own life the same kind of scrutiny that I give to others. It differs from most autobiographical essays, however, because I contrast my life to that of a close friend whose life took a different path. Of course, our two lives have no particular historical importance, and the reader is welcome to skip this chapter or save it for later. Chapters two and five give the basic theoretical ideas that tie this book together. The remaining chapters can be read in any order without losing more than an occasional reference.

Recollections of a Turncoat

Quaker Childhood. My parents were Quaker pacifists who favored racial equality and opposed militarism before it was popular to do so. As a small child growing up in the Michigan suburbs, I returned from playing with the girl next door full of comments about "niggers." This was a decade before the civil rights movement, but my parents were quick to lecture me on the importance of racial equality. There were no Negroes in our neighborhood, but on a trip to downtown Detroit I had the opportunity to prove how well I'd learned the lesson, shouting out for everyone to hear, "Mommy, I just held the door open for a Negro!"

Having been born in pre-baby-boom 1942, when my pacifist father was not away in the army, I became aware of political issues in the late fifties, when the nation was emerging from McCarthyism and the positions my parents believed in were on the upswing. Racial segregation, nuclear fallout, and the Vietnam War were all problems the nation could have avoided if it had listened to the Quakers. When we moved to New Jersey, the committee to organize northern New Jersey's first peace march met in my living room. "Ted Goertzel, Montclair High School" appeared among the list of sponsors of the march, because the organizers hoped this might help them to reach out to the conformist youth of the fifties.

The march itself wasn't very exciting. We gathered a few miles from a Nike missile base on a cloudy Saturday morning and walked slowly carrying placards denouncing nuclear weapons and calling for peaceful negotiations with the Russians. Our group included a number of colorful individuals with long hair and disheveled clothing, as well as Quakers whose nonconformity was expressed only in their dissenting beliefs and their proclivity for giving public witness to them. No one took much notice of our march. The Nike base was inconveniently located in a remote area with little auto traffic and no pedestrians. The only press coverage was one small story in a local paper, which claimed that a passing motorist threw a dead skunk at us. I didn't see this happen, nor did I hear anyone mention it at the time. It seems an unlikely thing for a driver to happen to have in his car.

Montclair was a safe, middle-class suburb with big old houses, lots of trees, and young people who were generally well behaved. I had skipped a year in grade school and was shy and socially inept and had difficulty making friends. There were a few boys who occasionally picked on me after school, just as they picked on anyone who seemed vulnerable. I was thin and wore thick glasses. I generally avoided situations where I might get involved in fighting, more because I thought I'd get beaten up than out of any pacifist principles.

I remember one occasion, however, when I passed a group of boys who were hassling a boy whose slight frame and poor coordination were not compensated by any quickness of mind. I succumbed to the temptation to join in, making some remark about his slowness. The other boys were eager for a fight to establish who was on the bottom of the pecking order. He got his courage up to come over and shove me, but when I shoved him back he slinked away. One of his friends later told me that he weighed only ninety-eight pounds. I was glad to have won something and secretly wished he'd put up more of a fight. At the same time, I thought I should have been true to Quaker principles and returned violence with love.

The unfortunate fellow called the next night when the peace committee was meeting in our living room to plan the march. When I picked up the phone, he said, "Goertzel, you are going to die," and hung up. I put down the phone and let everyone assume it was a wrong number. When I later described my pugilistic predicament to my mother, she seemed pleased and expressed the opinion that pacifist principles didn't necessarily apply to the school yard. Her desire to see me protected from harm or unhappiness meant more than abstract ideals. My father was more self-critical and more true to pacifist principles in his personal life. The best I can say for myself is that I never bothered the boy again.

I was usually quick to expose the flaws in other people's logic, but I chose not to confront my mother on her lapses in ethical consistency. I never had a convincing answer to the question usually put to pacifists: "What would you do if someone broke into your house and threatened to kill your family?" I knew that there were circumstances when I felt justified in using violence. The people I talked with were unfortunately too polite to push me very far on these issues. When I raised them with my parents they just said that these were difficult questions and I should respect other people's views. Politeness is the bane of skepticism, allowing each person the comfort of his convictions, however bizarre, so long as he has the good taste not to question anyone else's. My mother's mother, an austere Indiana farmer's wife, had sent her daughter away to college with the admonition that she should never discuss politics or religion.

In the Quaker culture, silent witness is preferred to rational argumentation. If God speaks to us in the silence, who are we to question the messages He sends to us? I wasn't sure what God was and certainly hadn't thought through the implications of a mystical, nonrational theology. Without thinking it through, however, I had strongly internalized the norm that it was admirable to make a public witness of one's convictions. One day, I simply decided that it was wrong to recite the Lord's Prayer and pledge allegiance to the flag of the United States of America. My allegiance was to humanity, not to a particular nation, and certainly not to a God who made no discernable effort to use his infinite powers to stop wars and injustice. Without discussing the issue with my parents or anyone else, and even without giving it much thought, I simply declined one day to stand for the classroom ceremonies. The teacher asked what was wrong. When I told her I didn't believe in it, she sent me to the principal. When he heard that I was a Quaker, he contacted my parents and found that they had no objection to my behavior. He then wrote the teacher a note stating that "Ted has a long history of Quakerism in his family" and that I should be allowed my unusual beliefs as long as I showed my respect for others by standing at attention. I can't recall if anyone at school ever mentioned the event again.

Much the same thing happened when I refused to take cover during air-raid drills, which we pacifists opposed because they gave people the false impression that they could escape a nuclear bomb by hiding under a desk or running to the basement. The tolerant response of the good citizens of New Jersey to my radicalism didn't bother me. I wasn't ready for a serious confrontation with authorities or even with a persistent group of teenage bullies. Later on, when the civil rights and Vietnam issues heated up, I experienced much greater hostility from authorities and from the general public. I think my Montclair experiences had a lasting effect on me, though. I never really expected any serious consequences for my radicalism. My greatest concern was with being ignored.

A Parental Script. When I was in high school, I had no idea how closely my experiences paralleled my father's, almost as if our lives were following the same script. Much later, in 1981, a brief comment appeared in the *New Yorker,* describing events at Los Angeles's Roosevelt High School:

> In 1930 and 1931, there was a bit of a free speech fight at the school—involving suspensions, demonstrations, lawyers and some battling on the campus. Students with names like Goertzel, Handler, Goldstein, and Schatz were being punished for accusing the school newspaper of "anti-working-class" and anti-Soviet attitudes and for refusing to salute the flag.[1]

The "Goertzel" in the story was my father, Victor, and the "Handler" was his step-sister, my Aunt Aida. The official school paper had written an editorial that Victor thought was an attack on the Soviet Union. When it refused to publish his reply, his radical youth group printed it and distributed it as a leaflet. Principal Thomas Elson professed to be a civil libertarian. He displayed the motto, "I disapprove of what you say, but I will defend to the death your right to say it," prominently on his office wall. Nevertheless, he suspended Victor, Aida, and several others, claiming that their "decidedly disloyal utterances" were impudent and revealed an attitude problem. Victor appealed to the motto on his wall, but to no avail. When they refused to recant after a few weeks suspension, Victor was expelled shortly before he was scheduled to graduate in the middle of the year. Despite these facts, Principal Elson insisted that "no one has ever been expelled from Roosevelt high school for radical views," only for "insolence and unpatriotic utterances."[2]

Victor wasn't upset about being expelled since he hadn't planned to go to college anyway and hadn't taken the college preparatory curriculum. He planned to be a factory worker, union organizer, and Communist Party functionary. After one day in an orange products factory, he abandoned this life plan. He learned his job in a few minutes and was bored before an hour was up. After loafing a few months, he decided to go back to school, and the Los Angeles Board of Education was quite willing to transfer his records to suburban Downey Union High School, which graduated him when the term ended.

My father inherited his Communism from his father, Sam, who grew up in Vilnius, Lithuania. One day Sam and a friend were playing by the river, and his friend fell in. Sam tried to save him but had to let go because the current was too strong. His friend's parents blamed him, and he had to leave the Jewish religious school and enter the Russian secular school. This experience may account for the fact that he became alienated from religious Judaism and was the only one of his brothers and sisters to become a lifelong believer in Communism.

Victor grew up in a community of leftist Jewish immigrants in Los Angeles and in New York and joined the Young Pioneers, a youth group sponsored by the Communist Party. The Pioneers was the "in group" whose respect he valued, and at the time he thought he had influenced his father to become a Communist, never realizing that Sam had been a Bolshevik in Lithuania. He was raised by his father because his mother, Anna, had never wanted to have children. She reluctantly cancelled her appointment with the abortionist when her young husband thought he was dying from an accidental gunshot wound and begged her not to flush his only descendent down the toilet. When they divorced she didn't contest custody. Anna was also a sympathizer with the Bolshevik revolution and even went to live in Russia for a while. Victor recalls that when he went for his driver's license examination, she asked whether he had given the examiner five dollars. When he insisted this wasn't necessary, she remarked that even in the Soviet Union you always had to bribe officials. This was, so far as Victor can recall, the only negative remark she ever made about Soviet society, although she voted with her feet by returning to live in New York.

Victor recalls demonstrating against the execution of Sacco and Vanzetti in Union Square in New York and feeling a rush of pride when he saw the hammer and sickle displayed on an issue of *Current History* on the occasion of the tenth anniversary of the Bolshevik revolution. He became restless with the Young Pioneers as an organization because it was too authoritarian. He was once called before the Central Control Committee in Los Angeles for the offense of playing tennis with a Lovestoneite, a member of a dissident faction within the party. His politics were not questioned, but he was not permitted to have social relations with "renegades." He joined the Young Communist League after he graduated from high school but became disillusioned with the trials of Communist leaders in Moscow. He couldn't believe that all the old Bolsheviks but Stalin were traitors. Even more central to his defection was his belief that the Communists were supporting the fascists in Germany on the theory that the workers would become class-conscious only if things got worse. He objected to being told to break up Socialist Party meetings in Los Angeles. He would gladly break up fascist meetings, but the socialists were well meaning, if naive.

My mother, Mildred George, was an Indiana farm girl who worked her way through Ball State Teachers' College in Muncie. Her parents weren't political, but her mother was supportive of Mildred's attempt to live a liberated lifestyle to the extent of urging her not to "waste all that education" by getting married. By the time they met in Chicago, Mildred was an orthodox socialist, while Victor was part of a Trotskyist faction that was engineering a "united front from below." They decided they were just canceling out each other's votes and dropped out of the socialist movement.

Victor had a problem with stuttering and had come to Chicago to seek the help of a nationally renowned expert on relaxation techniques, Edmund Jacobson, M.D., author of the books *Progressive Relaxation* and *You Must Relax*. The Indiana farm girl he'd just met, whose maternal instincts may have been revived by concern about her advancing biological clock, thought that unresolved feelings of rejection by his mother might be to blame. She tried holding his head on her lap and reading him nursery rhymes. The stuttering rapidly came under control, and they married, abandoning both of their jobs in the midst of the Depression to take off on an extended honeymoon in Mexico. There they met Babette Newton, wife of the American Friends Peace Secretary Ray Newton. She informed Victor that Quakers were not just a historical group but still existed in the modern world. He found that the Quakers shared many of the ideas he had developed independently, especially the emphasis on nonviolence. A few days later my parents happened to meet Arthur Morgan, a prominent Quaker who had been the first chairman of the Tennessee Valley

Authority and President of Antioch College. Victor told Morgan, who he knew only as a "farmer from Ohio," all about Quakerism. Morgan listened patiently while Victor voiced his newfound enthusiasm, never revealing that he had heard about it before. They moved to Berkeley, California, and became lifelong Quakers.

At about this time, Victor read Aldous Huxley's book *Ends and Means,* which he still remembers as an important statement of the validity of the pacifist position. This was probably the source of the argument, which I heard Victor offer in various forms when I was young, that good ends cannot come from evil means. Huxley argues that military sanctions are "intrinsically bad and so incapable of producing any but bad results."[3] Today, I regard this as a metaphysical error, falsely assuming that the outcome of real world events can be predicted by analyzing the meaning of a word. On the basis of this argument, Victor was a conscientious objector during World War II.

College in the Sixties. Antioch College, which I entered in 1959 at age sixteen, was a distinctive and distinguished liberal arts college, full of "red diaper babies" and sensitive, serious students who wanted a change from high school.[4] My freshman roommate, Karl Grossman, was a spirited, outgoing, cocky Jewish New Yorker who had read up on populism and prairie socialism in preparation for his venture into the Midwest. He had great curiosity and was always looking for something interesting to observe and talk about. He found Ohio a bit tame and took to riding around the countryside on a motor scooter, which he parked outside the window of the dormitory. During the winter quarter, which we both spent at the Antioch Center in Guanajuato, Mexico, he impressed me with the amount of confidential information he had amassed about the program director's marital problems. Twenty-five years later, I learned that he had become an investigative reporter, publishing in the *Nation* and the *New York Times* op-ed page, as well as teaching journalism. In a questionnaire that I circulated to 128 members of my college class, he was one of only three who reported no change in their opinions on any of fourteen attitude items.

Each academic quarter, the fifty or so of us who were inclined toward activism organized political groups and tried to find some action we could take to make the world a better place. I joined the Antioch Committee for Racial Equality and was one of the agitators who urged for several quarters that we should follow the example of southern students and stage a sit-in at Gegner's Barber Shop. The barber shop was Yellow Springs's only segregated establishment. Mr. Gegner stubbornly refused to cut the hair of blacks, claiming his was a personal service, and in any event he hadn't been trained to cut that kind of hair. We secretly sent in a white student with tightly curled hair, and he cut it without objection. Numerous legal complaints were filed, one of which finally ended in a trial; Gegner was found guilty of discrimination and fined one dollar. I was part of the faction that insisted on direct action, much against the urging of the fatherly dean of students, John (Dudley) Dawson, who counseled moderation, and the local courts, which passed an injunction prohibiting all demonstrations within one hundred yards of Yellow Springs's main street. Yellow Springs was so small that the injunction covered the whole town, including the college.

We were joined by a large number of black students from Central State and Wilberforce Universities, and the police fired tear gas and packed us off to jail. Spending the night in the Greene County Jail was interesting mostly for the chance to meet the regular prisoners. My cell mate was in for buying too much cough syrup with codeine, and he thought the jail food was pretty good compared to other jails he'd known. I bailed myself out the next day, and the cases were never brought to trial, probably because the prosecutor knew the injunction would never hold up on appeal.

I met my first wife, Carol Zwell, at an Antioch political meeting. Shared political views were central to our relationship. She was also involved in the Gegner's sit-in and traveled with me and a number of Antioch students to Selma, Alabama, to participate in the Selma-to-Montgomery civil rights march. We also agreed on opposing American intervention in Vietnam. After living together for two quarters, Carol's absence from her dorm room, which she had to pay for, was detected by the college officials, and we decided that getting married was the logical solution to our housing problems. Our parents thought nineteen was too young to make such a commitment, and looking back from middle age I would have to agree. Even at the time, I felt a need to date other women, which probably had its origin in a deeper need to mature socially and develop self-confidence instead of relying on a woman to solve my problems. I believe there were repressed doubts hidden behind my certainty about both the marriage and my prescriptions for saving the world.

In my political involvements, I was never quite satisfied with the groups or organizations I joined, often criticizing them in a cynical tone. I had inherited a good bit of skepticism from my father, and I never expected my life to be transformed by a political event such as universal disarmament or socialist revolution. I remember a discussion with another activist who couldn't understand why I remained active in the movement when I didn't expect us to win, at least not any time soon. I was making a moral witness, not trying to win anything, through politics. This may explain why I continued through school to obtain a Ph.D. and a sinecure as a college professor instead of devoting my major effort to politics. It wasn't that I didn't want success, I just didn't expect to get it through politics. Instead of sacrificing my career, I let my neuroses play themselves out in my marriage.

My experiences strengthened my confidence that the political values I had inherited from my parents were sound and that I was right in using militant nonviolent tactics in expressing them. The supposedly wiser adults, such as Dean Dawson, were simply holding up the march of progress. This is a view that has been largely confirmed by history, at least with regard to the civil rights movement. I am not aware of anyone who has recanted and come out in favor of segregation. This self-confidence carried over into other issues, such as opposing the increasing American involvement in Vietnam or the blockade of Cuba during the missile crisis.

This cocky sense of being in the vanguard of history made me self-righteous and something of a purist. My Federal Bureau of Investigation file reports that Yellow Springs police chief James McGee told them I was "a very unreasonable type person." It doesn't say why he thought so. McGee was the only black police chief in Ohio at the time, and I thought we were on good terms.

The FBI files also recount the following incident at Washington University in St. Louis, where I went for graduate work:

TED GOERTZEL was present at a Students for a Democratic Society (SDS) meeting held at Washington University on October 29, 1965, and at this meeting interrupted a speaker who at the time had the floor and made the announcement that he had some literature to distribute. He was told by the chairman that he was out of order and could not distribute the literature until the speaker who had the floor was finished. GOERTZEL apparently lost his temper and threw the literature he had in his hand to the floor.

I can't remember what this incident was about, or imagine why it interested the FBI. It does say something about my tendency to be highly critical of other people and of organizations, including those to which I belonged. Political groups served as a place to meet people and have a sense of belonging. While I looked down on people who joined fraternities (we didn't even have them at Antioch), I now see some sense in meeting one's social needs by joining an organization openly dedicated to that purpose instead of one focused on a political cause. With my family background, however, that would have been difficult. When my younger brother, Penn, told our father he was thinking of joining a fraternity, Victor became so angry he threatened that he wouldn't contribute "a red cent" to Penn's education if he did so.

The fact that my social needs were met through political organizations led me to compromise my political convictions in order to maintain my friendships. I did this fairly easily since my politics was based more on intuition than on rigid logical arguments. The cautiously pacifist Student Peace Union (SPU), which I supported for several years, died out as activists shifted to the more radical Students for a Democratic Society. I followed the crowd, joining the Washington University chapter of SDS when my SPU chapter dissipated. We continued our weekly demonstrations against the war, occasionally driving through the night to a bigger demonstration in Washington. We ruffled the university administration's feathers by chanting on the sidewalk in front of the auditorium when Vice President Hubert Humphrey spoke on campus, but I never abandoned my liberal, civil libertarian principles by actively disrupting a speaker.

I reluctantly conceded that pacifism wouldn't have worked for the Jews in Germany or the Vietnamese revolutionaries, but I wasn't persuaded that bombing campus buildings in the United States was justified. Where to draw the line? While I waffled on these issues, the FBI decided that my actions did not show the "requisite intention to violate the sedition statutes" and took me off their active surveillance list.

When some committed themselves full-time to the movement, I was one of many who held back and maintained my status in graduate school. I found academic Marxism attractive as a social theory, but I couldn't identify with the Weathermen and Progressive Laborists, who were taking over SDS. They were going back to the ideas that my parents had already rejected, for good reasons, in the forties. My wife had a baby, who conveniently maintained my draft exemption, while I did dissertation research for two years in Brazil, finished my Ph.D., and got a job teaching sociology at the University of Oregon.

For the first few years at Oregon, the student movement was at its peak and radical faculty were much in demand as speakers and organizers. When Nixon invaded Cambodia in the spring of 1970, the university administration actually had to end classes early so the students could canvass against the war. Hundreds of students even attended a faculty meeting, which had to be held in the gymnasium, where I was cheered when I introduced a resolution that the faculty go on record opposing the "incursion" in Cambodia. I was still part of the vanguard, leading society into the future. The very next fall, however, the masses of students were tired of activism. I still remember the first freshman who told me proudly, "we are the quiet generation." Thus began my long slide from vanguard to rearguard.

Remembrance of a True Believer

Albert Szymanski. The 1969 meetings of the American Sociological Association were held in the sterile towers of the San Francisco Hilton. The meetings were particularly incongruous at the climax of the social upheavals of the sixties. While blacks rioted in the streets and students bombed draft boards, the sociologists hid in their dummy variables and multiple dimensions, speculating about the functions of conflict and the need for values to maintain the social equilibrium. Colorless men in business suits read bland papers full of theoretical frippery and statistical fastidiousness. Al Szymanski was an oasis of genuineness in this desert of scholasticism.[5] He dressed casually in faded jeans and a work shirt, with a disheveled mop of dishwater-blond hair topping his large round head. He was only a few months older than I, having been born in 1941. At six-foot-two and 190 pounds, he was the largest of a small group of radicals who stood quietly in the back of a meeting room holding up a sign saying "bull shit" whenever the speaker made a particularly galling remark. The shy grin on his cherubic face revealed his embarrassment with this tactic, which he had agreed to as an experiment in ethnomethodology.

Al quickly recruited me into the sociology radical caucus, which gave me a support group of other young professors to replace the political groups I had belonged to as a student. We were committed to direct action and had little patience with the stuffy professionalism of academic sociology. We had missed the deadline to place a resolution condemning American involvement in Vietnam on the agenda for the business meeting. Courtesy resolutions, on occasions such as the death of a colleague, could be introduced at any time, however. Ho Chi Minh, the North Vietnamese leader, had died during the meetings. We felt that he was our colleague and sought to extend the courtesy to him. When our parliamentary maneuver failed, we simply marched to the front of the room and held our ceremony anyway. The officials wisely retreated to resume their deliberations in another room, allowing our action to fizzle out gracefully.

Al was the son of a Polish-American Rhode Island lobster fisherman who loved to work with his hands and never really understood his son's intellectual and political inclinations. It was his strong-minded, deeply religious, Italian-American mother who nurtured his precociousness, taking him to get his first library card as soon as he became eligible, on his sixth birthday. When he first entered school, she told him that "other children could be cruel to another child who was different because of color or how he dressed and if he saw anyone alone or rejected to become a friend to them."[6]

Al read Freud and Marx at the University of Rhode Island and tried to shock his mother first with the revelation that he had loved her unconsciously as a child, then with his discovery of Marxism. She professed to be flattered by the first revelation and did her best to understand the second. She believed he was true to the fundamental values she had taught him and defended his right to political views she did not share.

Al became involved in a group called Students for Democratic Affairs in 1963, writing a letter to the Providence *Journal* advocating that students be allowed to visit Cuba. He argued that students might return finding that Castro was not as bad as they had been told, or they might return as staunch anti-Communists. In any event, they would be better off with first-hand knowledge instead of repeating sterile clichés composed by people who had never left the state of Rhode Island.[7]

On April 14, 1963, he organized an appearance by Hyman Lumer of the Communist Party on the Rhode Island campus. Al thought the Communist system was a "tremendously important ideology in the world today." The *Worker* quoted him as stating, "if, after eighteen years of being schooled in the American way, two hours of listening to Dr. Lumer could change a student's political views, something would indeed be wrong with our system."

Al abandoned physics for sociology as an undergraduate major and went on to do a doctorate at Columbia University, where he organized a radical sociology journal. He was a compulsive worker who produced a massive, two-volume dissertation on Chile. He also found time to travel to Orangeburg, South Carolina, where he was arrested in a demonstration protesting a "slow down" by voting registrars. He was also arrested in a demonstration at Fairweather Hall, Columbia University, in 1968, but the case was apparently dropped, and the FBI never got his fingerprints. They suspect he was at times affiliated with Youth Against War and Fascism, the Workers World Party, the Weathermen, the Worker Student Alliance, the Progressive Labor Party, the Revolutionary Youth Movement, the People's Coalition for Peace and Justice, the Venceremos Brigade, and the Revolutionary Union, but his file includes few details. Both of our FBI files are heavy on hearsay and newspaper clippings. They did, however, uncover both of our "aliases." Mine was Ted Goerge Geortzel (instead of George Goertzel); his was John Albert Szymanski (instead of Albert John) or sometimes simply "Al."

By the time I met Al in San Francisco, he was finishing up at Columbia and looking for a job. Oregon was hiring, and we brought Al out for an interview. His charisma and intellectual brilliance were apparent to even the most stodgy of Oregon's senior professors, who accepted his assurance that he would not advocate armed revolution until social conditions had reached a point that made it unavoidable.

Al had been involved in the Sociology Liberation Movement for several years before I met him and had helped to edit the *Human Factor*, a radical journal produced by students at Columbia. In an article titled "Toward a Radical Sociology," Al stated that the journal's goal was to "explain how badly the present society functions, how people's frustrations stem from the social structure, how unnecessary and oppressive the present institutional arrangements are and how much better an alternative social order world work."

When Al came to Oregon, he brought the Sociology Liberation Movement's newsletter, the *Insurgent Sociologist,* with the intention of turning it into a journal of socialist scholarship. We formed a collective with interested graduate students, solicited articles, collated and addressed the copies, and mailed them out free to anyone who'd signed a list at an annual meeting. The costs were covered by a film series that we ran on the Oregon campus. The mailing parties were fun, probably the only cooperative work most of us had ever done, and spouses and children joined in. When somebody asked my son if he knew what his daddy did for a living, he said, "yeah, he puts things in piles to go to different cities."

We agreed that the *Insurgent Sociologist* should be open to a wide range of radical and socialist perspectives, instead of trying to define a narrow political line. A similar agreement enabled Al and me to work together for many years, despite the fact that I was a "wishy washy social democrat" while he was a staunch Leninist. What made him so intriguing was his insistence on combining theoretical orthodoxy with exhaustive empirical work. While many radicals retreated into theoretical speculation or utopian visions, Al focused on the difficult issues others ignored such as human rights in the Soviet Union. He relied largely on mainstream specialists for factual information, always carefully footnoted, and made the best case possible for an orthodox Marxist interpretation. His books are most fascinating when they defend positions I find outrageous, such as supporting the Polish government against the Solidarity movement.

Coping with Disillusionment

Buzzing Doubts. While the *Insurgent Sociologist* was successful, the left in general, and in Oregon, began to split and crumble. Many of the antiwar activists, including Al Szymanski, became involved in sectarian Marxist-Leninist groups that I thought were out of touch with reality. I saw no evidence that socialist revolution was on the agenda in the United States, nor was I even convinced that it would be a good idea. Al, his wife Sue Jacobs, Carol, and I were involved in the New University Caucus, which was an organization of New Left graduate students and young faculty who wanted to continue their activism while pursuing academic careers.[8] The women in the group were primarily interested in feminist issues, and we white males were expected to repent our ways. Even when we did so, after a fashion, the unmarried women tired of dealing with men altogether and split off into their own women's organizations. My wife became involved in radical feminism, telling me I was a representative of the gender that had caused most of the problems in the world. She also became enthusiastic about the Chinese cultural revolution and began studying Chinese. We no longer had much in common ideologically or participated in many of the same activities.

The conflicts within the University of Oregon sociology department became more complex when issues of preferential hiring for women and minorities were added to the splits between Marxists and mainstream sociologists and between Leninists and cultural Marxists. As an untenured white male Marxist with an "abrasive personality," my future in the department didn't look good, and the gloomy winters began wearing on my psyche. I left for safer and sunnier climes at Rutgers University in Camden, New Jersey, where everything was peaceful and my personality was unproblematic. Al remained, got tenure at Oregon, and took over my role as the department's scapegoat. He gradually became more and more isolated from his colleagues, especially from the feminists and the cultural Marxists.

My marriage finally broke up as Carol deepened her commitment to feminism and I envied the swinging singles. I dealt with the divorce by getting involved in humanistic psychology and personal growth, sampling the singles' scene, and eventually remarrying. For Al, personal life was always secondary to political and intellectual projects. I can remember him telling me that he feared his wife's getting pregnant as he would have only nine months to complete the book he was working on. I already had two small children at the time, and no book. He also divorced, but responded by becoming more and more involved in his work.

The annual American Sociological Association (ASA) meetings were a pleasure largely because I would get to spend time with Al. He would stay the full five days at the meetings, but would only attend one or two sessions, spending the rest of the time sitting at a table selling copies of the *Insurgent Sociologist*. It was a great way to meet interesting people and find out what was going on around the country. We also helped to organize the radical caucus at each year's ASA meetings and prepared resolutions on all the burning issues for the business meetings.

The peak of our movement came in 1976 when we nominated and elected our senior statesman, Alfred McClung Lee, to the presidency of the ASA. Lee put together a program that was stimulating and exciting, a real model of what a gathering of sociologists could be. His presidential address, delivered to a packed plenary session in the enormous, ornate ballroom of the New York Hilton, was a ringing indictment of the sociological establishment, many of whom walked out in dismay.[9]

After Lee's presidency, everything we did seemed anticlimactic. We tried nominating other radical sociologists for the presidency, but none of them were at the right stage of their careers to be electable. I had done the paperwork necessary to establish a section on Marxist Sociology, which gave us our own space on the program every year. This took much of the spontaneity and excitement out of our movement. There was no need for a radical counter-convention when we could give our papers in the official hotel and get our universities to pay our airfare to the conference.

As the radical movements around us waned, we became more professionalized, and I felt that our sessions often weren't any more exciting than the traditional ones. Academic Marxists were retreating into scholasticism, debating obtuse points in Marxist theory or developing complex conceptual schemes to disguise the fact that the world really wasn't evolving as we had expected. Much of the Marxist work was, in my view, just as obtuse as the worst of the establishment sociology we had protested as students.[10]

The Struggle to Keep the Faith. As a tenured professor, I could have gone on giving the same lectures year after year, but I began to feel that I was more of a relic than a revolutionary. I moved on to other interests, but Al remained loyal to Marxism-Leninism. He knew that few students were persuaded by his arguments, but he took comfort in what he called the "lazy dog effect," which meant that years later, when social contradictions had reached a peak, they would think back to what their radical sociology instructor had said, and the truth would "click" in their heads. He also continued to search for a Marxist-Leninist movement that would follow the correct line and bring revolutionary consciousness to the masses. For years he was involved with a group that was centered in Philadelphia, and he kept asking me if I had heard about its activities. I had to tell him it was a minor sect with no real political influence, and I teased him about his eternal quest for a nonsectarian sect. When the Philadelphia group fell apart, he grudgingly acknowledged that there was truth to my remarks.

I knew Al was disappointed in political trends, but he seemed personally contented when I saw him at the 1984 International Institute of Sociology meetings in Seattle. He conceded at a panel that he had no idea how to bring about a revolution in America, but he was good-natured about it and insisted that we go out drinking afterwards. He was even quite charming on a brief visit to my parents' home, taking an interest in my mother's work on health-food faddism.

It was a complete shock when I got a call from my ex-wife the next March with the news, "Al Szymanski has committed suicide." She'd heard from his ex-wife, who gave her no clue as to why he did it. As the reality of his death sank in, I felt worse and worse. Losing a friend my own age, forty-three, was bad enough. But Al was someone I genuinely admired, not just as a scholar but, more importantly, as a man who lived for and by his convictions. What principle could have led him to this? I realized that the writing I was doing at the time was meaningful to me largely as part of a dialogue with Al. Why should I go on if he had decided it wasn't worth living for?

After the burial, Al's girlfriend told me he had been taking antidepressants for a long time but had avoided psychotherapy or even medical attention for what he had thought was liver cancer but was only gallstones. I remembered conversations years ago when he urged me to keep a gun in the house in preparation for the revolution. Carol and I wouldn't consider such a thing with small children in the house, even if we had believed that a violent revolution might someday be necessary. We certainly never anticipated that Al would keep his gun by his bedside to comfort himself during bouts of depression, then, finally, one lonely agonizing weekend, use it on himself.

Many people asked if I knew why he had done it. I wasn't sure. If he had intended it as a political statement, he would have written a political testament. All he left was a three-by-five card asking that his retirement money be divided among a number of radical journals and a small fund for his dogs. Looking back, my biggest regret is that I didn't urge him to encourage his wife to have children even if it meant delaying his book a year or two. At least I could have responded more seriously, in later years, to his questions about my successful second marriage and encouraged him to talk more freely about his difficulties in establishing a committed relationship. I don't know that talking with me would have helped, but at least I would have the comfort of knowing that I had done everything I could to help. There is a sense in which the personal is political, but Al went too far in subordinating his personal life to his politics.

Although Al was my own age, he was also something of a mentor for me because of his brilliance, personal charisma, and strong sense of commitment. He shared my disillusionment with the scholasticism in Marxist sociology and insisted on dealing with difficult political and empirical issues. In a sense, his death was the end of my youth. I realized that we weren't young people having a good time tweaking the establishment's nose. This was real life.

A trip to China with a group of sociologists in 1983 contributed to my growing disillusionment with socialism. We talked to a great many people who recited the horrors of the cultural revolution period from their personal experiences. The success of capitalist reforms, particularly in agriculture, was apparent, and no one was interested in talking about socialism except a few of the Americans. I was particularly struck by the contrast between the repressive reality of the Maoist era and the idealized picture of it, which I had heard over the years from Carol and her friends.

For a number of years, I had been a member of the Democratic Socialists of America (DSA). This organization, led by Michael Harrington, essentially allowed me to continue to think of myself as a "socialist" while actually believing in democracy and a mixed economy. I went to monthly DSA meetings and attended an occasional Socialist Scholars conference in New York. I also kept up a membership in the local Nuclear Freeze group, which gave me a feeling of continuity with my history in the peace movement. These political affiliations, however, played a minor role in my life as I found friends elsewhere. In my academic work, I pursued other interests. I was glad when the introductory sociology textbook Al and I had written went out of print, since I had found it awkward to use the book in my own classes.

Loss of Belief. My final break with thinking of myself as a "socialist" came at a meeting of the DSA Peace Committee in Philadelphia. A speaker was presenting a slide show about her trip to El Salvador. She noted with pride that the guerrillas had blown up the highway bridge over a major river and showed a slide of local residents driving slowly over the ties on a railway bridge. I asked whether the people didn't resent having their bridge destroyed and noted that the same slide might be used as evidence against the guerrillas. As the presentation went on, I continued to question many of the speaker's remarks, which I thought idealized Communist movements and societies. At the end of the evening, one of the members, Russell Kleinbach, a sociologist at a Philadelphia College of Textiles and Sciences, politely objected to my role. He acknowledged that I was very well informed and that the members didn't have answers to my objections. Instead of suggesting further study or discussion, he made it quite clear that he wanted me to accept the group's line or stop coming to the meetings. His final remark was, "I don't know what happened, you used to be a socialist." I realized he was right.

At about this time, I decided to seriously reconsider pacifism. After a long search through obscure volumes, I found that I agreed most with a Catholic philosopher who carefully dissected the flaws of a doctrine that makes no distinction between justified and unjustified killing.[11] I thought her rationality contrasted favorably with the mysticism of my Quaker heritage. At a meeting of the Nuclear Freeze group I still belonged to, I found myself agreeing with Congressman James Florio's remarks and felt embarrassed by the group members who advanced simplistic anti-American views. I realized I didn't really belong in a movement that was essentially an odd alliance of Quaker pacifists and Marxist-Leninists.

The Turncoat and the True Believer. A number of things may help to explain why I became a turncoat while Al died a true believer. My father set a precedent with his apostasy from Communism and his skepticism about ideologies. Al rebelled against his father's beliefs and lifestyle much more consistently than I rebelled against my father. His father bragged that he had never finished a book; mine had a Ph.D. in psychology. Al spent his life trying to convert the working class to Leninism but he had no hope of convincing his own lobsterman father. This may have locked him more firmly into his position since any wavering would have meant giving into the old man.

Al was much more committed to Marxism than I was. He had visions of himself as the Lenin of the twentieth century and kept assuring us that the time would come when "power will be lying in the streets, and we must be ready to pick it up." When that glorious day kept receding further and further into the unknown future, he clung to the belief that nuclear war was imminent and that it was his duty to organize so the left could seize power in the aftermath. He became a survivalist, squirreling away food, medicine, bullets, and supplies in the hope that Eugene, Oregon, would be far enough from the bombs to survive. He had so much invested in his Marxism that it was impossible for him to accept failure. The drive and commitment that made him such a powerful writer and organizer dug him into a hole he wasn't able to climb out of. In this respect, his death parallels those of Eleanor Marx and Abbie Hoffman, which are discussed later in this book.

I was always more of a skeptic, unable to commit myself fully to Marxism or anything else. When I was in graduate school, my teacher, the Marxist economist James O'Connor, correctly observed that I really couldn't make up my mind whether I was a liberal or a Marxist. I enjoyed finding the flaws in other people's beliefs while avoiding committing myself fully to anything.

Moving away from the University of Oregon gave me a chance to redefine myself without making concessions to my opponents. Getting involved with the human potential movement after my divorce gave me an alternative reference group as well as a chance to develop interpersonal skills. In the larger urban world of greater Philadelphia, it was easier to drift away from radical sectarianism into new circles and organizations.

It is impossible to be certain whether any of these factors accounts for the differences between our lives. Al's depression may have had a chemical origin; he was seeing a psychiatrist who had treated him with pills. A little talk therapy might have helped him to lessen his dependence on politics as a source of meaning and fulfillment in his life. If he had lived to see the collapse of Communism in 1989, he might have changed his views as well. I don't think he would ever have abandoned Marxism, though. He might have become a reforming democratic socialist in the style of Boris Kagarlitsky.[12] If he had remained strongly committed to political sectarianism, he would probably have adopted a dogmatic defense of Maoist orthodoxy such as that of William Hinton.[13]

Al and I can be seen as examples of different ideological scripts. Although we were both leftist protestors, I was more of a survivor and a skeptic while Al had a much stronger commitment script. These ideological scripts will be explored in the next chapter.

Chapter Two

Ideologies as Life Scripts

*One of the curious things about political opinions is how often
the same people line up on opposite sides of different issues. The
issues themselves may have no intrinsic connection with each
other . . . yet the same familiar faces can be found glaring at each
other from opposite sides of the political fence, again and again.
It happens too often to be a coincidence and it is too uncontrolled
to be a plot.*

—Thomas Sowell, *A Conflict of Visions*

This book spares no sacred cows as it probes the reasons why Jim Jones
and Abbie Hoffman committed suicide, Saddam Hussein invaded Kuwait,
Ayn Rand seduced her leading disciple, Linus Pauling became a vitamin
faddist, Arthur Butz denied the Nazi holocaust, and Margaret Mead spun
fantastic tales of utopia in the South Seas while Karl Marx prophesied
a socialist utopia in industrial Europe. It reveals the personal psychology that shaped the biographies of people as fascinating and diverse as
Adolph Hitler, Mohandas Gandhi, Bertrand Russell, Phyllis Schlafly,
Woodrow Wilson, Winston Churchill, Betty Friedan, Auguste Comte,
Eldridge Cleaver, John Stuart Mill, Michael Harrington, Edward Bellamy,
and George Bush. It explores the rise and fall of communism from the
personal perspectives of Marx, Lenin, Trotsky, Castro, Stalin, and Gorbachev. It probes the reasons why some people believe the Armenian and
Nazi genocides never took place, while others believe utopia can only be
built in giant pinwheels in outer space.

All these people were deeply committed to political ideologies, which
gave meaning to their lives and enabled them to shape the world in which
we live. Many people have given their lives, or taken the lives of others,
in pursuit of their ideological commitments. But few people have a good

understanding of the psychological roots of their own political beliefs, let alone of what motivates the beliefs of others.

Most of us have had political arguments with people whose ideological assumptions are fundamentally different from our own. In these arguments we list facts that support our point of view, and they list facts that support their point of view. Occasionally we disagree about the accuracy of the facts, but more often we disagree about which facts are important. Seldom is anyone's point of view changed in these discussions. If the debate continues, we are likely to become angry and defensive, more certain of the correctness of our views and the obstinacy of our opponent. At best, we agree to disagree.

We may denounce our opponents for having a "knee jerk reaction" or using a "stock argument," but most of us actually do remarkably little study and analysis of a social problem or conflict before taking a position on it. We simply focus on the facts that fit our ideological preconceptions and try our best to ignore the uncomfortable facts that do not.

As the twentieth century comes to an end, however, many people are having nagging doubts about their ideological beliefs. The collapse of state socialism in eastern Europe has besmirched an ideal that many people held dear. The end of the Cold War has made the conflict between hawks and doves seem increasingly obsolete, and the recent Gulf War found many people reevaluating their accustomed position on military action. Conflict over affirmative action, racial quotas, and "political correctness" on college campuses has induced second thoughts for many people who are committed to equal rights for all. In the United States, the savings and loan crisis and other economic problems have raised doubts about many of the economic innovations of the Reagan era. In the Soviet Union, Mikhail Gorbachev has gone from hero to scapegoat in less than a decade.

In this epoch of rapid ideological change, the time is ripe for a better understanding of the psychosocial origins of ideology. Ideologies may seem stale and lifeless when they are ossified in party platforms, pamphlets, or textbooks, but they were created by people who cared deeply about them and whose lives make fascinating reading. Their biographies offer a sensitive and personalized view of what each ideology meant to the people who created it. The chief merit of biography as a genre is that it treats "the historical individual as a free and unique subject, not just the object of history."[1] That is why existentialist philosopher Jean-Paul Sartre chose to spend the last years of his career as a biographer.

Although each biography has its unique aspects, a book of comparative biography cannot simply treat each individual as a special case. If we wish to find general patterns in the biographies of large numbers of people, we need sort people into categories with similar beliefs and similar personalities. As Kenneth Boulding has pointed out, "we have to classify in order to be able to use language at all. We cannot talk about each of the 5 billion human beings separately."[2]

Systematic thinking requires categories, and choosing the right set of categories can be very important. The science of chemistry, for example, was greatly advanced when chemists stopped classifying elements into four categories—earth, air, fire, and water—and broke them down into their component parts. Political psychology is in need of a similar breakthrough. Traditionally, ideologies have been classified into two broad groups: "left" and "right." But simply classifying each of our subjects as "left" or "right" would be too crude and simplistic to capture the real diversity in their views and their personalities.

The left-right dichotomy is outdated, but what should we put in its place? I believe it is useful to think of ideologies as life scripts. Script theory in psychology and sociology is based on the metaphor of the individual as an actor in an improvisational theater, playing the scenes of his or her life.[3] A script is a set of guidelines that people develop and use to understand their role in the world around them.[4]

Biographies are fascinating because, unlike actors in a theater, people in real life have the freedom to write and rewrite their own scripts, and the choices they make may indeed be stranger than fiction. Biographies tell a life story by describing the scenes that were important in the subject's life. We learn what the subject thought and felt about each scene and what he or she chose to do in the circumstances. Of course, even the most comprehensive biography can describe only a tiny fraction of the scenes of the subject's life. By selecting scenes that were emotionally meaningful and that illustrate the scripts the individual used most regularly, the biography enables us to understand the person.

We use ideological scripts to respond to the political questions we face in life.[5] When Iraqi soldiers occupied Kuwait in 1990, people around the world reacted according to their ideological scripts. Some thought Iraq's invasion was an unbridled aggression that had to be stopped. Others denounced America's response to it as a cynical defense of greedy oil companies. Some thought Saddam Hussein was another Hitler, others thought that a better analogy was to Vietnam. Some rushed to join the armed forces, others became protestors or conscientious objectors. Some just hoped the whole thing would go away.

But why do some people prefer one script and others another? Script choices are rooted as much in emotional needs as in life experiences or rational interests. Silvan Tomkins defines an ideological script as an "organized set of ideas about which human beings are at once both articulate and passionate and about which they are least certain."[6] Facts or theories that everyone accepts as true are seldom central to ideological beliefs. As Kenneth Boulding notes, "it would be hard to build an ideology around the multiplication table, for nobody would be against it."[7] We use ideological scripts to make decisions when there are too many unknowns and uncertainties for an objective analysis.

Why all this passion about the uncertain? Because one central psychological function of ideological beliefs is adding drama and meaning to our lives. As Boulding observes:

> An image of the world becomes an ideology if it creates in the mind of the person holding it a role for himself which he values highly. . . . To create a role, however, an ideology must create a drama. The first essential characteristic of an ideology is then an interpretation of history sufficiently dramatic and convincing so that the individual feels that he can identify with it and which in turn can give the individual a role in the drama it portrays.[8]

A Typology of Ideological Scripts

In this book we will discuss nine principal ideological scripts: the utopian-dystopian, the survivor, the committed, the hawk, the dove, the authoritarian, the protestor, the skeptic, and the pragmatist. Each of these scripts defines a role for the believer in the drama of political life. The nine ideological scripts are listed in Table One, together with the names of some of the individuals discussed in this book whose lives followed each script. It must be stressed, however, that scripts are not psychological types in the sense of incompatible alternatives.[9] There is often no psychological conflict or difficulty in using more than one script. A person who uses multiple scripts simply has a larger repertoire of beliefs and behavior, and a greater tolerance for ambiguity, than someone who always follows one script. Some of the people in Table One are hard to classify because they frequently followed more than one script. Some people followed one script quite rigidly early in their life, then switched to another in later life. This pattern is indicated in the chart by the words "early" and "late."

Table One
IDEOLOGICAL SCRIPTS

The Utopian-Dystopian—Seeks to transform the world to prevent disaster and realize an idyllic vision. Examples: Edward Bellamy, Ignatius Donnelly, August Bebel, Jim Jones, Tom Hayden, Ayn Rand, Nathaniel Branden, Karl Hess, Murray Rothbard, Marija Gimbutas, Margaret Mead, Gerard O'Neill.

The Survivor—Seeks to move with the flow as a cork floating on the river of history. Examples: Bertrand Russell, Ignatius Donnelly, Mikhail Gorbachev, Jerry Rubin.

The Committed—Seeks meaning in life through commitment to a cause. Examples: Eleanor Marx, Woodrow Wilson, V. I. Lenin, A. J. Muste, Michael Harrington, Sidney Hook, Linus Pauling, Abbie Hoffman.

The Hawk—Seeks strength and security as a defense against outside threats. Examples: Adolph Hitler, Winston Churchill, Saddam Hussein.

The Dove—Seeks peace and love through conciliation and cooperation with outside groups. Examples: Mahatma Gandhi, Vera Brittain, A. J. Muste, Kenneth Boulding, Joan Baez.

The Authoritarian—Seeks a strictly disciplined world in which everyone must conform to established doctrines or powerful authority figures. Examples: Adolph Hitler, Joseph Stalin, Fidel Castro (late), Jim Jones, Bernard Coard, Eldridge Cleaver (late), Peter Collier and David Horowitz (late), Phyllis Schlafly.

The Protestor—Seeks to defend the powerless and oppressed from exploitation by elites. Examples: Bertrand Russell, Leon Trotsky, Fidel Castro (early), A. J. Muste, Abbie Hoffman, Jerry Rubin, Philip Agee, Maurice Bishop, Tom Hayden, Betty Friedan, Eldridge Cleaver (early), Peter Collier and David Horowitz (early), Kate Millett, Germaine Greer, Valerie Solanis.

The Skeptic—Seeks to base political decisions on objective truth confirmed by scientific evidence. Examples: John Stuart Mill, Auguste Comte, Bertrand Russell, Max Eastman, Jeffrey Masson, the *God that Failed* writers.

The Pragmatist—Seeks to accomplish practical, short-term goals. Examples: Mikhail Gorbachev, George Bush.

The Utopian-Dystopian. The dystopian anticipates an imminent disaster that threatens to destroy the world as we know it. The utopian seeks to realize a vision of a better world. Utopian and dystopian thinking usually go together, however, so these scripts can be treated together. Usually the utopian believes that disaster is certain unless his or her remedy is adopted, in which case everything will be peaches and cream.

Utopian visions draw our attention to the deficiencies of existing society and help us to think of alternatives. They motivate people to work for social change. Utopians often write novels that give their visions a feeling of reality. In these fictional utopias and dystopias, everything works out exactly as the writer chooses.

Realizing utopian visions in the real world is much more difficult. Some mechanism is needed to bring about the desired transformation. Perhaps the best mechanism is the voluntary experimental community, but results of these experiments seldom meet expectations. Utopianism is dangerous when adherents impose their vision on unwilling participants by force. We will encounter this phenomenon on a small scale in the Jonestown disaster and on a large scale in Leninist societies.

Utopian scripts appeal to people who are creative and imaginative, prone to flights of fancy and building castles in the air. They find existing reality boring and confining and prefer possibilities to realities. The utopian believes that "a man's reach should exceed his grasp, or what's a heaven for?"[10] Perhaps the most beautiful expression of the utopian vision is the following poem written by German socialist Heinrich Heine in 1844:

> A new song, ay a sweeter song,
> My friends, I'll sing to you:
> The dream of heaven, we'll make sure,
> Shall here on earth come true.
>
> Men will be happy here on earth;
> To starve is not our fate.
> The idle rich no more shall feast
> On what the poor create.
>
> There's bread enough upon this earth,
> Enough for all—and more.
> There's beauty, roses, myrtles, joy,
> And sugar-peas galore![11]

The Survivor. The survivor inhabits a world of constant flux with much change and transformation but little predictability.[12] Survivors believe that "there is nothing permanent except change"[13] and that "certainty generally is illusion, and repose is not the destiny of man."[14] They feel like a "cork on the river of history."[15] Survivors may make contingency plans and try to anticipate the flow, but they are always ready for sudden turns and unanticipated disasters.

Inconsistent parenting in early childhood is sometimes thought to be the origin of this script. People with strong survivor scripts are likely to be fearful that all good things must come to a tragic end, which makes it difficult for them to make lasting commitments. They often use emotional aloofness as a defense against unpredictable change. They cultivate indifference to praise or criticism and are often insensitive to the feelings of others. At the same time, they may use displays of emotion to influence others. Sometimes they get carried away by exaggerated emotion not based on deep convictions. They are reluctant to rely on others, since they believe people cannot be counted on to behave consistently.

The Committed. People with commitment scripts seek meaning in life through commitment to a cause. This is often combined with a protest script, but the commitment can be to any kind of cause. It need not be a protest against authority. People with a need for commitment often go through a period of searching before settling on a cause. Once they choose a cause and invest their energies in it, their commitment often becomes the dominant theme in their lives. Aphorisms that express a commitment script are "to thine own self be true"[16] and "faith and loyalty are still able to raise common men to greatness."[17]

Committed people sometimes identify so closely with their causes that they have difficulty separating their personal worth from the cause. They may become seriously depressed if the cause does not succeed. Suicidal feelings are one of the risks of the commitment script. Eleanor Marx, Adolph Hitler, Jim Jones, Albert Szymanski, and Abbie Hoffman are examples of people whose strong commitment scripts ended in suicide.

The Hawk. Hawks seek security by defending their group from other groups. In childhood, the group may be a neighborhood gang. Later on it becomes a racial, ethnic, religious, or national group. "Our country, right or wrong"[18] and "Patria o Muerte, Venceremos"[19] are slogans that express a hawk script. Hawks are often hostile and aggressive because of repressed anger or an inability to empathize with their enemies. They have a tendency to split positive and negative aspects of themselves and others into "all good" or "all bad" categories. Hawks have been responsible for many genocides throughout history and have a remarkable ability to deny that any such thing ever took place.

On the positive side, hawks can be hard-nosed realists who face up to harsh realities that the squeamish doves deny. After being denounced for decades as a warmonger, Winston Churchill was redeemed when his warnings about the Nazi threat turned out to be true. Ever since then, hawks have been greatly inspired by his model. Like any other ideological script, a hawk script need not be based on deep emotional needs but may reflect the environment in which a person lives. It can be based on a realistic appraisal of an objectively threatening situation. Albert Einstein and many other pacifists changed reluctantly from doves to hawks when faced with the Nazi threat. There was no change in their fundamental values or personality patterns.

The Dove. Doves seek peace through conciliation and cooperation. Their vision is of a nonviolent world when people shall "beat their swords into plowshares."[20] Doves have a more optimistic view of human nature than the hawks, believing that problems can and must be solved through negotiation and compromise. They seek the good in other people and have faith in the better side of human nature. Their slogans are "Make Love, Not War" and "Love Conquers All."[21] As the horrors of war have increased, the dove script has become more compelling.

Dove scripts appeal to people who would rather suffer themselves than inflict suffering on others. Since their desire for peace and conciliation is so strong, doves have a tendency to deny unpleasant or threatening realities about enemy groups. In their haste to avoid conflict, doves sometimes end up as the de facto allies of groups that have nothing but contempt for their values. Often, doves join in social movements with protestors. This can be an awkward combination since protestors often support the use of violence by oppressed nations or groups.

The Authoritarian. Authoritarians seek a world with hierarchy, discipline, and order where everyone is made to conform to rigid values.[22] They seek strong leadership as a means of enforcing discipline. Authoritarian scripts appeal to people who repress their feelings and do not trust themselves to behave correctly. Authoritarians are inclined to project their repressed hostilities onto vulnerable groups and to seek strong leadership to punish others for their own faults. Authoritarians have much in common with hawks and the two scripts are often combined. It is possible, however, to combine authoritarian and dove scripts as in the case of fundamentalist pacifist sects.

Authoritarians often identify with powerful and aggressive forces as a means of protecting themselves. When feeling threatened or vulnerable, the authoritarian "pretends not to be in danger of being the victim by mentally changing into a sort of facsimile of the aggressor."[23] Thus, the authoritarian is deferential toward the powerful, but hostile and aggressive toward the weak and vulnerable. This is sometimes called the "bicycle personality" because the head is bowed towards those above while the feet are kicking those below. Being abused as a child is a likely source of the pattern. It is the same pattern observed in men who defer to their boss but beat their wife or children.

The leader of an authoritarian movement is carefully tuned to these emotional needs in his followers but does not incorporate their feelings of weakness into his own personality.[24] This enables him to manipulate the feelings of the masses, often through dramatic and emotional oratory. The authoritarian hero is a "man on a white horse" who serves as an ego ideal for people who are too frightened or inhibited to express their anger directly. In a classic passage, Karl Marx described the relationship of authoritarians to their leader as follows: "Their representative must at the same time appear as their master, as an authority over them, as an unlimited governmental power that protects them against the other classes and sends them rain and sunshine from above."[25]

Psychologically, the authoritarian leader has a grandiose self-concept, perhaps as a defense against feelings of vulnerability or inferiority. He may be an individual who was abused by his father but whose mother doted on him, giving him a contradictory self-image. Adolph Hitler, Fidel Castro, and Saddam Hussein are the leaders in this book who best fit this model. Paradoxically, much of their apparent ego strength seems to have been based in suicidal feelings. Not fearing death, they were able to take dramatic and dangerous actions, which symbolized strength and power. The hero and the martyr are closely related. The tragedy is that authoritarian leaders often martyr their societies along with themselves.

Not everyone who follows an authoritarian script, however, can be shown to have these psychological traits. People may adopt an authoritarian script because it is the most common one in their social environment, because their knowledge of alternative scripts is limited, or because they believe it is necessary in a given social situation. Authoritarian scripts appeal to many people during periods of social chaos and unrest. Aspiring leaders may use authoritarian rhetoric because they think it is what the masses want to hear rather than because of their own psychological needs.

The best point of the authoritarian script is its contribution to self-control and self-discipline. Authoritarian scripts can help people to endure difficult conditions. Their worst point is their emphasis on scapegoating and victimizing vulnerable minorities.

The Protestor. Protestors empathize with the suffering of people on the bottom of the social order and seek to free them from exploitation by powerful elites. The exploited group may be a social class, racial or ethnic group, gender or age group, disability group, or some other group.

It may even be nonhuman as in the case of animal rights and environmental groups. Indeed, an environmentalist newspaper, the *Green Letter,* in San Francisco advocates that the United States adopt a constitution in which "trees, wolves, all beings could vote. The planet herself should have a major voice."[26]

Protestors often externalize their feelings of vulnerability onto these other groups. Rather than facing his or her own anxieties, the protestor worries about distant and vulnerable nations or about oppressed groups and classes to which he does not belong. When externalization is strong, a person may be completely unaware of his own feelings. As Karen Horney observed:

> not only one's faults are experienced in others but to a greater or less degree all feelings. A person who tends to externalize may be profoundly disturbed by the oppression of small countries, while unaware of how much he himself feels oppressed. He may not feel his own despair but will emotionally experience it in others. . . . Further, he will ascribe not only his disturbances but also his good moods or achievements to external factors.[27]

Sympathy for the unfortunate is an essential part of a protest script, but it is not all of it. Protest scripts also include hostility towards elite groups and an analysis of suffering as part of a larger system. Without these elements, sympathy for the unfortunate can better be expressed in voluntary charitable activities.

Protestors frequently are not members of the oppressed group to which they dedicate their efforts. Members of the oppressed group may join with the protestors for pragmatic reasons, of course, but their motives are more practical. Protest organizations are usually an alliance of people who are participating for pragmatic reasons and protestors who are ideologically motivated.

Protestors have helped to organize movements, such as the abolitionist movement, the labor movement, the civil rights movement, the feminist movement, and the human rights movement, that have greatly improved the human condition. Their effectiveness is sometimes limited, however, by psychological traits that are commonly associated with protest scripts. Psychologically, protest scripts can serve to express anger and frustration against authority. For this reason, they are more popular with young people than among the middle aged.

Although protest scripts are assertive, people with protest scripts are often losers in political struggles. Winning undermines the psychological function of the protest script as an expression of hostility against authority.

Protestors sometimes notice that their support for a candidate in an election is a "kiss of death," which really means that they select candidates who are more concerned with expressing values than with winning power. If a protest candidate should happen to win, the demands of office make it likely that he will betray the principles that made him attractive to the most idealistic of the protestors.

The unanticipated collapse of Communism in eastern Europe propelled human rights protester Vaclav Havel into the presidency of Czechoslovakia. When he met with some of his fellow protestors at the 1990 meeting of the Helsinki Citizens' Assembly, he remarked, "There are some among us who contend that there is an inherent contradiction between conscience and power, the moral demands of anti-politics and the practical ones of office. 'Are you not naive?' they ask me. 'Are you not the oppressor now? Are the structures of power not the same?' "[28]

The Helsinki Citizens' Assembly is a meeting of protestors from groups such as the Green party in West Germany, the New Forum in the former German Democratic Republic, and the left wing of the Civic Forum in Czechoslovakia. These groups were courageous and effective in opposing the Communist regimes in their countries. When Communism collapsed, however, they found themselves in the unfamiliar and uncomfortable position of winners. They quickly retreated into their protest scripts by espousing ascetic and moralistic "socialist" policies at a time when the people wanted nothing more than political freedom and a chance at Western affluence. They were abandoned by their pragmatic followers, and their vision was rejected in "country after country, election after election."[29] The tendency to "snatch defeat from the jaws of victory" is a weakness of protest scripts.

Because protest movements so often fail, protestors must develop a strong commitment script if they are to continue to be active in protest movements over their lifetime. Without this strong sense of commitment, people are likely to become discouraged and drop out of protest movements. Most protest movements have large numbers of participants who participate at peak moments when the movement seems likely to succeed, but who drop out when the going gets tough.

Although protest and authoritarian scripts are opposites in their choice of emotional objects, they have a great deal in common in their deeper structure and in their psychological appeal. Both develop elaborate theories that divide the world into good and evil forces. Adherents of both are often self-righteousness in imposing their views on other people. Although protestors are indignant about abuses of power by the authorities, they are likely to repeat the same or worse abuses themselves if they win power.

The Skeptic. Skeptical (or scientific) scripts are rooted in a desire to know the truth about the empirical world. Skeptics strive to use only evidence that can be objectively observed, counted, and analyzed with rigorous logic. Often, skeptics are disillusioned turncoats from other ideological scripts. Two of the people discussed in this book, Auguste Comte and John Stuart Mill, are important largely for creating skeptical scripts. Mill was able to live with skepticism. Comte was not and converted his beliefs into a bizarre utopian secular religion.

Living with a skeptical script means living with uncertainty and ambiguity, depending only on information that can be verified with empirical observation. As Comte said, "we have no knowledge of anything but phenomena; and our knowledge of phenomena is relative, not absolute."[30] This means acknowledging that anything we believe may be proven wrong. For the skeptic, "it is certainly not the least charm of a theory that it is refutable."[31] Scientific scripts can provide reliable and consistent knowledge, but sometimes at the expense of focusing on the trivial, commonplace, or routinized aspects of reality. This seems to be the case especially in the social sciences, where skeptics must accept their inability to answer many fundamental questions. Skeptics can be a drag when activists are trying to build enthusiasm for a cause.

Skeptical sociologist Peter Rossi decided to do a rigorous survey to find out how many homeless people there were spending the night on the streets of Chicago. He set up a rigorous sampling plan and hired off-duty police to accompany researchers into the streets, alleys, hallways, basements, roofs, and parked cars of the city. His estimate was 2,344 (with a standard error of 735). A follow-up with a larger sample estimated 2,020 and reduced the standard error (a measure of the likely sampling error) to 275.

Advocates for the homeless were outraged by his survey. When he gave a presentation of his results to the Mayor's committee on the homeless, the "talk was greeted by a torrent of criticism, ranging from the purely technical to the accusation of having sold out to the conservative forces. . . . Those two hours were the longest stretch of personal abuse I have suffered since basic training in the army." Rossi was ostracized when he flew to Los Angeles to speak at a conference. He became "a nonperson wandering through the conference, literally shunned by all." A convinced skeptic, he found it "particularly galling to have to defend our carefully and responsibly derived estimates against a set of estimates whose empirical footings were located in a filmy cloud of sheer speculation and guesses." For their part, homelessness protestors felt his report was a "serious disservice to the cause of the homeless." They accused him of deliberately underestimating the numbers.[32]

Similar outrage was directed against Michael Fumento when he wrote articles and a book arguing that there was not likely to be an epidemic of AIDS among the nondrug-using heterosexual population in the United States.[33] Fumento argued that AIDS activists relied on exaggerated projections and scare tactics to frighten the public and secure large amounts of funding. They generally opposed rigorous studies to determine the incidence of AIDS in the population, preferring to rely on what he called "advocacy statistics." Skeptics are often the bane of protestors and utopians because they question both their use of scare tactics and their exaggerated or unsupported claims for their solutions.

The Pragmatist. The pragmatist is concerned with short- or moderate-term, practical, achievable goals. Pragmatic scripts appeal to survivors and skeptics who feel that it is unrealistic to put much faith in long-term strategies and commitments. Pragmatism also appeals to people who are generally satisfied with the status quo and see no need for major changes as well as to people who simply have no taste for abstract causes and prefer to focus on more tangible projects. They believe that "an acre in Middlesex is better than a principality in Utopia"[34] and "the road to Hell is paved with good intentions."[35]

Most practicing politicians are pragmatists (or opportunists if you prefer a pejorative term). This accounts for the generally low opinion of politicians among the public at large, who tend to admire people with strong value commitments. The public nevertheless elects pragmatists in the hope that they will serve their interests. In totalitarian systems the pragmatist must be a sycophant, since cultivating the favor of the powerful is the only way to win. If conditions change, however, the pragmatic leader may abruptly change his tune. A strong pragmatic script explains how leaders such as Mikhail Gorbachev and George Bush are able to change their ideological colors as the opportunity presents itself. Pragmatists are "winners" in contrast to protestors, who would rather "be right than be president."

Ideological Scripts in the Life Cycle

In a very general way, ideological scripts correspond to cognitive patterns that develop at different stages in the life cycle.[36] Table Two shows how the script choices correspond to life-cycle stages. Utopian scripts are rooted in the narcissistic thinking of infants. Infants view themselves as the center of the universe and expect the world to cater to their needs. When it does, they are completely happy. When it does not, they are very unhappy. This corresponds to utopian and dystopian views of the world. The infant is not consistently utopian or dystopian, but swings abruptly from one to the other depending on his comfort level. Similarly, most utopian writers present both utopian and dystopian imagery. Revolutionary utopians typically advocate an abrupt transition from a dystopian to a utopian state. This does not mean that utopians are infantile personalities, simply that they are in touch with a way of thinking that first develops at that stage in the life cycle.

Table Two
IDEOLOGICAL SCRIPTS IN THE LIFE CYCLE

Approximate Life Stages	Typical Ideological Script Choices		
Infant:	Dystopian	——+——	Utopian
Toddler:	Survivor	——+——	Committed
Latency:	Hawk	——+——	Dove
Adolescent:	Authoritarian	——+——	Protestor
Adult:	Pragmatist	——+——	Skeptic

As the infant becomes a toddler and learns that he is not the center of the universe, he develops a model of the world around him. If it is stable and reliable, he is able to form trustworthy commitments to the people and objects in it, counting on them to respond consistently to his behavior. This provides the basis for a commitment script. If the world is chaotic and unpredictable, the child draws back from commitments in an attempt to survive. Of course, no child's environment is completely predictable or unstable, so these scripts are a matter of degree.

In the latency period, children develop stronger self-concepts, and in so doing they must deal with positive and negative images of themselves. Feelings of inferiority are a persistent problem at this life stage. Angry and hostile feelings develop and must be controlled in some way. One method is to project them onto enemies, which is the origin of the hawk script. Another way is to deny them or to repress them and turn them inward, which is the origin of the dove script.

In adolescence, these hawk and dove scripts become more generalized as the young person develops an understanding of the broader world around him or her. Adolescents need a way to understand who they are and how they relate to the rest of the world. At this point, hawk scripts are likely to develop into authoritarian scripts, while dove scripts are likely to develop into protest scripts. These scripts are more complex and sophisticated with abstract principles, which help to meet the adolescent's growing need for identity. They give the individual a principled role in the struggle for a better world.

Pragmatic and skeptical scripts are more typical of middle-aged adults whose emotional lives are settled and who may have become disenchanted with the limitations of other scripts. A person can fairly easily be both a pragmatist and a skeptic. The skeptical script appeals more to people with intellectual and intuitive inclinations, while pragmatic scripts appeal to people who are more concrete and practical in their thinking.

It should be emphasized that the fact that an adult uses a script that develops early in the life cycle does not mean that person is immature or childish. Just as it is healthy in our personal lives to remain in touch with the "child within," so too is it useful in political life. Utopian scripts, for example, can provide energy and vitality, which are sorely lacking in individuals who are limited to pragmatic or skeptical scripts. One definition of ideological maturity might be the ability to draw on a wide number of ideological scripts instead of being locked into a single one.

Detecting Ideological Thinking

Ideological analysis probes the irrational and emotional factors in political thinking. These factors usually lie buried beneath a veneer of logical and rational argumentation. Detecting the ideological core of a belief system can be difficult because people become defensive when the basis of their beliefs is questioned. The veneer of rationalizations becomes rigid and brittle, cloaked in a barrage of stock arguments and other defense mechanisms. I believe that these defenses, rather than the content of the arguments per se, are the most important clues that a person is following an ideological script.

Ideology as False Beliefs. Not everyone agrees that looking for defensive argumentation is the best way to detect ideological beliefs. Distinguished theorists as diverse as Karl Marx, Raymond Aron, Talcott Parsons, and Raymond Boudon have defined ideologies as false beliefs.[37] They hope that ideological analysis will help them to uncover the "objective truth" buried under the veil of ideological distortion. This definition has proved to be a dead end because it begs the difficult philosophical issue of how we know the truth. Trying to draw a line between "objective truth" and "ideological bias" gets one caught in a web of epistemological contradictions, which can be fun but not very helpful.

Ideological thinking focuses on issues where the objective truth simply is not known. Ideologies are more about future potentialities than current realities. They are often so vague and ambiguous that it is difficult to know what they mean, let alone whether they are true. Ideological beliefs are often concerned more with feelings and values than with verifiable facts. For all these reasons, ideological analysis is not best approached as a search for objective truth but simply as a search for the psychosocial motivations for belief. Persistence in testing for the truth of beliefs, even when the truth is unknowable or irrelevant, is a clue that a person is locked into a skeptical script.

Ideologies as Group Interests. Another approach is to analyze ideologies sociologically. Theorists such as V. I. Lenin, Louis Althusser, Edward Shils, Clifford Geertz, and Karl Mannheim define ideologies as beliefs that reflect class or group interests or that play a political function.[38] These writers have a useful point. People do use ideologies to advocate for their interests as group members. If they do so in a self-conscious, effective, and productive way, they are following pragmatic scripts. Such cases are not difficult to understand. Everyone readily understands why workers believe wages should be higher, capitalists favor deregulation, students believe in low tuition, property owners favor lower taxes, and so on.

Ideological analysis is most needed, however, to understand beliefs that do not rationally reflect objective group or class interests. Many of the most fervent ideological issues such as war, abortion, the environment, and animal rights, do not have much to do with the objective interests of any social class or group. Everyone presumably benefits from saving the environment and preventing war, yet very few people become ideologically involved in these causes. All women of child-bearing age have an objective interest in free choice on abortion, but many women nevertheless become involved in the anti-abortion movement. It is not being a woman that makes a person a feminist, but acceptance of feminist ideology and joining a feminist organization. The same is true for other ideological groups.

Another problem with a purely sociological approach is that it is often very difficult to know whether a belief actually reflects the interest of a group or whether the believers falsely believe that it does. Even if an individual appears to be advocating a group's interest, it is important to probe more deeply. In a controversy with John Dewey over Marxist ethics, for example, Leon Trotsky argued that "a means can be justified only by its end. But the end in turn needs to be justified. From the Marxist point of view, which expresses the historic interests of the proletariat, the end is justified if it leads to the increasing power of man over nature and to the abolition of the power of man over man."[39]

In response, John Dewey argued that Marxists such as Trotsky seldom make the kind of analysis that this kind of argument requires. To be true to his argument, Trotsky should have undertaken a "scrupulous examination of the means that are used, to ascertain what their actual objective consequences will be as far as it is humanly possible to tell— to show that they do 'really' lead to the liberation of mankind."[40]

Dewey was a pragmatist and a skeptic, while Trotsky was a protestor and a utopian. Dewey insisted on collecting as much solid evidence as possible to determine what was most likely to work. Trotsky felt an urgent need for revolution and didn't think history could wait until a bunch of middle-class academic philosophers pulled their noses out of their books and smelled the gunpowder. Trotsky believed he was advocating the historic interests of the working class, but ideological analysis can offer many other useful perspectives on his thinking and behavior. These are explored in Chapter Nine.

Passionate Belief. Passionate belief is often an indicator of ideological thinking. Bertrand Russell once argued that "No opinion should be held with fervour. No one holds with fervour that seven times eight is fifty-six, because it can be known that this is the case. Fervour is only necessary in commending an opinion which is doubtful or demonstrably false."[41]

Avoiding passion, however, is hardly possible or desirable. In his own life, Bertrand Russell was totally unable to follow his own advice, as we shall see in the next chapter. A resolution to be completely objective and scientific applies better to judgments about factual or mathematical matters than to moral or value judgments. Most people passionately believe that it is wrong to murder or torture even though this cannot be proved logically. Many of the most important issues are simply not amenable to logical solution, and we use our ideological scripts to take positions on these issues. Even beliefs about apparently factual questions are often emotionally charged because they include, or are assumed to include, implicit value judgments. The statement, "women are just as intelligent as men," for example, makes a factual claim, but many people would get quite angry at anyone who disagreed with it.

Passionate belief is a sign of ideological thinking when the passion is attached to the ideology itself instead of to the underlying moral or value issues. For many people, the feeling of knowing how the world works and how they fit into it is emotionally rewarding. For this reason, they become emotionally attached to a theory or point of view and cling to it even when the facts go against it.

Adopting an ideology can be very exciting, particularly for a young person who is struggling to define his or her identity in a confusing and threatening world. Ayn Rand's Objectivist philosophy has been highly inspiring for many young people, particularly those who feel suffocated by religious beliefs that allow little room for individuality.[42] Her novel

The Fountainhead tells of a heroic architect who blows up a housing project he had designed after a meddling socialist administrator corrupted his plans for the building. Nathaniel Branden, who later became Rand's leading disciple, says that:

> between the ages of fourteen and eighteen I read and reread *The Foun-tainhead* almost continuously, with the dedication and passion of a student of the Talmud. It was the most important companion of my adolescence. When I opened its pages, I was transported into a world where the issues I cared about really *mattered.* . . . To keep faith with the best within yourself was clearly *selfish* and clearly a *virtue.* I knew what a break from the beliefs of the people around me this way of seeing things represented and I welcomed that.[43]

This kind of passionate attachment to a belief system can be dangerous, particularly if the person becomes deeply committed to it. In Branden's case, it led him to destroy his marriage and devote many years to preaching a doctrine he later thought to be defective.

Sudden Insight. Ideological belief often comes as a sudden flash of insight. Arthur Koestler reported that:

> By the time I had finished with Engels' *Feuerbach* and Lenin's *State and Revolution,* something clicked in my brain and I was shaken by a mental explosion. To say that one had "seen the light" is a poor description of the intellectual rapture which only the convert knows. The new light seems to pour from all directions across the skull; the whole universe falls into pattern like the stray pieces in a jigsaw puzzle assembled by magic at one stroke. There is now an answer to every question; doubts and conflicts are a matter of the tortured past when one had lived in dismal ignorance in the tasteless, colourless world of those who *don't know.*[44]

This feeling of sudden discovery can be a clue in detecting ideological thinking, but it is not a reliable indicator. Ideological belief can come suddenly, but it can also grow slowly and prosaically. Furthermore, flashes of insight are not limited to ideological thinking but also occur in areas such as science and mathematics. Henri Poincaré, for example, reported that after trying for fifteen days to prove that there could not be any such thing as what are now called Fuchsian functions, he unaccustomedly drank a lot of black coffee in the evening and could not sleep. During the night "ideas rose in crowds; I felt them collide until pairs interlocked, so to speak, making a stable combination. By the next morning, I had established the existence of a class of Fuchsian functions, those which come from the hypergeometric series."[45]

Sudden flashes of insight are part of the creative process, as the mind puts aside old ideas and adopts new ones. They often occur when someone thinks intensely about a topic for some time, then pushes it out of his or her conscious mind. The unconscious mind continues processing the topic, sometimes in ways that lead to new combinations and insights. The flash of understanding comes when this new insight suddenly breaks into consciousness. It may be triggered by a chance occurrence or by an emotionally charged event such as Bertrand Russell's sympathy for a three-year-old boy frightened by his mother's heart attack.

Flashes of insight, which come as "bolts out of the blue," are a sign that the unconscious mind has been at work. The key question is why this has happened. In the case of ideologically sensitive issues, ideas are often repressed into the unconscious because of emotional resistance. In scientific thinking, the unconscious may be at work simply because the conscious mind has tired of struggling to solve a difficult problem. In either case, the flash of insight is a useful phenomenon, which should be welcomed. The difficulty comes if the insights are clung to for the excitement they bring, instead of being subjected to critical evaluation.

Polarized Thinking. Splitting the world into two groups is a common way of thinking. People frequently say, "there are only two kinds of people in the world," and go on to mention their pet peeve of the moment. The function of splitting the world in this way is usually to express anger or distaste for one group while praising the other. This kind of thinking is central to many ideological scripts. Whenever people start splitting the world into opposing groups, good clues as to their ideological scripts are likely to follow.

Polarized thinking is easy to detect in a written text. It will read like a polemic or a legal brief, which lists all the points on one side and none on the other. Occasionally, ideological splitting is explicitly advocated. For example, a law review article by Mari Matsuda elaborated a theory of "outsider" (minority or feminist) jurisprudence.[46] If this should become law, members of oppressed groups would receive special rights not to be shared with others. For example, Matsuda argues that the Constitution should prohibit racist slurs or insults. She is not content, however, to prohibit racist insults in general but only those by white people. She explicitly argues that black people should be allowed to hurl racist insults against white people. She also favors repressing groups such as the Holocaust revisionists and scholars who argue that blacks are genetically inferior, since their arguments are generally recognized as wrong and are part of a historical pattern of oppressing a group. The whole thrust of her argument is to divide the world into good and evil forces and to advocate whatever she believes will benefit the good.

In talking with an ideological thinker, one can detect polarized thinking by simply stating a point or two in favor of a group the speaker dislikes. In doing so, of course, one risks being exposed to a long diatribe or even a certain amount of abuse. Rather than actually responding to objections from their critics, polarized thinkers usually change the topic to any one of a number of other points that put their side in a better light. They have so many points to make in defense of their views that they never have time to think about the other side.

Biased Selection of Evidence. Perhaps the most general and important indicator of ideological thinking is a tendency to rigidly defend a consistent position regardless of any evidence that may be offered. If a particular line of argument proves ineffective, the ideological thinker simply discards it and looks for another way to defend the position. Facts are chosen selectively to illustrate and defend ideological beliefs.

As a child, Beatrice Webb observed the eminent philosopher, and family friend, Herbert Spencer at work:

> she was fascinated to watch the way in which Mr. Spencer used the specimens brought to him to prove this or that theory. Her sharp eyes were quick to spot that he only noted those which endorsed the point he was making. The rest was discarded. All his theories were built up in this way. He began with his proposition or principle and found the facts to prove it afterwards. His method of writing a book was unique. He would arrange his title headings on foolscap paper on the floor in a semicircle about his chair. Seated in the centre, he threw, from a pile collected by his secretary in order to prove his point, each "fact" on its appropriate chapter. Any unwanted ones fluttered away to oblivion.[47]

Biased Choice of Analogies. Reliance on a narrow set of well-chosen analogies is a frequent, although not often noted, characteristic of ideological thinking. Ideological thinkers often use analogies when they have difficulty in defending untenable positions. The analogy is used to shift attention away from the troublesome case at hand to another case where the evidence better suits the speaker's viewpoint. Whenever a speaker or writer switches to an analogy, the ideological analyst should be alert for a strong clue.

For example, in defending the thesis that the husband must be the final authority in the family, Phyllis Schlafly drew an analogy between a marriage and a country or a large corporation. The United States has a President and corporations have a chief executive officer, therefore, if a marriage is to succeed, "it must likewise have an ultimate decision maker, and that is the husband."[48] Schlafly is an authoritarian who deeply believes in hierarchy and discipline. When she found it hard to defend this script in discussing marriages, she simply switched to discussing corporations and the U.S. government.

Of course, the use of analogies is not inherently ideological. Analogies are useful in generating ideas and in illustrating points. The ideological thinker, however, selects the analogy that best supports his or her preconceived idea, not the analogy that is closest to the situation at hand. Schlafly, for example, ignored the differences between an intimate relationship and the complex administrative problems of a large organization. She chose not to draw a more appropriate analogy between marriages and two-person business partnerships, which often function quite well without an "ultimate decision maker." Nor did she even consider the possibility that the wife could be the "ultimate decision maker" in a marriage. Considering some of these possibilities would have been a creative use of analogies. Ultimately, however, the merits of egalitarian versus patriarchal marriage have to be addressed by examining marriages, not by drawing analogies or relying on other ideological devices.

William Gamson has shown that certain analogies are used routinely by adherents of particular ideological scripts.[49] In listening to speeches or reading newspaper columns, one can usually determine the ideology of the author by noting the analogies used. For example, protestors are likely to mention the overthrow of Salvador Allende in Chile in 1973, the U.S. intervention in Vietnam, and the invasion of Nicaragua by the U.S. Marines in the thirties. Hawks mention the appeasement of the Nazis, the Soviet invasions of Hungary and Czechoslovakia, or the overthrow of the Communists in Greece. Pacifists refer to the bombings of Hiroshima and Nagasaki. Hard-nosed pragmatists refer to the Cuban missile crisis. In his content analyses of group discussions, Gamson can code ideologies reliably based on the analogies that are used.

Rhetorical and Semantic Argumentation. Rhetorical devices are central to ideological argumentation. When the ideological thinker cannot avoid thinking about disturbing facts, as in a debate with an insistent opponent, various logical and rhetorical devices are used to discount their importance. Incidental or unimportant linguistic flaws in the opponent's arguments are seized upon and carefully demolished, while important points are ignored. Definitions are debated, metaphysical assumptions are analyzed, and the validity of the factual information is questioned. The motivations of the opponent are attacked. If all else fails, the opponent may be crudely ridiculed, jeered, physically attacked, or simply asked to leave.

Semantic rigidity is particularly common among intellectuals. On American college campuses, people who use "incorrect" words may be denounced as "racist," "sexist," "classist," "ageist," "ableist," "heterosexualist," or "insensitive" to the needs of a particular group. New "politically correct" terms are continually being invented to replace the old "biased" ones. The disabled become the "differently abled" or the "mobility challenged"; Negroes become "blacks," "Afro-Americans" or "people of color," but never "colored people"; minorities become "outsiders"; AIDS patients become "persons with AIDS"; American Indians become "native Americans"; Jews become "Jewish persons"; women become "womyn" or "wimmin"; seminars become "ovulars"; and the elderly become the "chronologically gifted."

It is not so much the new terms that are important in defending an ideology as the insistence that anyone who uses the old words is biased and insensitive and in need of immediate correction by the enlightened. This is done even when members of the groups involved prefer the old terms or don't care one way or the other. Sorority members at the university where I teach, for example, were publicly lambasted for posting a leaflet inviting "girls" on campus to a party. Needless to say, they were not encouraged to find out more about feminism.

Although these new terms are advocated as measures to lessen bias and prejudice, psychologically they serve to give protestors opportunities to put down other people while drawing attention to their superior sensitivity and consciousness. Writers who use masculine pronouns as generic terms referring to both genders get their manuscripts sent back for revision with a clear message that they better shape up if they want to publish in the correct journals. Journalists are told to consult the *Dictionary of Cautionary Words and Phrases* to make sure they avoid offensive terms such as "burly," "buxom," "stunning," "elderly," or "swarthy."[50] The *Dictionary* offers no guidance to the journalist about how to interview a black leader, noting than "Afro-American" is a term preferred by some, but it "may be objectionable to those persons preferring black."

In ideological debates, great importance is often given to words that symbolize adherence to a particular ideological script. These words come to be valued for themselves, independently of their meaning. They serve as shibboleths or code words, which affirm membership in a particular group, much as the word "God" is used to claim membership in the community of religious believers, even though believers often mean very different things by the word. When people's beliefs change, they often cling to the old words as a means of assuring themselves and others that they have not reneged on their commitments.

Sigmund Freud noted this phenomenon with respect to religious apostates:

Philosophers stretch the meaning of words until they retain scarcely anything of their original sense. They give the name of "God" to some vague abstraction which they have created for themselves; having done so they can pose before all the world as deists, as believers in God, and they can even boast that they have recognized a higher, purer concept of God, notwithstanding that their God is now nothing more than an insubstantial shadow and no longer the mighty personality of religious doctrine.[51]

In exactly the same way, old socialists such as Irving Howe and Sidney Hook have redefined the word "socialism" in such a way that it has lost its original meaning. Howe argued that "socialism is not to be 'defined' as a society in which private property has been abolished; what is decisive is the political character of the regime exercising control over a postcapitalist or mixed economy."[52]

Writing in his eighty-third year, Sidney Hook reported that "I am not aware of having undergone any serious conversions from the days of my youth."[53] This was a remarkable conclusion to a book that describes his transition from Trotskyist Communism to anti-Communism, yet he insisted that:

because our support of socialism as an economy rested on moral grounds, the very meaning of socialism changed once we abandoned serious advocacy of collective ownership of *all* social means of production, distribution and exchange. . . . the term *socialism* seemed to have changed its meaning to signify the responsibility of the state to intervene in the economy to provide a safety net for those able and willing to work . . . [while] preserv[ing] the free enterprise system.[54]

So defined, socialism hardly differs from democratic capitalism. Yet the term socialism has strong emotional significance to these writers, because of their personal histories, so they continue to use it to refer to beliefs that are in fact very different from the ones they held in their youths.

Although ideological thinking is based on strong emotions, this does not mean that ideological rhetoric is always openly emotional. The absence of apparent emotion, particularly when dealing with an emotionally sensitive issue, can also reflect a strong ideological script. Ideological thinkers sometimes use logic as a defense against having to question strongly held beliefs. Hannah Arendt, for example, commented on the "ice cold logic" of Adolph Hitler.[55] Hitler believed that "he who says A must say B" and was fond of syllogisms such as "culture is the only protection of the human race against nature, the Jews are the destroyers of culture, therefore the Jews are the enemy of the human race."[56] This kind of thinking provides absolute certainty so long as the premises are assumed to be true "by definition" or are defended with selective or biased evidence. Anything that is "true by definition" cannot be a statement about the empirical world. The substitution of semantic metaphysics for empirical observation is one of the hallmarks of ideological thinking.

All-Inclusive Systems. All-inclusiveness is a tell-tale sign of ideological thinking. Ideas that have validity when applied to specific problems are used as if they were the key to the universe. The greater the pretentions of a belief system to explain everything under the sun, the greater the likelihood that its advocates will rely on faulty logic, emotional rhetoric, and social pressure to persuade and discipline its adherents. Principles that purport to explain everything must necessarily be quite vague and abstract. If they were concrete and specific they would be testable and their limitations would readily become apparent.

All-inclusive systems often seem quite banal to the nonbeliever. Ayn Rand's hero defied the world on the basis of "a single axiom, which is the root of our moral code . . . the axiom that *existence exists.*"[57] Rand also advanced the "rule of all knowledge: A is A." These doctrines seem too silly and obvious to be the basis of an ideology, but they have a remarkable hold on the minds of true believers. After being purged from Rand's movement, Nathaniel Branden published a best-selling pop psychology book based on the thesis that "if man is to live, he must recognize that facts are facts, that A is A, that *existence exists.*"[58] Twenty years later, although criticizing Rand's "inadequate attention" to values such as benevolence and kindness, he continued to believe that her work "abounded with philosophical wisdom."[59]

Marxism, also, is often viewed as an all-inclusive system. Heinz Brandt reports that as a young man coming of age in Weimar Germany:

> everything was crystal clear to me. I knew exactly what held the world together in its innermost being. The law of social development lay before me like an open book. Past and present were scientifically analyzed; the future was fathomable in advance. Everything was laid down, everything was described. All one had to do was to glean correctly the works of Marx, Engels, and Lenin, employ these guides to action, and develop them further creatively.[60]

Dogmatic Use of Texts. Reliance on a hallowed text, such as the *Quotations of Chairman Mao* or Ayn Rand's novels, as a source of truth is a common feature of ideological scripts, particularly of the authoritarian variety. Of course, political ideologizes have this in common with religons and even with belief systems that aspire to scientific status. Freud and

Marx both aspired to scientific thinking, but their writings have been misused as sacred texts and are quoted authoritatively in settling disputes about empirical reality. When more attention is paid to what Marx or Freud said than to what is going on with the society or the patient, ideology has replaced science.

Glassy-mindedness. Denial of information that does not fit the ideological preconception is a classic characteristic of ideological thinking. Max Eastman referred to this phenomenon as "glassy-mindedness" in his account of his own resistance to assimilating the news of the Bolshevik's slaughter of the Kronstadt sailors who demanded free elections to the workers' councils in 1921. By glassy-mindedness, he meant, "offering a hard slippery surface to any datum or idea which, if it penetrated to one's inmost thought, would unsettle a firmly held belief."[61] It was not that he thought about the incident and rationalized it in some way. He simply put it out of his mind and didn't think about it, at least consciously. Of course, the thought was repressed into his unconscious mind, or at least pushed out of his awareness, or he would not have remembered it to put it in his autobiography. Many sudden apostasies and conversions, such as Eastman's, take place when resistance breaks down and repressed thoughts come back with a vengeance.

When Arthur Koestler visited the Soviet Union during the famine in the Ukraine, he was shocked when mothers held starving babies up to the train window in the hope of getting food. Despite the poignancy of this evidence of Soviet genocidal policies, Koestler accepted the argument that these were rich peasants who had refused to cooperate with the collectivization process. The Russian trip did undermine his beliefs, but only with a "delayed action effect, as it were. My Party education had equipped my mind with such elaborate shock-absorbing buffers and elastic defenses that everything seen and heard became automatically transformed to fit the preconceived pattern."[62]

Denigration and Censorship of Nonbelievers. An ideological script is undoubtedly present when members of an organization are required to accept a certain belief system. Ideological groups use defense mechanisms to maintain a boundary between believers and nonbelievers. This is particularly critical with apostates, former believers who have lost their faith. They must be firmly excluded before their doubts infect others.

The denunciation of nonbelievers is an important clue to ideological scripts. We do not angrily denounce someone who insists that $2 + 2 = 5$ or that the moon is made of green cheese. We get angry when someone denies beliefs that are emotionally important to us, particularly if we have some buried doubts about those ideas ourselves.

Soon after Max Eastman defected from Leninism in 1934, he picked up the *Daily Worker* to read the following:

I have never turned away from a friend who lost his path through drink, disease, or personal weakness. But Max Eastman, former friend, you have sunk beneath all tolerance! You are a filthy and deliberate liar! . . . you have aligned yourself with the white guards. . . . Nay, you are worse, since you yourself were once the Bolshevik leader of a generation of young intellectuals. The world has always loathed the Judases more than it did the Pontius Pilates.[63]

When Sonia Johnson founded Mormons for the ERA to defy the Mormon Church's opposition to the Equal Rights Amendment, the following letter was among hundreds she received:

Mrs. Johnson, you are a whore for the Secular Establishment. . . . You are a toady, a vile toady pandering to a morally bankrupt, anti-Christ world. . . . Your lying soul has fornicated with the vulgar mob-intelligentsia, and like a robot, you obediently spout off all the feminist buzz words, snatching headlines and getting patted on the back, stupidly. . . . You are a classic case of the born-in-the-faith Mormon gone ratfink—a brainless sycophant to the world, selling your "true confessions" for a rumor hungry, anti-religious society. . . .[64]

When feminist researcher Susan Steinmitz published a research review that concluded, "the data reported suggest that at least the intention of both men and women towards using physical violence in marital conflicts is equal," she was subjected to a torrent of criticism from feminist authors.[65] This went beyond the normal and appropriate publication of criticism in scholarly journals. There was an organized letter-writing campaign urging that she not be granted tenure at her university. She and her family also received threatening phone calls, and there was a bomb threat when she spoke at a conference.[66]

When Jeffrey Masson defected from the classical Freudian theory on infantile sexuality and defended Salvador Ferenczi's conclusion that many of Freud's patients actually had been abused as little girls, a true believer in Freudianism rose at a meeting and objected:

Your paper shows that you are as paranoid as Ferenczi. I am, as you know, a child psychiatrist and I know that children do, in fact, invent tales of sexual abuse. Freud was right, Ferenczi was wrong. . . . The fact that you, Jeff, can take up Ferenczi's views after all these years of clinical wisdom had demonstrated there was no truth in them shows . . . that you are dangerously mentally ill. In fact, Jeff, I believe you should spend some time in a psychiatric hospital. I have to go even further: I am prepared to commit you tonight if one of the gentlemen in the room will second my opinion.[67]

No one volunteered to second the opinion, and Masson took it as a joke since the speaker had been a friend of his. His friend wasn't smiling, however, and said, "Jeff, I'm serious."

Fortunately, in democratic societies psychoanalysts usually cannot commit people for criticizing established dogmas any more than political parties can imprison them or religious inquisitions can have them burned at the stake. The psychological dynamics of censoring, suppressing, and excluding dissidents, however, are persistent features of ideological belief systems.

The recent controversy over "political correctness" on college campuses has drawn attention to a number of attempts to denigrate and suppress people who publicly disagree with protestors' views of race and gender issues.[68] Opponents of "political correctness" say that this protest movement has degenerated into an authoritarian orthodoxy that refuses to tolerate disagreement or to permit questioning of any of its presuppositions. They are concerned that college classes will be converted into stale indoctrination sessions in which only approved arguments can be expressed.

At Harvard University, for example, Professor Stephan Thernstrom was attacked for reading aloud from the memoirs of a colonial slaveholder in a history class.[69] Unfortunately, the slaves published no memoirs and his critics accused him of presenting a "benevolent" picture of slavery. Thernstrom is a progressive historian who focuses on social history from the perspective of people on the bottom of the social order. He thought he had made every attempt to "present factual material in an objective and dispassionate way."[70]

Thernstrom's attempts to defend his teaching went unacknowledged, however, as he was used as an object for the angry feelings of the advocates of political correctness. The head tutor in the Afro-American Studies department told a campus newspaper that "by convention there are certain things that are forbidden to be spoken in the classroom."[71] Lacking support from the administration, Thernstrom stopped offering his course on "The Peopling of America." Also at Harvard, a woman dean who chose not to identify herself as a feminist was attacked for "doing violence to herself."[72] And dining hall workers who held a "Back to the Fifties" party were denounced for celebrating an incorrect decade.[73]

Students who disagree with feminist positions are often ridiculed and ostracized. A Women's Studies professor at the University of Washington began her class with the statement that the traditional American family is dysfunctional. When some students o jected that their own families had functioned well enough, she had her teaching assistants drown them out with shouts of "denial, denial." The next day, she had two police officers on hand to haul away a male student who had disagreed with her.[74]

Black writer Julius Lester was a Professor of Afro-American Studies at the University of Massachusetts at Amherst for almost two decades until he published a book about his own conversion to Judaism, in which he criticized anti-Semitic remarks by novelist James Baldwin.[75] All fifteen members of his department signed a lengthy statement asking that he be expelled from the department. He had to move to the Department of Judaic and Near Eastern Studies.

Barnard feminist scholar Rosalind Rosenberg had the courage to testify in court in support of Sears's claim that many women historically did not wish to take certain kinds of jobs.[76] The judge found her testimony well informed and reasonable in contrast to the sweeping and unsupported generalizations offered by the other side. Rosenberg was denounced in leading feminist journals, and a professional organization of feminist historians passed a resolution criticizing her for using her scholarship against the interests of women.

In actions reminiscent of the restrictions of the McCarthy era, a number of prominent universities have gone so far as to pass codes outlawing speech that they deem to be racist or offensive to certain groups. The University of Michigan passed a policy prohibiting "any behavior, verbal or physical, that stigmatizes or victimizes an individual on the basis or race, ethnicity, religion, sex, sexual orientation, creed, national origin, ancestry, age, marital status, handicap, or Vietnam-era veteran status."[77] (Presumably veterans of other wars could be stigmatized at will.) The American Civil Liberties Union took the university to court in defense of an instructor who said he was unable to express his views in class for fear of punishment. Meanwhile, students at Stanford University argued that "we don't put as many restrictions on freedom of speech as we should" and called for the university to "Muzzle the Stanford bigots."[78]

Dinesh D'Souza observes that "on virtually every campus, there is a de facto taboo against a free discussion of affirmative action or minority self-segregation, and efforts to raise such a discussion are considered presumptively racist."[79] In Orwellian fashion, a booklet at Harvard denounces the "myth" that "affirmative action means applying a double standard," when D'Souza argues that "in the case of Berkeley and other schools, it is unequivocally the case that affirmative action involves displacing and lowering academic standards in order to promote proportional representation for racial groups."[80]

At the University of Michigan, Professor Reynolds Farley was attacked in the student newspaper for supposedly racist remarks in a sociology class. He was attacked for calling Malcolm X a "red-haired pimp." Farley, a liberal with a progressive record on racial issues, says he mentioned that although Malcolm was an important figure, he had a "checkered career." Indeed, Malcolm X discusses his career as a pimp at some length in his own autobiography. Farley believes that the complex issues concerning racial differences on test scores and the differences in black and white family structures simply cannot be discussed in University of Michigan classes.[81]

Using the Typology of Ideological Scripts

The typology of ideological scripts, in Table One, is very helpful in detecting ideological scripts. If we keep the typology in mind, we will be sensitive to a wider range of ideological scripts, including those in our own thinking. Table Two puts the scripts in a developmental order. The scripts that are hypothesized to develop later in the life span are sometimes more difficult to detect because they are more subtle. Their followers are likely to use more sophisticated defense mechanisms. Also, some of the clues we have discussed work better with some scripts than with others. The pragmatic and skeptical scripts, in particular, are quite different from the others and may be detected with different clues. In the following sections we will suggest some clues that are helpful in detecting particular ideological scripts.

Detecting Utopian and Dystopian Scripts. Utopian and dystopian scripts split the world into positive and negative images, but these are seldom articulated fully. The rich descriptions of the writers discussed in Chapter Six are exceptional. More commonly only the negative half of the picture is made explicit while the positive half is implied. A believer may enumerate a long list of the evils of the existing social system, for example, on the implicit assumption that a superior alternative will emerge as soon as the evils are done away with. If pushed, they may respond that "there has to be something better than this mess" or "after the revolution the workers will decide on a better system." Their pragmatic critics fear that they are in danger of "jumping from the frying pan into the fire."

Another clue to utopian scripts is the explicit or implicit belief in a powerful force or "transformational object," which will transform the world from one extreme to the other. This can be a positive force such as a revolution, a new consciousness, or even an extra-terrestrial visitor. Or it can be an impending catastrophe, which will bring the mundane world to a crashing halt. Transformational objects of this sort include the debt crisis, the environmental crisis, the energy crisis, global warming, the population bomb, the racial crisis, the generation gap, the crisis of capitalism, nuclear holocaust, the drug crisis, and so on. Of course, each of these has a reality behind it, and dramatic social transformations do occasionally occur. Adherents of this kind of "crisis mentality," however, find it hard to believe that most "crises" are actually persistent but manageable problems and that societies are usually able to muddle through. They tend to exaggerate these crises, using them to justify their deep belief that the existing world is fated either to be destroyed or to be transformed into something much better.

Detecting Survivor and Commitment Scripts. These scripts are difficult to detect without examining the evolution of a person's beliefs and commitments over a period of many years. People's response to adversity is a useful clue. Commitment scripts are often strengthened by adversity, since it increases the believer's investment in the script. They are often surprised when other people are frightened away by the rigors of life in service of the cause. Committed believers become very skillful in using defense mechanisms to protect their beliefs. They often have rote answers available to respond to the most frequent criticisms of their beliefs.

By contrast, the life history of a survivor is likely to show frequent changes from project to project. Survivors are reluctant to throw good money after bad. Survivors may be more prone to sudden flashes of insight, perhaps interpreted as mystical or religious revelations, which set them off in new directions. With maturity, the survivor is likely to develop into a pragmatist. This requires being able to make limited, well-chosen, tentative commitments. Drawing the line between survivors and pragmatists can be difficult, but the true survivor has more difficulties in forming stable relationships and commitments. Bertrand Russell's life, as described in the next chapter, illustrates a survivor script with few pragmatic qualities.

Detecting Hawk and Dove Scripts. These scripts split the world into good and bad objects. The hawks adamantly defend their own group against any criticisms or perceived threats while ascribing all malevolent intentions to their enemies. The doves, by contrast, give every benefit of the doubt to outsiders while maintaining great suspicion and cynicism about their own nation and its leaders. Both groups tend to be highly emotional in their argumentation, particularly in their attacks on the people they believe to be evil. They ascribe the worst possible motivations to these people, sometimes creating elaborate conspiracy theories to prove that their enemies are evil, even when they appear to be doing good.

They discount anyone who doesn't share their perceptions as naive and gullible.

The thinking of hawks and doves is usually long on specific facts and illustrations and short on general principles. They are not so likely to have elaborated their beliefs into complex, abstract theories. They often have long lists of illustrative arguments at the tip of their tongues, ready to respond to anyone who doubts their script. If they use analogies as a form of argumentation, they are easily identified by the analogies they choose.

Detecting Protest and Authoritarian Scripts. These scripts are often more complex and developed elaborations of hawk and dove scripts. In addition to analogies and lists of examples, these believers have complex theories, all-inclusive systems, dogmatic texts, and often a remarkable level of glassy-mindedness. They become quite sophisticated in selecting evidence to fit their views. The existence of a well-developed ideological doctrine, usually available for purchase in books, journals, newspapers, and pamphlets, is a common feature of authoritarian and protest scripts. These doctrines have good guys and bad guys, but they also offer a sophisticated and complex analysis of how the world works. This aspect makes these scripts attractive to many intellectuals.

The authoritarians are much less likely than the protestors to be introspective. There are no revealing autobiographies by prominent authoritarians. They are much more likely to simply insist on the validity of their own views and to focus on denigrating their opponents. While this is also true of many protestors, the ranks of the protestors have included a great many introspective and empathetic persons who have evolved into skeptics and pragmatists. Their autobiographical writings are especially rich.

Skepticism and Pragmatism: The Anti-Ideological Ideologies. Skeptics and pragmatists strive to be free of the biases that characterize other ideological scripts. They seek to put emotion aside and stick strictly to the facts and the tasks at hand. Nevertheless, it must be recognized that skepticism and pragmatism are ideological scripts. Ultimately their principles must be taken on faith. One cannot prove that scientific data are better than beautiful visions or that it is more important to build housing projects on earth than to build castles in the air.

Skepticism and pragmatism differ fundamentally from other ideological scripts in their focus on empirical evidence and practical results. For this reason, many of the clues that reveal the presence of other ideological scripts do not apply to them. Indeed, in many cases, skepticism and pragmatism are suggested by the opposite of these clues. Skeptics and pragmatists are threatening to true believers who depend upon unquestioned dogma, vague visions, or angry emotion. They have a hard time dealing with protestors and authoritarians, who put principle ahead of practice. They are more comfortable with survivors. Indeed, the pragmatist can be understood as a mature survivor who has found a way to keep uncertainty within practical limits.

Skeptics urge people to follow scientific rules for collecting and interpreting data. Many questions can be answered with reasonable confidence in this way. If a question cannot be answered with empirical research, the skeptic can only say that the answer is unknown. This is the greatest weakness of the skeptical approach. It often seems that the more important the issue, the less the likelihood that it can be resolved with empirical evidence. This can be frustrating to skeptics who are often strongly committed to skepticism as a principle. People who are locked into a skeptical script may find themselves unsure of how to act on questions that are of great importance to them. Some skeptics, such as John Stuart Mill, have been able to live with this. Others, such as Auguste Comte, have not.

To the extent that good objective information is available about an issue, skepticism can be a useful antidote to ideological distortions. If good information is not available, or if the point at question is fundamentally one of values, skepticism will only force us to acknowledge our ignorance. This limitation of the skeptical script makes it vulnerable to misuse as a defense mechanism for true believers who wish to deny uncomfortable facts. These true believers suddenly become rigorous skeptics whenever someone raises facts that they wish to deny. They insist on the most rigorous standards of evidence, which often cannot be met because the irrefutable information they demand simply is not available.

In the social sciences, methodological criticism is often used to discount unwelcome evidence. When confronted with an unwelcome finding, critics typically find flaws in the statistical methods or sampling techniques or criticize the theoretical or methodological assumptions. This kind of criticism tends to be selectively applied. Studies that report findings sympathetic to the writer's ideas are often cited repeatedly, even when their methods are no more rigorous. For example, when confronted with Susan Steinmetz's findings about husband abuse, feminist reviewers Wini Breines and Linda Gordon responded with an attack on all "empiricist" research using quantitative measures.[82] As Murray Straus points out, however, they went on in the same essay to cite findings from other equally "empiricist" studies that supported their point of view.[83]

This kind of misuse of skepticism as a defense mechanism can be difficult to distinguish from honest skepticism. The critical difference is that skeptical denial is used selectively only on the issues the believer wishes to deny. Another clue is an insistence on harping on weaknesses in their opponents' arguments instead of doing the best possible analysis they can with the data available. The holocaust and genocide deniers discussed in Chapter Fourteen are an illustration of the misuse of skepticism as a defense mechanism.

Risks and Benefits of Ideological Analysis

Sensitivity to ideological scripts can be helpful in several ways. We may be able to predict other people's behavior more effectively if we understand their ideological scripts. In Chapters Seven and Eight, for example, I will argue that many well-intentioned doves misunderstand hawks such as Adolph Hitler and Saddam Hussein because they fail to recognize the differences in their ideological scripts. This kind of misunderstanding can actually lead to the very wars the doves want to prevent.

An understanding of ideological scripts may help us to communicate with people with whom we disagree. Instead of simply denouncing our opponents as malevolent, foolish, or ill-informed, we may be able to actually discuss our fundamental differences. This is more difficult than it may seem, however, since communication between people with different ideological scripts often leads to angry arguments. It takes a good deal of maturity to recognize that someone with fundamentally different beliefs has a reasonable position worthy of some respect.

Uncovering ideological scripts can be frustrating if one expects people's thinking to change once the ideological nature of their arguments has been explained to them. If this happens at all, it is likely to take a long period of time. People almost never abandon an ideological script during an argument. At best one can hope to impress them with the reasonableness of alternative points of view and to sow a few seeds of doubt. Atheist George Smith has written a useful guide to this kind of conversation, based on his experience in arguments with religious believers.[84]

It is also helpful to understand some of the deeper emotional needs that motivate people to cling to ideological scripts. Change may be difficult unless these emotional needs are addressed. Script analysis helps us to identify cases where strong emotional needs may be present, but it does not always tell us what those needs are. Freudian and other psychological theories can be helpful here. Many of these deeper emotional issues will become clear as we review the lives of the turncoats and true believers in the chapters that follow.

If we are more aware of our own ideological scripts, we can become sensitive to the rigidities in our own thinking. In approaching a new issue or problem, we may stop and think before assuming that it can be readily fitted into pre-existing patterns of thought. Listening carefully to our more thoughtful opponents, instead of dismissing them out of hand, can be very helpful in this effort. We may also find it helpful to consider how the problem would be viewed from several different perspectives. Using multiple scripts may not guarantee complete objectivity, but we may at least be able to choose the best of the available biases.

Because of its power in probing the emotional roots of belief, ideological analysis can be risky. Lynda Davies uses ideological analysis as a technique in her work as a professional organizational consultant. She finds it useful to "watch out for anger in response to your suggestions. This may be through sarcasm or through more direct emotional revolt." Probing into sensitive ideological issues can be a risky technique for a consultant who wants to keep her clients. Davies warns that one should not "push it beyond the point of 'forgiveness' but do note what it was in relation to. You may well be challenging a core belief."[85] One must be particularly careful in asking probing questions while studying authoritarian groups that are prone to violence.

It is much safer, and also often more efficient, to rely on published sources such as autobiographies, biographies, and memoirs. In reading these materials, one looks for clues that suggest the presence of a particular ideological script. If an autobiographer is sensitive and introspective, these clues may be quite explicit. But even if an autobiographer is not sensitive to psychological issues, one can infer a great deal from the way he or she chooses to organize the incidents of his or her life. With biographies there is the added complication of the author's ideas about the subject's life.

Psychologically oriented biographers provide a great deal of insight into their subjects' lives. Even if their theoretical orientation is different, the information they provide can usually be reinterpreted in terms of script theory. These issues will be addressed in more depth in chapters to come. Chapter Three, especially, explores the differences between script theory and more traditional psychoanalytical approaches in examining the biographies of Bertrand Russell and Woodrow Wilson. Chapter Seven explores this issue with regard to Adolph Hitler.

This book questions ideological assumptions of all kinds, and many readers may find themselves getting angry at times. One reviewer of an early draft denounced it as "distasteful and immature dreck wrapped up in high-falutin clothing."[86] Apparently I pushed that draft beyond the point of forgiveness, and I hope this version is more tactful. It is not possible, however, to avoid the problem altogether. One who lets sacred cows lie will never uncover the ideological bull. If this book is well balanced, there should be something to anger almost anyone. If you find yourself getting angry at any point, it may mean that your own ideological preconceptions are being questioned.

Chapter Three

Survival and Commitment:
Bertrand Russell and Woodrow Wilson

Lord Bertrand Russell, scion of one of England's most distinguished aristocratic families, was a radical who spent his life attacking many of the
ideological conventions of Western societies. Although he was one of the
greatest logicians of all time, his life was torn by strong emotions, which
he was powerless to understand or control. At different times his life illus-
trated a survival script, a skeptical script, a protest script, a dove script,
and a utopian script.

Woodrow Wilson was the son of a Presbyterian minister whose brilliance and charisma brought him to the White House, but whose self-
defeating character traits caused him to sabotage many of his most cherished goals. He was a political scientist who wrote successful books on
democratic governance, yet he had great psychological difficulty implementing his own ideas. His life illustrates the difficulty of reconciling a
commitment script with the pragmatic needs of a practicing politician.

Bertrand Russell: Survival and Skepticism

During his ninety-seven-year life span, Bertrand Russell made several
dramatic changes in his political views. As a logician he was strongly committed to basing his judgments on objective logic. He was also a crusading moralist and social reformer whose life was governed by three "passions . . . the longing for love, the search for knowledge, and unbearable
pity for the suffering of mankind."[1] The contradictions between these
three passions plagued his life, blowing him "hither and thither, in a way-
ward course, over a deep ocean of anguish, reaching to the very verge

of despair."[2] His survival script, which was deeply rooted in early childhood experiences, made it difficult for him to form relationships that could satisfy his need for love on a sustained basis. The contradictions between his skeptical script and his protest script account for much of his colorful political life.

Russell abandoned Christianity reluctantly and only after a careful search for some rational grounds for belief. He was unwilling to rely on faith without a sound logical foundation, and he could find none. Having abandoned Christianity because it failed his logical test, Russell wanted very much to find some objective basis for ethical belief. He could not. He fervently believed that it was wrong to kill in war, but he could find no logical basis for this belief. He concluded that "an ethical judgment does not state a fact; it states . . . some hope or fear, some desire or aversion, some love or hate."[3]

Despite his desire to be logical and scientific, Russell found himself adopting strong beliefs quickly and without careful analysis. His adherence to pacifism came during a five-minute rush of emotion provoked by his sympathy for a three-year-old boy whose mother was suffering an angina attack. In his autobiography, Russell described this emotional experience quite vividly:

> Suddenly the ground seemed to give way beneath me, and I found myself in quite another region. . . . At the end of those five minutes, I had become a completely different person. For a time, a sort of mystic illumination possessed me. . . . Having been an imperialist, I became during those five minutes a pro-Boer and a pacifist. Having for years cared only for exactness and analysis, I found myself filled with semi-mystical feelings . . .[4]

Although Russell does not say so, he must have been troubled by these issues for some time prior to his dramatic conversion. He must have repressed his doubts about his previous convictions, only to have them triggered by the emotional incident. Russell's parents both died when he was a small child, which may have made him especially empathetic to the feelings of a small child. His strong commitment to a skeptical script, which valued objective evidence and rational logic, made it difficult for him to accept his own strong feelings.

Although Russell's pacifism came upon him suddenly and emotionally in 1901, it proved an enduring (if qualified) commitment for which he bravely suffered persecution and a jail term during World War I. His attachment to Soviet Marxism was much more fleeting. In 1920 Russell boldly proclaimed his support for the Bolshevik revolution in the pages of the New York radical journal the *Liberator*. The then thirty-eight-year-old philosopher frankly conceded that "Bolshevism has temporarily flouted two ideals, which most of us have hitherto strongly believed in: I mean, democracy and liberty." Yet he argued:

> Are we on this account to view it askance? I think not. . . . The Bolshevik reign of terror has of course been used to make our flesh creep, but it differs from the others solely in its purpose. . . . throughout the world we are faced by a clash of naked force. . . . in these terrific epochs, a man must be prepared to back his own faith. . . . there is something a trifle pedantic in applying to the circumstances of Russia the sort of arguments and principles which are valid for ourselves in ordinary periods.[5]

Rather than maintaining scientific objectivity, Russell adopted the utopian script with which most progressive intellectuals of the era understood the Russian revolution. Then he took a trip with a labor delegation to Soviet Russia. He was overwhelmed by the experience of the reign of terror, which he had so lightly dismissed from the comfort and safety of England:

> Cruelty, poverty, suspicion, persecution formed the very air we breathed. Our conversations were continually spied on. In the middle of the night one would hear shots, and know that idealists were being killed in prison. . . . I felt that everything that I valued in human life was being destroyed in the interests of a glib and narrow philosophy, and that in the process untold misery was being inflicted upon many millions of people. With every day that I spent in Russia my horror increased, until I lost all power of balanced judgment.[6]

Russell was remarkably forthright about admitting his mistakes. On his return from Russia, he renounced his apology for Bolshevism, which was "still floating like a flag almost from the masthead of all pro-Bolshevik publications throughout the western world," and wrote a popular book attacking Bolshevism in the most vigorous terms.[7]

Russell's conversion from fellow traveler to freedom fighter was remarkably quick and decisive. Most people who abandoned Communism took several years or as long as a decade to sort things out in their minds. Russell's 1920 book, *The Practice and Theory of Bolshevism,* anticipated many arguments that others arrived at much later on. He denounced Bolshevism as "a set of beliefs held as dogmas, dominating the conduct of life, going beyond or contrary to evidence, and inculcated by methods which are emotional or authoritarian, not intellectual."[8] He was able to reprint the book without change or embarrassment in 1948 and again in 1964, something which could be said of almost no other contemporary writer on the subject. Indeed, he anticipated most of the key points that are being raised by contemporary critics of "political correctness."

The trip was the catalyst for Russell's change, but it is the exceptional political pilgrim who changes his ideology during a trip to the "promised land."[9] Most find precisely what they expect to see. Russell's traveling companion, labor leader Robert Williams, reported that "all my previous hopes and expectations were more than borne out by my actual contact with Soviet affairs."[10] Russell observed that his girlfriend, Dora Black, who made her own trip to Russia when he refused to take her along, "regarded my objections to the Bolsheviks as bourgeois and senile and sentimental. I regarded her love of them with bewildered horror. She had met men in Russia whose attitude seemed to her in every way superior to mine."[11]

Why did Russell perceive basic flaws in Bolshevism that were missed by most others in 1920? His observations of economic and social realities in Russia, although perceptive and insightful, were not distinctive. He had no fundamental disagreement with his traveling companions about the factual realities observed. Nor did he differ on economic theory. He believed that capitalism was bankrupt and that socialist central planning was the wave of the future. The basic difference was his skeptical frame of mind, his intense commitment to logical reason, and his abhorrence of dogmatism. He was horrified when he heard Bolshevik leaders quote the holy texts of Marx and Engels to prove their points or pander to the emotionalism of crowds instead of using cold logic and empirical arguments. Other members of his tour group probably dozed during the dull speeches or got swept up in the emotional enthusiasm of the crowds at the inspiring ones. They were more interested in tangible phenomena such as model factories or crime-free streets. For Russell, the logic of the system was paramount. He reported that he "went to Russia a socialist; but contact with those who have no doubts has intensified a thousandfold my own doubts, not as to socialism in itself, but as to the wisdom of holding a creed so firmly that for its sake men are willing to inflict widespread misery."[12]

Russell's antidogmatic position kept him from ever fully identifying with any established ideology such as socialism or pacifism. He remained active in pacifist circles during the thirties, but in World War II he thought that armed resistance to Hitler was justified and publicly supported the war effort. After the war, he wandered so far from pacifism as to repeatedly advocate that the United States should threaten to attack the Soviet Union with nuclear weapons to force the Soviets to disarm.[13] Once the Soviet Union got its own nuclear bombs, he converted to nuclear pacifism and denounced the leaders of the nuclear powers as a "murderer's club."[14] Instead of retracting his own previous statements, he simply forgot them. In October 1953, for example, he denied in the *Nation* that he had ever "supported a preventative war against Russia," insisting that the whole story was "a communist invention." He continued to deny the reality of these statements for several years. When finally confronted by the published evidence of his statements, he conceded that "I had, in fact, completely forgotten that I had ever thought a policy of threat involving possible war desirable. In 1958 [two writers] brought to my notice things which I said in 1947, and I read these with amazement. I have no excuses to offer."[15]

Russell also softened his opposition to Communism in old age, at least to the extent of opposing American involvement in the Vietnam War. Following his protest script, he organized an International War Crimes Tribunal, which denounced offenses on only the anti-Communist side of the conflict. Rather than making a serious analysis of the war in Vietnam, he lent his name to simplistic propaganda leaflets that denounced the American leaders as "brutal bullies, acting in their own economic interests and exterminating any people foolhardy enough to struggle against this naked exploitation and aggression." He was full of suspicion about American motives, but he accepted at face value the claims of the "Vietcong" to be a "broad alliance . . . including all political views ranging from Catholics to Communists."[16] As Sidney Hook observed, "what is curious about this document, issued in the name of one of the most distinguished minds of our century, is the simplism of its thought and the virulence of its language, matching the crudest Communist propaganda leaflet."[17] In Russell's defense, some have suggested that his statements during his final years, when he was over ninety years old, were manipulated by his secretary, who seems to have written much of his correspondence.[18] He recorded the same views, however, for broadcast over Radio Hanoi, and he had expressed similarly simplistic anti-American views earlier in his lifetime.[19] The tendency to view the world as polarized between good and evil forces is a recurrent feature of his protest script.

In addition to his atheism and pacifism, Russell was well known as a crusader against conventional marriage. He conceded that marriage was a useful institution for the raising of children, but thought it inconsistent with people's emotional needs. His advocacy resorted to dubious facts, personal biases, and tendentious arguments such as the claim that it is "a well-known fact that the professional moralist in our day is a man of less than average intelligence" or that "women are on the average stupider than men."[20]

Since Russell's attack on marriage was so vehement and poorly reasoned, it seems likely that it was motivated by his own personal difficulties. His own sexual life was the source of much unhappiness for himself, his partners, and his children. He fell into and out of love with reckless and uncontrollable abandon for reasons he was completely at a loss to understand. Writing his autobiography in old age, he recognized the irony of being a self-proclaimed expert on love and marriage who could not manage his own love life and frankly conceded that "I do not know what I think now about the subject of marriage."[21]

Psychoanalyzing Russell. In his psychobiography of Russell, Andrew Brink argues that Russell's emotional problems were caused by the loss of his mother and sister at age two and his father eighteen months later, and inconsistent parenting after that.[22] His parents were freethinkers who asked that he be raised as an atheist, but the courts overruled their will and gave custody to his grandmother. She was a liberal on many issues, but also a strong Christian believer who told him that his parents were better off dead because of their lack of belief. She was a rigidly moralistic woman who was known as "Deadly Nightshade" to her husband's friends. Russell seems never to have been allowed to mourn adequately for his parents, nor to have established a satisfactory attachment to a replacement parental figure.

Russell's upbringing was dominated by his grandmother, who was continually mourning for a succession of family members. He was cared for by nurses, nannies, and tutors. His marital troubles, in Brink's view, originated in his childhood experiences with domineering women. He externalized these problems in his works on marriage and morality, writing as if his own difficulties with intimacy characterized the human species as a whole.

Russell's grandmother was a controlling figure who used rational arguments to dominate the child, and he honed his argumentative skills as a means of being able to answer her. Russell recognized that his interest in mathematics was in large part an escape from emotional involvements. This, of course, does not in any way detract from his accomplishments; indeed much outstanding creative work may be an externalization of emotional needs. It may explain why he found this work unsatisfying and turned to popular writing, which enabled him to express his personal feelings. He said that the only real pleasure he received from *Principia Mathematica* was turning the manuscript in to the publisher. He found the work so exhausting that his "intellect never quite recovered from the strain" and that he was "less capable of dealing with difficult abstractions than I was before."[23]

Psychoanalyst Harry Guntrip believes that Russell's difficulty was the "basic psycho-dynamic problem, the initial failure or early breakdown of primary experiences of 'relationships' in which the beginnings of a coherent developing ego could arise, with the result that no secure 'self' exists capable of owning the body, using its appetites, having motives and impulses, or entering into relationships."[24]

Both Brink and Guntrip believe that Russell had a "schizoid" condition, which made it difficult for him to establish and sustain meaningful emotional relationships. It is highly debatable, however, whether he at any time met the technical criteria for "schizoid personality disorder" as defined in psychiatric manuals. It seems better to say that he was following a survival script, rooted in his childhood experiences, which caused him considerable unhappiness in his personal life. Russell was aware of these unhappy feelings and wrote of the "loneliness of the human soul [being] unendurable," but he did not seek therapy or systematically psychoanalyze himself.[25] If he had, Guntrip believes he might have developed a deeper psychoanalytical theory than that of Freud, who focused on the "Oedipal" problems, which he experienced in his own upbringing in a two-parent family.

Woodrow Wilson: Commitment and Self-Defeat

Woodrow Wilson's life was plagued by a pattern of self-defeating behavior caused by a rigid commitment script, which made it difficult for him to reach reasonable compromises. It is not uncommon for psychological difficulties of this kind to mar the careers of otherwise brilliant and creative people. As writer Edmund Wilson (no relation) observed:

> It is possible to observe in certain lives, where conspicuously superior abilities are united with serious deficiencies, not the progress in a career or vocation that carries the talented man to a solid position or a definite goal, but a curve plotted over and over again and always dropping from some flight of achievement to a steep descent into failure.[26]

This pattern of initial success followed by self-defeating behavior leading to failure is common in lives that follow commitment scripts. Wilson's career followed this pattern as he progressed from president of Princeton University to governor of New Jersey and President of the United States. Historian Arthur Link noted that:

> a political observer, had he studied carefully Wilson's career as president of Princeton University, might have forecast accurately the shape of things to come during the period when Wilson was president of the United States. . . . in both cases he drove so hard, so flatly refused to delegate authority, and broke with so many friends that when the inevitable reac-

tion set in he was unable to cope with the new situation. His refusal to compromise in the graduate college controversy was almost Princeton's undoing; his refusal to compromise in the fight in the Senate over the League of Nations was the nation's undoing.[27]

On appointment to the presidency of Princeton University, Wilson demanded that the trustees give him complete power over appointments and promotions. They acceded to this unusual request because of their great hopes for his leadership. He seemed to justify their confidence when he succeeded brilliantly in his proposal to set up a tutorial system similar to that of English universities.

Buoyed by his initial success, he formulated a plan to reorganize the campus into "quadrangles," modeled on English universities, where students would live and take their meals together with a faculty and preceptors. He thought the eating clubs where most students took their meals were elitist and frivolous, encouraging students to fritter their time away with social chatter instead of engaging in serious academic conversation. This plan, however, would have cost a great deal of money for new construction, and the trustees were not convinced that it was worth it. A study showed that the eating clubs did not inhibit studying and that they could easily be reformed to make them more democratic. Instead of accepting this outcome, Wilson took it as a "complete defeat and mortification" and almost resigned.[28]

He could have accepted this setback and welcomed acclaim as the president who brought graduate study to Princeton, if only he had been able to share the credit with Professor Andrew West, who had written the proposal and raised the money. This Wilson was unable to do. He had written a laudatory preface to the book in which West proposed his plan, and everything was ready to go. Yet Wilson kept stalling, perhaps in the hope of saving the money to finance the quadrangle plan. When Professor West became discouraged and thought of accepting a post at another college, however, Wilson led a movement to urge him to stay. He seemed to need West as an enemy on campus, even though he could not collaborate with him.

Wilson clothed his opposition to the graduate school in high moral principles. He focused on West's plan to build the school on the golf course at the edge of the campus, arguing that this was undemocratic because the graduate students would not interact with the undergraduates. He traveled the country asking Princeton alumni, "Will America tolerate the seclusion of graduate students? Will America tolerate the idea of having graduate students set apart? Seclude a man . . . from the rough and tumble of college life . . . and you have done a thing which America will brand with contemptuous disapproval."[29]

This dubious issue failed to stir the alumni, let alone American people at large who surely had other things to worry about. West's plans for building the graduate school as a separate college were, ironically, based on the same arguments that Wilson had used for the quadrangles. In Wilson's mind, however, the issue of the location of the graduate school building became a crusade for democracy against elitism. When the trustees proposed a compromise solution, putting some of the graduate buildings on the center of the campus and some on the edge, Wilson completely reversed himself by arguing that the location was of no importance. He now claimed that the problem was that the proposal espoused Professor West's ideals, and these were the wrong ideals. With the right ideals, which would be Wilson's ideals, the faculty could run a successful graduate program anywhere in Mercer County.

The difficulty with this argument was that no one could discover any difference in educational philosophy between West and Wilson. When asked why he had written a laudatory preface to West's proposal, Wilson falsely claimed he had never read it. The leading historian of Wilson's rise to power, Arthur Link, was bewildered by Wilson's irrational and self-defeating behavior:

> Who can explain the reasons that led Wilson finally to propound this interpretation of the graduate school controversy? The vagaries of his mind during this period are unfathomable. . . . there was no basis in fact for Wilson's charges. No evidence exists that West, Pyne or any other person supporting them wanted to make the graduate college an exclusive social club.[30]

When a large bequest provided a surplus of funds, Wilson recognized that he had no hope of killing the graduate school project. He never accepted the defeat emotionally, however, and continued to be angry with West for the rest of his life. The Princeton trustees were fed up with him by this time, but his career was rescued in the nick of time when feelers he had extended to New Jersey political leaders paid off and he was offered the opportunity to run for governor.

To be nominated for governor, Wilson had to make a commitment to the leader of the New Jersey Democratic Party machine, "Boss" James Smith. At this point, Wilson abandoned his commitment script for a pragmatic script. He promised Smith, in writing, that he would do nothing to upset his organization, so Smith went against his instinctive dislike of the "Presbyterian priest" and believed him. After all, a man with such strong moral and religious scruples should be good to his word. Wilson, however, believed that lying was justified for two reasons: to defend the honor of a woman or the interests of the nation. And he was convinced that the nation needed nothing so much as the leadership of Woodrow Wilson. As soon as he was elected, he turned against the Smith machine, building a reputation as a crusading reformer. Smith, whose pragmatic political script was based on the pursuit of self-interest through personal relationships, was dumbfounded that a moralistic college professor had out-manipulated him.

In order to win the governorship of New Jersey, Wilson made a fundamental shift in his political ideology. He shifted from a militant conservative opponent of government regulations to a left-of-center progressive. He never explained the reasons for this change. Indeed he tried to hide it until after winning the nomination in the hopes of appealing to both groups. During the campaign he was forced to take a stand and came out clearly for progressivism. One has to read his speeches closely, however, to observe the ideological change, which was obscured as much as possible in his rhetoric.[31]

Oddly enough, the change in fundamental political philosophy did not evoke anything like the emotional intensity in Wilson's life as the trivial fight over the location of the graduate school. His ego was on the line in the graduate school issue, since he had made a strong personal commitment to it. Getting elected governor would be a realization of his lifelong dream to be a statesman. These self-esteem goals were more important to him than broad philosophical concerns.

As governor of New Jersey, Wilson repeated his "temperamental inability to cooperate with men who were not willing to follow his lead completely."[32] This, and his frequent absences from the state, limited his effectiveness as governor. He was, however, able to use his image as a progressive governor and his charisma as a public speaker to win nomination and election to the presidency of the United States.

As president, Wilson followed an authoritarian script by surrounding himself with sycophants who praised him unstintingly. The most important was Colonel Edward House who catered to Wilson's narcissistic needs, writing him that "you are the bravest, wisest leader, the gentlest and most gallant gentleman and the truest friend in all the world."[33] Wilson exuberated, "what I like about House is that he is the most self-effacing man that ever lived."[34]

When Wilson led the nation into World War I, after campaigning for reelection on the slogan "He Kept us Out of War," he convinced himself that the war was a holy crusade to make the world safe for democracy and prevent future wars. He couldn't justify fighting the war for more mundane grounds of national interest. The difficulty with his position was that the war aims of Britain and France were much less lofty. They wanted to divide up the German and Ottoman empires while Wilson was committed to self-determination.

After the war Wilson was viewed as a savior by many Europeans. This may have fed into an unconscious identification of himself as Jesus (with his father as the Almighty). That, at least, was the view of French statesman Georges Clemenceau, who said, Wilson "thinks he is another Jesus Christ come upon the earth to reform men."[35] British leader Lloyd George remembered Wilson offering the following defense of his actions: "Why has Jesus Christ so far not succeeded in inducing the world to follow His teaching in these matters? It is because He taught the ideal without devising any practical means of attaining it. That is the reason why I am proposing a practical scheme to carry out His aims."[36]

Unlike the Princeton fight, the negotiations over the Versailles treaty involved an important ethical principle. In Europe, Wilson honestly wanted a just peace that would recognize the legitimate aspirations of all peoples. The allies were largely motivated by narrow national interests. Historians differ in their appraisal of Wilson's effectiveness in the negotiations.[37] Freud and Bullitt argue that just when a stand on principle was called for Wilson backed down and allowed the allies to impose their unjust war aims.[38] Arthur Link claims that Wilson made concessions only when necessary to avoid worse evils and describes the treaty negotiations as "Wilson's finest hour."[39] What is clear is that Wilson placed excessive importance on establishing a League of Nations. This led him to make concessions on less dramatic but more consequential issues such as German war guilt and reparations. He allowed himself to be persuaded that the League of Nations would correct these unjust treaty provisions and establish a just world order. His love of rhetoric and lofty principles took precedence over more important issues. This had the most serious consequences, since the unjust treaty provisions contributed to the German resentments that led to World War II.

The final tragedy of Wilson's life was his inability to get the United States Senate to ratify the League of Nations treaty, which was the culmination of his life's work. This failure was unnecessary. He took the opposition led by Senator Henry Cabot Lodge as a personal affront and refused to accept even the most minor of the reservations the senators wanted to place on the treaty.

In Wilson's defense, it must be conceded that Lodge hated Wilson and was actively scheming against him. But Lodge was a more effective pragmatic politician than Wilson, whose utopianism and commitment script led him to place principle over achievement. Lodge relied on his appraisal of Wilson as a man who would be incapable of making the compromises needed to pass the treaty. Instead of opposing the treaty on principle, Lodge insisted on adding reservations to correct certain passages. This was nothing more than a tactic to defeat the treaty, which was highly popular with the general public. One of Lodge's allies, Senator James Watson, remarked to him, "suppose that the President accepts the treaty with your reservations. Then we are in the League, and once in, our reservations become purely fiction." Lodge replied, "but my dear James, you do not take into consideration the hatred that Woodrow Wilson has for me personally. Never under any set of circumstances in this world could he be induced to accept a treaty with Lodge reservations appended to it."[40]

Lodge's assumption that Wilson would be unable to compromise was correct. Wilson's difficulty, however, was not so much his hatred of Lodge but an ego, which had become identified with his specific proposals. He could not compromise on policy without compromising his self-esteem. Even the historians who are most sympathetic to Wilson recognize that his self-defeating intransigence prevented him from making the compromises necessary to win ratification of the treaty.

Psychoanalyzing Wilson. Wilson, along with Moses and Leonardo da Vinci, was one of the select individuals favored with a psychobiography by Sigmund Freud himself.[41] It was not much of an honor. The biography, which Freud coauthored with one of his patients, diplomat William Bullitt, was a vicious character assassination. It has been severely criticized by psychoanalytic writers, who accuse Freud and Bullitt of projecting their own difficulties as analyst and patient onto Wilson.[42] Freud acknowledged that he did not care much for Wilson when he started the book and that "this aversion increased in the course of years the more I learned about him."[43]

Perhaps because of these strong biases, the book is quite interesting. Bullitt collected as much information as he could in 1932, before the more definitive biographies were available. Information on Wilson's childhood was, however, limited. Where there were gaps in the information, they filled them in with facts, which "psychoanalysis has found to be true with regard to all human beings."[44] Based on this skimpy evidence, Freud and Bullitt argued that Wilson's self-defeating behavior was caused by an unresolved Oedipal complex. He had failed to adequately express his hostile feelings for his father, so he took them out on Professor West and Senator Lodge.

The Oedipus conflict is the most important of the "facts" Freud had found to be true of every man, and, since Wilson did not evidence much, if any, conflict with his father, they assumed that he must have repressed it. This is clearly a case of using "the same Oedipal key for every lock."[45]

Both as a child and as an adult Wilson was quite unconscious of any hostility towards his father and, in fact, seems to have idolized him. The dedication to his first book read: "To the author's father, the patient guide of his youth, the gracious companion of his manhood, his best instructor and most lenient critic, this book is affectionately dedicated by the author."[46]

Freud and Bullitt interpret Wilson's idealization of his father as a reaction-formation against unconscious feelings of hostility. They argue that his failure to resolve this Oedipal conflict caused him to view men who conflicted with him as father figures. They do not, however, explain why Wilson's unresolved Oedipal conflict failed to inhibit his dealings with "Boss" Smith, only to recur in his dealings with Senator Lodge.

The other major psychobiography on Wilson was published in 1956 by Alexander and Juliette George.[47] Their key argument was that his self-defeating behavior as an adult was due to a poor self-concept, which had its origin in his father's excessive teasing and criticism. In their view, Wilson attempted to compensate for this low self-concept by seeking political power.

What are the facts and conjectures about Wilson's childhood upon which these analyses are based? "Tommy" Woodrow Wilson lived with both of his parents in a stable, middle-class American household. His father was a tall, handsome, and successful Presbyterian minister, well known for his dashing oratorical performances in the pulpit. Tommy idolized his father and thought himself puny and ugly by comparison with his protuberant ears and the eyeglasses, which slid down his beaked nose. It is known that he took comfort in the following limerick, which he repeated over and over:

> For beauty I am not a star
> There are others more handsome by far.
> But my face I don't mind it,
> For I am behind it,
> It's the people in front that I jar.[48]

As an adult, he continued to joke that he was the homeliest man on earth, and once told a photographer that taking his picture would smash the negative.[49] He was actually a reasonably attractive man with a "strong face" and largish ears, not significantly less handsome than his father in photographs taken at comparable ages.[50]

Tommy had a close relationship with his father, but the nature of the relationship is disputed. Some accounts portray his father as a harsh taskmaster, making him write and rewrite essays about any misbehavior and pedantically correcting him whenever he misused a word. His father had a caustic wit and teased him, but there is a disagreement about whether this teasing was excessive or damaging. It is agreed, however, that his father also shared confidences and intimate moments with him and that Tommy felt very close to him.

The Oedipal interpretation does not hold up very well in the light of evidence now available about Wilson's relationship with his father and with women as a young adult. In reviewing developments during Wilson's law school days, when he was courting Harriet Woodrow, who declined his proposal of marriage, and Ellen Axson, who accepted him, psychoanalyst Joseph Bongiorno concludes that:

> an Oedipal formulation runs into difficulties. That Woodrow went on to success after his failure rules out a success neurosis. Further, he gave little indication of guilt over his attractions to either Harriet or Ellen. He wrote to Ellen freely and often of kisses and caresses. And finally at no time did he show disgust or revulsion, the presence of which would suggest the danger of gratifying a repressed, forbidden impulse. Rather, Woodrow's experiences and feelings in these years are familiar to us now from patients who have experienced some disturbances in their self development: low self-esteem, poor tension regulation, and the need for personal relationships to maintain a manageable balance in each.[51]

This seems as good a psychiatric diagnosis of Wilson as is possible, based largely on a careful analysis of his quite personal and revealing correspondence with his fiancée and with his father. The letters suggest that Tommy's father was overinvested in him, and he also thought of himself as playing a Godlike role. When Woodrow was in trouble because of unexcused absences at the University of Virginia, his father wrote:

> we are as truly identified—*my* heart at least being the judge—as if we were one and the same person. What *you* have done, therefore, I feel as if I had done—and my head bows and my heart saddens accordingly. . . .
>
> My own precious son, I love you, and believe in you. God bless you now and ever: and that He may do so, seek more and more His guidance who is yr. *supreme* father
>
> Your affc. (earthly) Father.[52]

A child whose parents are so closely identified with him often becomes "enmeshed in his parent's needs [and] has difficulty developing a full, continuous, separate sense of self apart from the parent."[53] This is a fuller description of Woodrow Wilson than the Georges' argument that he had a "low self-concept" for which he compensated by attaining political power.[54]

His self-concept may have been fragile because it was so dependent on approval from his father and mother, but it was also inflated by their idealized estimate of him. This pattern is common in political leaders who find satisfaction in having their inflated, narcissistic self-concept confirmed by the adulation of crowds. A "low self-concept" without the narcissistic features, is not likely to lead to outstanding achievement and recognition.

Neither Freud and Bullitt nor the Georges paid much attention to Wilson's relationship with his mother. Wilson's mother, who was often depressed, was very supportive and overprotective of her son, which may have contributed to his excessive overconfidence as well as his shyness and dependence on women as an adult. He remained financially dependent on his parents until his late twenties.

One of Wilson's defenders has argued that Wilson suffered a series of strokes beginning as early as 1900 and that these largely accounted for his lapses in political judgment.[55] A number of prominent medical specialists have disputed the diagnosis, however, finding no reason to disagree with the specialists who examined Wilson at the time.[56] He may also have suffered from developmental dyslexia as a child.[57] He did not learn the alphabet until he was nine and could not read at all until he was eleven. His spelling and handwriting (with both hands) were excellent as an adult, however, which argues against the dyslexia hypothesis.

Parental Scripts. Many of Wilson's behavior patterns follow scripts modeled on or taught by his parents. In addition to helping with his reading, his father shared his love of fine phrases and lofty principles, and this became a central feature of Wilson's life script. In their Calvinist faith, morality was all important. Nothing was more admired than taking a stand on a moral issue. His uncle, Dr. James Woodrow, was fired from his position as Professor of Political Science at the Columbia Theological Seminary because of his insistence on teaching Darwin's theory of evolution. Wilson's parents held him up as a model for his courage in standing up for his ideals.

Wilson's father went through a self-defeating career episode, which was remarkably similar to Wilson's experiences at Princeton. He was professor of rhetoric at Columbia Theological Seminary in South Carolina and preached part-time at the local Presbyterian church. When the church let him go because it decided it needed a full-time minister, Wilson's father demanded that the Seminary require its students to attend Sunday services on campus instead of at the church in town. He was unable to offer a convincing rationale for this and left in disgrace when the faculty finally voted down his proposal. Although he went on to have a very successful career, it is reported that "he never fully recovered his self-confidence and self-esteem after this defeat."[58]

Wilson built his life goals around these stories and around a desire to make his parents proud of him. He was mesmerized by an article about British statesman William Gladstone and made a conscious decision to model his life after him. He set himself a goal of achieving a lofty position in life and tenaciously stuck to it. He first entered the law profession because he thought that would lead to a political career. His law practice failed to attract a single client (except his mother), and he retrained as a political scientist. After a very successful academic career, he was offered the presidency of Princeton University, which gave him the first opportunity to play his cherished role of statesman.

Although Freud and Bullitt and the Georges place great emphasis on his failure to confront or disagree with his father, there was one very important exception. He stuck to his commitment to become a statesman instead of following his father into the Presbyterian ministry. Who is to say that this act of independence was not enough to satisfy his Oedipal needs for rebellion?

As a leader, Wilson had many of the traits that have often been found in leaders of revolutions.[59] He was an ascetic who tended to confuse the boundary between his own personal needs and the interests of the community or the nation as a whole. He tended to see other people either as disciples or as enemies and had a hard time recognizing that someone might disagree with him on an issue without being motivated by personal animosity. He was a charismatic speaker who was skilled at influencing the feelings of others to suit his aims. He might have been happier as the leader of a revolutionary society, which would have given him absolute power and unquestioning admiration.

In his book on *Constitutional Government in the United States,* Wilson had advised that an American President must "establish intimate relations of confidence with the Senate on his own initiative, not carrying his plans to completion and then laying them in final form before the Senate to be accepted or rejected . . . in order that there may be a veritable counsel and a real accommodation of views instead of a final challenge and contest."[60] Despite his clear intellectual understanding, he was emotionally unsuited for the compromises and concessions necessary to accomplish his goals in the American system.

Comparison of Life Scripts: Russell and Wilson

Script theory begins with the common-sense observation that people model their lives on their parents and the other role models available to them. It allows for the fact that people make conscious choices in developing their personalities. Much sense can be made of Russell's and Wilson's lives with these straightforward assumptions. Depth psychology is most useful when people behave in self-defeating and irrational ways or when their choices are governed by strong feelings that they themselves do not understand. It helps to explain why both Russell and Wilson became locked into scripts that frustrated their own objectives.

In Russell's case, it is uncanny how closely he followed his deceased parents' skeptical and protest scripts as dissenting freethinkers and sexual radicals, given the fact that his grandmother made every effort to steer him in other directions. His parents, for example, believed that it was right for his mother to have sexual relations with a tutor they employed who was dying of tuberculosis and would have no opportunity to marry. When Russell grew up and coedited a volume of his parents' papers, he was shocked to find out how much he resembled them.[61]

Russell had an extraordinarily strong commitment to a scientific script and an exceptional willingness to submit his beliefs to empirical tests. He was remarkably open about expressing his feelings in his voluminous correspondence and in autobiographical writing, which helped him to cope with his emotional problems. His skill in externalizing his problems produced a lot of creative work, but discouraged him from seeking therapy, which might have helped him to enjoy his life more fully.

Woodrow Wilson's battle with Professor West and his failures at Versailles came about because the need to protect his narcissistic ego clouded his judgment about the moral issues involved as well as about practical political considerations. Wilson was willing to compromise certain of his ideals to the demands of practical politics, so long as he had not become emotionally committed to a specific project or proposal. Once his ego was involved in a project, however, he lost much of his ability for rational judgment.

Many of the differences in Wilson's and Russell's life stories can be understood by viewing them as examples of survivor and commitment scripts. Survivor scripts are often formed during a traumatic childhood when good and bad scenes are repeated in an exaggerated way. The death of Russell's parents, and his upbringing by a grandmother who strongly opposed many of his parents' core values, led him to view the world as an unpredictable and unreliable place where great pleasures were followed by terrible disappointments.

The roots of this script in Russell's childhood experiences is confirmed by the way his conversion to pacifism was triggered by sympathy for a three-year-old boy whose mother was suffering a heart attack. His relationships to women during his adult life also followed a survivor script and can easily be explained as resulting from childhood experiences with controlling and unreliable female caretakers. These experiences certainly colored his views of political and social issues, but not necessarily for the worse. His ability to abandon his idealization of Bolshevism so quickly and decisively when confronted with new information was facilitated by his survivor script, which helped him to accept the fact that seemingly good things are likely to go bad.

Wilson had a childhood in which religious values were strongly reinforced by parents who were supportive. Even if family life was sometimes unpleasant, he could always rely on his parents. The benefits of the family relationships to him greatly exceeded the costs. In such a family, a child learns to defer gratification in the pursuit of long-term values. This kind of commitment was strongly valued in his family.

Wilson was eager to stand up for principles, but had difficulty doing so because his insecurity created an exaggerated need for approval and because his fragile narcissistic overconfidence made him insensitive to realistic constraints. Being president and surrounding himself with sycophantic associates provided him with tremendous ego support, but it was apparently not enough. He tended to fall out of touch with political realities and to remain committed to positions he had taken when there was no realistic possibility of putting them into effect.

Wilson's married life also followed a commitment script. He was devoted to his first wife. Fortunately for him, she was equally committed and devoted her life to meeting his every need. When she died he was miserable and had difficulty functioning as president until he found someone to replace her. While there is evidence that he had an affair at a time of particularly great stress, he seems also to have felt tremendously guilty for this violation of his commitment to his wife and his religious values.[62]

One of the major functions of many ideological scripts is to divide the world into good and evil, into enemies and allies. Bertrand Russell used protest scripts for this purpose. For him, good and evil were social forces such as socialism, capitalism, and militarism. His enemies were political figures such as Lenin, Hitler, and Lyndon Johnson, not people from his personal life. One can dispute some of his judgments. Today, for example, few see Kennedy and Khrushchev as evil men out to destroy the world, although the militaristic social forces they were trying to manage certainly threatened to do so. But Russell was critical of his own judgments and was able to change them when conditions or evidence warranted.

Woodrow Wilson suffered from a tendency to make enemies of people who disagreed with him in the normal interplay of democratic politics. He was so strongly committed to his policy proposals that he could not tolerate anyone who questioned them. Viewing people from one's personal life as ideological enemies is a common trait, of course, but one ill suited to a statesman or a practical politician. Wilson was much more flexible in his attitudes toward social groups such as big business and organized labor, adjusting them to suit his political advantage. This, of course, is a trait that distinguishes the pragmatic scripts of politicians from the protest scripts of moralists and activists, such as Bertrand Russell, who are more concerned with expressing their values than with winning power.

When people have a strong desire to accomplish a goal that seems objectively very difficult, they often resort to utopian scripts in the hope that some dramatic and powerful force will intervene to transform the world. For a time Russell believed in socialism as a utopian force that would transform and save the world. He supported the Bolshevik regime because it promised this kind of transformation, even though it had "temporarily" violated many of his most fundamental values. He abandoned this utopian vision when confronted in a direct way with the realities of the Bolshevik regime.

Most utopians are much more persistent than Bertrand Russell in retaining their faith in utopian transformations. To an extent pacifism replaced socialism as a utopian vision in Russell's thinking, but he compromised it also when it came into conflict with his understanding of political realities in Nazi Germany. Russell's survivor script, which caused so much personal grief, served him well in helping him to abandon his most strongly held beliefs when they failed to meet real-world tests.

Wilson's utopianism can be seen in his idealized image of the League of Nations as a transformational force that would save the world from future wars. He greatly exaggerated its realistic potential while he compromised on the issues that actually led to another world war. He idealized the League so much that he was unable to allow it to be sullied by congressional amendments or reservations, even though this meant the United States would not join it at all.

Bertrand Russell and Woodrow Wilson are two of the people whose ideological scripts have shaped the world and who served as models for many others. In the chapters to come, we will learn about many more such people, their life experiences, their thoughts and feelings, and the impact they had on the world.

Chapter Four

The Dynamics of Skepticism: Auguste Comte and John Stuart Mill

Auguste Comte and John Stuart Mill were important because they dedicated their lives to skeptical scripts. In the end, however, Comte gave up his commitment to skepticism because he could not tolerate the ambiguity it entailed. He replaced it with a novel positivistic religion of which he was the high priest. Mill remained true to skeptical principles, despite the psychological strain they imposed, and followed them where they led.

Comte and Mill were pioneers in the movement to apply scientific thinking to political affairs.[1] Comte's principal claim to fame is his invention of sociology as an academic discipline, which would make the social system as rational and predictable as the solar system. Comte was eight years older than Mill, having been born in France in 1798, and for a time Mill was the leading English advocate of Comte's ideas. They had a personal friendship, and Mill raised money among his English friends to support Comte when he was unable to hold down a job. They grew apart when Comte's proclivity for all-inclusive systems led him to propose an authoritarian utopia guided by a Religion of Humanity of which he was to be the supreme Spiritual Power. Mill moved in the opposite direction, breaking out of the dogmatic Utilitarianism in which he was raised to become a preeminent exponent of liberty and women's rights.

The psychosocial factors in their lives are suggestive of many of the difficulties with scientific scripts. Both men had significant emotional problems, including a breakdown while they were in their twenties, and a tendency to an exaggerated dependency on women. The origin and nature of these psychological difficulties, and their possible relevance to their work, is a matter of some dispute. Both had difficulty reconciling their commitment to skeptical thought with their feelings.

Auguste Comte

Isidore-Auguste-Marie-Françoise-Xavier Comte's parents were conservative Catholics and cautious Monarchists in postrevolutionary France.[2] His father was an unassuming but honest civil servant who followed a strict schedule, rising each morning at five, breakfasting at eight, arriving at the office at nine, and leaving at five.[3] He was a devoted family man, who seldom left his home and garden except to go to work. His mother, who never told her children that she was twelve years older than her husband, was a gushing and overprotective mother, who doted on her "pet Isidore" and was devoted to all her children.

Their income was meager as Comte's father was honest and hard working, but he refused to get involved in the politics required to advance in the civil service. Indeed, he finally lost his job because of a failure to show sufficient interest in the election campaign.[4] Young Isidore Auguste's only hope for advancement was a scholarship to the Lycée, which he won at nine years of age. It was a kind of military school where the students wore drab uniforms, marched to drums, and studied hard. He was short, reaching only five feet, two inches as an adult, and his face was marred by smallpox. He missed his family and was unhappy in school and got into a lot of fights. He was known for a phenomenal memory, with the ability to memorize entire pages on only one reading. His academic success won him admission to the mathematics department at the Ecole Polytechnique where he was part of a student uprising demanding that a geometry teacher change his authoritarian ways. When the director tried to punish the six leaders, the students went on strike and the government sent in troops to shut the school down. Comte never applied for readmission when the school reopened, and never got a degree, which made it difficult for him to earn his living as a mathematics teacher.

He did find a job as secretary to Henri de Saint-Simon, an early socialist-industrialist who was more of an activist than a systematic thinker. He also fell in love with a young woman, Caroline Massin, whose mother had encouraged her to become the mistress of a wealthy lawyer. They married and the lawyer ended up supporting them both as he signed up to study algebra with Comte. His wife was registered with the police as a prostitute and was inclined to return to this profession whenever their money ran out.

Lacking a university appointment or other adequate source of income, Comte announced a private course in Positive Philosophy, which was to cover all of human learning in seventy-two lectures. He worked night and day to prepare until he had a nervous breakdown characterized by irrational attacks and violent rages. Caroline was forced to run from him in fear several times. He was hospitalized for eight months in a prestigious private clinic, which released him as incurable. On the ride home he attacked the friend who was accompanying him, insisting that they were not in Paris but in Constantinople.

In the "personal preface" to the sixth volume of his *Cours de Philosophie Positive,* Comte explains that his illness was the result of the "fatal concurrance of great mental or moral pain *(peines morales)* with a violent excess of work."[5] He claims that his illness would have run its course naturally if he had not been sent to the mental institution, where "the most absurd treatment delivered him rapidly to a very characteristic alienation." The proof of this is the fact that he soon recovered at home, due to the "intrinsic power of his own organization assisted by affectionate domestic attention," which was provided by his wife and by his mother.

His treatment at the asylum consisted mostly of blood letting, baths and showers, and enemas, together with an attempt at supportive talk therapy. This treatment was the state of the art at the time, under the direction of an eminent specialist, Dr. Esquirol. Comte was diagnosed as a megalomaniac.[6] As defined by his psychiatrist, mania included symptoms such as the exaltation of ideas, disorientation with regard to time and space, disparate associations of ideas, belief in bizarre images, a tendency to strange discourse, and an inclination to the most ridiculous actions.[7] Comte may have been correct about the limitations of the therapy, but his wife and friends thought he required institutionalization because he was a danger to himself and others. He insisted, for example, on jumping into a lake with his wife despite the fact that he had never learned to swim. He also attempted suicide by throwing himself into the Seine in 1827.

After recovering from his mental crisis, Comte worked on elaborating his course on Positive Philosophy into a six-volume book, a task that took twelve years. He kept his manic tendencies largely under control during this time with strenuous mental discipline. He continued to have outbursts of rage throughout his life and had several minor breakdowns, which largely explains why the French universities found it so easy to do without his services. In his autobiographical essay, he described a world polarized between friends and enemies, and he blamed his problems on the forces of theology and metaphysics, which opposed his scientific outlook. He denied the seriousness of his psychological problems and externalized the responsibility for his career problems.

Two years after finally breaking up with his wife, he fell madly in love with a Madame Clotilde de Vaux, who refused to become his mistress. He idolized her and was with her constantly for a year as she was dying of tuberculosis. This love affair improved his spirits tremendously, with disastrous consequences for his scholarly work. He abandoned his attempts at scientific rigor for bizarre and eccentric religious and utopian speculations.

No Freudian psychobiographer has written about Comte, but the basic patterns seem clear. A psychodynamic account of his life would focus on his having been sent away to boarding school at nine years of age, which doubtless interrupted the normal working out of his Oedipal conflicts. This led him to direct his aggressions toward his teachers and school authorities. This account fits reasonably well with Comte's self-analysis. He believed that his father was a small man, unworthy of having been the father of the grand priest of humanity. He also resented having been "torn as a child from the normal emotional environment of his home and placed in a baneful (*funeste*) scholastic environment."[8]

Throughout his life, Comte had a pattern of forming close friendships with other men, then breaking with them in anger. This happened in the most important relationship with a man in his adult life, his apprenticeship with Saint-Simon. Saint-Simon was thirty-eight years older than he and could be viewed as a father figure, although there is no evidence that Comte thought of him in that way. He did rebaptize himself on the occasion of beginning work with Saint-Simon, dropping Isidore for Auguste. He broke with Saint-Simon a few years later, angrily accusing Saint-Simon of taking credit for his work. This kind of accusation is impossible to assess in a situation where one man is working as an assistant to another. It is clear, however, that many of Comte's major ideas were anticipated by Saint-Simon in works published before Comte came into his life.[9] Comte's contribution was to elaborate these ideas into a comprehensive formal system.

Comte's lifelong idealization and excessive devotion to women could be explained as an unconscious attempt to complete the rebellion against his father and win his mother's favors. He made the worship of women a central focus of his Religion of Humanity, yet he advocated that they should be denied the right to earn an income so that they would be completely dependent on their husbands or fathers.

Intellectually, Comte's vision was to bring about a day when all the sciences, including sociology especially, would be as rigorous and deterministic as mathematics. He adopted this mission when he was only fourteen and "passing spontaneously through all the essential degrees of the revolutionary spirit, I already felt the fundamental need for a universal regeneration in both politics and philosophy."[10] Why would a fourteen-year-old boy feel such passion instead of pursuing more typical interests such as girls and sports? It seems likely that he felt a need for a doctrine that would help him to control his own violent and sometimes self-destructive impulses.

Even after recovering from his breakdown in 1826, Comte continued to struggle against a recurrence of his manic tendencies and against attacks from the enemies who he believed to be conspiring against him. The nature of his thinking is conveyed in the following letter, which he sent to John Stuart Mill after completing the final volume of his *Cours de Philosophie Positive:*

> my miserable enemies, in addition to wanting to reduce me to indigence, have also, I know, always confusedly strained to cause, by means of a coordinated attack on my work, a recurrence of the terrible and irreparable episode of 1826, discussed in my preface; but their abominable hope will be, I dare to affirm, always completely illusory, thanks to the constant discipline which I exercise over my emotions and my conduct.[11]

Comte divided the sciences into six levels, each of which had its own laws: mathematics, astronomy, terrestrial physics, chemistry, biology, and sociology. Glaringly absent from his hierarchy of the sciences is psychology, which he included as "cerebral physiology" under biology. Comte firmly believed that individual behavior was determined by biological and social forces. He looked forward to the day when sociologists would be able to predict social events as precisely as astronomers predict the movement of the planets. He relied on phrenology, the study of the shape of the skull, for guidance into cerebral matters. One of his tenets was that individuals go through the same three stages in their thinking—from theological to metaphysical and on to scientific thought—as societies. Once society became truly rational and scientific, psychological problems, including his own, would no longer exist.

At this point, the reader may be wondering why Comte was an influential thinker or why he is worthy of attention today. And I haven't even mentioned his more bizarre ideas, such as burning all books except for one hundred great works; exterminating all plant and animal species not domesticated by man; concentrating all political and economic power in the hands of three bankers and a High Priest; or replacing the Christian father, son, and Holy Ghost with the mother, wife, and daughter to symbolize the three virtues: veneration, attachment, and kindness. These creative fantasies, however, came after the 1845 love affair with Clotilde de Vaux, which seems to have released him from the need to rigorously control his emotions and flights of fancy. His most lasting contributions were in the six-volume *Cours de Philosophie Positive,* which was written during his struggle against his manic tendencies.

The scientific script, which Comte elaborated in these tediously wordy volumes, may have been partly motivated by a need to control his own psychopathology, but it also spoke to society's need for a framework to understand the social changes, which were accelerating as a result of the industrial revolution. Many historians of social thought list Comte as one of the thinkers who was most influential in shaping modern society.[12] Historian Isaiah Berlin argues that Comte's:

> views have affected the categories of our thought more deeply than is commonly supposed. Our view of the natural sciences, of the material basis of cultural evolution, of all that we call progressive, rational, enlightened, Western . . . our view of history itself, owes a good deal to his teaching and his fame. His grotesque pedantry, the unreadable dullness of his writing, his vanity, his eccentricity, his solemnity, the pathos of his private life, his insane dogmatism, his authoritarianism, his philosophical fallacies, all that is bizarre and utopian in his character and writings, need not blind us to his merits.[13]

Other historians focus on the flaws in his work, arguing that "his reputation has not assigned him to the first rank of thinkers" and that "few people in France bothered about him then [ca. 1900] and everyone makes fun of him now [1926]."[14] A thorough historical study of Comte's influence shows that positivism peaked in the last two decades of the nineteenth century and then declined rapidly. This was partly because "familiarity with it tended to breed contempt. It became less and less possible for outsiders to ignore the unsympathetically bizarre details of Comte's social and religious utopia."[15] The reactionary aspects of positivism became better known, while "for the 'progressive' generation in both countries a new social prophet was available of equal scientific pedigree and greater immediate applicability, Karl Marx."[16]

Unlike many physical scientists who aspire to apply scientific methods to social problems, Comte was strongly opposed to what is now called "reductionism." He insisted that sociology would have to develop its own laws, not use laws from other sciences such as physics or biology. Sociology as an academic discipline has struggled to live up to this mandate. Comte's influence in sociology has been indirect, primarily through the exemplary works of his follower Emile Durkheim, who replaced Comte's utopian speculation with rigorous research demonstrating that scientific generalizations could be made about sociological phenomena.[17] To the extent that Comtian thinking has a more direct influence in sociology, it is largely in reinforcing the discipline's penchant for tendentious world historical speculative theorizing and its taboo against biological or psychological explanations. Sociobiologist Pierre van den Berghe argues that "most sociologists have no clear perception of what reductionism means, but they are firmly against it. . . . In sociology, reductionism has been an epithet, first popularized by Durkheim, who kept insisting that social phenomena were not reducible to individual motivations or actions."[18]

This defensiveness serves to protect the discipline's boundaries against psychology, but at the expense of a trend toward "sterile, abstracted scholasticism. . . . attempts at general sociological theory have filled library shelves with failures or platitudinous truisms."[19] For contemporary sociologists, as for Comte, the taboo against psychology can serve as a defense against introspection into the sociologist's own feelings. Unlike psychologists and psychiatrists, for whom introspection and concern with "countertransference" are part of the professional training, sociologists have a professional bias against considering their own feelings in the course of their work.[20]

Research methodologies such as survey research, demography, and historical comparative analysis tend to isolate the sociologist from meaningful interaction with the people he or she studies. In her biographical study of a major figure in the history of American sociology, Barbara Laslett argues that the stress on quantitative methodology is rooted in male gender roles, which stress unfeeling objectivity against introspection and empathy.[21] To the extent that this characterizes sociology as a discipline, it can be traced back to Comte's rigid defensiveness and sexism.

John Stuart Mill

While Comte used his scientific script as a means for disciplining his manic tendencies, John Stuart Mill used his to liberate a psyche that was oppressed by dependence on a controlling father. Unlike Comte's shy and unassertive father, Mill's father was a powerful and dominating influence who completely shaped Mill's life through adolescence. Mill shared Comte's need to orient his emotional life around dependency on an idealized woman, although his relationship with his mother was distant and cold. He was strongly committed to scientific objectivity in dealing with social problems, but he did not believe that psychological problems could be solved through sociological analysis.

Mill's autobiography begins with the information that he was "the eldest son of James Mill, the author of the History of India."[22] His mother is not mentioned in the book, although in an early draft he mentioned that she "worked from morning till night for her children" and that "That rarity in England, a really warm hearted mother, would in the first place have made my father a totally different being and in the second would have made the children grow up loving and being loved."[23]

James Mill was a leading advocate of Jeremy Bentham's Utilitarianism, which advocated that social policies should be designed to achieve the greatest happiness of the greatest number. Indeed, the Mills lived with the Benthams for much of John Stuart's childhood. For Bentham, the utilitarian principle was little more than a "rough and ready criterion for judging the utility of legislation," but James Mill used it as a philosophical principle, which enabled him to defend each of his arguments "as if it embodied a universal and eternal principle."[24]

The flaw in Utilitarianism is that there was actually no way of being certain which policies would lead to the greatest happiness for the greatest number. Although the utilitarians were proud of their commitment to rationality and empiricism, they "made little effort to check [their] premises by observation."[25] On a practical level, their commitment was to the political and economic interests of the middle class to which they belonged and which they believed to be the most rational and productive element in society.

James Mill sought to make his firstborn son the embodiment of his principles, raising him in such a way as to assure that he would contribute the maximum to the cause. He educated his son at home, and kept him out of contact with boys his own age, in order to maximize his potential. He began his study of Greek at age three, working with a Greek-Latin dictionary, although he knew no Latin. He also learned arithmetic as a young child and read extensively in history and philosophy as he grew up. His mother, presumably preoccupied with the eight other children she bore her critical, domineering, and unaffectionate husband, left John Stuart's upbringing to his father.

Since John Stuart was kept apart from other children, he did not know that his accomplishments were exceptional and, indeed, usually believed himself to be behind in his studies. When he was fourteen, his father informed him that as he went out into the world he would find many who would praise him for his learning, but that he should not be proud since everything he had accomplished was due to his good fortune in having such an exceptional father.

Freudian theory would suggest that a boy raised in such complete dependency on his father would have an especially strong need for Oedipal revolt. John Stuart never openly rebelled against his father, which should have left him with a need to project these needs into his intellectual and political life. Certainly his need for freedom from his father was much greater than that of many revolutionary leaders who, psychobiographers have argued, made revolutions as a way of expressing their Oedipal frustrations.[26]

Several authors have interpreted Mill's life in terms of the Oedipus complex. These writers suffer from the usual difficulties of psychoanalyzing someone who is known only through his writings or through the writings of other people. No information is available about any sexual feelings Mill may have had in early childhood. He seems to have had a low sexual drive throughout his life, as evidenced by his belief that population could easily be controlled by having married couples refrain from sex. Bruce Mazlish suggests there may be significance in the fact that Mill fell in love with a married woman, Harriet Taylor, who had the same first name as his mother and was married to a man with the same first name as his father.[27] He and Harriet had an intense Platonic love affair for "though we did not consider the ordinances of society binding on a subject so entirely personal, we did feel bound that our conduct should be such as in no degree to bring discredit on her husband, nor therefore on herself."[28] They finally married when John Taylor died, but Harriet was suffering from a paralysis at the time. Bruce Mazlish believes that the paralysis was probably hysterical and that Mill probably never experienced carnal intercourse in his lifetime. Of course, this cannot be proven and most of their friends at the time assumed they were having an affair. Nevertheless, it is easy to see how biographers might conclude that "in Mill's unconscious, Harriet was . . . his mother as a desired Oedipal object. She was also his mother as a maternal figure. Everyone has noticed Mill's dependency on her . . . and how he constantly noted down for Harriet the symptoms of his illnesses, as if he were a child with its mother."[29]

Mazlish argues that Mill's feminism was due to a sublimated desire to emancipate his mother from his father. His unconscious desire, however, was not to possess his mother sexually but to "place her beside himself as an equal."[30] His lack of desire to have his mother for himself, in Mazlish's view, was because Mill was bisexual and also because he thought of her as unloving and unmotherly. While other men feared that liberated women would lose their femininity, Mill was unconcerned because he felt his mother did not have much femininity to lose.

Peter Glassman argues that Mill "obsessively detested his mother" and argues that he suffered from an "inverted Oedipus complex."[31] In other words, he longed for his father and wanted to do away with his mother. The fact that competent psychohistorians cannot agree whether he suffered from a classic or an inverted Oedipus complex highlights the speculative nature of this kind of analysis. This kind of speculation may be useful for a therapist, who can check the interpretations out with her client, but historians can never really know what was going on in Mill's unconscious mind. It seems very reasonable to assume that he, like many Victorian youth, longed for freedom from his father.[32] But, if so, even this desire was unconscious. At no point in his *Autobiography* did he express a desire for liberation from his father.

For Mill as a young man, the "principle of utility," which he learned from his father and from Jeremy Bentham was:

> the keystone which held together the detached and fragmentary component parts of my knowledge and beliefs. It gave unity to my conception of things. I now had opinions; a creed, a doctrine, a philosophy; in one among the best sense of the word, a religion; the inculcation and diffusion of which could be made the principal outward purpose of a life.[33]

This doctrine was his father's core value, and like many young people John Stuart defined his own identity by expressing parental values in as pure a form as possible. In his early twenties, he was the leader of a utilitarian study group, edited a utilitarian journal, and was active as a utilitarian speaker and debater. He became dissatisfied, however, because the doctrine provided no outlet for his feelings. Benthamites were often accused of being "mere reasoning machines," and he felt that, for two or three years of his life, this description was "not altogether untrue" of him. He understood that his father's doctrines "tended to the undervaluing of feelings," since his father was offended by people who justified policies with feelings instead of with rational arguments.[34]

His movement away from the utilitarian doctrine was gradual and did not involve any open confrontation with his father. One day he was reading Condorcet's *Life of Turgot* and came across the phrase "he regarded all sects as noxious" as an explanation for Turgot's keeping himself distinct from the Encyclopedists as a group. This phrase "sank deeply into my mind. I left off designating myself and others as Utilitarians, and by the pronoun 'we' or any other designation, I ceased to *afficher* [display] sectarianism. My real inward sectarianism I did not get rid of till later, and much more gradually."[36]

Finally getting rid of sectarianism required going through a "mental crisis" caused by the failure of the belief system, which had given him "an object in life; to be a reformer of the world. My conception of my own happiness was entirely identified with this object."[36]

One day, when he was twenty years old, he woke up feeling depressed, and it occurred to him that even if the changes in opinion and in society that he was advocating were put into place the next day, they would not make him happy. He seemed to have "nothing left to live for." The depression lasted several months until he happened to be reading Marmontel's *Memoires* and came upon a passage in which the Marmontel relates:

his father's death, the distressed position of his family, and the sudden inspiration by which he, then a mere boy, felt and made them feel that he would be everything to them—would supply all that they had lost. A vivid conception of the scene and its feelings came over me, and I was moved to tears. From this moment my burthen grew lighter.[37]

To one Freudian analyst this scene suggests that Mill's depression was caused by "repressed death wishes against his father."[38] At the least, it suggests a desire to be free of his father's domination. In the early draft of his *Autobiography,* Mill remarked that "another evil I shared with many sons of energetic fathers. To have been, through childhood, under the constant rule of a strong will, certainly is not favorable to strength of will."[39]

In any event, Mill developed the strength of will necessary to move away from Utilitarianism, which he viewed as a sectarian doctrine that neglected the emotional dimensions of human life. He was determined, also, not to sacrifice his new found freedom by adopting another ideological doctrine:

if I am asked what system of political philosophy I substituted for that which, as a philosophy, I had abandoned, I answer, no system: only a conviction that the true system was something much more complex and many-sided than I had previously had any idea of, and that its office was to supply, not a set of model institutions, but principles from which the institutions suitable to any given circumstance might be deduced.[40]

Mill's decision to avoid commitment to any system contrasts sharply with Comte's resolution to build an all-inclusive system. The contrast is made even sharper by the fact that Mill was in touch with Comte at the time and was entranced with his system. He shared Comte's fundamental goal of building a social science, which would provide objective, scientific answers to social issues. He also thought that Comte's law of three stages was an important insight and agreed that human societies had to be viewed as entities with their own laws of development, not as arbitrary arrangements, which could be changed at will to fit utilitarian schemata.

The most important thing Mill took from Comte, however, was his model of the logic of the social sciences.[41] Comte wanted sociology to be a rigorous scientific discipline such as physics or chemistry with a generally accepted core of theory from which empirical hypotheses could be deduced and tested. The only problem was that no such body of sociological laws existed. Comte's solution was to work inductively, seeking to find regularities in the observable world. Once these regularities were found, he tested whether or not they were consistent with preexisting theory. If so, the theory was confirmed and specified; if not, the theory had to be modified. Mill called this the "inverse deductive method," distinct from the "direct deductive method," which he thought to be characteristic of physics.

This is a perfectly reasonable way of doing research in the social sciences, but the results are usually disappointing if one is hoping to discover general laws that will answer important policy questions. Comte was unwilling to live with this inadequacy. He believed that when the available data left things indeterminate, social scientists were justified in "embellishing" their scientific thoughts in conformity to their need for a more ideal system (*besoin d'idéalité*). In his view, social scientists should follow their "instinctive predilection for order and harmony" in filling in any gaps in the evidence.[42] In order to avoid contaminating his theories with unwelcome facts, Comte adopted a discipline he called "cerebral hygiene," which meant that he simply did not read any new books or journals to avoid contaminating his mind.

Mill thought that Comte's willingness to disregard unwelcome evidence was "a complete dereliction of the essential principles which form the Positive conception of science; and contained the germ of the perversion of his own philosophy which marked his later years."[43] Comte's defenders argue that he was a visionary, not a scientist, and that his work was intended as an elaboration of his intuitive insight, not as a description of science as it actually functioned.[44]

Mill's commitment to scientific evidence forced him to limit his conclusions on many important issues, such as the question of socialism or capitalism. In choosing between "communism with all its chances, and the present [1852] state of society with all its sufferings and injustices," he could only conclude that the experience of humanity to date did not provide enough evidence to reach a definitive conclusion. He thought that it was necessary to compare "communism at its best, with the régime of individual property, not as it is, but as it might be made."[45]

Mill did take a strong stand, however, in support of human rights in *On Liberty* and *The Subjection of Women*. His emotional commitment to liberty was so strong that only very strong evidence would have convinced him to limit freedom. Comte was convinced that biological and sociological evidence proved that women were inherently inferior to men since females were subordinate to males in other species and women had made no historical accomplishments comparable to those of men. He insisted on these ideas very strongly in a series of letters to Mill.[46] Mill was unwilling to reduce psychological differences to biological factors and denied that past history could be used to know what might be possible in the future. He insisted that it was "impossible in the present state of society to obtain complete and correct knowledge" on the question of the natural differences between the sexes, although "almost everybody dogmatizes about it."[47] Given the lack of certain knowledge, he thought the only fair thing to do was to allow women the freedom to choose whatever roles in society they wanted. Comte, by contrast, believed it a scientific fact that women's proper role was to be supported and idolized by men and proposed to arrange matters so that they would have no choice but to be dependent on men.

Comparison of Ideological Scripts

Comte began his political life as a student protestor, rebelling against a harsh academic regime. He continued all his life to rebel against the demands of academia and never obtained a graduate degree or a professorship. As he matured intellectually, he became enamored of science and skepticism and was one of the most influential advocates of a scientific worldview. He sought to be a true skeptic, but he idealized science and expected it to provide answers to all of his and society's problems. He thought that he personally could master all the essential scientific knowledge in every discipline and that this would enable him to reach definitive answers to the world's problems. He was unable to accept the fact that his scientific knowledge, although formidable for his time, was inadequate to the task. He therefore abandoned true skepticism for an authoritarian pseudoscientific cult, which claimed to have all the answers. Like many youthful protestors, he became authoritarian once he had the opportunity to exercise power, if only over a small band of sycophantic disciples.

Pseudoscientific cults such as scientology, astrology, and sectarian Marxism view science as a source of definitive and irrefutable answers to all questions. Mary Baker Eddy, the founder of Christian Science, for example, asserted that "there is neither place nor opportunity in Science for error of any sort."[48] This is the opposite of a true scientific philosophy, which is always open to refutation and correction of errors. Auguste Comte observed that there is no room for debate among astronomers over when and where the sun will go into eclipse. He thought that there should be as little doubt among the scientists of society about the proper role of women or the best way to structure an economy. Sociology offered no such certainties.

Psychologically, authoritarian scientism appealed to Comte because of his need for strict discipline to control his manic tendencies. Mill, on the other hand, was highly disciplined and inhibited, and he sought to escape from the sectarian doctrine in which he was raised. He began his political life as a protestor advocating utilitarian reforms, but he found this dogma too confining and adopted a skeptical script, which resonated with his need for freedom.

Comte began his career with an admirable commitment to scientific principles. He ended it as an authoritarian utopian who closed his mind to new evidence and built castles in the air. His final book on mathematics was the most absurd result of this unfortunate degeneration of an important scientific thinker. In it he named the earth the *Grand Fétiche* (great fetish) and argued that in some distant past it had deliberately adjusted its orbit with a series of planned explosions in order to provide a more suitable environment for people. He realized that this was a fiction, but felt that it was useful to fill "the gaps in our scientific notions with poetic fictions . . . the world being conceived as aspiring to second mankind in ameliorating the universal order under the impulse of the *Grand Etre* (Great Being)."[49]

Mill's skeptical approach to science saved him from absurd speculations, at the expense of conceding that scientific knowledge did not offer answers to many fundamental social questions. He used his logical skills and scientific knowledge to debunk metaphysical speculation and scientistic pretensions. As Iris Mueller concludes, "in a real sense, Mill remained a positivist while Comte became a dogmatist."[50]

Chapter Five

The Ideological Group

While speaking at a mass meeting in Russia in 1917, Leon Trotsky found that:

> At times it seemed as if I felt, with my lips, the stern inquisitiveness of this crowd that had become merged into a single whole. Then all the arguments and words thought out in advance would break and recede under the imperative pressure of sympathy, and other words, other arguments, utterly unexpected by the orator but needed by these people, would emerge in full array from my subconsciousness. On such occasions I felt as if I were listening to the speaker from the outside, trying to keep pace with his ideas, afraid that, like a somnambulist, he might fall off the edge of the roof at the sound of my conscious reasoning.[1]

Strong group beliefs, norms, and assumptions can emerge spontaneously from the chaotic and unstructured behavior of crowds.[2] These beliefs infect both speakers and audiences, leaders and led. Rumors spread and people share their feelings, thoughts, and observations. Quickly, a common definition of the situation emerges and is used to mobilize the group for action. Revolutionary leaders play a key role in the process of defining group norms because of their sensitivity to the feelings of the group. In speeches such as the one described by Trotsky, the talented leader senses or anticipates the crowd's reaction to slogans and phrases and offers words that articulate and magnify the group's feelings. Gifted orators such as Fidel Castro or Jim Jones can sometimes hold such a crowd mesmerized for hours. These leaders also become potent symbols in their own right. Identifying with the same charismatic leader is often one of the main things that holds group members together.

Peaks of emotional intensity are rare for groups, just as they are for individuals. An ideological group may emerge in a time of spontaneous mass enthusiasm, but it must develop an organizational structure with regular patterns and procedures if it is to survive. As ideological groups develop, they must deal with the same organizational issues as other groups. This chapter begins with a discussion of the stages of group development as they apply to ideological groups. The tragic history of the New Jewel Movement in Grenada will be used as an example of the powerful impact group dynamics can have on ideological politics. After this case example, we will examine the role of leadership in ideological movements. We will again use a tragic and extreme case, that of the People's Temple, to illustrate these processes.

Group Dynamics and Ideological Polarization

Studies of group development have found that groups go through developmental stages and that they use social defense mechanisms analogous to those used by individuals.[3] These phenomena can be seen most clearly in laboratory groups where things are simplified for research purposes. In these laboratory groups, the leader often intentionally refuses to perform many of the normal leadership functions in order to force the group to develop more quickly.[4]

Of course, political groups are much more varied than laboratory groups, and the group dynamics are more complex. Nevertheless, similar developmental stages and defense mechanisms can be observed, although with less predictability and regularity. The parallels between laboratory groups and political groups are close enough that members of ideological groups would benefit greatly from paying more attention to them. Many political organizations have destroyed themselves because of poor handling of these group-dynamic processes.

When a laboratory group is first organized, the members are likely to be anxious and uncomfortable, simply because they are in an unfamiliar situation. They seek a way to defend themselves from these anxious feelings. Most members eagerly call upon the leader to provide security and structure. In group-dynamics jargon, we would say that the group uses a "dependency assumption" as a social defense mechanism, which simply means that the group members find security in behaving as if it were necessary for them to defer to a strong authority figure.[5]

At this early stage of group development, the members' anxiety is similar to the "basic anxiety" felt by a small child who is unable to care for herself. Karen Horney argues that people respond to this kind of anxiety in three basic ways.[6] Some people cope by demanding mastery or control over others. Others respond by becoming submissive in a quest for acceptance and love. Still others distance themselves from the group. In the early stages, dependent submission to the leader is the most frequent response. A group may remain stuck in a dependency mode for a long time if the leader has a strong need for mastery while the other members have strong dependency needs. Members who are not comfortable with this pattern may simply drop out.

Ideological groups often differ from laboratory groups in that at the beginning there is no formally defined or generally accepted leader. Anxiety may also be masked in an amorphous crowd situation where people feel safety in numbers and anonymity. Unless the crowd simply dissipates, however, the group must organize itself, and then there is a strong demand for leadership. Once leadership emerges, dependency on the leader is often very strong, perhaps as a means of defending against guilt for having violated societal norms. Leadership cults are a recurrent feature in ideological groups, even those that are theoretically opposed to it.

Moving beyond dependency on the leader is difficult, in both laboratory and ideological groups, but necessary if the group members are to develop their individuality and initiative. Without this development, the group will seem increasingly stifling and repressive disciplinary measures may be needed to keep people in line. In the laboratory group there is not time for this process to develop naturally, so the leader usually forces the group to develop by refusing to meet the members' dependency needs. The members naturally find this disturbing. Depending on their personality type as categorized by Horney, members react in three characteristic ways. Some become highly submissive or "overdependent." They assume that the leader has some secret wisdom or plan, which they try to infer from any remarks or gestures he or she may make. Other members have a tendency to become rebellious or "counterdependent." Still others withdraw and wait for someone else to do something.[7]

As the group progresses and more people become frustrated, the rebellious or counterdependent members are likely to become dominant. In this case, the group adopts what Bion calls a "fight/flight" assumption as a social defense mechanism. This means that the members behave as if they are in great danger and must fight or flee from an enemy.[8]

Group members can also defend against anxiety by adopting ritualistic behavior and rigidly adhering to past procedures or established doctrines. In political groups, this often takes the form of ritualistic adherence to the group's founding ideology as if it contained magical solutions to all their problems. It can also take the form of rigid adherence to parliamentary procedures in meetings or the continuation of activities, which may no longer be effective, merely because they were done in the past.

Table Three

STAGES OF GROUP DEVELOPMENT
LABORATORY GROUPS AND IDEOLOGICAL GROUPS COMPARED

Stages	Laboratory Group	Ideological Group
Primitive	Group initiated by appointed leader Initial anxiety Dependence on leader as social defense	Initial anxiety Spontaneous emergence of beliefs Emergence of charismatic leader Dependence on leader as social defense

Transitional	Leader withdraws
	Group splits between:
	    overdependents
	    counterdependents
	    withdrawn
	Revolt against leader
	Fight/flight assumption and parliamentarism as social defenses
		Group splits between:
		    orthodox, radicals, or purists;
		    revisionists or pragmatists;
		    dropouts
		Power struggle over leadership
		Fight/flight assumption and ideological dogmatism as social defenses

Mature	Revolutionary euphoria Declining energies Building interpersonal relationships Focus on tasks	Revolutionary euphoria Declining energies Routinization of factional conflict and leadership succession Focus on tasks

None of these defenses can work indefinitely, however, if the group is not accomplishing its mission. Covert coalitions develop among members who have similar feelings about the group. These coalitions reinforce each other's feelings and form a nucleus for subgrouping. At some point, the coalitions become explicitly identified and the group is likely to split into two warring factions. Typically, these factions disagree about some issue of policy and procedure. In a laboratory group, the overdependents usually want to elect leadership and establish a formal agenda and procedures, while the counterdependents resist these ideas in favor of expressing feelings or enunciating principles. In an ideological group, the conflict is likely to be between the orthodox purists, who want to stick to the founding principles of the group, and the revisionists, who want to keep the group open to new ideas.

Splits within groups serve as a social defense mechanism, helping members to reduce anxiety by projecting their unwanted feelings onto the other group faction. The group's problems can then be blamed on the other faction instead of being analyzed impartially. Political groups that are unable to achieve their objectives often fall into this pattern as a means of denying their larger problems. When this defense mechanism becomes dominant in a group, the members spend all their time fighting with each other and little or no time fighting the group's supposed enemies or accomplishing its appointed tasks.

Table Four

DEFENSE MECHANISMS IN GROUPS

Dependency Assumption—the group follows an unconscious assumption that it must defer to a strong authority figure.

Fight/Flight Assumption—the group follows an unconscious assumption that it must fight or flee from a threatening enemy outside its boundaries.

Pairing Assumption—the group follows an unconscious assumption that its salvation will come from the unity of a pair of leaders, leading to a dramatic transformation or rebirth of the group.

Covert Coalitions—enduring patterns of behavior governed by dependency, fight/flight, pairing, or other unconscious basic assumptions are maintained among clusters of individuals within the group.

Factional Splitting—arbitrary boundaries are drawn between factions (often originating in covert coalitions) within the group, so that anxiety can be reduced by externalizing unwanted feelings onto another faction.

Organizational Rituals—established policies and procedures are rigidly adhered to even when they are not effective.

Doctrinal Dogmatism—the group's founding ideology or sacred texts are used rigidly to provide simplistic and authoritative answers to problems.

When a training group reaches this point, someone is likely to suggest that the leader leave so that the members can work out their own affairs. This person tends to become a group hero. In ideological groups, there are several common outcomes. The people in the minority faction may leave or the group may split into two groups, each of which begins from scratch with its new leaders. Or the two tendencies may develop norms, which enable them to coexist as factions while they work on their common problems.

After resolving their dependence on the leader in one way or another, groups focus on developing interpersonal relationships among their members. This is analogous to the stage of individual development when children break away from dependency on their parents and focus on peer relationships. At the beginning there is a myth of mutual acceptance and harmony as the group celebrates its independence. An idealized, narcissistic image of the group is created and used to distract attention from remaining problems. This is similar to the period of revolutionary euphoria, which sweeps over an entire country after the overthrow of a tyrannical leader.

And, just as the revolutionary euphoria dissipates in factionalism and apathy, the training group tires of the illusion of harmony, and members express their need for individual autonomy with boredom, absenteeism, and complaining.[9] At this point, the group may once again split between overdependents and counterdependents, but this time the issue is interdependency within the group rather than dependency on a leader. The dependents sometimes express their needs with ideological concepts such as Christian love, sisterhood, or communalism, while the counterdependents elaborate individualist doctrines emphasizing privacy and individual achievement. If the members are successful in sharing their feelings about these issues, the anxieties will subside, and the group will be able to go on to effectively work on collective and individual tasks.

Ideological groups often have difficulty getting beyond the stage of factional infighting to a level of mature and productive work on their goals. Many fall apart before reaching this stage or even regress into dependency on a strong leader. To get beyond this stage, they need to develop regular procedures for conducting factional conflicts and dealing with leadership succession.

The New Jewel Movement

The New Jewel Movement in Grenada provides a dramatic illustration of many of the phenomena we have been discussing.[10] Grenada is a small island in the Caribbean, just north of Trinidad. Its population of 110,000 in 1980 was 80 percent of African origin, with the remainder largely East Indian or of mixed racial background. Its principal exports are cocoa, nutmeg, and bananas. Slavery was abolished in 1883 and, due to the widespread availability of land, the plantation system declined as most of the peasants settled on smallholdings. Half of the 120 industries on the island in 1977 employed fewer than five people, usually family members. The largest, a brewery, employed seventy-six.

Despite its small size and limited resources, Grenada was strongly influenced by the nationalist, populist, and socialist ideologies current in the Caribbean and in the third world generally. In 1951 Eric Matthew Gairy organized a successful strike of plantation workers, which overcame the opposition of the British colonial government and established him as "the undisputed hero of the working class and the most powerful trade union leader on the island."[11] Gairy was a former school teacher, of peasant origins, and he used nationalist and populist rhetoric, favoring both free enterprise and increased wages. His Labour Party alternated in power with the middle-class National Party until Gairy was overthrown by the New Jewel Movement in 1979.

During his period in power, particularly after full independence in 1974 freed him from fear of British intervention, Gairy "continued to accumulate property for himself, disburse official funds at whim, force sexual favors from women in the civil service, and indulge with great ostentation his fascination with the supernatural."[12] He established a repressive police force, and many people thought he was bent on establishing a personal dictatorship similar to that in Haiti.

The New Jewel Movement (NJM), organized in 1973 by a group of young lawyers and intellectuals, can be seen as a typical movement of "Young Turks" against an aging dictator. Its most charismatic leader was Maurice Bishop, a twenty-six-year-old man who had studied law in London and been influenced by the writings of radical intellectuals such as Nkrumah, Fanon, Malcolm X, and Che Guevara. Other leaders were Bernard Coard, a young British trained economist with more orthodox Marxist-Leninist views, and Hudson Austin, a defector from Gairy's small army. At this time the NJM avoided Marxist rhetoric and focused on opposition to the Gairy dictatorship with emphasis on public-sector development. Gairy ordered the NJM leaders beaten and jailed and was so confident of his power that he took off to New York to try to persuade the United Nations to set up a commission to investigate one of his major interests, unidentified flying objects. An armed band of forty-five NJM members succeeded in freeing Bishop from prison and overthrowing the government in 1979.

Having won power, the NJM adopted a series of self-defeating policies, culminating in the murder of Bishop and his supporters by a faction led by Coard and Austin in 1983, followed by an American military occupation. Supporters of the NJM naturally denounce the United States for the invasion and for economic measures taken against the NJM government. While these complaints may be valid, everyone also recognizes that the NJM played its hand very poorly. In the words of one of the NJM's strongest supporters, Fidel Castro, "the Grenadian revolutionaries themselves unleashed the events that opened the door to imperialist aggression. Hyenas emerged from the revolutionary ranks."[13]

Perhaps the most fundamental problem was that the NJM's Marxist-Leninist ideology really did not fit the realities in Grenada. In the 1990s it is commonplace to doubt that it fits anywhere, but in 1979 it was understandable that a group of young progressive intellectuals were inspired by Cuba and African socialist movements and the Marxist theories, which they had learned at British universities. They understood very well, however, that Grenada with its small population of predominately small farmers, located in an area of strong American military dominance, was ill suited to socialist revolution. In the confidential "Line of March for the Party," which Maurice Bishop prepared on September 13, 1982, he stated that:

> All comrades know of course that we inherited a backward, undeveloped economy with a very low level . . . of technological and economic development [which] resulted in very undeveloped class formations. . . . The question we must now pose comrades is whether a society such as ours with their primitiveness, with so little infrastructure, with so little development of productive forces, with such a small working class can really build socialism.[14]

Bishop's answer was that it was impossible to establish state socialism on the Cuban or Soviet model, but that they could work toward socialism by building a mixed economy with a dominant state sector. In order to do this, they had to make an alliance with non-Marxist business and professional people who had needed skills and resources. These people had to be fooled into thinking that the NJM was not really intent on building socialism, so that they would remain in the country and use their connections to bring in foreign capital and economic aid. But party members should understand that all power remained with the NJM, which, at the appropriate time, would "crush, oppress and repress the recalcitrant minority."[15]

This "Line of March" is intelligent and insightful; even with the benefit of hindsight it would be difficult to prepare a better strategy for a group intent on imposing a Leninist state on a society such as Grenada. For the first few years, things went well enough under Bishop's leadership. A number of economic and social reforms were instituted without challenging capitalist institutions on the island. Serious internal conflicts developed within the NJM, however. These focused on two issues: dissatisfaction with Bishop's leadership and with the failure of the movement to develop an orthodox Leninist pattern of organization.

A split developed between a group of radicals, centered around Bernard

Coard, and a more pragmatic group, centered around Bishop. The minutes of several key meetings were captured by the U.S. invasion force and provide a valuable account of the ideological and group-dynamics processes involved.[16] All agreed that the party was in trouble because, in the words of Comrade Ewart Layne, "there is great dispiritiveness and disaffection among the people. . . . the party is crumbling, all mass organizations are to the ground, organs of people's democracy is about to collapse."[17] Supporters were leaving the country; comrades were afraid to speak up because they would be stigmatized with an ideological label ("termed in different ways"). People were not attending mass rallies or party meetings, even when party organizers made extensive efforts to "mobilize" them. The roads were not being maintained, the economy was in a shambles, and so on.

At no time in the four days of almost nonstop discussion did anyone suggest that the fundamental problem might be with the party's long-term strategy of imposing Leninism in a society that they recognized to be dominated by "petite bourgeois" attitudes. Bishop thought that the party had become too bureaucratic and that the leadership was out of touch with the membership and the masses. His opponents, who were in the majority, thought the problem was that Bishop, despite his charismatic appeal to the masses and popularity with international audiences, lacked the necessary leadership qualities, which were "a Leninist level of organization and discipline, great depth in ideological clarity, and brilliance in strategy and tactics."[18]

From a group-dynamics standpoint, the NJM had clearly moved from a stage of dependence on Bishop as a leader to a transitional phase characterized by ideological polarization and struggle over leadership. The majority faction adopted ideological orthodoxy and scapegoating of Bishop as social defenses, which protected them from having to examine the fundamental strategic issues. They quoted extensively from Lenin's writings on party leadership, as if they could guarantee success by following a formula contained in them.

The conflict placed a great emotional burden on the participants. Comrade Ventour, for example, "took the opportunity to explain to the Central Committee that his illness was to a large extent more psychological than physical. Since he came back the situation had effected him which reflects a P.B. [petit bourgeois] character of lack of staunchness." Bernard Coard claimed that "he cannot take emotional conflict situation that saps his energies . . . unless the Central Committee is prepared to manners [discipline or rectify] all petit bourgeois responses, he will withdraw." Bishop was at first unable to attend a general meeting on September 25, because he was "relatively confused and emotional. There are several things that concern him and thus require a lot of mature reflection."[19]

Despite the open acknowledgment of emotional strain, and even the high rate of psychosomatic illnesses among Central Committee members, the discussion of personality issues was taboo. Comrade Layne insists that "the attempt to draw the Central Committee in a personality discussion is a P.B. [petit bourgeois] childish attitude." In his view the correct form of leadership must be "scientifically decided" based on the facts and Marxist theory. The correct scientific solution was to have joint leadership, with Bishop as Prime Minister and spokesperson for the revolution and Coard holding the real power as party and ideological leader.[20]

This joint-leadership model was almost unanimously selected, despite the obvious conflict between the two men. In group-dynamics theory, a group belief that salvation will come from the joining together of a pair of leaders is called a pairing assumption.[21] It is rare that one finds such a clear example in an ideological group. Another unusual thing about this case is the extent to which Bishop accepted the criticisms of the group, remarking that "he picked up an overwhelming sentiment that the qualities required are not possessed in him. He agreed that the points are correct especially correct application of strategy and tactics which cannot be achieved except the other qualities are fulfil [sic]." Bishop apparently lacked the ability to defend against introjecting the group's criticism into his own feelings, an essential skill for a revolutionary leader who wishes to control his party instead of being controlled by it. When he was accused of sins such as arrogance, "onemanism," "right opportunism," and defending the class interest of the bourgeoisie, he became increasingly contrite and promised to do better.[22]

At the end of the general meeting on September 25, everyone had accepted the solution of joint leadership. Bishop said that his problem had been that "so many things were going on through his mind . . . but all these things are now behind his back . . . his desire is now to use the criticism positively and march along with the entire party to build a Marxist/Leninist party that can lead the people to socialism and communism." Falling completely under the sway of a pairing assumption, the group as a whole "broke into singing and members filed past to embrace Comrades Bishop and Coard."[23]

Despite the seeming reconciliation, it was apparent that Bishop still had doubts. Observers reported that "the prime minister's behavior throughout this period was akin to that of a man without firm direction and deeply disturbed by events taking place around him."[24] At this crucial point he left the country for a scheduled two-week international tour, during which time Coard strengthened his position. On his return Bishop said that he wanted to reconsider the leadership question and was placed under house arrest. At a meeting on October 23, he was purged from the party. Those attending reported that "the tenor of this meeting was quite abnormal for the NJM, being highly virulent and very antipathetic to the prime minister."[25]

Bishop refused to accept a figurehead role and moved to rally support from the masses. A group of school children occupied the airport chanting "No Bishop, No School." Further demonstrations were planned, and Bishop went with a large crowd of followers to take over the army's communication center at Fort Rupert. At this time army units arrived and fired on the crowd, killing several people. They placed Bishop and his supporters against:

> a wall marked with the slogan "Towards a Higher Discipline in the PRA [People's Revolutionary Army]." Jacqueline Creft [Education Minister and Minister of Women's Affairs] screamed, "Comrades, you mean you're going to shoot us? To kill us? [Captain Lester] Redhead's alleged reply was to the point. "You fucking bitch," he shouted, "who are you calling comrades. You're one of those who was going to let the imperialists in."[26]

Bernard Coard and his supporters had one revolutionary leadership trait Bishop apparently lacked: the willingness to order their closest friends killed in cold blood. This despite the fact that before the revolution and for the first few years after it, Coard and Bishop "had co-operated closely and harmoniously and defended one another when they came under criticism."[27] They shared a commitment to Marxist-Leninist values and generally agreed on policy issues. Prior to the organizational crisis of the party, there was no sign of a personality conflict between the two men. Indeed, they seemed a perfect team with the tall, slender, handsome Bishop dazzling the masses and foreign fellow travelers while the shorter, stocky, theoretician Coard planned strategy and settled organizational matters.

Despite their apparent toughness, the people who took power after Bishop was killed were clearly frightened. After venting their fury on their comrades, they sent telegrams to the U.S. and British imperialists assuring them that they were for peace, friendship, a mixed economy welcoming foreign investment, and a broad-based civilian government. This message had no impact on the Reagan administration, which had already decided that Bishop's murder provided the ideal opportunity for an invasion. The invasion, although in violation of international law and largely condemned by other nations, was warmly welcomed by the Grenadian masses, who "hardly believed that their popular prime minister could have been executed by those who once applauded him."[28]

A case such as this can be interpreted in several different ways, largely because we can never have full information about the motivations of the participants. The most popular interpretation was that there was a well-planned conspiracy by Bernard Coard and his group. After examining the case quite carefully, Payne, Sutton, and Thorndike rejected this hypothesis on the grounds that Coard was aware that he "lacked the charismatic leadership qualities, so admired by an impressionistic and psychologically dependent society."[29] Coard and Bishop worked well together for many years, and Coard was highly flexible in his economic policies. It would have taken extremely skilled actors to simulate the intense emotions expressed in the minutes of the NJM meetings, including the joy at the unanimous agreement on the joint-leadership model.

It is more plausible to view the events as "a struggle for the control and direction of the revolution in a deteriorating economic situation which, because of the specific circumstances of Grenada, inevitably involved strong personality clashes."[30] The political culture of Grenada, with its strong stress on charismatic leadership, contributed to the outcome.[31] But quite similar events have taken place in revolutionary parties in nations with quite different cultures and circumstances. Bishop and Coard were, for example, playing in many ways the same roles as Trotsky and Stalin in Russia or Ben Bella and Boumedienne in Algeria.

Group-dynamics research shows that the tendency toward splitting and factional conflict is present in all groups. The (nonviolent) revolt against the leader is a regular occurrence in laboratory groups where the stakes, motivations, and culture are entirely different. Revolutionary movements are particularly vulnerable to these tendencies because of their strong reliance on charismatic leadership, their lack of established procedures for resolving factional conflicts, and their tendency to rigidly adhere to ideological doctrines.

Leadership in Ideological Groups

Freud conjectured that the earliest human groups may have been led by a dominant male who monopolized all the women. When the younger men banded together to kill this leader, they felt guilty or afraid and replaced him with an idol, which was the beginning of religion. Of course, Freud's suggestion that young men are angry because the leader has monopolized all the women must be taken as an allegory if we are to apply it to real-life situations in the modern world. Freud himself recognized that it was a "Just-So Story . . . like so many others with which archaeologists endeavor to lighten the darkness of prehistoric times."[32] Revolutions are not fought out of sexual frustration. Far from monopolizing the women, for example, Nicolae Ceausescu urged his subjects to marry and reproduce and even imposed tax penalties on women who failed to have a child by age twenty-five. Sex was one of the few pleasures that was not denied to Romanians under his dictatorship except to the extent that it was inhibited by the prohibition of birth control devices.

Nevertheless, many revolts do fit the pattern of a father figure being overthrown by a younger generation, one of whom eventually assumes the mantle of "father of his country." When Freud was writing his essay, he may have been thinking of the overthrow of Sultan Abdul Hamid II by the "Young Turks" in 1908. Abdul Hamid had several hundred women in his harem and is known to have ordered one of them drowned because she had sex with his oldest son.[33] Of course, the Young Turks were not after the women. In fact, they found them an awkward burden and tried to get their families to take them back. They were motivated not by sexual resentment, but by frustration with an archaic and rigid political system, which denied them the opportunity to play appropriate leadership roles.

After a decade of conflict and war, the role of national father figure was assumed by Mustafa Kemal, who took the surname Atatürk, which means "Father Turk."[34] Revolutionary leaders typically become father figures after assuming power. In the Russian and Chinese cases, the overthrown Tsar and Emperor were replaced by leaders who were not only idolized while they were alive but were actually mummified and placed on display as totems in new secular religions.

Neither Atatürk, Lenin, nor Mao lived long enough to be overthrown, but it is not impossible that under different conditions they might have suffered the fate of Nicolae Ceausescu, a man who indulged in such paternalistic prerogatives as turning off the national television station at 11:00 so his subjects wouldn't stay up too late and cutting their food rations so they wouldn't suffer from overweight.

In his study of Lenin, Trotsky, and Gandhi, Victor Wolfenstein argues that men become leaders of revolutions because they have unresolved Oedipal conflicts with their fathers.[35] This seems to trivialize the revolutionary experience, and Wolfenstein concedes that he has no real evidence that unresolved Oedipal conflicts are more common among revolutionary leaders than among other men.[36] Nevertheless, he offers some useful observations about the personalities of revolutionary leaders and a plausible hypothesis about the origins of the personality pattern.

Lenin's father died when he was quite young, and his older brother, who assumed the leadership of the family, was killed as a terrorist by the Tsar. At age sixteen, Trotsky had a bitter disagreement with his father, which was never resolved, over his father's desire that he become a civil engineer. Neither Lenin nor Trotsky wrote about his feelings for his father, so we can only speculate about how these early experiences were related to their adult behavior patterns. Gandhi was consumed by guilt because he was in bed with his child bride when his father died.[37] Austrian Marxist leader Ernst Fischer described a scene that occurred when he was eight or nine years old:

> mother fled from the conjugal bedroom . . . to take refuge with me. Clad only in her nightgown, she knelt panting beside my bed, her body shaken by spasmodic sobbing. She was holding me close in her arms and the odour she gave off was unfamiliar and disagreeable. Instinctively I knew from what it was she had fled. . . . Hideous images thronged my brain. The little turrets crowned with fat knobs, phallic ornamentation of this marriage bed, were instruments of violation. He had used them to impale my mother. "Shall I go and get a knife?" I asked my mother.[38]

A well-educated Viennese, Fischer naturally considered the possibility that this incident revealed an Oedipus complex. He concluded, however, that "though I worshipped my mother, I never desired her. What my father stirred up in me was not jealousy, but rather the hatred felt by the weaker for the stronger."[39]

Fischer's father was a conservative army officer, twenty years older than his mother. His mother had gone against her husband and sought money from her father to send Ernst to the seashore to recover from a heart ailment. While she had no defined political ideology, Fischer thinks that loyalty to her may explain why he grew up to revolt against his father's world of "officers, bull-necks and riding whips." Of course, a Freudian psychohistorian would argue that Fischer was simply unaware of his repressed sexual desire for his mother. Certainly his imagery shows that he viewed the incident as sexual, not simply as an assault.

Freudian theory posits that in the normal course of development the Oedipal conflict is resolved when the boy learns to identify with the father. If this fails to take place, perhaps because the father is particularly distant or hostile, it may happen that the issue remains unresolved and can become externalized into the ideological realm. In Fischer's case it could be that the strong conflict between his parents and the close relationship with his mother, caused by his physical disability, explain why he became first a left-wing socialist and, after the defeat of Austrian socialism, a leader in the Communist International.

Even if we cannot prove its origin in Oedipal conflicts, there is certainly much truth in Wolfenstein's description of the personality of the revolutionary leader. Revolutionary leaders tend to be preoccupied, not with their own personal problems, but with the struggle between good and evil in the larger world. They dichotomize the world into enemies and friends, and they feel intense love for their cobelievers as a group. Personal friendships and romantic attachments outside the group are rare.

Revolutionaries' hatred of authority is more ambivalent than their love of their allies, as if they had residual feelings that authority might be benevolent and that it might be wrong to rebel against it. Often they are ascetic, as if to prove their moral worth and to reassure themselves that their rebellion against authority is not selfish. They also tend to identify with some alternative authority figure, such as an older revolutionary leader, as well as with an authoritative doctrine, which provides justification for their action. The most effective revolutionary leaders incorporate the revolutionary ideology into their own personality so that they seem to identify themselves with it. This gives them great superego strength, which enables them to withstand criticism and failures and to project an image of tremendous strength to their followers.

In a comparative study of Cromwell, Robespierre, Lenin, and Mao Tse-tung, Bruce Mazlish found that they fit a pattern similar to that described by Wolfenstein.[40] Mazlish called this type the "revolutionary ascetic." The revolutionary ascetic is a narcissist, a person with an exaggerated self-love that masks a deeper insecurity. They are also highly disciplined individuals who have few loving ties to other people, but displace their emotions onto abstractions. In Mazlish's view, "narcissists . . . do not become revolutionary leaders unless they are also able to displace their self-love onto an abstraction with which they then totally identify. Thus it is the Revolution, the People, Humanity, or Virtue which the leader glorifies and extols; only 'accidentally' does he happen to embody it."[41]

In Mazlish's view, the revolutionary leader serves as an ego-ideal for his followers. By identifying with him, they are able to externalize needs for self-assertion, which they have not been able to actualize due to personal deficiencies and/or social conditions. The revolutionary leader is extremely sensitive to his followers, yet he is able to avoid having his own emotions shaped by them. He is, therefore, highly effective in manipulating his followers' emotional reactions. (Trotsky may have been somewhat weak in the ability to defend his own feelings against influences from others, which may explain his losing out in the struggle with Stalin.)[42]

The People's Temple

The collective suicide of almost one thousand men, women, and children at the People's Temple agricultural project in Guyana, South America, on November 18, 1978, was naturally viewed as a bizarre cult phenomenon. Yet, before it reached this tragic end, the People's Temple was perceived quite positively by many respected people. Before leaving for

Guyana, the People's Temple leader, Reverend Jim Jones, had established strong connections with progressive circles in the San Francisco Bay area. After he delivered a significant block of votes in the 1975 elections, San Francisco Mayor George Moscone made him chairman of the housing authority. Governor Jerry Brown spoke at the church, and Jones received letters of praise from national leaders. Jane Fonda said that "the church that I relate to most is called the People's Temple . . . [which provides] a sense of what life should be about."[43]

Jim Jones was born in 1931 in the small, all-white town of Lynn, Indiana, where blacks were made unwelcome after sunset. His childhood was "marked by loneliness. His father . . . returned from World War I with a severe lung problem and could no longer work. . . . His ill health affected his relationship with his son—Jim spent most of his youth without a father."[44]

His mother was much younger than her husband and was forced to work to support the family. Queried many years later, some residents say she was a loner, others not. She was known for proficient cussing and for having walked down Main Street smoking a cigarette. She was also "dark-complected" according to one informant. Jones's father was a member of the Ku Klux Klan.

Not much is known of Jones's relationship with his mother, but neighbors believe she tolerated his walking down the street shouting obscenities and saying, "good morning, you son of a bitch," to everyone he met. One informant stated that as a boy Jim would gather together about ten children from the neighborhood, line them up, make them march, and hit them with a stick. They would scream and cry, and he would preach sermons to them. Nevertheless, the kids would come back to play the next day, as they found him exciting.

In high school, when other boys were becoming interested in girls, Jim had a one-track mind: religion. He experimented with a number of churches, including the Pentecostal "Holy Rollers," who spoke in tongues and "whooped and hollered all night."[45] His roommate says that he was "maladjusted and ignored" at Indiana University in Bloomington. He dropped out to work as a hospital orderly and to sell monkeys door to door. At eighteen, he married an attractive nurse, four years older than he, who remained with him until the end.

In 1950 Jones moved to Indianapolis and got a preaching job. He quickly became known for his liberal views on civil rights. Nothing is known of how he acquired these views; it seems likely that he sympathized with his "dark complected" mother against his racist father. In any event, he began referring to himself as "biracial" on the grounds that his mother was a Cherokee, although he appeared white and had been so categorized in Lynn. He also adopted several children of different races. He made weekend trips to watch famous preachers and was especially impressed by Philadelphia's Father Divine whose preaching style he mimicked. He also followed Divine's model by establishing an "interrogation committee" in his church to screen members.

When Indianapolis became more and more hostile to him and his multiracial congregation, he decided to move to Ukiah, California, because he had read that this would be one of the safest places in the event of a nuclear holocaust. Over one hundred church members moved with him, and he rapidly built a following in California, expanding into the San Francisco Bay area where he began to combine religious and socialist rhetoric in his sermons. Again, he built a congregation that was racially integrated and drew from all social classes.

Jones was the only white leader in the Bay area who could produce significant numbers of black supporters at leftist demonstrations. At first, few were inclined to criticize him for his charismatic personality or the revival-meeting atmosphere at his services. But there were persistent rumors of chicken gizzards being pulled from people's throats in phony "cancer cures" and of poor people giving up their homes and most of their income to the Temple.[46] Disaffected former members claimed to have been beaten and threatened with death, and there were suspicious deaths among former members as well as evidence that the leadership was stealing from the Temple. An exposé in *New West* magazine in 1977 was especially damaging, and Jones made arrangements to move most of his congregation to an agricultural settlement in Guyana, South America.

Ukiah teacher Steven Katsaris was concerned when his twenty-four-year-old daughter, Maria, moved to the agricultural settlement in Guyana. At first he was supportive and telegramed at her request to protest the forthcoming *New West* magazine article. But he became concerned when he read the article and when several other critical stories appeared in the press. Maria reassured him in a letter:

> It is absolutely incredible how the press can print such a filthy bunch of lies and are allowed to get by with it. They refuse to print what we have had to say or to show the truth. I guess the other makes for more sensational reading. I am not surprised though. A society that is based on economic inequality and classism is certainly not going to let an organization advocating economic and racial equality exist too easily. . . . most people believe everything they hear on the news and read in the papers.[47]

This is the kind of defense typically offered by a true believer whose idol is being attacked, but Maria was on the scene, and she cited a lot of details to support her claim that the agricultural settlement was achieving many of its utopian goals. People's Temple attorney Charles Garry returned from a 1977 visit reporting, "From what I saw there, I would say that the society that is being built in Jonestown is a credit to humanity. I have seen paradise."[48]

Steven Katsaris remained suspicious and insisted on visiting his daughter, despite objections from the Temple. When he and some diplomats were finally able to see her, she was accompanied by four Temple members, and she seemed agitated and was unable to look him in the eye. She was, however, an adult and appeared to be there of her own free will, so there was nothing he or the officials from the U.S. Consulate could do. A few months later, she died in the mass suicide.

The People's Temple is an extreme case, but it has enough in common with other intentional communities to disturb students of utopian experiments.[49] Utopian movements are usually founded by a charismatic leader such as Father Rapp at Harmony, Robert Owen at New Harmony, John Humphrey Noyes at Oneida, "Mother Ann" and the Shakers, and John Frederick Rock at Amana. They often have strong religious beliefs and tend to draw a sharp boundary between themselves and the rest of the world. They often break up traditional family and sexual relationships and demand hard work from their participants. Even the mass suicide bears some similarity to the suicides of the Jewish Zealots at Masada, the Christian Dukhobors in nineteenth-century Russia, the Caribs at Sautuers in Grenada, and the Japanese on Saipan at the end of World War II.

Emigrants to Guyana were promised "an idyllic garden spot, trees laden with fruit, land waiting for the planting of harvests to come, universal love among men and women of all faiths, all races, all educational and economic backgrounds."[50] What they found was a tropical gulag with forced labor eleven hours a day in 120-degree heat, restricted rations with meat only for the elite, and a "relationships committee," which governed choice of sexual partners. Children who misbehaved were lowered into a well and dunked repeatedly while they cried out, "I'm sorry father, I'm sorry father." Their passports and money were taken away, and armed guards threatened any who thought of escaping through the jungle.

Reverend Jones claimed his choice of sexual partners, male and female. He told an old girlfriend, "I like to have sex for several hours with an individual. In the process their personalities are destroyed and they become just barnyard animals."[51] Regular suicide drills were held when everyone drank "poisoned" fruit drink to prove their willingness to die for the cause. Until November 18, the poison was not real, but Jones told his followers, "Everyone has to die. If you love me as much as I love you, we must all die or be destroyed from the outside."[52] One of his followers knew better, claiming, "We'll all die tonight, but father will raise us from the dead tomorrow."[53]

If the Jonestown story had been a work of fiction, it would seem a crude caricature of Freud's concept of the leader as an oppressive, all-powerful figure, dominating sex as well as other aspects of life. Jones presented himself as an all-powerful transformational force, able to cure cancer and heal people's troubled lives, if only they would commit themselves totally to him. People who were not inclined toward dependency on a strong father figure would not remain long in such a church. Those who did remain were seduced with kind words and concern about their problems. At first they were asked for only the modest financial contributions typical of any church. As they became more committed, their tithes were gradually increased to the point where they were eventually expected to give everything they had. This commitment script was offered as an organizational imperative and was appealing to many people whose previous lives had been chaotic and unsuccessful.

Abandoning a commitment script is difficult, but many people did leave the People's Temple, even after long periods of membership. The loss of autonomy and opportunity for personal growth in such a setting is stifling, while the rewards are much less than anticipated. In California, Jones resorted to blackmail and physical intimidation to keep people. In Guyana, guns and geographical barriers were used. People also had the possibility of winning power and privileges by rising within the hierarchy, another typical feature of authoritarian utopias.

The People's Temple shows the dark side of utopia in its starkest and most revealing form. In this case, truth is sadder, if not stranger, than fiction. Jonestown was worse than any of the classic fictional dystopias. The only cases that have been worse, in the quantity of death, if not the quality of life, are those where utopian ideals have been imposed on a national scale. These utopias have been plagued by many of the same problems that were found at Jonestown: concentration of power in a charismatic leader, inequality and exploitation, economic failure, and lack of freedom or respect for basic human rights. The leaders blame the failures on the outside world or on traitors within, and they use force to suppress dissent and maintain their own privileges.

Organizational Dynamics in Ideological Groups

Extreme groups such as the New Jewel Party and the People's Temple are useful because they offer a stark and exaggerated version of the organizational dynamics of ideological groups. The same processes can be observed in less extreme form in many other groups. A few examples will suffice to illustrate this point.

Oddly enough, groups of psychoanalysts have been especially susceptible to organizational splitting. Karen Horney's daughter observed that "organizational schisms are characteristic of psychoanalytic organizations the world over. They are symptomatic of what one might call a constitutional or genetic factor inherent in the discipline of psychoanalysis."[54] Psychoanalytic schools of thought are established by a founding father or mother who is idealized by the followers. Eventually, this idealization wears thin, and the less dependent members of the group make revisions and modifications in the received doctrine. At this point, a split emerges between the orthodox followers of the original doctrine and the revisionists.

When Karen Horney and her friends split from the New York Psychoanalytic Institute, they claimed that "reverence for dogma has replaced free inquiry; academic freedom has been abrogated; students have been intimidated; scientific sessions have degenerated into political machinations."[55] Robert Knight, speaking to the American Psychoanalytic Association in 1952, observed:

> The spectacle . . . of a national association of physicians and scientists feuding with each other over training standards and practices . . . calling each other orthodox or deviant . . . is not an attractive one to say the least. Such terms belong to religious or to fanatical political movements and not to science and medicine. . . . Perhaps we are still standing too much in the shadow of the giant Sigmund Freud to permit ourselves to view psychoanalysis as a science of the mind rather than as the doctrine of its founder.[56]

Splits in political groups are commonplace, even among those that make a special effort to avoid dogmatism and elitism. Usually, these splits fall at least roughly along a line between orthodox true believers and revisionists. In the German Green Party, for example, there is a fundamental split between the pragmatic "realos" and the orthodox "fundis."[57] The American right-wing is split between pragmatic "neocons" and orthodox "paleocons."[58] Bitter disputes between purist and pragmatic feminists had much to do with the failure of the movement to win the struggle for ratification of the Equal Rights Amendment, as we shall see in Chapter Eleven. Ideological splits destroyed the leading organization of radical students in the sixties, only a few years after it promised to do away with the ideological hairsplitting of the old left, as we shall see in Chapter Ten. In Chapter Fifteen, we will argue that adroit management of organizational dynamics within the Soviet Communist Party largely explains Mikhail Gorbachev's rise to power and the limits to his ability to bring about fundamental changes in the system.

The sexual excesses of Jim Jones's leadership of the People's Temple were extraordinary, but sexual abuse by people in powerful organizational positions is hardly uncommon.[59] This is true in anti-authoritarian progressive organizations as well as in traditional ones. Todd Gitlin argues that the male "heavies" in Students for a Democratic Society enjoyed "staffs that were, in effect, serial harems." One participant at the time observed that "the movement hangs together on the head of a penis."[60]

Sigmund Freud thought there was a close analogy between individual and group development.[61] He thought that group leaders played the role of father figures and that group members needed to rebel against the leader to develop, just as adolescents need to rebel against their parents. Only after they overcome their dependence on the leader are group members free to develop mature interpersonal relationships and to work productively as responsible adults. As we have seen, research on group dynamics has confirmed much of Freud's hunch about how groups function. Bennis and Shepard, for example, observed that there is an "interesting parallel" between the rebellion against the leader in laboratory groups and "Freud's discussion of the myth of the primal horde."[62]

But it is not only the Freudians who have observed irrational, childlike behavior in political groups. In *"Left-Wing" Communism: An Infantile Disorder,* Lenin "again and again rebuked the 'Left' for confusing its own subjective desires with objective reality, which led it to sectarian errors, to running far in advance of the masses."[63] Perhaps the members of the New Jewel Movement would have benefitted from including this pamphlet in their study program. Lenin thought that "infantile" radicalism was characteristic of the lower middle class as a group, because it was insecure due to its declining role in the economy. This doubtful historical observation is the origin the New Jewel Party members' belief that weakness or vacillation was a "petit bourgeois" trait, an unfortunate stigmatization of a class that made up the majority of their nation's population.[64]

Actually, the tendency to infantile thinking is present in people of all social classes who feel insecure and threatened, including members of Marxist-Leninist vanguard parties, which have lost touch with reality. Indeed, a certain amount of this kind of thinking is essential to provide energy and enthusiasm for political activism. Mature realism can be stifling and boring. Socialist Dorothy Healey observed that "without a vision the daily struggle can consume us without any nourishment."[65] As a young woman, Healey believed that Communist Party doctrines were scientific verities. When she finally became disillusioned and left the Party for a social democratic organization, she found that:

> with an organization that doesn't claim to have a monopoly on truth and doesn't inspire its members with the belief (even if it's an illusion) that no matter how irrelevant you are today tomorrow you're going to be the vanguard . . . you can't keep members enthused and willing to sacrifice their time and energies on the basis of an amorphous perspective or one that says "I don't know the answer, but hopefully we'll all find out together."[66]

If a certain amount of childish energy and enthusiasm is necessary to launch and sustain any ideological group, a healthy dose of adult realism is needed to avoid the kinds of catastrophes we saw in the People's Temple and New Jewel Movement cases. Charismatic leaders have a role to play, particularly in mobilizing a group, but it is also necessary for a group to move beyond the stage of leader worship. The stages of group development are unavoidable. The organizations that prosper are those that learn to manage them effectively.

Chapter Six

The Utopians

Long-haired preachers come out every night
Try to tell you what's wrong and what's right
But when asked how 'bout something to eat
They will answer in voices so sweet:
   You will eat, bye and bye
   In that glorious land above the sky
   Work and pray, live on hay
   You'll get pie in the sky when you die

—Joe Hill

Joe Hill was a radical organizer in the early twentieth century who ridiculed religious utopias for fooling people into putting up with suffering in this world in return for a worthless promise of utopia after death. By the end of the century, the Marxist promise of utopia after the socialist revolution was widely viewed as equally worthless. The parallels between religious and political millenarianism are obvious.[1] Political millenarians portray the revolution as an event of unique importance that will transform the world into an idyllic state, just as religious millenarians predict a transformation after the return of Jesus or the Messiah.

Utopian and dystopian (or cataclysmic) thinking are found in all human cultures, often in the form of myths about birth and death, destruction and resurrection.[2] Jungian psychologists believe that utopian archetypes are "based on the phantasy of recreating in adult life the blissful security of a Golden Age (the primal relationship)."[3] This thinking is rooted in memories of the experience of being a newborn infant, completely dependent on parents with the power to transform it from a miserable, dirty, and hungry state of existence (dystopia) to a blissfully comfortable and satisfied one (utopia).[4] Indeed, psychohistorian Lloyd deMause traces these patterns back to fetal life, as the infant reacts to variations in the placental oxygen supply.[5]

In many ways, the infant's belief that the parents can solve all problems is realistic. But it can lead to irrational expectations when the belief in parental omnipotence is exaggerated or prolonged beyond infancy. For example, my mother has told me of the first time she took me to the seashore. I became angry when the waves kept washing down the castles I was building in the sand and insisted that she should make them stop. Her insistence that she could not do so was simply incredible to me. I was reminded of this story when, during the 1988 presidential campaign, candidate Pat Robertson claimed that as a Christian preacher he was uniquely qualified because he could pray to God to turn hurricanes away from the American coast. The devastation of the southern American coast by hurricane Hugo in 1989 may have been our punishment for refusing his services.

As adults we may retain an unconscious memory of this all-powerful parental force, which Bollas calls the transformational object.[6] In his psychiatric practice, Bollas finds that many people associate this unconscious memory with people or ideas in their adult lives, leading them to have unrealistic expectations:

> Once early ego memories are identified with an object that is contemporary, the subject's relation to the object can become fanatical, and I think many extremist political movements indicate a collective certainty that their revolutionary ideology will effect a total environmental transformation that will deliver everyone from the gamut of basic faults: personal, familial, economic, social, and moral. It is not the revolutionary's desire for change, or the extremist's longing for change, but his *certainty* that the object (in this case the revolutionary ideology) will bring about change that is striking to the observer.[7]

Utopian doctrines serve as transformational objects. They give our wishes and fears an exaggerated and idealized but apparently tangible form, which serves as an object for the projection of our feelings. We may believe in a God who is all-knowing and all-powerful, who can be called upon to intervene on our behalf. Perhaps we can be "born again." Or we may become convinced that a change in jobs or communities or romantic partners will transform our lives. We may attribute transformational power to a charismatic leader or to an ideology such as socialism, libertarianism, fascism, or democracy. Or, for that matter, to a therapist who allows us to lie down on the couch and expose our childish feelings.

Since transformational objects do not actually exist, they are most convincingly portrayed in works of fiction. Novels such as *Looking Backward, Gulliver's Travels, Island, Erewhon, The Shape of Things to Come, Walden Two, Ecotopia, The Dispossessed, Caesar's World, Animal Farm, Brave New World, We,* and *Nineteen Eighty-Four* are expressions of utopian and dystopian themes, which have had a wide appeal at particular times in history.[8] Some portray the bliss of utopia, others the agony of dystopia, but all share an assumption that dramatic transformation from one extreme to the other is possible.

Utopias are more dangerous when they are not expressed openly as fiction, but hidden in scientific monographs or political manifestos. In these forms, it is difficult to distinguish between fantasy and reality. People may try to force the world to fit their utopian dreams, with dystopian consequences.

This chapter begins with a portrait of two of the most influential utopian authors, Ignatius Donnelly and Edward Bellamy. Their utopias were products of their own minds, but their popular acclaim shows that they reflected collective consciousness as well. We will then examine two utopian movements that have had a major effect on twentieth-century societies: Ayn Rand's Objectivism on the right and Marxism on the left.

Case Comparison: Ignatius Donnelly and Edward Bellamy

Ignatius Donnelly. Ignatius Donnelly was born in Philadelphia in 1831, the youngest son of an Irish immigrant who succeeded in obtaining a medical degree only to catch typhus from a patient and die after two years of practice. A biographer notes that the passing of his father "had no marked effect upon his youngest son," which suggests that he repressed his feelings.[9] Although she was only thirty-one when her husband died, Cathrine Donnelly never remarried, but devoted her life to raising her children and running the pawnshop she had opened to finance her husband's medical education. Ignatius received a good education at Philadelphia's Central High School, despite the nativism and bigotry against Irish immigrants, which threatened his community. The Kensington riots, when mobs surged through the streets and burned Catholic churches, made a lasting impression.

In Philadelphia, Donnelly studied law and became involved in real-estate development schemes, but he was not very successful as either a lawyer or a businessman. He also became involved in Democratic Party politics and in political writing, beginning with a phrenological analysis of *New York Tribune* editor Horace Greeley. Phrenology, the inference of character traits from the shape of the head, was only the first of Donnelly's scientific enthusiasms.

Donnelly was generous with his impecunious legal clients, but he was accused of fraud in his real-estate dealings. Accusations of fraud followed him throughout his life. While they were often untrue, in the judgment of his biographer, there were occasions where he was clearly involved in dishonest schemes.[10] Despite his dislike for Greeley, Donnelly took his advice to "go west, young man" and moved to Minnesota, where he invested in a planned community to be called Nininger City. He brought his new wife, Kate, with him and remained a devoted husband until she died.

Nininger City never succeeded, and Donnelly was eventually forced to farm the land he had bought. His political efforts were more successful, and he served two terms as a Republican lieutenant-governor and three terms as a Republican congressman in Washington. At the time, the Republicans were considered to be more radical than the Democrats, particularly because of their antislavery stance. When fallings out with more powerful Republican politicians caused him to lose office, Donnelly served two terms in the Minnesota legislature as an Independent and then became involved in the Farmer's Alliance and the Populist Party. His political career peaked in middle age, and he never again held elected office. Many of his real-estate investments also went bad. On his forty-ninth birthday, he told his diary, "a sad day it is. . . . all my hopes are gone, and the future settles down upon me dark and gloomy indeed. . . . my life has been a failure and a mistake."[11]

In Donnelly's survivor script, however, despair was always followed by a new enthusiasm. Taking his wife to Philadelphia for medical treatment, he hit upon the idea of writing a book to prove that the lost continent of Atlantis was not a myth but a scientific reality. Atlantis was first mentioned in Plato's *Timaes* where he told the tragic tale of a lost island or continent where the people:

> were obedient to the laws, and well-affectioned towards the gods . . . uniting gentleness with wisdom in the various chances of life, and in their intercourse with one another. They despised everything but virtue, caring little for their present state of life, and thinking lightly of the possession of gold and other property, which seemed only a burden to them.[12]

Sadly, this island paradise was destroyed when it sank into the sea, perhaps as a punishment for not listening to its philosophers. The surviving manuscripts of Plato's story break off abruptly in the middle, and it is not certain whether Plato believed that Atlantis ever actually existed. Aristotle thought it was a fictional account designed to persuade the ruler Dionysus the Younger of Syracuse to implement Plato's ideas for an earthly Republic ruled by a philosopher king. Since Plato believed that ideas were more real than empirical observations, the distinction between history and speculation may not have been important to him. Although Plato claimed that Atlantis had existed 9,300 years before he told the story, no mention of anything like it has been found in any historical records dating before his time.[13]

Despite Plato's warning that Dionysus's realm might sink into the sea as Atlantis did, he ignored Plato's pleading. The Atlantis story faded into the background with other ancient myths, appearing only in works of fiction such as Jules Verne's *Twenty Thousand Leagues Under the Sea,* until Donnelly decided to prove that it was real. He threw himself into the research at the public library, combing works of history, archeology, and mythology, looking for "facts" to prove his thesis. He worked like a lawyer constructing a legal brief, collecting the facts that suited his argument and ignoring those that did not.

In his book, published in 1882, Donnelly argued that Atlantis had been on the Atlantic Ocean near the mouth of the Mediterranean and that it was exactly as described by Plato. It ended in a terrible convulsion of nature during which the whole island sank into the ocean, with only a few inhabitants escaping on rafts. Some of these survivors reached Mexico, the Amazon, Europe, and Africa. This, in Donnelly's view, accounted for the discovery of similar cultural forms in all these areas, such as sun worship in both Egypt and Peru and supposed similarities between the Phoenician and Mayan alphabets.

Donnelly's book was poorly received by the archeological community and would have had little influence if not for its immense popular following. By the early 1900s there were numerous "clubs" dedicated to a literal acceptance of Plato's Atlantis. Over two thousand books and articles were published on the subject, many in the specialized journals *Atlantis* and the *Atlantis Quarterly.*[14] Serious scholars were skeptical because many of the claims of amazing cultural similarities in different parts of the ancient world were hoaxes or were based on sloppy fieldwork.[15] Donnelly, for example, thought that the Egyptian and Mayan pyramids were the same and that both societies used the arch. Actually, the Maya did not have a keystone arch, and their pyramids differ in many ways from those in Egypt. Far from using the Phoenician alphabet, Mayan writing was hieroglyphic. Other remarkable "coincidences," such as the existence of flood mythology in both Hebrew and Babylonian scriptures, could be explained by the fact that the Hebrews were familiar with the Babylonian beliefs. Donnelly thought that the flood stories, which occur in many cultures, were references to the sinking of Atlantis, dismissing the fact that many parts of the world do, in fact, have floods.

The Atlantis scholars assumed that the existence of common myths or cultural artifacts in two different cultures proved that they had to have the same source, and they used Atlantis as a convenient explanation for the existence of many similarities, which would not otherwise be explained within this "diffusionist" theoretical framework. In time, diffusionist theory in anthropology was supplemented or replaced with evolutionist theory, which offered an alternative explanation of the fact that similar developments occur in different societies at different times.[16]

After writing his book on Atlantis, Donnelly wrote *Ragnarok: The Age of Fire and Gravel,* which argued that the earth's deposits of gravel, sand, and clay were the residue of a giant comet, and *The Great Cryptogram,* which argued that when Francis Bacon wrote the plays attributed to Shakespeare he included a secret code, which could be used to decipher hidden messages. Both of these books made scientific allegations, and Donnelly had great difficulty defending them. He admitted that *Ragnarok* was speculative, but he was sure he would be able to solve the cryptogram. After months of painstaking work, however, his ciphers were so complex that it took a professional astronomer six weeks to figure out how to use them. Even then, they did not work precisely but required adjustments. Donnelly also found it difficult to make his political points with scientific arguments. He thought of Bacon (who had been his father's favorite author) as an honest debtor and crusading politician, while he believed Shakespeare was a greedy moneylender. *Ragnarok* was linked to a Scandinavian myth of a divine cataclysm punishing a sinful world.

Donnelly's next book was a work of fiction, which he published in 1890 under a pseudonym to avoid tainting it with his tarnished reputation. *Caesar's Column: A Story of the Twentieth Century* was inspired by the success of Edward Bellamy's utopian novel, *Looking Backward,* which had come out two years before. *Caesar's Column,* however, is a classic dystopian novel, projecting the disasters of Donnelly's life script onto society. It had an enormous success, selling almost 700,000 copies by 1899. It tells of an America in 1988 that is polarized between a small wealthy class, composed largely of Jews, and the impoverished masses, whose wages have been reduced to the level of bare survival.

The novel appealed to Donnelly's populist constituency, as it fixed the blame for society's ills on the monopolies and big government. There is a revolutionary movement in the book, but it becomes consumed by violence, and the society ends in genocidal mob violence. Had it been set in Germany in 1938 it would have been more prophetic.

The hero of *Caesar's Column* is a visitor from the mountain Republic of Uganda, which has avoided all these problems by adopting policies identical to the platform of the American Populist Party: paper money; government ownership of the railroads, mines, highways, and telegraph lines; and government control of all wages. The Ugandan "Garden in the Mountains" is almost entirely rural, with only a village as capital. Government is split into three houses: one for the workmen, one for the merchants and manufacturers, and one for the intellectuals who hold the balance of power when the other two do not agree.

Edward Bellamy. Edward Bellamy's *Looking Backward,* published in 1888, is an idyllic portrayal of the society of the future.[17] Bellamy has been largely forgotten today, but when philosopher John Dewey, historian Charles Beard, and editor Edward Weeks were asked in 1935 to name the twenty-five most important books of the preceding century, each ranked *Looking Backward* second after Karl Marx's *Das Kapital.*[18] In addition to spawning Donnelly's *Caesar's Column,* Bellamy's book inspired Thorstein Veblen to become a social scientist, influenced Mark Twain in writing *A Connecticut Yankee at King Arthur's Court,* and introduced Norman Thomas to socialism. It was enthusiastically read by anarchists, feminists, and socialists in Europe and the United States, who found its vision inspiring, even though they often disagreed with details.[19]

Edward Bellamy was born in Chicopee Falls, Massachusetts, in 1850 and lived almost his entire life in that area.[20] His father was a Baptist minister who was too tolerant and liberal to believe in eternal damnation. He eventually left the ministry under some pressure. His mother was more orthodox and spiritual, and she talked with Edward mostly about religion. He and his brothers abandoned their mother's orthodox faith but retained her life script of commitment to a spiritual cause. She was tolerant enough to appreciate Edward's moral commitment, even though it was directed toward secular causes. She is reported to have said that Edward was the most Christlike man she had ever known.

At age seventeen, Edward planned to devote himself to a military career. He was devastated when he failed the physical examination for West Point. He then studied law and was admitted to the bar, but gave up that profession when his first assignment at a prestigious law firm was to evict a tenant. Instead of seeking a more humanistic legal practice, he decided that he could not reconcile himself to "earn my daily bread at some plodding business such as men ply all about me," because he could not "turn my heart from the great work which awaits me."[21] At twenty-two he wrote, "I had thought myself to be something greater than other men, and find that I am but after all a mediocre person. Well then, I am weary and could wish to die. . . . if I am not more than other men I would be nothing."[22]

Five months later, he reread this diary entry and dismissed it as nothing more than the winter blues, perhaps complicated by too much liquor, which he gave up (temporarily) in February of the same year. Gradually, he perfected his literary skills with a view to a career as a journalist and writer. When he failed to break into Manhattan journalism, he returned to his hometown, which remained his base for the rest of his life.

Seeking a faith to give purpose and meaning to his floundering life, Bellamy read Auguste Comte as well as American figures such as Emerson, Whitman, and Henry James. He wrote an essay, "The Religion of Solidarity," to define his new religious insights.[23] Reminiscent of Comte's Religion of H manity, it is a vague rumination on man's affinity with nature and on the centripetal forces of universal solidarity, which bind people together, and the centrifugal forces of individuality, which keep them apart. He never published the essay, but many of its ideas were worked into the texts of *Looking Backward* and its sequel, *Equality,* where they were portrayed as the religion of the future.

Having satisfied his spiritual quest, Bellamy earned his living as a journalist for Massachusetts newspapers and published his first novel in 1878. His novels focused on altered states of being and personal transformation, often accomplished through mind-altering technologies or mystical visions.[24] Bellamy continued to experiment with altered consciousness in his own life, writing *Looking Backward* with a cup of coffee at one hand and a glass of whiskey at the other. Temperance was one cause of his era that he never incorporated into his visions of the future.

Looking Backward's appeal was its glowing vision of an idyllic future. A contemporary reviewer wrote, "Men read [Plato's] *Republic* or [More's] *Utopia* with a sigh of regret. They read Bellamy with a thrill of hope."[25] *Looking Backward* and *Equality,* published in 1897, described an affluent society where everyone's income was equal, and all consumer needs were met by giant department stores, which employed statisticians to keep track of market trends. To make sure minority needs were met, the state was required to produce anything out of the ordinary that any consumer requested.

In contrast to Donnelly's pastoral Garden of Eden, Bellamy's ideal was an urban, technologically advanced, affluent society. *Looking Backward* was set in Boston and included technological innovations such as cable radio and disposable clothing. This required that Bellamy show how such an economy could be run without economic incentives or market mechanisms. His solution was a military model. Everyone would serve in an industrial army from ages twenty-five to forty-five and would do the tasks assigned. After a three-year period of general labor, people would be assigned to specialized trades in keeping with their abilities and preferences. Anyone who refused to work would be put in solitary confinement on bread and water.[26] While everyone's pay would be the same, there would be differences in rank and status, which would motivate hard work and initiative. Women and cripples were to be organized in separate armies. Political power was to be exercised by the retired men. These features brought criticism from feminists and anarchists, and Bellamy eliminated many of them in *Equality*. His vision was hailed by many feminists for giving women complete economic equality and independence from men.

One of Bellamy's historical inspirations was ancient Peru, as described in Prescott's *Conquest of Peru*. This is not as odd as it may sound. Idealization of ancient societies is a common utopian theme, and Bellamy's image of Peru was based on well-known historical accounts.[27] Bellamy admired the military way of life for its discipline and idealism. He also shared the conviction of other utopian thinkers that an economy centrally planned by experts would be more efficient and productive than one regulated by markets.

From the perspective of the late twentieth century, Bellamy's faith in the omniscience and disinterestedness of central planners seems naive, as it did to Peter Kropotkin and other anarchist critics of his time.[28] The labor army was not central to Bellamy's literary purpose, however, and he modified it along decentralist lines in keeping with anarchist criticisms in the sequel. In *Equality,* instead of being locked up on bread and water, conscientious objectors were allowed to build their own communes in the woods. Bellamy was willing to "almost" give up on having police and prisons, on the assumption that few crimes would be committed in paradise, but he insisted on having a central administration of technocrats to manage the economy.

Bellamy assumed that life would be simplified without bothersome disputes among private interests and that little would need changing from year to year. Bellamy's time traveler was told that "the fundamental principles on which our society is founded settle for all time the strifes and misunderstandings which in your day called for legislation."[29] State legislatures would be abandoned and Congress would meet only every five years, since few new laws would be needed. Any that might be passed would be delayed for reconsideration by the next Congress, just to make sure they were not hasty.

This vision of the future has been criticized as stale and authoritarian.[30] One of the criticisms of utopias in general is that life in them sounds boring. Readers, however, found *Looking Backward* exciting and inspiring. If we examine *Looking Backward* as a literary text, it is clear that the theme is transformation, not stasis.[31] The transformational object is the underground vault in which the hero spends a 112-year hypnotic trance, awakening in utopia. The contrast between old and new is what gives the book its excitement, and many readers were excited by the prospect that the book itself would serve as a transformational object as soon as enough people read it and were persuaded to make the effortless, nonviolent transition to a Nationalist utopia.

Bellamy was familiar with European socialist theories, but he was repelled by the specter of class hatred and thought that European socialism was overly materialistic and not sufficiently radical in its visions. He thought the word "socialist" tarnished by its association with extremists and working-class militancy and used the term "Nationalist" instead. Of course, in his time the word nationalism did not have the meaning it has today. For Bellamy and his supporters it meant, "the progressive nationalization and municipalization of industries."[32] In his 1894 introduction to a volume of Fabian essays, Bellamy stated that "Nationalists are socialists who, holding all that socialists agree on, go further, and hold also that the distribution of the cooperative product among the members of the community must be not merely equitable, whatever that means, but must be always and absolutely equal."[33]

Looking Backward was written in the voice of a time traveler in the year 2000 who explained that Nationalism had been installed by a nonviolent "revolution" after everyone had been persuaded of its merits. The book sold over a million copies and led to the formation of "Nationalist" clubs all over the United States. The Nationalist movement was in large part dominated by members of the mystical Theosophist movement, who found Nationalism a useful vehicle for their advocacy of universal brotherhood based on a synthesis of Hindu, Christian, and Neoplatonist principles. Theosophists believe that evil results from the quest for finite goods and that it can be overcome by complete absorption in the infinite.

Most of the articles in the *Nationalist* were written by Theosophists, and Theosophists held most of the leadership positions in the important clubs. While they were in general agreement with Bellamy on philosophy, they differed in insisting that political reform could come only after a reform in human nature. They wanted to keep all discussion of politics or class consciousness out of the Nationalist meetings, insisting that "the charm, the universal drawing power, of Edward Bellamy's *Looking Backward* was the absence of 'class consciousness.' The emphasis was placed upon the transition from the nineteenth-century condition to the ideal state without class conflict, hate or injustice."[34]

Bellamy was dissatisfied with this apolitical stance and split off to start his own newspaper, the *New Nation.* The Theosophists decided to pursue their spiritual proselytism under their own name. There seemed to be little need for a separate Nationalist political movement, since its planks differed hardly at all from existing populist and socialist groups, such as the People's Party and the Socialist Party. Bellamy's books were available in all Industrial Workers of the World meeting halls, and there was clearly a resonance between their view of a world run by "one big union" and Bellamy's Nationalism. Bellamy, himself, became active in the populist movement, where he joined forces with other utopians such as Ignatius Donnelly. The Nationalists as a distinct organization died out in the late 1890s, perhaps because Bellamy's melding of spiritual and socioeconomic utopianism was more viable in a novel than in a social movement.

Bellamy's writings continued to have an influence on the Populist and Socialist movements, however, and had a considerable revival in the 1930s. A Utopian Society was organized in California in 1929, and it filled the Hollywood Bowl with a mass meeting in 1934.[35] Bellamy Clubs again grew up around the country, and Bellamy was a major influence on Upton Sinclair's socialist race for the governorship in California and on the emergence of the Townsend Plan, which proposed to end the Depression by giving every American over sixty years of age a pension of $150 a month. Bellamy also appealed to progressive engineers in the Technocrat movement in the United States and the Industrial Party in the Soviet Union during the 1920s. Many people in the leadership of Roosevelt's New Deal were familiar with Bellamy's work. Arthur Morgan, Bellamy's first biographer, for example, was the Chairman of the Tennessee Valley Association. While it is difficult to evaluate the impact of any one book, Bellamy clearly had a significant impact in inspiring social democratic, anarchist, and feminist politics in the United States and Europe.[36]

Comparison of Life Scripts: Donnelly and Bellamy. Donnelly's life was a roller-coaster ride, with rising expectations and peak experiences inevitably followed by disaster. Despite very limited information about his childhood, it is easy enough to see how this survivor life script could have originated in the death of his father. His close relationship with his mother could explain why this pattern did not carry over into his married life, as it did for Bertrand Russell. Of course, the ups and downs of Donnelly's career could also be attributed to economic and political forces, but he did choose to become a real-estate developer and politician instead of a school teacher or journalist.

Donnelly was ambivalent about enemy imagery. In his journalism and political campaigns, he consistently spoke against anti-Semitism and racism of all kinds, insisting that "we are fighting Plutocracy not because it is Jewish or Christian, but because it is Plutocracy."[37] He wrote a fantasy novel, *Dr. Huguet,* which attacked racial prejudice. Yet, when it came time to describe the ruling class of his dystopia, he made them predominately Jewish, explaining that this was because persecution by the Christians had caused them to evolve into a superior race. It seems reasonable to suppose that he had anti-Semitic feelings, which went against his conscious values.

Perhaps the most interesting thing about Donnelly is his quest for novel solutions to scientific and scholarly riddles. He put tremendous energy into collecting facts about Atlantis and trying to decipher Shakespeare's plays. Certainly this served as a diversion for him at a low point in his life, just as Bertrand Russell's mathematical work did. He lacked the ability or training to make a real scientific contribution, but his forthright advocacy of dissenting theses brought him the kind of notoriety and book sales that Russell obtained from his popular writings. Both appealed to the public's appetite for simple, moralistic solutions to life's puzzles and problems.

Donnelly's survivor script is expressed in both *Atlantis* and *Caesar's Column,* and they probably appealed to readers who shared his assumption that no virtue would long go unpunished. Biographer Martin Ridge concludes that "because his nature was strong, misfortune, the poison of the weak, seemed to be his tonic."[38] Donnelly's survivor script provided a way of dealing with misfortune, by abandoning the failed ventures and starting anew. More strength may be required, however, of those whose commitment scripts lead them to remain loyal to their causes no matter how bad their fortunes.

Edward Bellamy's quest for a cause to which he could fully commit himself contrasts sharply with Ignatius Donnelly's enthusiasm in taking up the many opportunities that came his way. The prospect of success in some mundane business or career was threatening to his image of himself as a special person with a mission in life. Donnelly would have been happy to get rich any way he could and would have been bored spending his life in one place or on one project.

People with commitment scripts often take a period of time before choosing a cause, just as they may take time in selecting a career or a romantic partner. Often, they choose a different cause from their parents even as they retain their parents' pattern of devoting their life to a cause. Bellamy created a fantasy society, which idealized his desire for harmony, equality, and moral integrity.

Ayn Rand and Objectivism

Alissa Rosenbaum was born in St. Petersburg, Russia, in 1905. Her family lived comfortably on her father's earnings as a chemist, sending the three daughters, of which Alissa was the eldest, to quality private schools.[39] This untroubled existence was shattered by the Revolution of 1917. The family hid in Odessa, and Alissa escaped into Victor Hugo's novels where strong heros struggled valiantly against adversity. When the Bolsheviks confiscated her father's drugstore and made it almost impossible for girls from "bourgeois" families to obtain a higher education, she managed to escape to "visit" relatives in the United States. On the way, she adopted the first name "Ayn" from a Finnish writer she admired and the last name "Rand" from her typewriter.

Under the circumstances, it is hardly surprising that Ayn Rand's bitter hatred of socialism lasted all her life. What is puzzling was her equally strong lifelong hatred for religion in any form. Her family was Jewish but not religious. She hated the atheistic Bolsheviks and longed to escape to live in America where living "under God" is part of the national identity. Yet, as an adolescent hiding from the Bolsheviks, she found the idea of humbling herself before God degrading and humiliating.

On a conscious level, Rand's atheism was part of her commitment to rationality and individualism. Unlike Auguste Comte, who replaced traditional religion with faith in altruism, Rand replaced it with faith in selfishness. Her "Objectivist Creed" stated that no one should "sacrifice himself to others, nor sacrifice others to himself."[40] Yet, in some ways she was curiously submissive. She believed that women were inferior to men and should subordinate themselves to them. She thought that women enjoyed sex most when they were violently raped. She wrote novels with heroines who refused to marry the men they loved because they preferred extramarital rape to marital love. If we take this masochistic streak as a clue to Rand's unconscious mind, we might speculate that her adoption of atheism was an identification with the oppressive, atheistic Bolsheviks.

Rand is influential because of her epic novels in which tall, handsome capitalists with strong jutting jaws prevail over flabby, weak-chinned socialists with names like Ellsworth Toohey and Wesley Mouch. Her heroines are tall, blonde, and willowy. She herself was short, dark, and stocky. The hero of her first major novel, *The Fountainhead,* was an architect who kept losing assignments because he would not compromise to the demands of corrupt bureaucrats and careerists. He won the love of the heroine when he raped her, but she married someone else out of disgust with herself and the world. She then snuck out to her true lover's bed on her wedding night. The architect finally blows up a housing project he had designed, when the corrupt builder failed to follow his plans. When he is arrested, he convinces the jury that it was his creation and his to destroy. He owed nothing to the people who expected to live in it. Biographer James Baker observes that *The Fountainhead* "advocates chaos by romanticizing anarchy, sadomasochism, and infidelity. It appeals to bored, frustrated, angry young people, particularly those with unearned money and unrealized talent."[41]

Rand's dystopian novel, *Atlas Shrugged,* is the tale of four heroic capitalists who escape from a socialistic America of the future to build a Utopia of Greed in a hidden valley. In this utopia, each man acts only for himself, trading his services for gold. The dollar sign was the community's symbol just as a gold dollar sign was Ayn Rand's favorite piece of jewelry. The novel gives few details of life in the Utopia of Greed. Rand's vision was of America during the period of 1815 to 1914, when capitalism was unrestrained by government regulations, but she never wrote historical novels about life in this golden era. Instead, she spun her tales of superheroes defeating nerdish bureaucrats.

The heroes of *Atlas Shrugged* were brilliant inventors and industrialists who refused to share their inventions with others. Instead of fighting the system, they shrugged their shoulders and walked away, leaving the incompetent "second handers" (those who live off of others' ideas), "whim worshipers" (religious believers), and "muscle mystics" (those who rule through intimidation) to flounder without them. Finally, one of the heroes, John Galt, returns to deliver a thirty-thousand-word radio address. This address, which took Rand two years to write, distills the essence of her philosophy.[42] Its essential wisdom is that A is A, that existence exists, and that man is capable of perceiving objective reality. To be free, each person must earn his own way and give up all mystical beliefs and all concern for the good of others. Rational thought must replace all mystical or emotional considerations. All must swear to follow the Objectivist Creed. Only then will the capitalists return to society.

Despite negative reviews when it appeared, *Atlas Shrugged* sold very well. Its appeal was so great that an Objectivist movement sprung up among its readers, dedicated to implementing its arguments.[43] The leading figure in this movement was Nathaniel Branden, who was also Rand's closest disciple.[44] Branden's name was Nathan Blumenthal when he met Rand, but he decided to change it. He insists the change had nothing to do with concealing his Jewish origins (as does Rand about her name change) and says he was surprised when a journalist observed that the letters in Branden could be rearranged to form the Hebrew words *ben rand,* which mean son of Rand.[45]

Branden, who is twenty-five years younger than Rand, discovered Rand's novels when he was fourteen. For the next four years, *The Fountainhead* was his constant companion. Looking back as an adult and bestselling popular psychologist, he believed that "no one can understand the appeal of Ayn Rand to youth who does not understand how profoundly she speaks, on many different levels, to the quest for individuation, autonomy, and self-actualization."[46]

Branden wrote Rand a fan letter when he was nineteen, asking her judgment on philosophical questions that were implicit in the novels. Ayn and her husband Frank were impressed by the letters and invited him over to their house. Nathaniel looks like one of Ayn's heroes: tall and handsome, with cascading hair, piercing eyes, and a strong chin. Ayn was as captivated with Nathaniel's earnest hero worship as he was with her brilliance. Ayn and Frank became very close friends with Nathaniel and his first wife, Barbara. Nathaniel felt as if they were his true family. It was a family without an Oedipal taboo, however, and Ayn and Nathan had a long sexual affair. Barbara, who had been a Rand fan since before she met Nathan, tried her best to accept the affair because Ayn told her it was "right and rational."[47] Still, it made her very depressed and drove Frank deeper and deeper into alcoholism.

With Ayn's support, Nathaniel established the Nathaniel Branden Institute to offer courses in Objectivist philosophy. Nathaniel lectured and Ayn came in at the end to answer questions. Objectivism was an all-inclusive philosophy, and Branden gave lectures on Objectivism and Politics, Objectivism and Economics, Objectivism and Art, Objectivism and Psychology, Objectivism and Sex, and Objectivism and Aristotle.[48] Ayn gave the Objectivism and Literature lecture herself.

Objectivism developed into a cult, much like Auguste Comte's Church of Positivism.[49] Like all cults, the Objectivist cult had a public creed, which it preached to the world, and an unspoken internal creed, which was quite different. Although the public creed required everyone to be a rational thinker, the unspoken creed was that the truth was whatever Ayn said it was, because Ayn Rand was the greatest person who had ever lived and *Atlas Shrugged* the greatest intellectual achievement. Ayn Rand was the final arbiter of the truth on any issue.[50]

Rand also imitated Auguste Comte's principle of "cerebral hygiene." Although she did not start writing philosophy until *Atlas Shrugged* was published in 1957, there is no evidence that she read any philosophical literature published since 1945.[51] She published a critique of the most influential contemporary work on ethics, John Rawls's *A Theory of Justice,* in which she bragged that she had not read the book but only a newspaper review. She openly stated, "let me say that I have not read and do not intend to read that book."[52] Why read other people when she was the greatest thinker who ever lived?

As with any cult, there were turncoats. Jerome Tuccille had been attracted to Objectivism as an alternative to the Catholic dogmatism in which he had been raised.[53] At first, the doctrine of rationalism seemed like just what he had in mind, but the longer he participated, the more Objectivism reminded him of his Catholic upbringing, with dogmas and catechisms. He simply could not believe that altruism was responsible for all the world's problems. Nor could he take Ayn Rand as his saviour.

He found that "to be in disagreement with the ideas of Ayn Rand was to be, by definition, irrational and immoral."[54] At one session he attended, everyone had to write an essay on the one person who had most influenced his or her life. Naturally everyone wrote about Ayn Rand, except for one naive young man. He wrote about Rocco Fantozi, a high-school friend who had helped him through his parents' divorce. He was purged immediately for heresy.[55]

When economist Murray Rothbard's wife could not be persuaded to give up her Christian beliefs, Rand and Branden suggested that he leave her and take a more rational mate.[56] He refused. At a later meeting, Rothbard was denounced for not smoking cigarettes. A purge trial was held, which Rothbard refused to attend. Rothbard left the cult and continued to fight the Randians in the Libertarian Party. In 1990 he offered the following analysis of the psychology of Rand's followers:

> what better way to rationalize and systematize rejection of one's parents, family, and neighbors than to join a cult which denounces religion and which trumpets the absolute superiority of yourself and your cult leadership, as contrasted to the robotic "second-handers" who supposedly people the bourgeois world. A cult, furthermore, which calls upon you to spurn your parents, family, and bourgeois associates, and to cultivate the alleged greatness of your own individual ego.[57]

Rand believed that cigarettes were a pro-life product produced by capitalists and that refusing to smoke was irrational. When her doctor suggested she quit, she countered, "But *why?* And don't tell me about statistics; I've explained why statistics aren't proof. You have to give me a *rational* explanation. *Why* should I stop smoking?"[58] As always, she insisted on logical, not empirical evidence. She finally quit when the doctor showed her X-ray evidence of a malignancy on one of her lungs, but she refused Barbara Branden's entreaties that she inform her followers of her change of heart.

The biggest scandal was when Nathaniel Branden himself was purged from Objectivism. This came as a shock to readers of the May 1968 issue of Rand's newsletter, the *Objectivist,* who were given only a list of vague accusations against Branden, including the statement that he had given Ayn Rand "a written statement which was so irrational and so offensive to me that I had to break my personal association with him."[59] She did not reveal the content of the letter, which was actually an attempt to end their romantic relationship. Rand used all kinds of threats to try to keep Branden, including promising to pressure the publisher to cancel his *Psychology of Self Esteem* book and telling him that if he had an ounce of psychological health he would be impotent for the next twenty years. Branden left the movement for these personal reasons, not because of any philosophical disagreement. He continued to promote many of the same ideas in his popular psychological self-help books. He did, however, become critical of many of the cultish aspects of the Objectivist movement.

Although Branden chose not to lead an organized factional fight against Rand, his fall from grace was disillusioning for many of Rand's followers. Rumors spread that the cause was a lovers' quarrel, and many admirers saw Rand as a human being with flaws for the first time. Rand insisted that all her followers accept her version of the events on faith. Anyone caught reading any of Branden's books or articles was immediately purged. This led to a split in the movement, cynically referred to as the Objecti-schism, between those who accepted the ostracism on blind faith and those who insisted that they needed more facts to make an independent judgment. When Branden moved to California, some joked that the Objectivist Church had split between Eastern Orthodox and Western Reformed.[60]

Psychologist Albert Ellis was impressed when he read *The Fountainhead,* and he later conceded that "it is possible that it influenced me somewhat as I developed my rational-emotive method of psychotherapy."[61] Many of his patients noticed that the two approaches were similar and urged him to join forces with the Objectivists. Ellis challenged Nathaniel Branden to a debate, which was packed with Objectivists who cheered Branden and ridiculed Ellis, despite Branden's efforts to get them to be courteous. Branden later came to see some value in Ellis's critique of Objectivism, although at the time the Objectivists hailed him as the "consummate intellectual warrior."[62] Ellis got his revenge in a book that denounced Objectivism as a religion characterized by dogmatism, absolutism, tautological thinking, intolerance, deification of heroes, anti-empiricism, punitive correction, obsessiveness, mysticism, and ritualism.[63] Ellis changed the name of his approach to rational-emotive psychology.

Ellis's intense anger at Rand and Branden was ironic since the essence of Ellis's psychological theory is that each person is responsible for his own feelings. According to Ellis's theory, it was not the Objectivists who angered him but his own assumption that they should have been doing something other than what they did. He may have felt that Rand was stealing his thunder, since, in fact, Objectivist psychology is quite similar to rational-emotive psychology.[64]

Actually, little of Rand's thinking is original. Her epistemology is

Aristotelian and Thomistic, and her political theory is warmed over classical liberalism. George Smith has shown that many of her central philosophical arguments read like paraphrases of paragraphs from earlier philosophers.[65] Since she rarely footnoted her texts, there is no way to know whether she reached the same conclusions independently or simply borrowed the ideas.

While disillusioned turncoats are eager to find flaws in the doctrine they once embraced, it is not the content of the ideas that gave Objectivism its "religious" or dogmatic nature. The dogmatism came from the authoritative way in which the ideas were expressed and the worshipful way Rand's followers used them as sacred texts.

As the Objectivist movement crumbled, some of its most prominent members simply moved away without making any public break. Economist Alan Greenspan has never publicly repudiated Objectivism, so far as I know, but has moved into elite Republican Party circles. Economist Murray Rothbard returned to his interest in the writings of Austrian economist Ludwig von Mises and became active in the Libertarian movement.[66] Ayn Rand could not stand either Libertarianism or von Mises because neither paid obeisance to her, not because of any real political or intellectual differences.

Marxism as Utopianism

The early socialist writers were unashamedly utopian.[67] Visionaries such as Henri Saint-Simon, Charles Fourier, and Robert Owen hoped to inspire people to create utopias by the beauty of their ideals and the clarity of their ideas. Their followers obliged by establishing model socialist communities, many in the United States. These experiments fell apart because of interpersonal and factional conflict, economic difficulties, and simple boredom with life in small isolated communities. The ones that survived the longest were those with a religious philosophy; the secular communities lasted on average only a few years.[68]

Perhaps because he knew of some of these failures, Karl Marx rejected the "utopian" label. He insisted that he was a scientist analyzing the inevitable course of history, not a visionary singing songs of beauty, joy, and sugar peas. This was a misunderstanding, both of his own psychology and of the popular appeal of his work. Marx never understood utopians such as himself, who rejected their bourgeois class origins and sided with proletarian revolution.

The core of Marx's political thought was the belief in a socialist revolution, which would end the "prehistoric stage of human society" and usher in a utopia where all would live in harmony and equality with no need of a state to enforce social order.[69] In such a society, no one would have to work on a particular job since:

> society regulates the general production and thus makes it possible for me to do one thing to-day and another to-morrow, to hunt in the morning, fish in the afternoon, rear cattle in the evening, criticize after dinner, just as I have a mind, without ever becoming a hunter, fisherman, shepherd or critic.[70]

This brief utopian paragraph, from a book published by Marx and Friedrich Engels when Marx was twenty-eight, is often cited by Marxists eager for some clue of their founding fathers' vision of the future. If they turn to the original book for more details, however, they are disappointed. This one paragraph is all there is about the economic institutions of socialism. There is no description of how things would be run or what life would be like. Marx and Engels claim that the state would no longer be needed because there would be no conflicts to be settled, but they say nothing about the mechanisms society would use to "regulate the general production."

There are scattered references in other texts by Marx and Engels, which help to fill out the picture a little.[71] The *Critique of the Gotha Programme* explains that with Communism each worker would simply draw whatever goods he needed from the common storehouse. Marxist slogans, such as the "from each according to his ability, to each according to his needs," "the withering away of the state," and the transition from "the government of men to the administration of things," were taken from the utopian socialists. In *Socialism: Utopian and Scientific,* Engels criticized the "utopian socialists" for assuming that socialism could be brought about through idealist dreaming, but went on to describe the socialist utopia as one in which production of commodities for the market is done away with and anarchy in social production is replaced by systematic organization. To Engels, socialism meant, "the ascent of man from the kingdom of necessity to the kingdom of freedom."[72]

Many socialists found inspiration in these abstract phrases, but others longed for a more concrete and detailed portrait of the society of the future. This was provided by August Bebel. Bebel was a respected leader in the German Marxist movement who was convicted of treason by the Bismarck government and spent two years in prison with Wilhelm Liebknecht. He ended his 1883 book, *Woman and Socialism,* with a detailed description of socialist society of the future.[73] He may have thought that women, practical beings that they are, would not be satisfied with vague

Hegelian concepts but would want to know details such as who would do the cooking. (It would be done in communal kitchens, the private kitchen being as anachronistic as the private workshop.) As it turned out, men were just as eager as women for the specifics about socialism, and his book went through fifty printings in Germany alone.

Bebel described a society in which women would be completely equal to men, forming sexual liaisons and entering into occupations or leadership roles with complete freedom. He assumed that children would never be a burden, because "nurses, teachers, women friends, the rising female generation, all these will stand by her when she is in need of assistance."[74] It did not occur to him that men might share in this joyful responsibility.

People would enter whatever occupation they chose, and, if an imbalance should come about, "it will be the duty of the administration to make the necessary arrangements to bring about an equalization."[75] All economic decisions would be made by administrators who would be trained in administrative science and would collect the statistics, which "are the most important auxiliary science in the new society, since they furnish the standard whereby all social activity may be measured."[76]

This utopia, ruled by bureaucrats and statisticians, may have appealed to Bebel because his own life had been so impoverished and insecure.[77] His father was a noncommissioned officer who died at thirty-five, leaving little for the family to live on. Bebel was treated harshly by a stepfather and had no money to pursue his dream of becoming an engineer. His fondest wish during childhood was to be able to eat his fill of bread and butter. He became a machinist and a leader in the labor and socialist movements, paradoxically solving his own economic problems by becoming a successful manufacturer. His business was periodically interrupted by stretches in jail because of his socialist activism. Jail served him as a forced sabbatical, allowing him to rest and study and to write books, such as *Woman and Socialism.*

A skeptic might wonder how a society that depends upon a central administration to resolve all its problems could do without a state. Bebel stated, "Together with the state will vanish its representatives: ministers, parliaments, standing armies, police, courts, lawyers and district attorneys, prison officials, collectors of taxes and duty; in short the entire political apparatus."[78]

The administrators will have no need of coercive power; they will play a purely technical function. Everyone will accept their recommendations willingly and enthusiastically, competing with each other only to be the most diligent and innovative in accomplishing society's collective goals. There will be no need for law enforcement since crime will disappear:

> Neither political nor common crimes will be known in the future. Thieves will have disappeared, because private property will have disappeared, and in the new society everyone will be able to satisfy his wants easily and conveniently by work. Nor will there be tramps and vagabonds, for they are the product of a society founded on private property. . . . Murder? Why? No one can enrich himself at the expense of others, and even the murder for hatred or revenge is directly or indirectly connected with the social system. . . . Arson? Who should find pleasure or satisfaction in committing arson when society has removed all cause for hatred? Counterfeiting? Money will be but a chimera.[79]

Rape and violence against women or children are not mentioned, an odd oversight in a book on *Woman and Socialism.* Lenin filled in this gap, explaining that members of the community would spontaneously apprehend and punish or treat anyone who violated socialist morality, making a specialized police force unnecessary.[80]

Bebel's book, which sold far better than any of Marx's writings other than the utopian *Communist Manifesto,* shows that utopianism was a strong theme in the Marxist movement despite the refusal of Marx and Engels to speculate about details. As in other utopian socialisms, the Marxist vision of socialism depended on an optimistic view of human nature. It assumed that once material affluence is achieved and the evils of capitalism are abolished, people will naturally be cooperative and unaggressive. Even the transition to socialism would be painless in Bebel's view since:

> at a given time, all the depicted evils will have developed to such extremes and will have become so evident and tangible to the great majority of the population, that they will come to be regarded as unbearable; that a general, irresistible demand for a thoroughgoing transformation will manifest itself, and that, accordingly, the quickest help will be considered the most appropriate.[82]

Paradoxically, Marx's scientific stance helped him to sustain his utopian vision. He used scientific skepticism as an excuse not to examine his utopian assumptions. When questioned about the viability of his proposals, he always denied any ability to predict specifics of the future. All problems would be worked out by the people at the time. Scientists could only analyze data that already existed. Yet he was adamant in predicting that a socialist future would inevitably emerge. He also refused to make moral judgments, insisting that people had no power to change history to suit their ethical predilections. He thought it foolish to debate whether socialism would be good or bad. It was inevitable. Yet his writings are saturated with moralistic rhetoric, expressing hatred of the oppressors and the belief that anything that undermined the existing social order was good.

As a young man, Marx had a strong need for something to believe in, a cause or mission to give meaning to his life.[82] His father, Heinrich, was a liberal, secular Jewish lawyer living in Trier, a town that was transferred from French to Prussian sovereignty just before Karl was born. France allowed full civil rights to Jews, but Prussia prohibited Jews from practicing law. Marx's father protested and tried to obtain an exception, but finally gave in and converted to Christianity in order to be able to practice his profession. His mother refused to convert until much later.

There is no record of how Heinrich felt about his conversion, nor about how he explained it to his son. His letters to his son at college reveal some conflict between pragmatism and idealism. He wanted his son to make contacts and advance his career, but also wanted him to have a good heart and be true to his ideals. Heinrich died when Karl was only twenty, and it may be that the conflicts they had were not adequately resolved for Karl to put them aside psychologically. David Felix argues that "Karl Marx never consciously connected his contempt for the liberals in general with his feelings for the liberal gentleman Heinrich Marx."[83]

If Karl felt contempt for his father, it was buried in the depths of the unconscious, which are revealed only to Orthodox Freudians and trance channelers. They had disagreements, but their correspondence was friendly, and Heinrich was generous and supportive. Away at the university, the young Karl Marx wrote his ill father of "the deep affection, the immeasurable love, which I often have not been able to express as I should like; in the hope that you too, dear and eternally beloved Father, mindful of my storm-tossed feelings, will forgive me when my heart must often have seemed to have gone astray as the burdens of my spirit stifled it."[84] Marx's letter to his father sounds like Woodrow Wilson's, and Heinrich, like Wilson's father, may have overidentified with his son and wanted him to achieve great things that he had been unable to accomplish. Nothing in Karl's later sexual life suggests that he was plagued by an enduring Oedipal crisis. He did have some animosity toward his mother who was critical and controlling. After Heinrich died, she controlled Karl's inheritance, and they argued over money. She wished he would stop writing about capital and accumulate some.

As a young student, Karl tried law, philosophy, and poetry in his quest for a meaningful calling. He wrote a nearly three-hundred-page treatise on the philosophy of law before deciding it was empty. He felt that his poetry was worthless: "the realm of true poetry flashed open before me like a distant faery place, and all my creations collapsed into nothing." He was so vexed that "I was for several days quite unable to think. Like a lunatic I ran around in the garden."[85]

Marx resolved his quest for purpose by converting to a belief in Hegelian philosophy. Hegel postulated that history was fundamentally a struggle between conflicting ideas, which he referred to as theses and antitheses. Out of this struggle, a synthesis developed, which transformed the nature of history. Hegelian philosophy appealed to the utopian longings of many young radicals, since it gave them faith that their criticisms of society would ultimately lead to a revolutionary transformation. Hegel's theory of history excused them from the tiresome task of stating exactly what that transformation would be like or explaining why it would be better than the existing way of doing things.

Marx had considered Hegelianism earlier and rejected it, in part due to pressure from his father who thought that Hegelians "screw their words up so tightly that they cannot hear themselves; because their torrent of words conveys no thoughts, or confused ones, they baptize it as a birth of genius."[86] At that time, Karl had found Hegel's "grotesque craggy melody unpleasing," but now he thought it might be an answer to his mental anguish. He turned to Hegel with "the definite intention of discovering our mental nature to be just as determined, concrete, and firmly established as our physical."[87]

Hegelianism gave Marx a feeling that he was part of a larger movement of history, that his feelings were not his own problem but were determined by historical forces. When he explained this to his father, Heinrich accepted his "transformation," since it appeared that "your philosophy satisfactorily agrees and harmonizes with your conscience."[88]

Becoming a Hegelian philosopher also offered Karl the prospect of a secure profession as a college professor—a profession that would not require him to compromise his values, as his father had done. This was a matter of great concern to him. As an adolescent, he had written that an ill-advised choice of a vocation was "an act which can destroy a man's entire life, defeat all his plans, and make him unhappy."[89] He plunged into a doctoral dissertation on *The Difference Between the Democritean and Epicurean Philosophy of Nature.*

By the time Marx completed his dissertation, however, the winds of academic politics had changed and Hegelians were no longer in much demand. He could not find an academic post, so he took a job as the editor of a liberal newspaper and became convinced that political journalism was a better vocation for a progressive philosopher. Here, again, he was frustrated when the newspaper was suppressed by the government. He emigrated to Paris and became immersed in French revolutionary theory and politics. In collaboration with his new friend, Friedrich Engels, he developed his own unique synthesis of Hegelianism and French radicalism, positing that the class struggle (not ideas as Hegel had claimed) was the motive force in history. His life would have meaning as part of the struggle of the working class to make a socialist revolution.

Never again would Marx have to worry about finding a career that would not compromise his values. His career was that of revolutionary writer and organizer. Not only would he refuse to sell out as his father had done, but he would build a world where no one had to do any work he did not want to do. His vision of a world where people could do whatever work they wanted, whenever they wanted, was taken directly from the writings of French socialist Charles Fourier.[90] Fourier was a bachelor traveling salesmen, who lived in grubby hotels and passed away the lonely evenings writing an elaborate fantasy of an idyllic community where sex was free and promiscuous, work voluntary, and all human passions carefully provided for. He also carefully analyzed the sex life of the planets. To make sure no passion was overlooked, he developed an elaborate theory of human nature, based on numerology and astrology, which divided people into 810 psychological types. Each of these was to be provided for in his utopian community.

When revolution spread throughout continental Europe in 1848, Marx thought that his predictions were coming true. Sadly, the revolutions were crushed, and he had to go on with his life. He emigrated to London and eked out a modest living as a part-time journalist. He had married the girl-next-door from his hometown and had a series of children, several of whom died in childhood. The Marxes were always in debt, unable to pay doctor bills or to take their sick children to the seashore when the doctor recommended it. This was partly due to poor money management, since their income, although less than that of their parents, was several times that of a skilled worker. Karl lived largely off charity from Friedrich Engels, who ran his family's textile business in Manchester, supplemented with inheritances and payments for articles he wrote for a New York newspaper. Marx once wrote to Engels in desperation, complaining that he could not go outdoors because his only coat was in the pawnshop.

The worse things got for Karl, the more he felt he had invested in his theories, and the more committed he became. He worked late into the night, even when his body was covered with painful carbuncles and the doctor said that only proper rest, exercise, and good diet would make them go away. He realized that he was ruining his health, but felt he could not explain to his doctors "the causes that *compel* me to these extravagances."[91] He smoked incessantly, despite a lifelong affliction with lung disease, which had kept him out of the Prussian army as a teenager. He kept trying to complete his book on economics but was not able to get the data to fit his theories. He knew his general theories about the capitalist economic relations were "contentless" if they could not explain actual trends in profits and wages. He wrote and rewrote, never satisfied with his formulations. Yet he could not abandon the underlying theory to which he had dedicated his life. He retained his Hegelian faith that a new revolutionary synthesis was inevitable.

Other political exiles in similar circumstances took jobs that paid the bills and still provided free time for their writing and politics. Marx refused to do this, although he realized that the difficulties that were agonizing his family and keeping him from finishing his book would disappear "tomorrow, if tomorrow I decided to engage in some practical business."[92] Instead, he stuck to journalism, which took a great deal of time and intellectual effort and paid poorly. He also spent a lot of time and energy on running the Socialist International before deciding that he could not carry on both this and his scholarly work.

Marx was, of course, aware that he had "sacrificed [his] whole wealth to the revolutionary struggle."[93] He also knew better than anyone that the cause was not going well. He wrote to Engels that "the pleasant delusions and the almost childish enthusiasm with which we greeted the revolution before February, 1848, are for the devil. . . . we now know what a role stupidity plays in revolutions, and how they are exploited by scoundrels."[94] Engels finally persuaded him to go ahead and publish the first volume of his book *Das Kapital,* even though he was not satisfied with it. He never completed the volumes, which were to show how the general theory, could explain the observable dynamics of capitalism. Engels pieced them together as best he could from Marx's notes after he died.

Marx was never overtly suicidal, but his lifestyle was self-destructive. Wilhelm Liebknecht wrote that "I am convinced—and the physicians who last treated him were of the same opinion—that had Marx made up his mind to a life in keeping with nature, that is, with the demands of his organism and of hygiene, he would still be alive today [1895]."[95] His wife suffered greatly from their money problems, and she died at thirty-nine of a stomach problem. He was devoted to his legitimate children, but he sent the son he had by the family servant out to be raised by foster parents rather than compromise his respectability.

Sadly, his self-destructive life script was imitated by his youngest daughter, Eleanor, who was closest to him politically and personally. She lived with a prominent socialist spokesman, Edward Aveling, who was utterly selfish and disloyal. Edward could not marry her because he was not divorced from his first wife, but he secretly married another woman who would not sleep with him otherwise. He never had any money so he borrowed Eleanor's illegitimate brother's life savings and never repaid him. Eleanor finally committed suicide with poison he had purchased.

Some say he killed her, others that they had a mutual suicide pact and he cheated. Her biographer, however, believes that her suicide was not motivated by his infidelities (which she had long tolerated) but by her frustration at the decline of the socialist movement to which she and her father had devoted their lives.[96] She had no way of knowing that Marxism would have a revival in the twentieth century.

Utopianism in Scientific Disguises

Utopianism is not confined to novels and radical political movements. It can also be found in scientific disciplines, which claim to be based on rigorous empirical evidence. In this section, we will examine utopian myths that are hidden away in several academic disciplines.

Archeology and Utopia. The discipline of archeology is particularly susceptible to utopian fantasies. People's imaginations run wild, filling in the gaps in our knowledge of long-dead societies. Archeologists find that many students are attracted to their courses by stories of "ancient astronauts, Noah's ark, psychic archeology, pyramid power, lost continents, harmonically converging ancestors, and more" gleaned from the "New Age" or "Occult" shelves of almost any bookstore.[97] Each of these myths include a transformational object such as extraterrestrials or a "harmonic convergence," which promises to totally change reality. A large survey found that about a third of American college students believe in myths of this sort.[98]

The Atlantis myth lives among those who prefer "inspirational" to "tape-measure" archeology.[99] The Theosophists, who believe that human beings evolved from astral jellyfish and four-armed egg-laying hermaphrodites, adopted the Atlantis myth and discovered a counterpart sunken continent called Mu in the Pacific Ocean.[100] In the 1940s, psychic Edgar Cayce predicted that much of the American east coast would be flooded by the reemergence of parts of Atlantis in 1968 or 1969.[101] And the "trance-channeler" J. Z. Knight has recently been in touch with the spirit *Ramtha,* who was born on Atlantis 35,000 years ago and now uses the wisdom gained through millennia of contemplation to provide investment counseling to Knight's customers.[102]

Sometimes the date of the forthcoming transformation is given, an error Marx carefully avoided. Art historian and author Jose Argüelles predicted that a "harmonic convergence" would occur on August-16, 1987, because of a critical conjunction of planets, energy beams, and extraterrestrial beings.[103] Argüelles believes that the Maya and Aztecs were extraterrestrial beings, and he used the Aztec calendar to predict the future. Hundreds of his followers gathered at sacred sites in the hopes of meeting the god Quetzalcoatl, or at least seeing some flying saucers, but nothing happened.

More troublesome is the evidence of utopianism in the work of reputable, even eminent, archeologists. In 1886 the eminent American Maya specialist Edward H. Thompson observed, "As I look over the result of archaeological work, this fact forces itself upon me: how hard it is for an investigator with a pet theory, to avoid molding the facts to suit his theory rather than to shape his theory to suit the facts."[104]

Ironically, one of the most influential examples of this phenomenon was the work of another Maya specialist with the same last name, British archeologist Sir Eric Thompson, with whom Edward Thompson is easily confused. Eric Thompson's book *The Civilization of the Mayas* became an archeological best-seller largely because it promised to answer the great enigma of the Mayas.[105] Why, after building huge cities and amassing considerable wealth and scientific knowledge, did Maya civilization abruptly collapse? In the first edition, published in 1927, Eric Thompson offered the conventional view that it may have resulted from either an invasion of groups from central Mexico or from agricultural failure. Apparently this was not dramatic enough. In the 1931 edition, despite a lack of any significant new evidence, he presented a model of Maya society polarized between two classes: an exploiting theocracy living in the cities and an exploited peasantry scattered throughout the countryside. He then speculated that a great peasant revolt may have overthrown the Maya civilization.

The problem with this explanation is that there is very little evidence for it.[106] Indeed, some research suggests that, far from being highly stratified, the ancient Maya may have been primitive communists. They may have followed the practice of contemporary Maya in Zinacatan where men rotate between being peasant farmers and priests.[107] Ongoing excavations show that Maya cities were much more populated than Eric Thompson thought. The sad fact is that we simply don't know why classic Maya civilization collapsed.

When there is a dearth of evidence, there is a great temptation for authors to fill the gap with projections of their own concerns. As an early twentieth-century Englishman, Eric Thompson came from a highly stratified society that was concerned about class warfare. End-of-the-world myths were also quite the rage. Becker notes that:

> Thompson grew up during the explosive first decade of the twentieth century [when] the idea of the lost city of Atlantis was in great vogue. The more rapidly the scientific revolution changed the world, the more the masses clamored for simplistic explanations and fantasmagorical

theories. . . . The Maya cities could be explained as being the products of the inhabitants of the lost Atlantis, who seemed to be forever doomed to be lost again. The lost city theme may have been a Freudian projection of what many in the landed classes felt to be a growing horror: "Urbanization." . . . The anti-urban people of 1910 found the idea of a cataclysmic end to cities to be an attractive and fitting end of a way of life which they were unable to tolerate.[108]

It is not clear to what extent Thompson believed the ideas expressed in his own popular books. He may simply have been catering to the popular audience. The peasant-uprising thesis does not appear in his scholarly articles intended for a professional audience. When questioned about this, he readily admitted that there was no real evidence for his speculations and mentioned, "you know, I never held a university appointment."[109] Although he was recognized as the "Great Panjandrum" of Maya studies, there were no teaching or research positions in a field that was traditionally thought of as a suitable occupation for gentlemen of independent means.[110]

Today, the classic Maya collapse is more likely to be attributed to overpopulation and resource exhaustion. While this might be more accurate, one must be skeptical of an explanation that is so conveniently "relevant" to contemporary concerns.

Feminist Utopias. Another common archeological myth is the belief in an idyllic classless society in which women and men were equal. Friedrich Engels used anthropological evidence from L. H. Morgan's book *Ancient Society* to argue that women were equal before the desire to pass private property on to their legitimate heirs led wealthy men to institute the sexual double standard.[111] Engels book served well as a manifesto for socialist feminism, but the anthropological evidence it relied on to prove that historically matriarchial society preceded patriarchal society is no longer accepted today.[112]

A similar myth is advanced today by University of California archeologist Marija Gimbutas who argues that six thousand years ago, women and men lived in harmony in Old European culture.[113] The key to their success was that society was focused on women and worshiped goddesses instead of male gods. This idyllic society was overthrown by Indo-European invaders between 4000 and 3500 B.C., and patriarchy has reigned supreme ever since.

A new "goddess religion" has become popular among some feminists who accept Gimbutas's theories as proof that feminism worked beautifully before the men took over and ruined it.[114] Several of these women to whom I have spoken insist that it is a proven historical fact that everything was wonderful under the goddess religion before the men messed things up. They do not want to hear otherwise and cite as their authorities eminent writers, such as mythologist Joseph Campbell and anthropologist Ashley Montague, who have applauded Gimbutas's work. Less visionary archeologists, however, claim that Gimbutas "amasses all the data and then leaps from it to conclusions without any intervening argument. Most of us tend to say, oh my God, here goes Marija again."[115] They offer evidence that, far from being peaceful feminists, the Old Europeans had hierarchies and forts, and they used weapons and practiced human sacrifice. Anthropologist David Anthony says that there is no real evidence for Gimbutas's fundamental thesis that women played a central role in the Old European societies or in their religions.[116] The archeological evidence for the "goddess religion" is little more than a few ancient stone carvings of female figures.[117] No one knows what they meant to the people who created them, which makes them perfect for utopian projections.

Gimbutas's work is applauded by many on the grounds that belief in an idyllic Goddess-worshiping past will help humanity create a non-sexist, egalitarian, nonviolent, ecologically sound future. Professor Gerda Lerner of the University of Wisconsin applauds Gimbutas's work because it offers an imaginative alternative to male-centered thinking, even though she agrees that it "can never be proven." Other archeologists recall that similar unsupported archeological myths were used by the Nazis to support their racist theories and object to distorting scientific evidence to advance ideological agendas, however laudatory they may be.[118]

Margaret Mead's Tropical Paradise. One might think that anthropologists would be too sophisticated to perpetuate the myth of a tropical paradise where life is free and the women are easy. Yet, in 1983 Australian anthropologist Derek Freeman shook the anthropological profession with a book that accused America's best-known anthropologist, Margaret Mead, of doing just that in her classic 1928 book, *Coming of Age in Samoa*.[119] In the preface to the 1961 printing, Mead herself noted, "Those who saw American society in the 1920's as a rapacious and consuming monster greeted this book as an escape—an escape in spirit that paralleled an escape in body to a South Sea island where love and ease were the order of the day."[120]

In debunking Mead's utopia, Freeman relied on his own research and on the research of Lowell Holmes, a young anthropologist who replicated Mead's field work in Samoa as his dissertation project. In his own book, Holmes criticizes both Mead and Freeman and offers his own middle-of-the-road perspective.[121]

Freeman argues that Mead was so eager to prove that culture, not biology, shaped behavior that she believed the tall tales of a group of adolescent girls who were teasing her. He cites statistics and case histories on rape to disprove Mead's claim that rape did not exist in Samoa. He claims that the cult of virginity is as strong in Samoa as anywhere on earth and that young men traditionally sneak into virgin girls' homes to deflower them manually while they are sleeping so that they will be despoiled and have no choice but to marry them. Mead was aware of the "curious form of surreptitious rape, called *moetotolo,* sleep crawling," but downplayed it as a practice indulged in by "youths who find no favor in maiden's eyes."[122] If the girl raises a fuss, Mead reported, the sleep crawlers are chased away by the family and become the laughing stock of the community.

The Samoans are alive and well and living in Samoa, so it might seem a simple matter to ask them which author is correct. Indeed, some of them are intellectuals who have written reviews of the controversy, and Lowell Holmes quotes a number of their comments on the dispute. Alas, some of them favor Mead, others Freeman. Most seem to agree that "Mead erred far too much on the side of free love and promiscuity, while Freeman errs on the side of sexual purity, strictness, and abstinence."[123]

Perhaps the only thing we can say for certain about the sex life of Samoan teenagers is that they do not like to talk about it with visiting anthropologists. Virginity is highly valued in the traditional culture, but that norm is often violated in Samoa as it is elsewhere. No contemporary authority accepts Mead's idealized, utopian picture of Samoan society. Yet, when her book was published in 1928, it was hailed as a great scientific contribution and was very widely assigned in college classes.[124] Bertrand Russell used Mead's findings to bolster his argument against conventional marriage, expressing his admiration for the way Samoan men, "when they have to go upon a journey, fully expect their wives to console themselves for their absence."[125] Radicals cited Mead as justification for their belief that the Soviet Communists were on the right track in promoting liberated sexual norms. Liberals cited her in support of less punitive child-rearing practices, and cultural anthropologists used the book to respond to those who claimed that human behavior was biologically determined.

Unidentified Flying Objects. If utopia never existed on a sunken continent, in ancient history, or on a south seas island, there is always the possibility that it exists somewhere in the heavens. Indeed, representatives of other planets or galaxies may be buzzing around the earth and transforming ordinary people into minor celebrities by offering them rides in space vehicles. After all, if God picked Jonah to deliver one of his messages, why shouldn't the spacemen choose handyman and "metaphysics" teacher George Adamski to deliver theirs?[126]

Sightings of Unidentified Flying Objects have been recorded periodically at least since 1561.[127] Their appearance has changed to suit the conceptual framework of the time. In the 1560s, they looked like suns with faces, while in the 1890s they looked like dirigibles with wings, sails, and/or propellers and traveled at the then phenomenal speed of two hundred miles an hour.[128] In the 1950s, they were seen as disks or cigar-shaped objects and traveled at speeds much greater than the fastest supersonic jet fighters. The "flying saucer" craze peaked in the 1950s and declined into a minor sect because the mass audience tired of waiting for the space travelers to make themselves known. There was, however, a resurgence of sightings in 1972 and 1973, and it seems likely that similar sightings will occur in the future.

Efforts by skeptics to study the UFO phenomenon have ended in frustration.[129] There are many sightings by seemingly objective observers such as airline pilots, some of which are confirmed by radar, but there are few photographs and only of very poor quality. Their existence cannot be disproved, and official agencies have decided that it is not worth spending more money to study the reports. Professional astronomers interested in extraterrestrial intelligence spend their limited funding on listening for electromagnetic signals and shy away from the "flying saucer" enthusiasts.[130]

The vulnerability of "eye witness" perception to rumors and group suggestion is well known and may account for the tendency of the sightings to occur in waves.[131] While some reports are hard to explain, others seem clearly illusionary, such as that of Mr. Adamski, who claims to have been taken on a trip around the moon in a few hours.[132] He observed that the far side of the moon had an atmosphere, trees, forests, and settlements much like the earth. No explanation was given for the moon's shyness in showing only its uninhabitable side to the earth.

Depth psychologist C. G. Jung analyzed UFO sightings in historical reports and in dreams reported by large numbers of people and found they shared archetypal symbolism consistent with his general theory of archetypes in the collective unconscious.[133] In his view, the UFOs are a modern version of the archetypal epiphany from heaven, similar psychologically to the appearance of visions of gods or other supernatural beings throughout history. The association of the birth of Jesus with a new, bright star in the heavens is a familiar example. The predominance of cigar-shaped and circular vehicles may be sexual symbolism. More central to the archetypal symbolism found in UFO reports, however, is the antithesis between Above and Below, between "an enigmatic higher world and the ordinary human world."[134]

Of course, the value one ascribes to this kind of analysis depends on one's opinion of Jung's general theory. It certainly doesn't prove that the UFOs are psychological hallucinations, as Jung readily admits, nor does it prove that any individual who sees or dreams about a flying saucer is seeking a religious epiphany. Jung's analysis does, however, fit well with an analysis of preoccupation with UFOs as a utopian social movement. UFOs are all-purpose transformational objects, since they have no certain features and seem to interact primarily with isolated individuals. They bring excitement to the mundane lives of ordinary people and seem to do no harm, other than distracting people from matters that they can actually do something about. As with other utopian movements, disappointment sets in when the promised changes do not actually happen.

Alvin Lawson has argued that UFO abduction reports are based on unconscious memories of the birth process.[135] Abductees report being trapped and going through a long, dark tunnel into a place with blinding light. The pictures they draw of spacemen do look a lot like fetuses. The imagery is similar to that reported by people who have near-death experiences or who enter into shamans' trances. The birth-trauma theory of "out of body" experiences is quite popular, perhaps because of its support from astronomer Carl Sagan, but there are good reasons to doubt whether infants really experience birth as going through a tunnel, or whether they are capable of remembering prenatal or birth experiences.[136] Of course, the large majority of UFO reports do not involve abductions, and it is always possible that the reports are similar because the people were actually abducted by the same spacemen. The archetypal concept of being reborn, however, is a common feature of transformational myths.

Space Colonies. An alternative to waiting for the spacemen to visit is to build a space utopia ourselves. Princeton physicist Gerard O'Neill has developed elaborate plans for giant pinwheel-shaped space colonies to be located at L5, the point where the gravitational fields of the moon and the earth intersect. From there it will be only a short trip to "homesteading the asteroids."[137] While O'Neill's engineering model for space colonies has value, his advocacy of space colonization as a solution for humanity's problems is a utopian fantasy. He argues that humanity has made a mess of life on earth, citing problems such as overpopulation, pollution, and nuclear war as documented in the writings of well-known social critics. He then assumes that life on space colonies will have none of these problems: resources will be plentiful, cultural diversity will be valued, and life quality will be high. Not only that, but the problems on earth will be relieved by exporting surplus population and industry.[138]

This utopian model can be appealing to people who have given up hope for life on earth. For example, an Argentinean woman, whose son "disappeared" during a period of military dictatorship, lost hope for an ideal society on earth, but she found comfort in the belief that as soon as people moved to the moon, where there were no people already there to exploit and tyrannize, the colonists would organize a truly just and humane society.[139] Many supporters of space colonization, who are organized in a group known as the L5 Society, are just as convinced of the idyllic nature of life at L5 as adherents of any other utopian myth. Unfortunately, there is no good reason to believe that problems such as piracy, religious or ideological conflict, fighting over scarce resources, and inequality will somehow go away because people are living in isolated, artificial environments.[140] These problems certainly existed in frontier societies on earth where resources such as air, land, and water were plentiful.

Conclusions

The people we have discussed in this chapter tried to be objective, rational thinkers. They thought of themselves as scientists and logicians, not utopian true believers. These claims were most persuasive when their utopias were new. As time passed, their works appeared less and less realistic, and their origins in the psychology of the authors became clearer. The fantasies are clearest in the nineteenth-century utopias, more obscure in the contemporary ones. When we read *Looking Backward* and *Caesar's Column* in the late twentieth century, it is obvious that both were elaborations of the concerns and perspectives of the writers, not impartial forecasts. This was not apparent to their authors. Bellamy wrote that "*Looking Backward*, although in form a fanciful romance, is intended, in all seriousness, as a forecast, in accordance with the principles of evolution."[141] Donnelly's Ugandan utopia followed exactly the same agrarian populist principles, which he advocated for America in his roles as politician and journalist.

Marxists have been aware of the utopianism of rival socialist sects and have striven to be different. Lenin claimed that:

> There can be no dogmatism where the supreme and sole criterion of a doctrine is its conformity to the actual process of social and economic development; there can be no sectarianism when the task is that of promoting the organization of the proletariat, and when, therefore, the role of the "intelligentsia" is to make special leaders from among the intelligentsia unnecessary.[142]

Many thoughtful people found this argument persuasive when Lenin wrote it in 1894, and Marxist intellectuals have tried very hard to be objective and scientific. Yet by 1990 it was apparent even to Soviet spokesmen such as Vladimir Pozner that:

there is a profound contradiction between the openness and thought-provoking character of Marxist philosophy and its practical implementation. In virtually every case, this philosophy has led to the destruction of the intellectual community, the ending of all discussion, and the emergence of a so-called Marxist state that was in effect the antithesis of Marxist thought; the replacement of debate and questioning by one point of view.[143]

Ayn Rand made rationality the center of her doctrine and espoused an Aristotelian theory of knowledge, which made the objective, empirical world the standard for judging the truth of any belief. Yet she did no empirical research, preferring the black-and-white world of utopian fiction where everything worked out as her "rational" arguments said it would. Her movement quickly degenerated into a utopian sect with her as the guru and her novels the sacred texts. We are fortunate that she founded no state and could do no more than purge dissidents from her ranks.

Margaret Mead went to Samoa to challenge the biases of the biological determinists with the hard facts of empirical fieldwork. She ended up writing of an adolescent sexual utopia. The fact that feminist scholars ignored her appalling apologetics for the rape of adolescent girls reveals their own selective indignation. If the same book had been written by a man, it would have been included in the lists of works routinely denounced as sexist.

If these intelligent and well-meaning people fell into the trap of utopianism, how can we be sure that we are not doing the same? How can we detect utopian illusions before they are tarnished by the passage of time or debunked by the scrutiny of critics? One way is to use the skeptical script. A healthy dose of skepticism is appropriate about all claims about the inevitable future or the prehistoric past. So too of claims of little-known foreign countries, distant planets, or ephemeral spacemen. The utopian literature relies heavily on ideological devices such as rhetorical argumentation, polarized thinking, and passionate belief. Utopias are all-inclusive systems that are resistant to discordant facts or analogies. Pointing these things out to true believers, however, is almost always futile. Utopian thinking is resistant to skepticism precisely because utopias are about the future and the unknown. Utopias are about possibilities, not actualities, and holding them to a strict scientific standard is inappropriate. Their function is to stretch the imagination. A good novel about life in a feminist utopia would be a real contribution to social thought, just as *Looking Backward* and *Women and Socialism* gave us a vision of what the socialists were after. Such a vision can be criticized, and alternatives can be presented. Dystopias such as *1984* and *Animal Farm* have been invaluable warnings of things that might happen, even though they have not been accurate as forecasts.

Utopias are harmless when they are clearly recognized as fantasies. People who misuse them as dogmatic imperatives are usually seeking a compensation for feelings of inadequacy. As a student struggling for an identity, Karl Marx shared with his father his painful discovery that "self-contempt is a serpent which eternally gnaws in one's breast, sucks out the heart's lifeblood, and mixes it with the poison of misanthropy and despair."[144] He found relief by identifying with the Hegelian Dialectic of History, just as countless young men (including this author) have found strength by identifying with the Marxian Dialectic of Revolution.

In reflecting on his own experiences, turncoat Ron Tuccille believed that Objectivism:

> is especially appealing to those in the process of escaping a regimented religious background—particularly young Jews and renegade Roman Catholics, ripe for conversion to some form of religion-substitute. The crumbling walls of doctrinaire Catholicism, or heavy-fisted Judaism, leave you with a feeling of vulnerability. . . . You realize you can't go home again, but where do you go? And then you discover Galt's Gulch at the end of *Atlas Shrugged* and you know everything is going to be all right forevermore. . . . You've become a devout Objectivist.[145]

These needs for self-affirmation may be most common in adolescence, but they can occur at any stage of life. Ignatius Donnelly's turn to utopianism came during a mid-life crisis caused by the failure of his business and political careers. Throughout their adult lives, Sidney and Beatrice Webb were rigorous social scientists as well as social reformers. They founded the Fabian movement, which advocated social reform through gradual-ism and "permeation" of existing social institutions. Beatrice thought of "a fondness for revolutionary action in the same category as a fondness for whiskey; as an addiction into which the addict was liable to relapse at any moment, and end up, ruined, in the arms of the Social Democratic Federation."[146]

Yet, when she and Sidney visited the Soviet Union in 1932, they were enthralled with the vision of revolutionary change and wrote a two-volume book heralding it as a new civilization.[147] Her niece's husband, Malcolm Muggeridge, shared her enthusiasm and took his wife to the Soviet Union with the intention of becoming citizens. He was disillusioned when he discovered the harsh living conditions, the famine in the Ukraine, and the Moscow purge trials.[148] He sent back highly critical reports, which were published in the *Manchester Guardian*. Their "Aunt Bo" dismissed his reports as "a hysterical tirade," preferring to believe the apologetic reports from *New York Times* correspondent Walter Duranty and others.[149] She had enough self-perception, however, to joke about their late-life conversion to Stalinism, remarking that "old people often fall in love in extraordinary and ridiculous ways—with their chauffeurs for example; we feel it more dignified to have fallen in love with Soviet Communism."[150]

One way to protect ourselves from utopian illusions is to be sensitive to political beliefs that have a strong emotional component. It makes sense to believe strongly in values and principles, but when we believe strongly that a certain theory is true or a certain future inevitable, we are confusing a utopian script for a scientific one. The same person can be both a utopian and a skeptic if he is careful to keep the two scripts distinct in his mind. Karl Marx was a skeptical scientist when he tried to puzzle out the dynamics of wages and prices in English capitalism or to understand the forces that caused the revolutions of 1848 to fail. He was a utopian when he insisted that history was inevitably marching toward an idyllic socialist future. As long as his believers were out of power, the socialist vision provided inspiration for political organizing and activism. When it was imposed as a scientific "fact" by a ruling elite, Marxism deteriorated into the dogmatism that Vladimir Pozner denounced.

Utopian visions can be evaluated for the richness of their imagery and the subtlety and plausibility of their descriptions. They are literary, not scientific, works. Perhaps because of their origin in infantile narcissism, utopias tend toward simplistic splitting between idyllic utopia and catastrophic disaster. Much utopian thinking is marred by the unconscious assumption that unmitigated evils must necessarily be followed by a transformation to utopian bliss. This ignores the common-sense warning against jumping from the frying pan into the fire.

The irrational assumption that if capitalism is flawed, then socialism must be perfect is characteristic of true believers who continue to espouse Marxist utopianism. They devote all of their efforts to denouncing capitalism and simply assume that all existing evils will be eliminated under socialism. Since the "actually existing" Marxist states have accomplished no such thing, these Marxist utopians strongly resist any effort to get them to describe the socialism they advocate so insistently.

At a Socialist Scholars meeting in 1989, for example, I raised the question of why so many participants continued to be committed to "socialism" after hearing so many panels about the failures of socialism in Eastern Europe. Did they perhaps mean a different kind of "socialism" such as that prevailing in Scandinavia? No, there were several panels on the problems of these societies and the consensus was that they also were seriously flawed. One woman assured me, with a beatific look on her face, that she was expecting something "different," something that had never been tried before.

At another meeting, I was surprised when a radical sociologist insisted that socialist revolution was imminent in the United States. I could not imagine what she meant and asked her what she expected American socialism to be like. She refused to answer, repeating over and over that "the workers will decide." Despite familiarity with all the problems of socialism in Eastern Europe, she had no doubt that whatever the workers decided on would be vastly superior to the existing American system. Nor was she impressed with the Swedish model, which she knew well because she had relatives in Sweden. It was too tangible and mundane to meet her need for a vision of immanent transformation. While this kind of thinking is frustrating to a skeptic, it can have positive value. This sociologist's optimistic, if intangible, vision gave her the strength to work tirelessly for social reform in her Appalachian community under conditions where a skeptic would give up in despair.

The weakest point in utopian visions is the transformational object, the mysterious mechanism that is needed to bring the utopia about. In science fiction, this can be solved with fantastic fantasies, and the silliest New Age utopianism is based on confusing these fantasies with reality. Perhaps authors such as Donnelly, Bellamy, Rand, and Marx can be forgiven for hoping that their books would serve this function, but societies based on the worship of holy books have generally not lived up to expectations. Marxist hopes for the emergence of revolutionary consciousness in the working class were more plausible, but ultimately misguided. Revolutionary transformations have more frequently been brought about by small groups of armed true believers, such as Leninist parties. Relying on such a mechanism usually defeats the purpose of the transformation. The utopians are most in need of advice from the skeptics when they decide on the steps to take in the real world to bring about their utopia.

Chapter Seven

The Hawks

Leopold Brezhnev's twenty-nine-year-old grandson describes the pleasure his grandfather took in keeping pigeons and doves—the symbols of peace—and hitting their cage to see them all fly around, terrified.

—Gail Sheehy, *The Man Who Changed the World*

For Saddam Hussein, the struggle in the Persian Gulf in 1991 was between "faith and infidelity; truth and falsehood; treason and commitment; justice and injustice, arrogance and aggression."[1]

This hawkish polarization of the world between good and evil is a recurrent theme in human history. Sam Kean has collected enemy images from cartoons, propaganda films, and posters from all over the world.[2] His collection shows that the same images occur again and again: the Stranger, the Aggressor, the Devil, the Barbarian, the Rapist, the Criminal, the Greedy Person, the Disease, the Skeleton, the Vicious Animal, and so on. The images on one side of a conflict are often the mirror image of those on the other side.

The doves view the hawks' splitting of the world between good and evil as a sign of psychological immaturity. The hawks, in return, view the doves as naive and foolhardy. Each group offers some valuable insights into the psychology of the other.

The Doves' Critique of the Hawks

The doves suspect that if the hawks did not have a real enemy they would create one. People often find it easiest to hate people who are similar to themselves. Groups such as Greek and Turkish Cypriotes, Catholic and

Protestant Irish, or Israelis and Palestinian Arabs are often indistinguishable to the outsider although they hate each other thoroughly. Perhaps we hate people who are similar to us because we unconsciously recognize our own unwanted traits in them. Nietzsche thought that "in a friend one should have one's best enemy. . . . But the worst enemy you can encounter will always be you, yourself."[3]

Sigmund Freud observed that "an intimate friend and a hated enemy have always been indispensible to my emotional life; I have always been able to create them anew."[4]

Why this need for an enemy? Psychoanalyst Vamik Volkan thinks that children whose self-esteem is fragile need the enemy as a repository for negative feelings about themselves.[5] If a boy is humiliated or hurt by a fall, for example, he may say that his doll fell down. Many young children develop a fear of strangers even though they have never been hurt in any way by one.[6] This generalized fear of strangers is similar to the generalized fear of outsiders or foreigners felt by many adults. The stranger is used as a target for hostile or angry feelings.

At the most primitive level, the stranger is viewed as not just an angry individual but as evil incarnate. In fables, films, and folktales for children whose thinking is on this level, evil is incarnated as an ugly witch or big bad wolf that threatens the good people or cute bunny rabbits. As we get older, this becomes too crude and simplistic. We recognize that the world is not divided into devils and angels, and we accept responsibility for more of our own feelings. During periods of stress, however, we may regress to the more primitive pattern.

There is an important distinction between viewing other people as *evil* and simply seeing them as *angry* or *hostile*. If we view another person as angry, we see him as a complex person whose feelings can change. We also realize that we can become angry at times, even though we may be unconscious of anger which we have repressed at a particular time.

Externalization of inner frustrations accounts for the "black and white" thinking of many hawks, particularly in ethnically divided communities such as Vamik Volkan's native Cyprus. These hawks are unwilling to analyze the thinking or behavior of their opponents in detail or to question their own motivations. They blame every problem suffered by their own group on the evils of the other group. This kind of thinking can tear a country apart, as we have seen in recent years in the Soviet Union, Yugoslavia, Romania, and other ethnically divided countries.

One sign that an enemy is serving a psychological purpose is the refusal to talk with him. Talking with an enemy implies recognition of him as a human being. It runs the risk that differences might be lessened or resolved, a possibility that cannot be accepted if the enemy is meeting important psychological needs. The hawk script may break down if the enemy is perceived as a person with complex thoughts and feelings. In international conflicts, getting the parties to the bargaining table is often more important than anything that takes place there since it means that the essential emotional issue has been overcome. Prenegotiation techniques designed to overcome these barriers are an essential part of diplomatic training.[7]

Refusal to talk is often justified in self-righteous language, which reveals the strong feelings of the true believer. When a French television station broadcast a program critical of some aspects of Cuban literary and artistic policies, for example, the Cuban leaders were especially outraged by the fact that Cuban exiles were interviewed. The Cuban media regularly denigrates these exiles as "worms" or "rats," a sign that they have been chosen as targets of externalization. When the French invited Cuban writers to take part in a televised debate with some of the exiles, the Cuban government insisted that:

> The Cuban Revolution and the writers and artists of the country are not prepared to become ensnared in a gross controversy promoted and encouraged by the United States, nor will they agree to debate under allegedly equal conditions set up beforehand with traitors or fakers, some of whom are not really artists. They will not do this for the same reason that the French might refuse to debate with those who are guilty of treason against France.[8]

The Cubans would have been willing to debate a panel of prominent French intellectuals. Their objection was not to defending their views but to appearing on a panel with Cubans whom they considered to be enemies.

When talking in 1983 with Palestine Liberation Organization Chairman Yassir Arafat, psychologist Herbert Kelman suggested that not much could be expected from the Begin government in Israel. Arafat interrupted, insisting that "you can't say that, they aren't all the same." He went on to talk about differences within Begin's cabinet. Kelman noted that:

> By contrast, on the same day a Palestinian scholar told me that there was no difference between Menachem Begin and Matti Peled (a leading Israeli advocate of a Palestinian state in the West Bank and Gaza and of negotiations with the PLO)—because "they are both Zionists."[9]

These delegitimizing beliefs, on both sides, are the psychological core of the Israeli-Palestinian conflict and present a formidable obstacle to the difficult task of resolving the real conflicts of interest.[10]

Although externalization is a primitive process developed in the first years of life, it continues to be used throughout the life span. Because of its simplicity, externalization is easily used by groups as a means of building a positive group image while deflecting bad feelings outside the group. The images that appear in war propaganda often are not much more subtle than the witches and wolves of the fairly tales.

In early childhood each boy and girl has his or her personal objects of externalization. One child's teddy bear means nothing to another. In later childhood, however, the peer group becomes much more important, and young people adopt group targets of externalization. They form into cliques and gangs for the purpose of elevating their own self-esteem at the expense of the others. This is the origin of the hawk script as a social phenomenon. At this stage of life, most people adopt the traditional enemies of their national or ethnic group as targets of externalization and link their positive feelings to patriotic symbols such as flags, emblems and anthems. Team sports, which provide a harmless and ritualized outlet for these needs, are particularly popular among young people.

The Hawks' Response

The hawks are not convinced by the doves' psychologizing. They insist that war is not a football game. Many enemies are not figments of our imagination. What about Munich or Pearl Harbor? On many occasions in history the hawks have been in closer touch with reality than the doves. Sometimes war is necessary for the national interest, and real men must not shirk their duty. Theodore Roosevelt feared that "if we seek merely swollen, slothful ease and ignoble peace, if we shrink from the hard contests where men must win at the hazard of their lives and at the risk of all they hold dear, then bolder and stronger peoples will pass us by, and will win for themselves the domination of the world."[11]

To hawks, the doves seem self-centered and childish. They live in a fantasy world where lions lie down with lambs and flower power is stronger than fire power. Hawks praise the manly virtues of courage, loyalty, discipline, and team spirit. Georg Frederich Hegel thought that militarism was needed to bind societies together and maintain their enthusiasm for their historical mission. He argued that "in order not to . . . break up the whole into fragments and let the common spirit evaporate, government has from time to time to shake them to the very centre by War."[12]

Many hawks link military values with masculinity. This is a view they share with the feminists, although the feminists don't see it as a virtue. Elizabeth Cady Stanton denounced the "male element" in civilization as "a destructive force, stern, selfish, aggrandizing, loving war, violence, conquest, acquisition, brooding discord, disorder, disease and death."[13] There is some evidence for the link between gender and hawk and dove scripts. Statistically, women are more dovish than men but by only a few percentage points.[14] Of course, there are certainly many exceptions. Most of the prominent militarists have been men, but so have many of the eminent pacifists.

Many veterans look back on their war experiences as the highlight of their lives. Journalist William Broyles believes that "most men who have been to war would have to admit, if they were honest, that somewhere inside themselves they loved it . . . as much as anything that has happened to them before or since." Of course, the veterans know better than anyone that war is "ugly, horrible, evil, and it is reasonable for men to hate all that."[15] But it is exciting. Soldiers know who their friends are, and they depend on each other for their survival. Individual inadequacies are submerged in the group. The danger makes other problems seem insignificant, and men feel freer to express their aggressive and sexual drives. Broyles claims that "most men who have been to war, and most women who have been around it, remember that never in their lives did they have so heightened a sexuality."[16]

War is also exciting for those on the sidelines, even for pacifists. When America went to war against Iraq, Americans of both genders and all political persuasions were glued to their television sets. The Cable News Network brought twenty-four-hour coverage into our living rooms and its ratings were pushed into the big leagues. The somnolent left was revived as it had not been since the Vietnam War. Protesting a war is much more exciting than struggling against homelessness, racism, or poverty, let alone trying to advocate for socialism in the America of the 1990s.

With all this going for war, it may seem remarkable that we have peace as often as we do. Of course, much of the excitement wears off as wars drag on and the casualties pile up. Public support peaks early in a war and declines steadily the longer it lasts.[17] The veterans who are nostalgic about their war experiences are usually realistic enough to hope that their sons do not have to repeat them.

In this chapter, we will discuss the psychology of war in the lives of three eminent hawks: Adolph Hitler, Winston Churchill, and Saddam Hussein. In the popular consciousness, Adolph Hitler is remembered as the "mad man" who caused World War II. Some historians think that he was mentally ill, others argue that he was just "the ordinary German writ large."[18] There are two questions here. First is the question of Hitler's psychology. Second is Hitler's influence on the course of history. The same issues are raised with Saddam Hussein and the Iraqi invasion of Kuwait in 1990.

Winston Churchill was maligned as a "warmonger" for most of his life and would have retired a failure had he not been called, at age sixty-five, to lead his nation in its "finest hour." He is the role model for hawks who see themselves as fighting to save their countries from dovish illusions. He is seldom if ever portrayed as a "mad man," although he did suffer from severe depression over much of his life.

Adolph Hitler

It is tricky to apply psychiatric diagnoses to any individual who holds power in a society. A person who believes he is the saviour of his race and seeks to kill or enslave everyone who does not fit into his schemes would usually be considered psychotic. But if he is able to win power and put his schemes into practice, who is to say that he is out of touch with reality? We could say that the society as a whole was mentally ill, but the analogy between a mentally ill individual and a defective society is not very close. And how do we expect sane individuals to behave when they find themselves in an "insane" society?

There are things about Adolph Hitler that suggest he did have mental health problems. He had suicidal impulses and apparently engaged in masochistic sexual practices. These mental health problems, however, may have been irrelevant to his political behavior. If he had had normal sexual preferences instead of apparently craving women who would squat over him and urinate on his face, would that have made him less obsessed with exterminating the Jews and conquering the world? There is no way to be certain of the answer if we consider Hitler as an isolated case. On a comparative basis, however, it is clear that deviant sexual practices are not necessarily found in hawkish or authoritarian political leaders. Hitler's closest ally, Benito Mussolini, for example, was quite conventional in his sexual practices. The same is true of the other hawks considered in this chapter, Winston Churchill and Saddam Hussein.

The attempts to psychoanalyze Hitler have been intriguing and suggestive, but not entirely persuasive.[19] The information about his childhood is quite limited.[20] Not surprisingly, some orthodox Freudians have suggested that he suffered from an unresolved Oedipal complex.[21] He was apparently beaten by his father, although probably not excessively by the standards of his society and his time. His father was away a lot, and Hitler sometimes slept in his mother's bed. There is one scene in *Mein Kampf* that can be interpreted as a recollection of having seen his parents having sex when he was three.[22] Unless one is an orthodox Freudian, however, there is no persuasive reason to believe that this "primal scene trauma" should have had lasting consequences. There were some doubts about his father's legitimacy, and he may have suspected that he had a Jewish grandfather. Robert Waite suggests that he may have grown his famous mustache to hide a "Jewish" nose.[23]

Hitler's father wanted him to follow in his footsteps and be a civil servant. Adolph wanted to be an artist, but he did not openly rebel against his father's expectations. He kept up with his school work while his "firm determination never to be a civil servant sufficed to give me complete inner peace."[24] His father died when he was fourteen, saving him from a confrontation over his career plans. Freudians would say that his Oedipal complex was never resolved. He was ill for a while, which interrupted his schooling, and then his mother allowed him to study art. His mother died from breast cancer when he was nineteen. She was treated for her long illness by a kindly family doctor who happened to be Jewish.

Adolph sent the doctor a hand painted postcard signed, "from your ever-grateful patient, Adolph Hitler." Robert Waite believes that Hitler "unconsciously perceived this Jew as 'he brutal attacker who had finally mutilated and killed his beloved mother."[25] We have to take Waite's word for this, however, since there is no direct evidence for it. At the time, Adolph was not consciously an anti-Semite. He says that his parents raised him to be a cosmopolitan and that he believed that Jews were Germans who differed only in religion. He believed that the "anti-semitic press was unworthy of the cultural tradition of a great nation."[26] Even after he became the world leader of anti-Semitism, he never accused the Jews of having killed his mother.

Hitler's first known expression of anti-Semitism came when he was rejected twice in his applications to the Academy of Art in Vienna. He found out that four of the seven judges who rejected his paintings were Jews, and he used them as scapegoats for his failure. He sent the director a letter promising that "for this the Jews will pay."[27] This is one of the ironies of history. If these Jewish art judges had had a crystal ball, they might have steered Hitler into an artistic career and prevented the Holocaust.

When support from his mother ran short, he was forced to seek work on a construction project. Here he came into contact with socialist activists. He sympathized with their desire to improve the conditions of the workers, but he was disturbed by their willingness to accept Slavic workers as equals. As the discussions became heated he:

> argued back, from day to day better informed than my antagonists concerning their own knowledge, until one day they made use of the weapon which most readily conquers reason: terror and violence. A few of the spokesmen on the opposing side forced me either to leave the building at once or be thrown off the scaffolding.[28]

At first, Hitler could not understand the dogmatism of the socialist workers. Perhaps the socialists could have recruited him to their cause if they had been a bit more sensitive to the needs of a troubled young middle-class man whose career aspirations had been blocked. They rejected him, however, and he soon found a satisfying explanation for his troubles in some anti-Semitic pamphlets that claimed the German workers had been led astray by a sinister Jewish conspiracy that was responsible for the disasters and defeats that had humiliated the German nation. This answer met his need for a scapegoat for his own failures. He now "understood the significance of the brutal demand that I read only Red papers, attend only Red meetings, read only Red books, etc. With plastic clarity I saw before my eyes the inevitable result of this doctrine of intolerance."

Hitler thought the German masses were like a woman who would "rather bow to a strong man than dominate a weak one." They longed to be dominated by a stern commander. Socialism, he was convinced, could only be conquered by another doctrine with "equal brutality of methods."[29] Hitler's anti-Semitic conspiracy theories were crude and fallacious, but his insight into the psychology of the German masses during the chaos of the Weimar Republic was terrifyingly acute. He adopted anti-Semitism as an ideological script because it met his emotional needs even though his personal relationships with Jewish people had always been good. During his period in Vienna, for example, he lived at times in a residence for homeless men financed by Jewish philanthropy. He used the Jews as a convenient and culturally acceptable target of externalization for his hostile feelings.

Nothing about Hitler's life to this point is particularly exceptional, which supports the idea that he was "the ordinary German writ large." Anti-Semitism was rampant in Austria at the time, and his beliefs were taken directly from readily available tracts. Vienna was full of frustrated young men with career problems. He may have had repressed homosexual tendencies, but if so that would hardly have been distinctive. The death of his parents may have placed him under exceptional stress, but it also freed him to spend his inheritance without parental restraints.

Of course, he had his personal idiosyncrasies. He was small and unimpressive physically and tended to be rigid and inflexible in his habits. He was compulsive about time. He was a bit of a dandy, spending much of his time dressing up and going to concerts. He admired monumental architecture and hoped to eventually get admitted to architecture school. He was also a strict vegetarian, not out of any principled concern for animals but because he found meat repugnant. When a girl he was dating ordered meat in a restaurant, he chided her for being a "corpse eater."

After Hitler took power his ideas about health and diet became part of the Nazi campaign to purify and perfect the German race. They promoted "organic medicine," whole-grain breads, breast-feeding, midwifery, and a diet with less meat and fats and more raw fruits and vegetables.[30] They also opposed pesticides and alcohol and smoking. No one could smoke in Hitler's presence.

World War I rescued Hitler from his empty Vienna existence. He had evaded Austrian military service before the war, possibly because he identified Austria with his father, an Austrian official. Austria was little and weak. But the German declaration of war offered him a noble cause and the chance to join a powerful force in a struggle against a clearly defined enemy. He fought bravely, won an Iron Cross, and was temporarily blinded by poison gas (or by a psychosomatic reaction to a gas attack).

Germany's defeat was a bitter pill for Hitler to swallow, and he readily fell in with circles that blamed it on traitors at home. He got a job as a military intelligence agent visiting political party meetings, and a tiny sect called the German Workers' Party appealed to him. Here he found his true calling as an orator, and he rapidly developed a personal following. When some members of the party attacked him for his "lust for personal power," he called a mass meeting of all the members (about 1,200). He delivered a mesmerizing speech, which brought the entire crowd to its feet cheering. From then on the National Socialist German Workers' Party was his personal fan club.

Hitler parlayed this tiny beginning into a mass movement with a ludicrous, quasi-suicidal gambit known as the "Beer Hall Putsch." He simply led a small group of supporters into a large meeting hall in Munich where a group of conservative leaders were reading dull speeches. He stood on a table, fired two shots into the ceiling with a pistol, and announced that the revolution had begun. He seemed an absurd, pathetic figure at the time. One observer noted that he was: "dressed in a morning coat, the most difficult of all garments to wear, let alone a badly cut morning coat, and let alone a man with as bad a figure as Hitler with his short legs and his long torso. When I saw him jump on the table in that ridiculous costume I thought, 'The poor little waiter!' "[31]

He was saved from absurdity by his electrifying oratory, which roused the crowd from its stupor. He ended with the dramatic promise that "tomorrow will find either a nationalist government in Germany or us dead."[32] Of course, neither happened. He was arrested and tried. At his trial he was allowed to give a four-hour oration, the judge finding himself unable or unwilling to interrupt him. A massive crowd rallied to his support, and he became a national figure. He served only nine months in jail, during which he dictated *Mein Kampf*. He worked late into the night

172 Turncoats and True Believers

and was served breakfast in bed by prisoners assigned to wait on him.

Mein Kampf was originally intended to be a denunciation of people within his own party who rejected his leadership. He was obsessed with the group dynamics of the National Socialist Party. The pettiness of his mentality at the time is reflected in its intended title: "A Four and One-half Year Struggle against Lies, Stupidity, and Cowardice: Settling Accounts with the Destroyers of the National Socialist Movement." As he dictated, however, he went beyond this topic to comment on his life, German history, the Jews, and assorted topics. Historians such as A. J. P. Taylor dismiss *Mein Kampf* as incoherent ramblings, others take it as a serious statement of his plans.

Both interpretations have an element of truth. In the beer halls of Munich, many unhappy men daydreamed about redeeming Germany's defeat or driving the Jews out of Germany. The unique thing about Hitler is that he actually did most of the things he promised to do. Hitler's incoherence and his quasi-suicidal willingness to risk everything on desperate gambles gave him the flexibility and foolhardiness to carry out plans that a more rational planner would have rejected as unfeasible.

Hitler's writing is incoherent in that there is often no logical connection between the paragraphs. He makes absurd allegations without evidence. He demonizes his enemies and magnifies his own importance. At the same time, his writing shows some psychological insight, although in a distorted and self-centered way. One of his observations was about the psychological appeal of ideological scripts. In *Mein Kampf* he recalled endless debates with Marxists where he "talked his tongue sore and his throat hoarse" thinking he could persuade them of "how ruinous their Marxist madness was."[33] The more he argued he found that they quoted platitudes and pretended not to understand what he was talking about. Whenever he tried to close an argument his "hand closed on a jelly-like slime which divided up and poured through your fingers, but in the next moment collected again." If they lost the argument in the eyes of the audience, they simply returned the next day and pretended it never happened.

Hitler was impressed by the persistence and cleverness of his opponents, which he attributed to their Jewish mentality. Like many anti-Semites, he envied the Jews in many ways and resented their accomplishments. He believed they were the "mightiest counterpart to the Aryans" and that they were "smart" in certain ways, as evidenced by their survival over the centuries. This smartness, however, was not their own but came from "visual instruction through foreigners," whatever that meant.[34] His thinking was thoroughly confused. "Sometimes I stood there thunderstruck. I didn't know what to be more amazed at: the agility of their tongues or their virtuosity at lying. Gradually I came to hate them."[35]

Instead of remaining stuck in his confusion, Hitler made a virtue of it. He decided that it was impossible to establish the truth. People needed answers, however, so he would give them answers. The purpose of propaganda "is not to make an objective study of the truth, in so far as it favors the enemy, and then to set it before the masses with academic fairness; its task is to serve our own right, always and unflinchingly." In discussing Germany's war guilt, for example, one should never admit that Germany shared any of the responsibility. One should "load every bit of the blame on the shoulders of the enemy, even if this had not really corresponded to the true facts."[36]

The fact that he was using the exact same techniques as his hated Marxist opponents did not bother Hitler in the least. His fundamental postulate was that his side was good and the other side evil. The important thing was to win. The way to win was to formulate an ideological script for his side and repeat it over and over, using the same rhetorical tactics as his opponents.

The script Hitler formulated was taken from the nationalist and anti-Semitic tracts circulating in Germany at the time. There was no need to be original, just persuasive. He articulated his views clearly in *Mein Kampf* and repeated them over and over in his speeches. One person who understood this script very well was Winston Churchill, who summarized it as follows:

> The main thesis of *Mein Kampf* is simple. Man is a fighting animal; therefore the nation, being a community of fighters, is a fighting unit. Any living organism which ceases to fight for its existence is doomed to extinction. A country or race which ceases to fight is equally doomed. The fighting capacity of a race depends on its purity. Hence the need for ridding it of foreign domination. The Jewish race, owing to its universality, is of necessity pacifist and internationalist. Pacifism is the deadliest sin; for it means the surrender of the race in the fight for existence. . . . Will and determination are the prime qualities. The individual who is born to command is more valuable than countless thousands of subordinate natures. Only brute force can ensure the survival of the race. . . .[37]

Churchill's understanding of Hitler's ideological script enabled him to predict Hitler's behavior better than the doves in the British government who assumed that Hitler would respond to their conciliatory gestures by lessening his hostility. Doves believe that fundamentally everyone is like them, that there is "that of God in every man" to which they can appeal. This may be true in the sense that every human being has the potential for expressing loving feelings. As a guide to predicting political behavior, however, relying on this potential can cause grave distortions of the personalities of other people. One well-meaning English pacifist, for example, argued that: "Hitler has a warm, even a soft heart, which makes him over sensitive to suggestions that he is not hard enough. . . . he does not want war, but he wants a peace in freedom, not a peace from impotence."[38]

Hawks, on the other hand, often believe that their enemies are fundamentally different from (and inferior to) them. Hitler saw his opponents as weak, lacking the backbone to stand up to him. This assumption served him well at first. He predicted that the pacifist leaders in power in England and France would not respond to actions such as the occupation of the Rhine, Austria, or Czechoslovakia. His success reoccupying the Rhine in 1936 was particularly impressive to the German High Command, since they knew that the French had the clear advantage in military strength, and they had assumed the French would repulse the German forces. In this case, Hitler succeeded because of his understanding of the dovish political psychology of the French and English leaders.

Ultimately, however, Hitler's belief in the weakness and inferiority of his enemies was his downfall. In 1941, he had defeated France and Poland. He dominated western Europe. The British empire was fighting alone. Instead of being satisfied with his conquests or focusing his resources on defeating Britain, he decided to launch a surprise attack on his Soviet ally. He confidently predicted that "we'll kick the front door in and the whole rotten structure will come crashing down,"[39] and he refused to invite his Japanese allies to join him in this attack, even though a combined German and Japanese attack would have virtually guaranteed success. The tendency to exaggerate one's own strength and resources and to minimize the resolve of one's enemies is the Achilles heel of the hawk.

Winston Churchill

Winston Churchill was an unhappy man who often thought of himself as a failure. A few years before his death he told his daughter, "I have achieved a great deal to achieve nothing in the end."[40] If he had retired at the usual age of sixty-five, history might have agreed with him. He was a prophet denied, foretelling disaster at a time when his countrymen sought escape through appeasement. After the Munich agreement, he told the House of Commons that "all is over. Silent, mournful, abandoned, broken. Czechoslovakia recedes into the darkness."[41] In response, he was almost recalled from office, winning a vote of his constituency organization by only a three to two margin.

But the tide of opinion was already turning. Many people felt guilt over Munich and distrusted Hitler. Churchill became the heroic prime minister who saved his nation in its "finest hour." He published many best-selling books, became an accomplished amateur painter, and had a devoted wife and children. Why then the depression in his old age? He had the misfortune to live to ninety-one, the last ten years spoiled by inactivity and despair.

Depression, which he called the "Black Dog," was a lifelong affliction for Winston. As a child he was neglected by his aristocratic parents. His father was too busy with affairs of state and his mother was a socialite who gave him little time or attention. His son observed that "the neglect and lack of interest in him shown by his parents were remarkable, even judged by the standards of late Victorian and Edwardian days."[42] He was left in the care of nannies and governesses, who fortunately supplied a substitute for the warmth that he longed for from his parents. At boarding school he was "an underling, bullied and beaten. He grew up full of apprehension and he spoke with a stutter."[43] His letters home included desperate pleas for attention, which went largely unanswered. He had suicidal thoughts, although there is no evidence that he ever attempted suicide. He did take reckless risks during World War I, which put others as well as himself in danger. Psychiatrist Anthony Starr concludes that "Winston Churchill was deprived by parental neglect of that inner source of self-esteem upon which most predominantly happy persons rely, and which serves to carry them through the inevitable disappointments and reverses of human existence."[44]

Churchill found relief from depression in intense activity and in a resolute determination to overcome adversity. He overcame his fearfulness at school by taking foolish risks to develop his courage. He was a natural writer, but speaking before an audience frightened him. Instead of hiding in his library or study, he set out to make himself a great orator. The struggle against adversity gave meaning to his life and distracted him from his inner doubts. He was absolutely determined to accomplish his goals, particularly if they went against his natural inclinations.

He preferred not to dwell on his feelings or to spend too much time thinking about things. He was extraverted and intuitive, making quick judgments based on minimal information. He had little patience for intensive study and usually asked his staff to present issues to him on half a sheet of paper. He dictated his many books quickly, based on research done by assistants. He was extremely ambitious and constantly sought the approval of others. He was not a good student in school, and he barely made it into the military college at Sandhurst after six months of coaching and three tries at the examination.

For Churchill, war was exciting. He was first under fire while visiting the Spanish forces in Cuba in 1895. As a lieutenant in India in 1896–97, he fought in frontier skirmishes. In 1898 he fought with British forces in India. His career as a journalist was built on his ability to communicate his sense of excitement in these battles. When he lost his first campaign for Parliament in 1899, he went to South Africa as a correspondent, was captured, escaped, and fought with the British forces. Returning as a war hero, he was elected to Parliament and began his long career in the English establishment. During World War I, he advocated and directed a disastrous naval attack on Turkey in the hopes of defeating Germany from behind its lines in France. He resigned from Parliament to command a battalion in France, and returned to the government in 1922.

Churchill's political positions did not follow a predictable left-right ideological pattern.[45] He changed from the Conservative to the Liberal Party and then back again. He supported social security insurance and labor legislation, but he ordered troops out to suppress strikers. He vigorously opposed British support for the Greeks in a conflict with Turkey in 1922, then just as vigorously supported rescuing the Greeks when the Turks were too demanding in victory. This switch caused him to be labeled a "warmonger," and he temporarily lost his seat in Parliament.

Although he is remembered as an enemy of appeasement because of his position in the 1930s, this was not a consistent position. At an imperial conference in 1921 he sought "an appeasement of the fearful hatreds and antagonisms which exist in Europe."[46] He generally supported a conciliatory position toward Germany after World War I and opposed the unrealistic and unfair reparations that were imposed. In 1950, when appeasement as a slogan had been completely discredited, he told Parliament that "Appeasement in itself may be good or bad according to the circumstances. Appeasement from weakness and fear is alike futile and fatal. Appeasement from strength is magnanimous and noble, and might be the surest and perhaps the only path to world peace."[47]

Although he was Adolph Hitler's most effective opponent and Hitler hated him thoroughly, he had remarkably little personal animosity for Hitler. In a book published in 1937, he expressed "admiration for the courage, the perseverance, and the vital force which enabled [Hitler] to challenge, defy, conciliate, or overcome, all the authorities or resistances which barred his path."[48] He thought Hitler was entitled to be a German patriot, but he was eloquent in denouncing his anti-Semitism and his persecution of leftists and trade unionists. Still, he hoped that Hitler might redeem himself, despite the horrible methods he had used to win power.

Churchill's real venom was reserved for communists. In the same book where he was hopeful about Hitler, he wrote a vicious character assassination of Leon Trotsky. Hitler was also an anti-communist, and many English anti-communists supported him as a bulwark against Bolshevism. In this situation, Churchill was well served by his lack of ideological dogmatism. He cared little for consistency except on a few fundamental values. In every situation, he based his position on a careful diagnosis of the situation existing at the time. Despite his anti-communism and his sympathy for Hitler's patriotism, he judged Hitler to be a terrible threat and acted accordingly.

When he took power in 1940 England's situation was very grim. The only choices were to fight or surrender. Churchill had a lifetime of experience with struggles to overcome adversity, and he took to this challenge with gusto. As Lord Moran observed:

> In the extraordinary circumstances of 1940 . . . we needed a very unreasonable man at the top. If Winston had been a reasonable man he would not have taken the line he did; if he had been a man of sound judgment he might have considered it his duty to act differently. A sage would have been out of his element in 1940; we got instead another Joan of Arc.[49]

Of course, any competent politician in the same circumstances would have recognized that the country needed an optimistic leader and done his best to offer upbeat speeches. Winston was a writer and historian, and he was well aware of the drama of the role he was called to play. What made him effective, however, was the fact that he truly felt excited by the challenge. In his speeches, he communicated his inner certainty that adversity could be overcome. His life history of struggling against depression gave him the psychological strength to rally the nation's spirits.

Saddam Hussein

When Iraqi forces moved into Kuwait on August 2, 1990, American President George Bush quickly labeled Iraqi President Saddam Hussein as another Hitler. Bush cast himself as Churchill as he resolutely opposed appeasement of a vicious aggressor. The opponents of Bush's actions saw it differently. They cast George Bush as Lyndon Johnson and themselves as the anti-war movement which brought him down.

As usual, these analogies tell us more about the ideological scripts of the speakers than they do about the realities of the situation at hand. Kuwait is not South Vietnam nor was the Iraqi conquest a civil war. Saddam Hussein was not a threat to the United States in the way that

Hitler was to Churchill's England. American interests in the Persian Gulf were much greater than in Indochina. George Bush is a cautious pragmatist, not an outspoken gadfly prone to dramatic rhetoric such as Churchill.

The analogy between Hussein and Hitler, as personalities, is more plausible. As with any comparison, there are similarities and differences, and analysts reach different conclusions depending on which they stress. Edward Mortimer argues that Hussein is a regional Hitler, although he lacks Hitler's power to threaten the major world powers.[50] Biographers Efraim Karsh and Inari Rautsi conclude that "Saddam Hussein is no Hitler," but they go on to observe that:

> to be sure, the two leaders share some striking similarities. Both Hitler and Hussein espoused a Darwinian worldview in which only the fittest survive, and where the end justifies all means. Both lacked the ability for personal empathy and possessed neither moral inhibitions nor respect for human life. As heads of ideological parties professing a mixture of nationalism and socialism, they transformed their countries into terrifying totalitarian systems, and embarked on large-scale aggression against external neighbors.[51]

In 1975 Saddam asked his Head of Intelligence to collect books on Nazi Germany, which he believed to be a useful model of "the successful organization of an entire society by the state for the achievement of national goals."[52] Hussein's book *Unser Kampf* (our struggle), published in Switzerland and Iraq in 1977, paralleled Hitler's *Mein Kampf* (my struggle) in important respects.[53] In his book Hussein advocated a war to expel the Jews from the Middle East. He argued that the Arabs under his leadership could split the Americans, Europeans, and Japanese over the oil issue. He dedicated himself to building Iraq's military strength to redress the outrages imposed on the Arabs by the European colonialists, just as Hitler rebuilt the German military to redress the humiliation of Versailles.

Given all these similarities, why do Karsh and Rautsi insist that Saddam is no Hitler? They argue that "Hitler was driven by a socio-political vision, however perverse, which he doggedly sought to achieve. Saddam, conversely, carries no ideological baggage whatsoever."[54] In terms of life scripts, they describe Hussein as a "ruthless pragmatist." He lacks Hitler's charisma as an orator or his willingness to sacrifice everything for the cause. Hussein's bottom line is his commitment to his own survival and personal power. Hitler transformed German politics to suit his ambitions and ideological visions. Hussein seized power within the established Iraqi political culture.

Brute force has been the only mechanism for political change in Iraq since the Hashemite dynasty was overthrown in a military coup in 1958. The bodies of leaders of the Hashemite regime were dragged through the streets by angry mobs. When the leader who succeeded the Hashemites, General Quassem, was overthrown five years later, his bloody corpse was shown on television so the public could verify that he was really dead. The Baath Party, which came to power for the first time when Quassem was overthrown, was itself overthrown only nine months later.

Purges, pogroms, and massacres have been recurrent in Iraqi history. In 1933 the Iraqi army slaughtered several hundred Assyrians who sought ethnic and religious recognition. The public held joyous celebrations throughout the country, going so far as to erect triumphant arches decorated with melons stained with bloody daggers to symbolize the heads of slain Assyrians. Almost the entire population of Baghdad turned out to welcome the returning heroes.[55] In 1969, in response to the Israeli six day war, the government rounded up seventeen members of an "Israeli ring of spies," thirteen of whom were Jewish. They were hanged in Liberation Square in Baghdad, amid patriotic speeches and much fanfare, and half a million people paraded, shouting "death to Israel" and "death to all traitors."[56]

Saddam Hussein rose to power in a political system dominated by conspiracies, coups d'état, and brutal repression. A western surgeon, who had been brought in to operate on Hussein, was asked whether he could do something about Hussein's headaches. He asked Saddam whether he was under any stress. Hussein responded with a lengthy recital of all the conspiracies that were out to get him. To the western surgeon, his account sounded like the ravings of a paranoid schizophrenic.[57] Given the realities of Iraqi politics, however, Hussein's account was probably realistic.

Saddam Hussein is not psychotic. If he were out of touch with reality, he could never have risen to power in the Iraqi system. Political psychiatrist Jerrold Post, however, classifies him as a "malignant narcissist," a disorder characterized by "messianic ambition for unlimited power, absence of conscience, unconstrained aggression, and a paranoid outlook."[58] He is a "judicious political calculator," who is highly dangerous because he functions effectively within an authoritarian system.

There is no mystery as to the origins of Hussein's worldview. From the age of ten he was raised by an uncle named Khairallah Tulfah. This uncle was the author of a pamphlet titled *Three Whom God Should Not Have Created: Persians, Jews and Flies.* The pamphlet calls the Persians "animals God created in the shape of humans" and the Jews "a mixture of the dirt and leftovers of diverse people." It offers no explanation for the flies. After he came to power, Hussein had the pamphlet reprinted.

Hussein's father either died or abandoned the family before Saddam was born or shortly thereafter. His mother remarried an abusive man who saw no need to send Saddam to school, but sent him out to work and steal. When Saddam saw that other boys his age were learning to read, he asked to be sent to school. His stepfather refused. He either ran away or was thrown out of the home and went to live with his uncle who sent him to school and introduced him to the world of Arab nationalist politics.

Like Hitler, Hussein suffered a tremendous blow to his self-esteem when he was rejected for admission to university. In Saddam's case, it wasn't art school but the Military Academy. As Karsh and Rautsi observe, "to Saddam, his failure to enter the Military Academy had been a personal disgrace, a humiliating reminder of his inadequacy vis-à-vis his uniformed colleagues and relatives, and an exclusion from one of the country's most powerful channels of social mobility."[59]

Rejected by the military, he found an alternative in the Arab Baath Socialist Party. The Baath Party was founded in 1940 with the aim of creating a unified Arab nation by defeating the imperialist powers that dominated the Arab world at the time. Hussein was fifteen when Nasser led a nationalist revolution in Egypt in 1952. Nasser became his hero, although he was also taught to identify with Nebuchadnezzar, who conquered Jerusalem in 586 B.C., and Saladin, who regained Jerusalem by defeating the crusaders in 1187. He joined the Baath Party when he was twenty and participated in a failed coup against the monarchy.

When General Qassem and fifty-eight army officers succeeded in overthrowing the Iraqi monarchy in 1958, Saddam Hussein was part of a group that tried to assassinate Qassem. The mission failed, although Hussein did kill a communist supporter of Qassem who happened also to be his brother-in-law. He had to escape to Syria. His escape on horseback and by swimming a river while nursing his wounds has become part of his mythic life story, although skeptics claim that he had a minor role in the assassination attempt and was helped out of the country by the party.[60] In any event, he went to study in Egypt and returned after the Baath overthrew Qassem in 1963.

Throughout his life, Saddam has played the role of tough guy. His favorite movie is *The Godfather*. He was arrested twice for violent acts while a student in Egypt. When he returned to Iraq in 1963, he got a job as a torturer working for the security services. One man who was tortured by Saddam personally says that "my arms and legs were bound by rope. I was hung on the rope to a hook on the ceiling and I was repeatedly beaten with rubber hoses filled with stones."[61] In another incident, he is reputed to have thrown a man into a vat of acid and stood watching while the body dissolved.[62] When the Baath was ousted by the army in 1963, all kinds of torture instruments, including electric pincers, pointed iron stakes, and a machine with bits of chopped off fingers, were found in the basement of the building where Saddam worked.

Saddam was not, however, a compulsive torturer. He let one man go, even though he was Jewish, because he had been a generous tipper when Saddam had served him as a newsboy. This is reminiscent of Hitler's befriending the Jewish doctor who had tried to save his mother from cancer. Both Hitler and Hussein tortured and killed without inhibition when it suited their ends, but there is no evidence that they were driven to it by sadistic compulsion.

Hussein is particularly adept at manipulating group dynamics within the Baath party. When the Baath first took power in 1963, they immediately split into the radical and reformist factions characteristic of ideological movements. President Bakr tried to reconcile the factions and maintain party unity, but he failed. First one group was expelled and then the other. This weakened the party to the point that it lost its grip on power.

Hussein, who was a young activist in the background during these struggles, spent a brief period in prison where he decided that the Party had lost because it was too factionalized and disorganized. In his view, it needed to be ruled by a single leader with iron discipline. When the Baath seized power again in 1968, he was not strong enough to become the dominant leader. Instead he took control of the security services where he set about building a network loyal to him and became President Bakr's second in command. As a pair, they benefited from Bakr's prestige and Hussein's ruthlessness. Potential rivals were lulled by Hussein's seeming reticence about assuming power. In group-dynamics jargon, we could say that the party was dominated by a pairing assumption, the unconscious belief that the Bakr-Hussein pair would lead to the birth of a new social order.

The Baath retook their power with the assistance of a military intelligence officer, Abdul Razzaz al Nayef. Within two weeks, Saddam had him arrested and exiled. He was gunned down in London in 1978. Since that time, Hussein has systematically eliminated anyone who was a threat to his power.[63] He went so far as to wire people's bedrooms and jail or kill them for making critical remarks to their wives in bed. One man was killed for not reporting antigovernment jokes told by others at a party he attended.

When Saddam finally persuaded President Bakr to retire in 1979, Saddam engineered the purge to end all purges. He held the families of a third of the members of the Revolutionary Command Council hostage while these men continued to hold office and sign papers. He finally killed them all together with around five hundred of the top leadership of his own Party. This mother of all purges was carried out during a mass meeting of some one thousand Party members. The meeting was videotaped and shown to Party cadres around the country. It begins with the confession of one man, Muhie Abdel-Hussein, who "admits" that he was part of a Syrian conspiracy to overthrow the regime. (Syria is ruled by a rival faction of the Baathist Party.)

After a long statement about traitors, Saddam began reading a list of names of people who should leave the hall. The remaining members of the audience, fearful of being included, cheered him on vigorously. One of his apologists reports that "the participants in the plot tried so hard to act naturally while the questioning of Muhie Abdel-Hussein was going on that they made themselves conspicuous."[64]

Saddam's methods were highly effective in consolidating his power. There had been coups d'état in Iraq since 1920, and Saddam made sure his would be the last. His action in purging the top leadership resembles that of Stalin in the Soviet Union, and his persecution of the Kurdish minority parallels Stalin's killings in the collectivization process. Hussein's repression, however, was not used in an attempt to fundamentally restructure the economy or social structure of the country. It was used to keep him and his sycophants in power and to build Iraq's military power so as to make it the dominant force in the region.

Like Hitler, Saddam's greatest vulnerability has been his decisions to go to war against enemies who turned out to be more powerful and more resolute than he anticipated. The reasons for his invasions of Iran in 1980 and Kuwait in 1990 are controversial. There is a long history of enmity between Iran and Iraq, and the Khomeini regime was supporting Kurdish and Shiite discontent within Iraq. Yet, Iraq was not forced to go to war over these issues. After reviewing the "objective" causes in depth, Samir al-Khalil is led to the conclusion that "the whole question of how this war began resolves itself into what was passing through Saddam Hussein's mind."[65]

What was passing through Hussein's mind was a combination of repressed fear, messianic ambition, and narcissistic self-aggrandizement. Karsh and Rautsi emphasize the fear, arguing that Hussein was led to war with Iran by "his insecurity, a gnawing fearfulness bred by the precariousness he perceived in his own regime and by Iraq's glaring vulnerability vis-à-vis Iran."[66] His insecurity was revealed in his reluctance to allow the Iraqi military to use tactics that would lead to heavy casualties and in his attempt to sue for peace a few weeks after the war began. He never anticipated the tenacity of the Iranian resistance, and he failed to take advantage of his initial military advantages. His narcissistic omnipotence and insecurity led him to direct the war personally from Baghdad instead of allowing his military officers to use their professional judgment. Only when the war was almost lost did he relent and allow the officers to act on their own initiative.

Hussein's admirers deny the fear and stress the messianic ambition. Fuad Matar states that Saddam went to war with Iran for a series of noble and rational objectives. In his view, Iraq stood to gain the restoration of territory taken by Iran, ending Iran's ambitions to topple the regime and export revolution. The war would make the great powers sit up and take notice of Iraq. Iraq would find out once and for all who its friends were and who its enemies were, test its army on the battlefield, and help it prepare for the holy battle with Israel.[67] Matar's book was written with Hussein's collaboration and probably reflects his thinking. His fear is deeper in his mind and accounts for his failure to pursue these goals as effectively as he might have.

The invasion of Kuwait came after an inconclusive end to the tremendously costly war with Iran. Iraq was deeply in debt, unable to continue its development policies, which had been the carrot accompanying his stick. The Kuwaitis were demanding repayment of their war loans and allegedly selling oil in excess of their OPEC quota. Some of this oil may even have been siphoned off from Iraqi oil fields. Historically, the Iraqi government had laid claims to Kuwait, although it had also acknowledged Kuwait's legitimacy and accepted its membership into the Arab League.

In selling oil in excess of their quota, the Kuwaitis were doing nothing that Iraq had not done before. In the 1970s, the Iraqi government made publication of their nation's oil sales to the West a capital offense.[68] Nevertheless, Hussein seemed genuinely outraged by the Kuwaitis' perfidy in pursuing their own interest. He saw Kuwait's oil wealth as the solution to his debt problems.

Before invading Kuwait, however, Hussein went out of his way to determine that the West would let him get away with it. He sought assurances from Washington that the Israelis were not going to attack him. In an infamous interview with American ambassador April Glaspie, he sought American understanding for his needs. In a classic dovish response, Glaspie sought to reassure him of America's good will and neutrality. She assured him that America had no position on border disputes such as his with Kuwait, receiving only a promise that Iraq would not attack Kuwait before talking with Kuwaiti leaders.[69]

Much has been made of this interview, some even suggesting that the Bush administration intentionally lured Iraq into attacking Kuwait. Ambassador Glaspie's supporters insist that she expressed opposition to the use of force to resolve the dispute. The tone of her language in the transcript, however, supports Karsh and Rautsi's conclusion that:

her servility in front of the Iraqi leader and the conciliatory language she used were construed by Saddam as an American "green light" for a movement against Kuwait. After all, did he not tell the Ambassador that Iraq "will not accept death," and did not Glaspie express her empathy with Iraq's economic plight, as well as her government's neutrality toward the Iraqi-Kuwaiti conflict?[70]

Glaspie's attempt to placate Hussein and appease his legitimate concerns was a typical dovish response to aggressiveness from a hawk. She appeared to assume that his fear and anger could be appeased by an honest attempt at empathy and reconciliation. As a hawk, Hussein took this as a sign of weakness. He was undoubtedly shocked by the strength of the American response and even more so by the united opposition of the major Arab powers.

Conclusions

Each of the hawks we have examined in this chapter personified an important strand in his nation's history. Adolph Hitler was in many ways an "ordinary German writ large." His sexual and dietary idiosyncrasies were unimportant. What was important was his nationalism, militarism, and anti-Semitism, and these were rooted in German culture and history. Winston Churchill was marginalized while his nation sought to appease Hitler and avoid war, then he became the right man at the right time. His hawk script, which had been vilified as warmongering, came to exemplify the toughness and determination of the Briton under attack. Saddam Hussein was simply the most clever and ruthless of a series of Iraqi leaders socialized in the same political culture.

Nevertheless, without these individuals history would have been different. The German military command opposed the occupation of the Ruhr on good rational grounds. Only Hitler's grandiosity, lack of inhibition, and willingness to gamble everything on risky operations enabled him to prevail in so many improbable initiatives. The same traits led him to his ultimate downfall. His generals were dumfounded when he called off their attack on the British troops retreating at Dunkirk. Even today his reasons for doing so are so difficult to fathom that Waite's argument, which states that Hitler had an unconscious will to fail, is the most plausible explanation.[71] The decision to exterminate the Jews made no sense in a nation desperately short of manpower and can only be explained by his psychological determination to throw caution to the wind. The decision to march on Moscow before finishing the attack on England was similarly grandiose.

In a democratic society, Churchill had less power to indulge his idiosyncracies. Nevertheless, it can be argued that without his personal leadership England would have made peace with Hitler after Dunkirk.[72] He reached the hearts and minds of the British people, enabling them to express determination and resolution, which were inherent in their character. Without his leadership, another side of their character might have predominated.

Less time has passed for historical evaluation of Saddam Hussein's regime. He holds absolute power in Iraq, so there is no question that he made the decisions to go to war against Iran in 1980 and against Kuwait in 1990. Another leader with the same political views but without his megalomania would probably have acted more cautiously. Syrian President Safez Assad, also a Baathist, is an example.

In each of our cases, leaders with exceptionally strong commitment to their ideological scripts served to mobilize and accentuate tendencies that were inherent in the mass psychology of their countrymen. Their personalities help us to understand some of the character traits that resonate with a hawk script. Both Hitler and Hussein had an exceptionally strong tendency to project hostile and aggressive feelings onto enemy groups. They mobilized these tendencies among their followers. While they were not psychotic in the sense of being grossly out of touch with reality or governed by uncontrollable impulses, their personalities often led them to overestimate their own power and to minimize the strength and resolution of their enemies. It is for this reason that aggressive hawks have, at least in the period since 1914, lost more conflicts than they have won.[73] They lack the capability for realistic empathy with their victims or their potential allies.

Winston Churchill's case demonstrates that a hawk script need not be adopted for these psychological reasons, but may be a realistic response to an objectively threatening situation. Leading Britain during the Second World War was undoubtedly good for his mental health, but he did nothing to provoke war for that reason. Indeed, war might have been avoided and certainly would have been less costly if the country had followed his hawkish inclinations a few years earlier.

The American war with Iraq, also, might have been avoided if the United States had firmly expressed its determination to protect Kuwait *before* the invasion. The best intentions of the doves sometimes fail because they find it difficult to accept how different the motivations of the hawks really are.

Chapter Eight

The Doves

The sweetness of the dove, some laugh. There are no crueler ani-
mals. I've had doves here that pecked to death a little hen-pigeon
they didn't like. They pecked her eyes out! Some symbol for the
peace movement.

—Pablo Picasso, 1949

French Communist Party leader Louis Aragon looked through a collection of Pablo Picasso's work for something that could be used on a poster for a World Peace Conference in 1949. He came across a delicate white pigeon on a black background, a lithograph that Picasso had made with no political symbolism in mind. Aragon remembered that a dove is really a small pigeon and that the dove was a traditional symbol of peace. Picasso thought, "Poor guy! He doesn't know the first thing about pigeons."[1] But Aragon understood political symbolism. The lithograph was renamed *The Dove of Peace,* and tens of thousands were distributed. On release from prison, Chilean Communist poet Pablo Neruda happily observed that "Picasso's Dove is flying around the world, and none can stop it in its flight."[2]

Before the second world war, "hawks and doves" was not used as a metaphor for pacifist and militarist ideological scripts. For rural people, familiar with both species of birds, "hawks and doves" would be a metaphor for "hunter and prey." As Alexander Pope wrote in the early eighteenth century:

> Say, will the falcon, swooping from above
> Smit with her varying plumage, spare the dove?[3]

The "hawks and doves" metaphor was first used in 1962 to describe a split between orthodox and revisionist factions in President Kennedy's National Security Council during the Cuban missile crisis.[4] The hawks favored air strikes; the doves wanted to negotiate. Both sides were sober members of the national security establishment who differed on tactics but shared strategic goals and assumptions. In the nuclear age, everyone recognized that the triumph of the hawks might have led to Armageddon.

More recently, "hawks and doves" has been used to symbolize the fundamental philosophical gulf between pacifists and militarists. During the Vietnam War era, these views became crystallized into rigid ideological scripts and reasoned discussion between the two groups became almost impossible. In observing a discussion between a Yale Faculty Arms Control Seminar and General Russell Dougherty in 1982, Jeffrey Klugman observed:

> The faculty group, mostly dovish, became increasingly agitated as its questions and the General's answers flew by one another. I am a psychiatrist, and I felt very much like I was in my office, except that I felt like one of the patients. How can well-informed and well-intentioned people disagree so vehemently, and at such length, without coming to a mutual understanding? The worldviews of hawks and doves are so different that reasoned discussion does not occur.[5]

Hawk and dove scripts appeal to people who use different strategies for dealing with aggressive feelings. In the last chapter, we argued that hawks project their hostile feelings onto suitable targets of externalization, while glorifying their own group. Doves do just the opposite. They project their compassionate and vulnerable feelings onto others who may not actually have them. At the same time, they often direct their hostile feelings against their own nation's leadership.

British psychoanalyst R. E. Money-Kyrle finds that hawks typically deny that they feel guilty about their aggressive impulses while doves deny that these impulses exist:

> Those who exalt the inevitability of conflict [hawks] deny their sense of guilt and develop a defensive pride in their freedom from all scruples. Those who cling to a vision of a world without strife [doves], or even competition, deny at least some part of the predatory aggression that threatens to disturb their relations with their fellows.[6]

The hawks become tough-minded "realists" who believe in a dog-eat-dog world where only the tough survive. Living in such a world, they can be proud of their own aggressiveness. The doves become tender-minded "idealists" who believe that love can triumph over hate, the lion can lie down with the lamb, and everyone can beat their swords into plowshares. Certainly this is an appealing vision, and the doves are often disappointed in the failure of their own government to live up to these principles. But they have faith that a way can be found to reach out nonviolently to people in other nations.

Externalizing either aggressive or loving feelings can cause a person to be out of touch with reality. Refusal to acknowledge a real enemy is just as irrational as seeing one who is not there. When the German army came to round up the Jews in a small Russian town in the fall of 1941, one man argued, "Listen, they will kill us, just as they killed others. There are only a few of them. There are a lot of men among us. We can overpower them and kill them first. Even if they kill many of us, they won't be able to kill us all."[7]

This plan depended on their accepting the likelihood that they were going to be killed instead of believing the Nazi's promises that they were being taken to work. They had heard of Nazi massacres in many other villages, but most of them denied this information. Perhaps they also knew of cases where Jews had been taken to labor camps. One elder hissed angrily, "you are an adventurist, you want to kill us all." Another murmured, "there are women and children among us, he wants us all to die." Finally, three young men despaired of rallying the group to revolt and darted into the woods. Two of them survived. That night all the remaining Jews of the village, close to three hundred men, women, and children, were burned alive in a church. One of the men who escaped felt so guilty for abandoning his community that he was able to tell his son this story only when his life was approaching an end.

In addition to reminding us that not all enemies are figments of hawkish imaginations, this vignette illustrates how anger can be directed away from a true but frightening enemy onto a more vulnerable scapegoat who may actually be an ally. This accounts for many of the angry splits and schisms within ideological groups, which put more energy into ritualized squabbling with each other than into the struggle with the more powerful enemy outside the group.

In many ways, the hawks and doves are opposite sides of the same coin, each acutely aware of one aspect of international relations while minimizing or denying the other. The hawks focus on boundaries and on differences between groups, while the doves focus on connections and similarities.[8] There is no simple rule of thumb for deciding which is closer to reality in a given situation.

In this chapter, we will examine the personal psychology of such eminent doves as Mahatma Gandhi, Vera Brittain, A. J. Muste, Albert Einstein, and Kenneth Boulding. We will also look at the mass psychology of the antiwar movement, focusing specifically on the movements against American involvement in Vietnam and in Iraq.

Mohandas Gandhi

Mohandas Gandhi was a shy and fearful boy, preoccupied with fears and inhibitions, and strongly attached to a saintly mother whose spiritual preoccupations distracted her from his needs.[9] She left him in the care of servants while she began each day with two hours of prayer and spent much of the rest of the day preoccupied with religious observance. Gandhi lived in reverence of his father, who was forty-seven when he fathered Mohandas by his fourth wife. His father was a distinguished provincial prime minister who was constantly surrounded by a bevy of officials and secretaries.

In keeping with Indian culture, Gandhi's father arranged for him to be married at thirteen, but he still lived in his parents' home and devoted himself to his parents after his wedding. He particularly idealized his father. When his father was injured in an accident, Mohandas became his nurse, helping him with his personal hygiene and massaging his legs each evening. The most dramatic incident of his life was his father's death when Mohandas was sixteen. On that evening, his uncle relieved him from the chore of massaging his father's legs, and he retired to his wife's bed. In only five minutes, he was called back to find that his father had died. He felt enormous and lasting guilt over his absence at his father's death:

> The shame of my carnal desire even at the critical hour of my father's death . . . is a blot I have never been able to efface or forget, and I have always thought that, although my devotion to my parents knew no bounds and I would have given up anything for it, yet it was weighed and found unpardonably wanting because my mind was at the same moment in the grip of lust. . . . I may mention that the poor mite that was born to my wife scarcely breathed for more than three or four days. Nothing else could be expected. . . .[10]

Wolfenstein argues that "one aspect of the Oedipal fantasy is that the son desires the elimination of the father and in adolescence feels that his developing sexual potency will be the instrument of that desire."[11] If this is so, then adolescent sexual activity has an element of hostility toward the father. It certainly seemed so to Gandhi, who also blamed his having had sex with his wife late in the pregnancy for the death of his first child. For the rest of his life he seemed to be atoning for his lust and self-indulgence with periods of fasting and sexual abstinence, as well as by devoting himself to the care of the needy.

Gandhi was an extraordinarily timid youth, fearful of ghosts in the dark and of other children during the day. He was afraid to go to school, and in high school made friends with a Muslim boy who served as his mentor and bodyguard. Under the influence of this boy, he experimented with meat eating, a major offense to his mother's religion. His stomach felt as if he had swallowed a live goat. He also let his friend talk him into visiting a brothel, as a young married man of fifteen, although he backed out and left in humiliation.

The death of his father left Gandhi without an idealized figure to model himself on or to rebel against. Throughout his life, he believed in the Hindu theory that true knowledge could only come through a Guru, an idealized teacher. He experimented with many relationships in hope of finding a Guru he could believe in, but at the age of fifty-six he wrote that "the throne has remained vacant and my search still continues."[12]

At the age of eighteen, he sought independence by traveling to London to study to be a barrister, a credential which would qualify him to follow in his father's footsteps. This meant leaving behind his mother, his wife, and an infant child. To reassure his mother, he promised to be true to her religious principles, including vegetarianism. Life in London was lonely at first, but he found companionship and support by becoming involved with vegetarianism as a cause. He published articles in vegetarian journals. He also dedicated himself to his studies as he never had before, even taking on unnecessary challenges such as reading Roman law in Latin.

On his return to India, he learned that his mother had died two weeks before his arrival. Once again, he had failed in his obligation to be present at a parent's death. He tried to practice law, but failed because he was too shy to speak in court. He worked as a clerk for two years, then emigrated to South Africa in the hope that a fresh start would enable him to overcome his emotional distress.

On arrival in South Africa he quickly suffered from racial discrimination, being forced out of his first-class seat on a train. Rather than suffer indignation in silence, he resolved to campaign for human rights. He studied the problems of Indians in South Africa and called a public meeting where he found the strength to speak brilliantly. Identification with a noble cause gave him strength that he could not find as a simple lawyer defending mundane cases. In consultation with a Quaker teacher, he developed a belief in nonviolent struggle, which made a virtue of his tendency to inhibit aggressive feelings. This ideological script gave him a dramatic role to play in the theater of history.

At this point, Gandhi felt strong enough to put aside European dress and manners and return to India and his Hindu roots. He developed the concept of *satyagraha,* combining the Hindi words for love (satya) and firmness (agraha). This doctrine empowered him to be assertive without compromising his humility or giving in to his aggressive drives. It made a virtue of suffering as long as it was combined with forceful action instead of submissiveness. It was a doctrine that resonated strongly with Hindu culture, which valued the ability to detach one's feelings from the physical world in the quest for spiritual goals.[13] By developing a doctrine consistent with his own personality, Gandhi became his own Guru and developed the inner strength to be a Guru to millions of people in India and around the world.

Gandhi's greatest innovation was to show how suffering and non-violence could be used as a tool for assertively demanding social change. He frequently fasted in order to put psychological pressure on the British and on his own followers when they failed to follow nonviolent principles. In this, he was adopting a technique used by his mother within the family, when she fasted as a means of pressuring family members to behave correctly. Gandhi's strong emotional commitment to this philosophy enabled him to become the charismatic leader of a mass movement for Indian independence. When British troops used violence against nonviolent resistors in India, their moral legitimacy as a force for civilization was undermined even in England. After a long struggle, Indian independence was achieved.

Vera Brittain and Albert Einstein

British feminist and pacifist Vera Brittain converted to radical pacifism in middle age.[14] She had experienced the horrors of war in her twenties as a nurse during World War I and became a leading proponent of collective security through the League of Nations. She was not, however, an absolute pacifist since she favored the use of force when necessary to enforce the rulings of the international body. In 1936, at the age of forty-seven, she converted to an absolute pacifist position, which she maintained throughout World War II.

In part, Brittain's change reflected the trends of the time. Pacifism was strong in Great Britain in the thirties, and she was part of the Peace Pledge Movement, which asked young men to renounce war unconditionally. Her conversion also reflected changes in her own emotional needs. It came at a time when she was looking for something to help her to "sublimate grief" caused by her father's suicide and the death of several close friends. Her efforts to become absorbed in her work or to distract herself through travel failed, so she sought to become immersed in "a political or social campaign."[15]

While she was in this frame of mind, Brittain was asked to speak at a peace rally, following the charismatic Methodist preacher Richard Sheppard. Sheppard's speech was inspiring, and Brittain observed that he could "play on the emotions of a crowd with a master's skill."[16] When she rose to speak, "I was panic-stricken. This Christian pacifist platform was like no other on which I had stood; here my customary little speech in support of collective security would strike a discordant note. Its basis was political, but the message of my fellow-speakers sprang from the love of God."

Afterwards Sheppard wrote inviting her to join the Peace Pledge Movement. In her autobiography, Brittain was quite insightful about the psychological processes at work. She thought that Sheppard's "long experience of the peace movement must have shown him that it contained many disciples of a type similar to mine. They suffered from the deficient confidence which is the root of all aggression, and in order to discipline their unruly selves required the inexorable standards of a spiritual creed."[17]

Max Weber thought that youth were likely to adopt an "ethic of ultimate ends" while mature adults were more likely to adopt an "ethic of responsibility."[18] Weber noted, however, that it was not age but "the trained relentlessness in viewing the realities of life, and the ability to face such realities and to measure up to them inwardly" that was decisive. He also recognized that there are times when even the mature person, who is acutely aware of realities and weighs them carefully, reaches a point where rationality fails and a decision must be made that "Here I stand; I can do no other."[19]

At such a point, pragmatism is no longer fulfilling, and the believer searches for a script with more dramatic idealizations. Vera Brittain had reached such a point in her thinking. She adopted absolute pacifism, recognizing that "it was a simple idea which derived its validity not from political calculation but from the prophetic challenge of an inner compulsion; it was the belief, for which Christ died, in the ultimate transcendence of love over power."[20]

Her husband tried to dissuade her with the practical argument that since the majority would not adopt pacifism it would not succeed in preventing the world war that was clearly threatening. Brittain, however, felt that she had to remain loyal to her "long-term policy" of pacifism even if it conflicted with short-term goals, drawing an analogy to Christ and his apostles who could hardly have expected to convert the Roman empire in their lifetimes. When asked to support the Spanish republic, she announced that "I detest fascism and all that it stands for, but I do not believe we shall destroy it by fighting it."[21]

Faced with the same historical situation, the forty-year-old Albert Einstein moved in precisely the opposite direction. In the twenties he had adopted a strong pacifist stand, based not on religious principle but on an emotional revulsion for war. When asked in 1929 what he would do if a war broke out, he stated that "I would unconditionally refuse all war service, direct or indirect, and would seek to persuade my friends to adopt the same position, regardless of how I might feel about the causes of any particular war."[22]

He felt very strongly about this issue and worried that others would lose their faith under pressure. In 1931 he told a group of American pacifists, "I fear very much that of those who, in a formal sense only, join in the renunciation of war in time of peace, many will become weak-kneed when the threat of war becomes a reality."[23]

Einstein was a Jew who was forced out of Germany by the Nazis. His close personal experience with the horrors of the Nazi regime may account for his change of views, which occurred "with the greatest reluctance and after a difficult inner struggle."[24] As a prominent advocate of the principle of conscientious objection to military service, he was asked to write in support of a Belgian who had been jailed for refusing induction. He urged the King of Belgium, whom he knew personally, to be lenient with such men and to offer them alternative service. Nevertheless, in 1933 he stated publicly that "Were I a Belgian, I should not, in the present circumstances, refuse military service; rather, I should enter such service cheerfully in the belief that I would thereby be helping to save European civilization."[25]

Einstein's change of position was not uncommon. Most of the young men who signed the Peace Pledge, or who adhered to the Oxford Union Resolution of 1933 "that this House will in no circumstances fight for King and country,"[26] changed their minds with the outbreak of war in 1939, as did Bertrand Russell. They thought that the responsible thing was to destroy fascism by fighting it. Almost 100,000 members of the Peace Pledge Union, however, joined Vera Brittain in refusing to compromise their principles even in response to the Nazi threat. Many of them were young men who served as conscientious objectors during the war.

Like many apostates, Einstein found it difficult to admit abandoning his beliefs. He used rhetorical argumentation as a defense, insisting that "I am not surrendering the principle for which I have stood heretofore."[27] He continued to refer to himself as a pacifist. He simply redefined the term to refer to someone who sought to abolish war through international institutions, not someone who would refuse to participate in a just war of defense against a nation such as Nazi Germany.[28]

Einstein's extensive writings on peace, consisting entirely of speeches and letters collected by others, are an excellent argument for intellectual specialization. He was deeply concerned about war and responded to many people who wanted his endorsement for a cause or who hoped that his scientific genius might find a solution to an intractable social problem.

Alas, he had no new ideas on the topic of war and wrote to Sigmund Freud for help, explaining that "the normal objective of my thought affords no insight into the dark places of human will and feeling."[29] In 1929, he frankly stated that "my pacifism is an instinctive feeling, a feeling that possesses me; the thought of murdering another human being is abhorrent to me. My attitude is not the result of an intellectual theory but is caused by a deep antipathy to every kind of cruelty and hatred."[30]

A. J. Muste

In his long and distinguished career as a social activist Abraham Johannes Muste may have set a record for the most ideological reversals.[31] He changed from to Christian believer in just wars, to a Christian pacifist opponent of American participation in World War I, to a leader of a revolutionary Marxist-Leninist-Trotskyist party, then back to Christian pacifism in time to oppose World War II. He ended his career as a New Left sympathizer of a revolutionary victory in Vietnam. In his memoirs he observed:

> In a certain sense, there is no "explanation" for the fact that one who had been so deeply convinced a pacifist as I was and who, furthermore, had seen some remarkable instances of nonviolence in American labor struggles like the Lawrence strike, ceased to hold that position. You simply have to take it as one of the "facts of life." No doubt analysts could come up with interesting and perhaps startling deductions.[32]

Despite his curiosity and intellectual sophistication, Muste never sought psychoanalytic or other psychological insight into his feelings. The son of Dutch immigrants who were deeply rooted in religious thinking, he interpreted the flashes of insight, which followed his periods of agonizing doubt, as revelations from God. Once he received a revelation, his doubts were gone and he felt called to spread the good word with what some thought "a self-righteousness which verged on fanaticism."[33]

Muste's confidence in the righteousness of his ideas, however, was not based in personal conceit or self-aggrandizement. He was a charming, compassionate man who made friends wherever he went and who had a remarkable ability to keep his friends even after he broke with them ideologically. When he and his wife were financially and emotionally exhausted after years of Leninist factional infighting, his Christian and Marxist friends took up a collection to send them to Europe on vacation. When he defected from Trotskyism, he was the only turncoat the Trotskyists didn't hate. They recognized that he was returning to his roots and that he was still deeply concerned with human betterment.

Muste's family emigrated from Zierikzee, Holland, to Grand Rapids, Michigan, in 1891 when he was six. Affiliating with a church was a first priority, and their relatives steered them to the Dutch Christian Reformed Church. When this Church refused to accept their transfer of membership from Holland, however, they switched to a more liberal church. They also pulled their children out of the school run by the Reformed Church when they found it sterile, dogmatic, and too expensive. Abraham enjoyed the public school, was good at sports, and seems to have fit in well with the other boys. One day he tripped a schoolyard bully in the classroom, getting him in trouble with the teacher. After school, the bully approached him menacingly with the accusation, "you tripped me." Muste's natural charm saved him; he simply looked the boy calmly in the eye and confessed quietly, "yes, I did."[34]

Muste's parents wanted him to be a preacher, and he accepted the idea willingly since he enjoyed church and religious thought. When he went off to New Brunswick Theological Seminary, however, he found the classes tedious and boring. The only advantage was the opportunity to get to New York for more interesting classes at New York University and Columbia. He did well at New Brunswick, however, and was chosen as speaker at the 1909 graduation. His speech denounced the low intellectual standards at the seminary. They graduated him anyway, and he was accredited as a minister by the governing body of the Fourth Reformed Church in Grand Rapids. He got a well-paying job as minister to a congregation in Washington Heights, New York City, which gave him the wherewithal to finally marry his longtime sweetheart, Anna Huizenga of Rock Valley, Iowa. He had met her while teaching at the Northwest Classical Academy, a Dutch Reformed Church school in Orange City, Iowa.

Everything was going beautifully for A. J., except for his nagging doubts about theological matters. He and his parents had always stressed the substance over the form of religious belief. The essence of Christianity was to be Christlike, not just to go through the forms while leading a comfortable life. He took classes at Union Theological Seminary, which reinforced his inclination toward liberal religious ideas. He was also inspired by the socialist movement and voted socialist in 1912.

Finally, he told the Fort Washington congregation that he no longer believed in the Virgin birth or the literal inspiration of Scripture. They responded by raising his salary and urging him to stay, which he did for two more years. They were years of great doubt and inner turmoil for A. J. and his wife, who loved him dearly but preferred to continue a comfortable life as the wife of a successful minister. Finally, however, he forced the issue by responding to a query from the governing body of the denomination with a statement that he did not believe in the inerrancy of Scripture. They reluctantly felt they had to let him go, and he moved to a more liberal Congregational church in Massachusetts.

Having made the break with his past, his sense of inner doubt and turmoil was resolved when he received a vision of a white light, which flooded the world with an image of "God being truly present and all-sufficient." This vision gave him "perfect religious certainty, a peace of mind, after a long period of doubt."[35] He and Anna rejoiced at the certainty that he had a new and greater Gospel to preach.

In Massachusetts, he began reading the Christian mystics and the Quaker scholar Rufus Jones. He was inspired by the pacifist commitments of these writers and felt that pacifism was an essential element that had been left out in his Christian education. When the United States entered World War I, he was not sure how to respond. Doubts and inner turmoil returned, and in his pre-Easter sermon he startled the congregation with the declaration that "I find myself at the point where I must feel myself doing something that costs and hurts, something for humanity, and God, or go stark mad."[36]

Finally he resolved his doubts and announced his opposition to the war. This was not well received by everyone in the congregation, especially those whose sons had been killed in the fighting. The church offered him a six-month leave of absence to work on war relief, but he felt this would be compromising with the war effort. At this point, Muste received his second mystical experience of God, which reassured him that he was doing the right thing. He offered his resignation, arguing that Jesus was a pacifist and that all Christians should be also. The church reluctantly accepted his resignation, giving him a three-month paid sabbatical.

The Mustes left Massachusetts and settled in Providence, Rhode Island, where A. J. was offered a post as an educator with the Quaker Meeting. Anna followed along, loyal to him despite her unhappiness at abandoning another comfortable position. A. J. became more involved with radical antiwar and socialist thought, and he made plans for a new preaching order that would travel the world in special uniforms calling upon rich and poor to "rebuke the old order and . . . enter upon a new."[37] When the textile workers struck in Lawrence, Massachusetts, in 1919, he wrote the Providence Quakers that "the Textile Strike has me in its grip far more securely than I have supposed possible," and he left for the opportunity to apply his spiritual ideals in the industrial realm. The Quakers appreciated his pacifism but had great doubts about his new labor militancy.

Muste took an important leadership role in the Lawrence strike, using his moral authority as a middle-class Christian minister to bring respectability to the strikers. When the strike was over in 1921, pacifism was no longer a controversial issue but labor militancy was. Muste took a position as the leader of the Brookwood Labor College in Katonah, New York, an innovative free school supported by labor unions to provide noncredit enrichment experiences for labor activists. It tended to attract radicals, although its primary financial support was from moderate American Federation of Labor unions. Muste managed the ideological conflicts as well as he could, but he found his own thinking moving steadily to the left.

In 1929, Muste joined in forming the Conference for Progressive Labor Action (CPLA) to agitate for progressive trade unionism. He abandoned non-violence because he found it "difficult to find any moral ground for objecting to the spontaneous violence that often occurs in strikes."[38] His militant advocacy of radicalism caused problems at Brookwood, where the faculty split between radicals who wanted to use the college as a vanguard for revolution and traditionalists who wanted to continue educating labor activists. In the course of this organizational schism, Muste lost his composure and denounced his opponents as "numbskulls," "traitors," "turncoats," "academicians," and "reactionaries." A faithful supporter recalls the "angry huskiness of his voice as he indicted his opponents." Another recalled how he would "waggle his long finger, his voice would tremble, and that evenness of temperament we'd all thought was an unchangeable characteristic of A. J. was gone." He taunted men and women who had devoted their lives to teaching with Bernard Shaw's aphorism that "those who can do, those who can't teach," and he moved to fire the faculty who did not support a merger with the CPLA.

Muste soon recognized that he had acted with arrogance and malice, but it was too late to patch things up and he left Brookwood. He became fully committed to Leninist politics, forming the American Workers Party in 1933, which absorbed the CPLA. His followers, known as Musteites at the time, criticized the Communist Party for its linkages to the Soviet Union and its remoteness from the American scene. They attempted to be the truly American revolutionary socialist movement. Their opposition to the Stalinists made them attractive to the Trotskyists, and the American Workers Party merged with Trotskyists to become the Workers Party, U.S.A. in 1934.

Muste's conversion to revolutionary socialist politics was without benefit of a spiritual revelation from God. It was a gradual experience as he become more committed to labor militancy and more attracted to radical socialists as a community of believers. In his memoirs he recalled that:

When you looked out on the scene of misery and desperation during the depression, you saw that it was the radicals, the left-wingers, the

> people who had adopted some form of Marxian philosophy, who were doing something about the situation . . . it was on the Left . . . that one found people who were truly "religious" in the sense that they were virtually completely committed, they were betting their lives on the cause they embraced . . . the Left had the vision, the dream, of a classless and warless world . . . in a sense it was the true church.[39]

Alas, the leftist church was plagued with acrimony and factional conflict. The Trotskyist leaders in Muste's new Workers Party wanted to join the Socialist Party as a faction instead of keeping the Workers Party as a separate organization. Muste fought this strategy vehemently on the grounds that it was dishonest and ineffective to infiltrate a party one did not respect. He may also have been unwilling to see the new Party he had created disappear. He was overruled when a letter arrived from Leon Trotsky approving the new strategy. Muste was deeply disillusioned with the "pettiness and duplicity and self-indulgence and ruthlessness and a lack of human sensitiveness and of moral standards in The Party itself."[40]

When Muste tried to support the Goodyear workers who were on strike in Akron, Ohio, the strike leaders told him they didn't want any interference from outside radicals. One of the leaders was a former student of Muste's at Brookwood, and she made it clear that she was still loyal to the practical strategies and ethical ideals he had taught before becoming a revolutionary. Brookwood had not paid back salary he was owed, Anna was ill, and the Mustes were broke. A. J., fifty years old, had to swallow his pride and write to an old friend and supporter begging for money to pay his rent. Almost eighty and running short on resources herself, she came to his aid despite her strong disagreement with his current politics. It was at this time, in 1936, that their old friends raised money to send the Mustes to Europe on vacation.

In Europe, the Mustes went first to Norway to meet with Trotsky, then to Switzerland for a rest. While walking alone through Paris, he happened to enter a church purely as a tourist. When he entered the sanctuary, he was overcome with a feeling of "deep and singing peace," which reminded him of the Biblical passage describing a time when "the morning stars sang together."[41] He instantly resolved to leave the Trotskyist movement and return to Christ. From this point on, he never again wavered in his Christianity, nor did he ever again allow doubts to disturb his inner tranquility. He remained a pacifist through World War II and a leader in the antiwar movement until his death in 1967 at eighty-two years of age.

Muste served as director of the Fellowship of Reconciliation from 1940 to 1953. He opposed American involvement in World War II on the grounds that both sides were imperialist powers out to defend their privileges so it made no difference which side won.[42] In 1940 he told his Friends Meeting that "if I can't love Hitler, I can't love at all."[43] This was a common position among religious pacifists during World War II, although many others "gradually came to realize that in fighting the Nazis the United States was fighting an evil without precedent."[44] This may account for the fact that once the United States entered the war there was no antiwar movement, except for a few desultory efforts to encourage negotiations. Muste and other pacifists sought "to wean our fellows from the desire to make war, not to interfere from without with their war efforts."[45]

In the postwar period, Muste had a hard time reconciling his suspicion and distaste for Communists with his belief in seeking dialogue and understanding with all people. He insisted that pacifists had to oppose Russian militarism as much as American militarism, yet he opposed collaboration with Communists since they "use deceit and violence at the behest of the Party. . . . they do penetrate organizations of all kinds . . . without hesitating to resort to the most egregious chicanery."[46] At the same time, he opposed McCarthyism and collaborated with Communists in 1957 to organize the American Forum for Socialist Education.[47]

A. J. Muste lived into the Vietnam era when he compromised his pacifist neutrality to support the Vietnamese revolutionaries. He argued that "politically sophisticated pacifists have to make a distinction between the violence of liberation movements (of people who, in a situation where they have no real possibility of democratic means, resort to violence) and the violence imposed upon these countries by the imperialist powers." He thought that he had to be "for the defeat of the United States in this war" instead of opposing the use of violence by all sides equally as he had in World War II.[48]

In the sixties the antiwar movement had the spirit of righteous indignation and total commitment, which Muste had found in the socialist movement in the thirties. This indignation, however, was not directed primarily against war as such but against the Americans as the aggressors. Violence on the part of the Vietnamese was widely accepted as necessary and even heroic in response to the aggression from America. Despite his long commitment to religious pacifism, Muste's need to be on the cutting edge of moral righteousness led him to accept this position.

Dissent from majority opinions, sympathy for the oppressed and downtrodden, and the quest for an idealistic community of true believers are the consistent themes of Muste's otherwise highly varied ideological history. The norm of commitment to a moral cause was strongly reinforced by his parents, and he found a quiet life as a pastor unsatisfying. He had to be where the action was. In a sense, one could say that he was addicted to the high he received from standing up for his principles. He had remarkably little need to belittle others or to aggrandize his own ego in these actions, although he could get angry at those who frustrated his aspirations.

Like many true believers, Muste tended to bury his doubts in his unconscious mind. He was highly intelligent, and his skeptical streak made it difficult for him leave his doubts buried indefinitely. The doubts seemed to plague him until he found a new belief to replace the old. He attributed these new insights to inspiration from God, which helped him to adopt them without reservations. His greater serenity in the years after his final conversion in 1936 came because he stopped trying to rationalize his beliefs and simply accepted them on faith.

Kenneth Boulding

Quaker economist Kenneth Boulding is one of a small core of religious pacifists who remained true to pacifist convictions throughout both World War II and the Vietnam War. Boulding was born into a Methodist working-class family in Liverpool, England, in 1910. His father, William, was a Liberal plumber with two or three men working for him, but his business was often in financial difficulties. His mother was deeply involved in religious life, but neither of his parents were pacifists.

Boulding's pacifism is based on profound religious feelings, which may be rooted in experiences he had as a child. His father was exempt from service in World War I, but an uncle returned with permanent damage from shell shock. He came to Kenneth's home covered with lice and had to throw all his clothes out of the bathroom window into the back yard where Kenneth's mother killed the lice with a hot iron. The only significant personal experience with violence Kenneth had as a child was at the age of nine when he observed a riot between Irish Protestants and Catholics outside his home.[49]

He became a pacifist at about the age of fourteen when:

> feeling as a result of my Methodist upbringing that I wanted to model my life on the teachings of Jesus, and remembering my experiences of the First World War, and also perhaps the sense afterwards of having been totally deceived and betrayed by the propaganda I was exposed to at that time, I was flooded by a strong feeling that if I was going to love Jesus, I could neither kill anybody nor participate in war.[50]

This sense of being flooded by a strong feeling is very similar to the experiences which led Bertrand Russell and A. J. Muste to become pacifists. Both Muste and Boulding interpreted such experiences as religious, but psychologists naturally suspect that such feelings are messages from the unconscious. Boulding's biographer, Cynthia Earl Kerman, has made a psychological interpretation of Kenneth's pacifism.[51] Kerman knew Boulding well, having been his secretary for two years as well as a member of the same Quaker Meeting. She persuaded him to take a Thematic Apperception Test, which he thought rather silly, and she went to England to interview people who knew Kenneth as a boy.

Kerman's English informants remembered Kenneth as a big and awkward boy who hated sports, games, and fighting. He went to some lengths to avoid bullies after school and seems to have grown up with a strong distaste for fighting and violence. He "would never let himself be 'organized or dragooned' into games," and has had a "lifelong aversion to competitive athletics."[52] An only child who grew up in an adult-centered home, he was deeply concerned with religious and philosophical questions at a time when most boys were spending their energies on the playing fields.

Boulding's mother went through a period of depression when he was five years old, and economic circumstances forced them to move back to Liverpool from a suburban community they much preferred. At this time, Kerman believes Kenneth may have suffered a withdrawal of the affection and attention to which he had been accustomed. Kerman suggests that Boulding's pacifism may be rooted in a strong need to control his aggressive drives. She quotes him as having once remarked that "I am consumed by the moral disease of anger" and that "if I wasn't so violent I wouldn't have to be a Quaker."[53] On a number of occasions, she observes, "he spoke or wrote so sharply to good friends, or to associates in Quaker groups, that there were hurt feelings, sometimes even a break in relationships, although when these came to his attention he usually tried his best to make amends."[54]

Boulding is not happy with a psychological analysis of his pacifism:

> I think it is frankly nonsense to say that my pacifism is related to a strong need to control my aggressive drive. It arose out of a conviction that war was an aspect of society in which I could not participate, no matter what the personal cost. I felt the same about drunkenness, licentiousness, slavery and crime. Personal abstention, of course, is not the same thing as solving the social problem, which is why I got into peace research. But there is nothing "irrational" about it.[55]

Boulding's objections are understandable. Most people find their own beliefs quite logical and unproblematic and see no need for probing for deeper psychological motivations. Boulding's equation of serving his nation in the armed forces with drunkenness, licentiousness, slavery, and crime is unusual, yet to him it seems perfectly sensible. Boulding is especially sensitive about psychological analyses of religious beliefs. Kerman reports that he has "carried on, for most of his life, a muted feud with Freud, beginning perhaps in response to a talk he heard at Oxford in 1930."[56] The talk was on psychoanalysis and religion.

Throughout his adult life, Boulding has avoided thinking about his own deeper psychological motivations. In later life, he has simply put many of the childhood incidents described in Kerman's biography out of his mind and has no recollection of them. His personality puzzled psychologist Else Frenkel-Brunswick who spent a lot of time talking to Kenneth and his wife Elise while they were all in residence for a year at the Institute for Advanced Study in Palo Alto, California. According to Frenkel-Brunswick's theories of authoritarianism, the reluctance to examine one's inner motives is a key sign of an authoritarian, dogmatic, racist, violence-prone personality.[57] Yet Kenneth was clearly the opposite of all these, bubbling over with creativity and humanistic charm. His only apparent problems were a certain amount of physical tension and a persistent stammer, but neither of these inhibited him in any way. He is perhaps the only person with a serious stammer who has learned to use it as a rhetorical device in a highly successful career as a public speaker. Frenkel-Brunswick gave up her attempt to analyze Kenneth, deciding simply to enjoy his company as a delightfully idiosyncratic individual.

Although Boulding is an exceptionally wide ranging scholar and one of the founders of general systems theory, he rarely incorporates a psychological dimension in his systems analyses. In a recent book he remarked that "the whole dynamics of human learning is clearly of great importance in the general theory of power—How did Hitler learn to be Hitler?— and I must confess I am deeply troubled by my own ignorance in this matter."[58] Of course, Adolph Hitler, who differed from Kenneth Boulding in almost every other way, had no use for Freud and thought his own beliefs to be perfectly logical. Since our goal is to understand what made Hitler Hitler and Boulding Boulding, perhaps we can be forgiven for probing into psychological motives.

As a child, Boulding's greatest strength was in academics. He was a brilliant student who won scholarships for university education at a time when this was almost unheard of for working-class children. He became an economist and obtained a teaching job in Edinburgh at the height of the Depression in 1934. He had problems, however, when he denounced Scottish university education as "ossified" and failed to be deferential to the senior professor in his department. He felt uncomfortable as a man of working-class origins in the stuffy, class-conscious British universities, so he emigrated to America, which he found much more open and congenial.

Boulding's commitment to nonviolence has been absolutely constant throughout his life, unlike his belief in socialism, which he adopted enthusiastically in adolescence and abandoned after mature reflection. He is highly skeptical about every other ideology, submitting doctrines such as socialism to scathing critiques, but his pacifism is exempt from skeptical examination. Although he describes himself as a "compulsive writer" who once almost thought of forming a Writer's Anonymous group for people such as himself, his dozens of books and hundreds of articles do not include a book or rigorous philosophical essay on the ethics of refusing to use violence even in self-defense.[59] Early in his career, Boulding recognized that for him pacifism "is a faith, and like all faiths it cannot be proved— it can only be lived." He resolved to "show that it is worth living."[60]

Like many pacifists, Boulding's faith was shaken by Hitler's inhumanity, and there was a time in May 1940 when he felt overwhelmed by hatred for the Nazis. He sat down and wrote a poem:

> I feel hate rising in my throat.
> Nay—on a flood of hate I float.
> My mooring lost, my anchor gone,
> I cannot steer by star or sun.
>
> Black are the fountains of my soul
> And red the slime on which they roll.
>
> I hate! I hate! I hate! I hate!
> I hate this thrice-accursed State
> I'll smash each bloodshot German face
> That travesties the human race![61]

His faith was clearly wavering, but it was saved by an inner illumination, which came not during a Quaker meeting for worship but while he was drying himself after a bath. It seemed almost as if he had a vision of the suffering that Christ had taken on for people no better than the Germans or the Bouldings. He saw the German boys he had known as friends and felt his kinship with all men in suffering, sin, and hope. He captured this vision, also, in poetry:

> Hatred and sorrow murder me.
> But out of blackness, bright I see
> Our Blessed Lord upon his cross.
> His mouth moves wanly, wry with loss
>
> "If I forgive, will ye not too?"[62]

These poems support Kerman's hypothesis that coping with anger and aggression is a strong emotional component of Boulding's pacifism. The Quaker religion, which Boulding joined soon after his conversion to pacifism as an adolescent, places great value on a peaceful, nonviolent personal style in personal relationships as well as in settling international disputes. Quakerism is based on silent meditation and listening to the quiet voice of God within the worshiper. Quakers acknowledge that their pacifism is ultimately a religious conviction, which must be taken on faith.[63]

Although their religious life emphasizes peaceful withdrawal from the surrounding culture, Quakers are renowned for their strong social concerns and commitment to nonviolent activism. Their religious commitment gives them faith that a nonviolent way can be found to resolve even the most difficult conflicts and to ameliorate even the most intractable human afflictions. This tradition suited Kenneth Boulding perfectly, giving him support in his fundamental ideological commitments while encouraging his creativity and intellectual curiosity. In addition to publishing many important books and hundreds of articles on topics of war, peace, and human betterment, including the classic *Conflict and Defense,* he collaborated with his sociologist wife of over fifty years, Elise Boulding, in helping to found the international peace research movement. He also played an important role in starting the *Journal of Conflict Resolution.*

Perhaps on some level Boulding was thinking of himself when he described ideologies as interpretations of history, which are "sufficiently dramatic and convincing so that the individual feels that he can identify with it and which in turn can give the individual a role in the drama it portrays."[64] His own pacifist ideology certainly provided much of the motivation for an exceptionally productive career as a scholar and activist. His unquestioned core commitment to nonviolence, which Kerman describes as the "deep root" of his psyche, freed him from self-doubt and enabled him to channel his energies into the ways that he found to be the most satisfying and productive.

Dovish Doubts: The Vietnam and Gulf Wars

Religious pacifists provided a core of organizational structure and committed activists in the movement against American involvement in the Vietnam War. Pacifists were joined in this struggle with leftist protestors whose opposition was not to war as such but to capitalist imperialism in the third world. This alliance of protestors and doves has often been difficult because agreement on immediate objectives cannot always overcome differences in ideological scripts. In the course of these struggles, pacifist leaders such as A. J. Muste, David McReynolds, and David Dellinger sometimes compromised their pacifist convictions by choosing to apply them disproportionately to the anti-communist side of the conflict. They felt they could not condemn terrorism or violence when used by oppressed third-world peoples even though they regretted it.

The dismay felt by traditional religious pacifists at this defection by their leaders is detailed in Guenter Lewy's book *Peace and Freedom: The Moral Crisis of American Pacifism*. Lewy argues that leading pacifist organizations such as the American Friends Service Committee, the Women's International League for Peace and Freedom, and the War Resister's League abandoned the pacifist opposition to all use of violence for a New Left ideology, which portrayed:

> America as the root of most of the world's problems. American foreign policy is said to be based on an irrational anti-communism, on the "myth of the Soviet threat," the defense of right-wing dictatorships, and the hunger for profit on the part of multinational corporations. The estrangement from American society, idealization of revolution and revolutionary regimes in the Third World—as long as these movements and regimes claim to be committed to some kind of socialism and are opposed to America. The unsavory record of many of these regimes with regard to political freedoms and human rights generally is denied or, if that is not possible, defended as temporary and the result of American hostility.[65]

This, of course, is a viewpoint that was held by many, including the present author, in the sixties. The pacifist leaders might argue that their views have been caricatured, but Lewy's portrait captures the concerns of traditional pacifists leaders such as Robert Pickus, Charles Bloomstein, Kenneth Boulding, and Jack Powelson, who found themselves fighting a rearguard action against the New Left trend.[66] Lewy's book extensively documents his claim that the pacifist organizations had adopted an ideological script that divided the world into demonized enemies and idealized allies, with precious little love lost on the enemies.

On a practical political level, of course, both the pacifist and the anti-imperialist camps agreed on opposing service in the American armed forces during the Vietnam War. The differences were on subtle issues such as slogans (should one call for an American withdrawal or for a cease-fire and negotiations) and on the propriety of joining in coalitions with Leninist groups. After the war, however, the failure of the Vietnamese regime to live up to the idealized expectations of many of the peace activists led to more bitter conflict. In December 1976, about one hundred former opponents of the war published an "Appeal to the Government of Vietnam" protesting its human rights violations. Other former activists published an advertisement praising the Vietnamese government for its moderation and efforts to achieve reconciliation.[67] The issue became especially poignant when Vietnamese Buddhist pacifists who were personal friends of American pacifists and members of the Fellowship of Reconciliation wrote claiming that "the peace organization closest to us, and to which we belong, is looking the other way. It finds something interesting and encouraging to say about the policies of our government, but treats us who were sisters and brothers as if we were invisible or *dead*."[68]

Among those who found it impossible to ignore or rationalize the events in Vietnam were eighty-four antiwar leaders, led by folk singer Joan Baez and including Daniel Berrigan, Bradford Lyttle, Allen Ginsberg, I. F. Stone, Staughton Lynd, and Ed Asner, who were deeply disturbed by reports of torture and confinement of activists in "re-education camps."[69] The persecution of Vietnamese Buddhist pacifists, many of whom had become personal friends of American activists, was particularly distressing to Baez and the other pacifists. They published an open letter of protest in the *New York Times* and four other leading newspapers.[70]

Other prominent antiwar leaders, including David Dellinger, Stuart Meacham, David McReynolds, Tom Hayden, Jane Fonda, and Daniel Ellsberg refused to sign Baez's open letter.[71] They used various defense mechanisms to dispute the facts she presented such as questioning her sources and motivations. Baez reported that:

> A campaign was launched to stop me. I felt as if I were living in a vise. People appeared from my past, "just wanting to talk." They tried everything to get me to stop the letter. I woke up in the middle of the night in cold sweats. The phone rang off the hook with ultimatums and suggestions that I was naïve, that Doan Van Toai [her chief information source] was a CIA agent, that I was being used by the right wing, that I had lost all judgment.[72]

None of the prominent activists who refused to sign Baez's open letter, however, signed the rebuttal letter organized by the U.S. Peace Council, which claimed that "Vietnam now enjoys human rights as it has never known in history."[73] Most claimed that they weren't certain of the evidence, or that they felt it wasn't politically opportune to make a public statement. They did not, however, make an effort to search out better information or elaborate a more appropriate political argument. They simply preferred to think about something else.

Joan Baez thought of herself as trying to view the issues without "ideological blinders," responding to human need regardless of the larger issues.[74] In 1979 she had remarked that "as long as I have a cause, something to put my energy into, it's all right."[75] She was briefly praised by conservatives such as William Buckley and Ronald Reagan, who apparently thought she had converted to conservatism, but lost their approval when she went to Argentina and Chile to visit the Mothers of the Disappeared in 1981.

The American-led war to drive Iraqi forces from Kuwait in 1991 posed an ideological dilemma for American doves because they found it impossible to idealize Saddam Hussein's Iraqi regime. The war was sanctioned by the United Nations in response to the Iraqi occupation of a recognized sovereign state. Doves are generally supportive of strengthening the United Nations as a step toward world government. Yet the war was led by the American government, which doves consider to be an enemy of world peace.

Few antiwar activists had any illusions about Saddam Hussein's regime. They knew of reports that he had used poison gas against Kurdish civilians and that his war with neighboring Iran had led to approximately a million deaths. Amnesty International and other sources reported that Iraqi troops had tortured and killed hundreds of innocent civilians in imposing their occupation on Kuwait.[76] How could the peace movement oppose American military involvement without becoming unwilling accomplices to a brutal dictatorship?

A number of prominent leaders from the Vietnam-era peace movements simply decided to opt out of the movement against the Gulf War. Leftist scholar Michael Walzer was torn by the issues in the war and stated, "I am not prepared to join an antiwar movement modeled on that of the Vietnam years, whose protagonists claim that a war against Iraq would be unjust. It might well be politically or militarily unwise, but that is not a matter for marching."[77] Sam Brown, who had played a key role in Eugene McCarthy's 1968 presidential campaign and in organizing the 1969 Vietnam moratorium, also opted out of the Gulf War movement. He said, "It's a real odd thing for an old anti-war person to be thinking, but there are wars and there are wars. Every time I hear a parallel to Vietnam, I blanch. I see the movement people gearing up, the same familiar faces, and I want to say, 'Hold on, Hold on.' It's a wholly different situation that needs to be analyzed on its own merits."[78]

Other doves tried to use their usual methods of nonviolent activism. Members of one pacifist organization, the Fellowship of Reconciliation, went to Iraq in the hope of establishing people-to-people communications.[79] They came up against a stone wall of Iraqi indifference when they tried to take a position independent of both the American and the Iraqi governments. No one they talked to was willing to disagree with Saddam Hussein on any topic. Certainly not the pistol-packing government spokesman who seemed like "someone out of central casting playing the executioner." Instead of meaningful dialogue, they were treated to concerts by school children singing, "Saddam you are our leader and we are your willing soldiers." One participant observed sadly, "they're singing 'Kill Them! Slaughter Them!' and us nonviolent types are clapping along."

Another group, the London-based Gulf Peace Team, tried to use nonviolent direct action to prevent war between the United States and Iraq. They set up a "peace camp" on the border of Iraq and Saudi Arabia. In this case, the Iraqi government was enthusiastic since the pacifists were in effect providing a cover for their occupation of Kuwait. Members were aware of the Iraqi motives, but felt that Saddam Hussein "may get some mileage out of it, but we'll get more."[80]

The pacifists were, of course, opposed in principle to the Iraqi invasion of Kuwait. But they had no practical way of acting against it and persuaded themselves that American intervention was the greater danger. They also stayed as glassy-minded as possible to information about Iraqi atrocities. One Peace Team member insisted that they were completely unaware of the Iraqi atrocities, despite the massive coverage given to them in the Western media.[81] They had a rather grandiose image of themselves as World Citizens holding the line against World War III. When the United Nations deadline of January 15, 1991, passed without war breaking out, they held a celebration in the belief that they had prevented war.

They were perhaps the only people in the world who did not know that the American-led attack would begin with air raids, not a ground attack. When it did begin a few days later, they felt depressed and ineffective. No one seemed to be noticing them. The Iraqis evacuated them after taking them on a tour of bomb damage in Baghdad.

When questioned about the Iraqi aggression and atrocities, peace activists typically responded that this was something for "the Arabs to resolve among themselves." The activists claim to be "responsible" for protesting the actions of their own countries, while leaving the Arabs to solve their own problems. This helped them to cope with the strain of being *de facto* supporters of Iraqi aggression, but at the cost of compromising their commitments as humanists and internationalists. Of course, drawing a boundary between Arabs and non-Arabs instead of between Kuwaitis and Iraqis is an arbitrary mechanism that ideological thinkers often use to avoid dealing with difficult problems. When responding to the problems in South Africa, for example, it is the supporters of apartheid who argue that the outside world should allow the South Africans to settle their problems on their own.

The doves' assumption of "responsibility" for American policies is a somewhat grandiose exaggeration of their influence. As Americans, they may have an unconscious identification with American power and strength even as they protest it. They feel guilty for what the American government does, which they cannot control, yet they rarely express any self-doubt about their own actions. They are satisfied that their *motives* are pure, while the government's motives are not. This focus on motivations enables them to avoid thinking about the actual consequences of their activities, which in this case may well have been to encourage Iraqi intransigence and thus to increase the risk of war. In a speech broadcast to the world on January 28, 1991, for example, Hussein said that:

> All the people of Iraq are grateful to all the noble souls amongst the United States people who are coming out into the street demonstrating against this war. To all the noble people in France, in Britain, in England, in Italy and everywhere demonstrating against this war. We follow with keenness this sublime level of humanity, which comes out to counter the policies of aggression which are being planned and decided through the corridors of evil penetrated and dominated by criminal Zionism.[82]

The activists' ambivalence about the Iraqi invasion was obvious at peace rallies. Remarkably, speakers tended to avoid the topic of the Gulf War, even though this was the purpose of the meetings. A few speakers made token comments opposing the occupation of Kuwait, but most moved as quickly as possible to other topics such as the American actions in Panama and Grenada, local labor struggles, homeless people in the streets, and so on. In effect, they gave their usual stock speeches, adding only a quick reference to the fact that all the money being spent on war could better be spent here at home. Some speakers went to great lengths to criticize past American policies in the Middle East. By doing so, they implicitly excused the Iraqi invasion by putting it "in the context" of a greater American imperialism.[83]

Much of this effort seemed forced, as if the activists did not quite believe what they were saying. They were following the same script as in the Vietnam days, but it did not quite ring true. In the Vietnam era, many activists saw the National Liberation Front as a force for freedom and democracy. No one seemed willing to make a similar claim for Saddam Hussein's Baath Party. President Bush quickly seized the moral high ground by quoting from the Amnesty International report on the invasion of Kuwait. Congress, which allowed itself to be manipulated into a cheerleader role in the Vietnam era, held meaningful and well-informed debates on Iraq and Kuwait. By contrast, the peace movement's debates seemed sterile and scripted.

James Zogby is the director of the Arab American Institute in Washington, D.C., a leftist organization dedicated to defending Palestinian rights.

He believes that the peace movement erred by stressing slogans such as "bring our troops home," "out now," and "no blood for oil," which ignored the "real human tragedy of what happened to Kuwait." In his view, the frequent attacks by activists on the Kuwaiti emirs as undemocratic oil barons were unfair. Kuwait was actually more advanced toward democratic pluralism than any of the other states in the area. In his opinion, "the so-called peace movement has adopted a rhetoric that you find in right-wing circles, picturing Arabs as little fat barbarians with too much wealth."[84]

Zogby's critique best fits the leftist wing of the peace movement. As in the Vietnam era, the peace movement in 1991 was split into two major factions, one representing the Leninists, the other the pacifists. The Leninist National Coalition for Peace in the Middle East took no position on the Iraqi invasion of Kuwait, explaining the invasion was "up to the Arab peoples to resolve."[85] Founded by Ramsey Clark, this group was heavily influenced by the Trotskyist *Workers World* party, which also supported the Chinese government's massacre in Tiananmen Square.

The larger pacifist National Campaign for Peace in the Middle East opposed the invasion of Kuwait and sympathized with United Nations sanctions against Iraq. It held separate demonstrations on different Saturdays in Washington, D.C., in the hope of distancing itself from the Coalition's anti-American slogans. In a deliberate effort to avoid repeating the mistakes of the Vietnam era, it avoided any criticism of the American troops, saying that the best way to support the troops was to bring them home. Despite these intentions, however, the major impact of its activities was to oppose American military action. It never took a clear policy position in favor of United Nations sanctions, which limited its political effectiveness.

This unhappy alliance of anti-Americanism and pacifism is inherent in the political logic of American peace movements, since opposing America's war efforts means helping the other side no matter how much the doves wish that were not the case. It is also inherent in the political psychology of many peace activists, who channel all their hostility and aggressiveness against the American government. This alliance between protestors and doves is easier to sustain when it is possible to idealize America's enemies.

Conclusions

To the hawk, the doves seem self-centered and childlike, living in a fantasy world where lions are vegetarians and flower power is stronger than fire power. French psychiatrist Marcel Boisot argues that the growth of pacifist movements in Europe in the 1980s resulted from the decline of the traditional family structure.[86] The image of the father and of authority were weakened, and families became child centered. In modern mass societies, people have become self-centered without strong commitments to the myths and ideals of their national group. Pacifism, in Boisot's view, represents the triumph of the pleasure principle over the reality principle, a regression to narcissism. Life becomes a permanent party, a sort of self-indulgent heaven on earth. Denial is used as a defense mechanism against the reality of geopolitical facts.

Boisot argues that the demand for peace is a response not only to the anguish of war, but also to the anguish of change. It reflects an unconscious desire to return to the womb, to the Garden of Eden, where we were the universe and there was no need to fear outsiders. For Boisot, pacifism is simply another utopian fantasy.

Boisot's analysis of the psychodynamics of pacifism may fit some anti-American, new leftist protestors. It does not fit the pacifists whose lives we have examined in depth in this chapter, all of whom had traditional upbringings in strong families. These doves fit much better into an analysis of pacifism as resulting from the inhibition of aggressive and self-indulgent feelings. Doves and protestors may often be allies in social movements, but their psychodynamics are quite different.

Of course, like any ideological script, pacifist views can be adopted for a variety of different reasons. Many people who do not have a deep emotional commitment to nonviolence nevertheless support nonviolent tactics when they seem likely to be effective in certain situations. And pacifists who do have a deep emotional commitment to nonviolence can also be concerned with pragmatic political success. Gandhi's pacifism may have originated in his need to overcome his shyness and inhibitions, but he used it effectively to win Indian independence. Nonviolence was certainly effective in the American civil rights movement, although most activists abandoned it when they became frustrated with its limitations.

It is very difficult, however, to argue that nonviolence can be effective in every situation or that it is the only ethically justifiable policy. A. J. Muste argued that nonviolent resistance might have saved the European Jews from the Nazis, but most thoughtful people agree with Albert Einstein on the necessity for armed resistance to the Nazis.[87] In one of the best-known defenses of nonviolence, Richard Gregg simply asks skeptics to "suspend judgment" on the Hitler case.[88] Pacifists such as Vera Brittain and Kenneth Boulding, who remained true to their principles during World War II, had to be willing to give absolute priority to expressing their values without regard for the practical consequences. Einstein, by contrast, placed less importance on value consistency than on his practical judgment that the consequences of not violently resisting the Nazis would be worse than the consequences of violently resisting them.

For A. J. Muste, commitment to values was important, but there was a stronger theme of anger against American society and a need to belong to a community of morally superior people. He tired of Christian pacifism during the interwar years because it simply was not a controversial issue, and so he became involved with a Leninist group because it was a community of true believers fighting the good fight against evil. His idealization of the Leninist movement, however, led to disillusionment and burnout.

The American peace movement is based on two conflicting feelings. The first is a revulsion for violence and killing. Freud, who thought of himself as a pacifist, thought this feeling had its origins in the strengthening of the intellect, which resulted in:

> an introversion of the aggressive impulse. . . . war runs most emphatically counter to the psychic disposition imposed on us by the growth of culture; we are therefore bound to resent war, to find it utterly intolerable. With pacifists like us it is not merely an intellectual and affective repulsion, but a constitutional intolerance.[89]

The other emotional source of the American peace movement is anger at American society and its dominant institutions. In adolescence, most young people learn to hate the traditional enemies in their culture. Turks hate Greeks, Iraqis hate Iranians, Americans hate Communists, and so on. Some people, however, reverse the imagery by idealizing their country's enemies and demonizing their own country's institutions. These individuals, who may be motivated by personal unhappiness, unfortunate life experiences, or socialization into a deviant counterculture, provide the core of leftist sectarian movements. The "peace movement" has been an odd alliance of adherents of these two quite different ideological scripts.

American opponents of the Gulf War used a number of defense mechanisms to deny the contradiction inherent in acting as unwilling allies of a brutal aggressor. They denied or repressed facts about Iraqi aggression and atrocities. They split themselves off from responsibility for anything that happened among Arabs, or even from responsibility for the consequences of their own actions, while assuming responsibility for the behavior of the American government as if they had control over it. This tendency to identify with the American "aggressor" may also explain the tendency for movement speakers to exaggerate American power, efficiency, and omnipotence.

These mixed motives were responsible for a number of self-defeating behaviors on the part of the peace movement during both the Vietnamese and the Gulf Wars. During the Vietnam era, for example, some protestors attacked American troops and carried enemy flags in demonstrations. They denied any legitimacy to American concerns about protecting democracy and stopping communist totalitarianism, portraying America as an evil imperialist motivated only by greed and aggressiveness. By taking this stance, they lessened their effectiveness, allowing the supporters of the war to mobilize a backlash against them.

Many of these mistakes were avoided in the Gulf War protests, but antiwar activists nevertheless failed to articulate their opposition as effectively as they might have. When opinion in the U.S. Congress was divided on the issue of continuing sanctions against Iraq as an alternative to driving Iraqi forces out militarily, the peace movement was unable to take a clear stand on the issue. Doing so would have meant supporting what was official American policy at the time and would have forced a break with the Leninist left. The demonstrators devoted more energy to venting their anger, and talking about other issues, than to advocating for a policy that might have minimized the killing.

Despite the efforts of Guenter Lewy and other committed pacifists, the pacifists have often failed to make a clear distinction between opposition to war as such and selective opposition to only those wars conducted by the United States and other "imperialist" powers. The willingness of even sincere religious pacifists to ally themselves with hostile and sometimes violent Leninist sectarians is puzzling. Their "introverted aggressive impulses" are too easily expressed as hostility against the nation to which they belong. Loving your enemy seems to be easier when one's angry impulses are redirected against one's own society and government.

Chapter Nine

Protestors and Authoritarians: Trotsky and Stalin

Protestors and authoritarians are opposites in many ways. Protestors identify with the oppressed and condemn the oppressor. Authoritarians identify with the forces of law and order and condemn deviants and nonconformists. Although they disagree about who the good guys and bad guys are, they share an inclination to deny the legitimacy of their opponents while they self-righteously demand that their own rights be scrupulously protected. Protestors who have won power have often proved to be more repressive than the old regimes that they despised.

There are many parallels in tactics between protestors and authoritarians. Anti-abortion protestors in the 1980s and 1990s use tactics copied from the civil rights and antiwar movements of the 1960s and 1970s. Both placed their convictions above the law and used nonviolent harassment and disruption in an effort to compel others to follow their beliefs. Radical feminists who oppose religious fundamentalists on abortion join forces with them in seeking to outlaw pornography.

The similarity of protest and authoritarian scripts is also suggested by the fact that a number of individuals have made dramatic shifts from one side to the other. In the 1940s and 1950s a great many dedicated Communists abandoned the "God that Failed." Some of them became militant anti-Communists. In the 1960s and 1970s conservatives such as CIA agent Philip Agee and Pentagon strategist Daniel Ellsberg defected to join the protest bandwagon. In the 1980s, a number of prominent leftists such as Jerry Rubin, Eldridge Cleaver, and David Horowitz switched in the other direction. In most cases, these individuals displayed the same personality traits and habits of thought before and after their change. They simply reversed the imagery, making good guys into bad guys and vice versa.

Marxism promised the "withering away of the state," but Marxist-Leninist regimes everywhere established states that were stronger and more oppressive than those they replaced. Was this due to the inherent logic of Marxism or to the psychological traits and needs of the leaders who won power? In the last days of the Soviet Union, a central debate focused on the question of whether the totalitarian Soviet state was Stalin's personal responsibility or whether it was inherent in the Leninist project.[1]

In this chapter, we will compare the lives of Joseph Stalin and Leon Trotsky, a pair who have been extensively studied and who had an enormous impact on world history. To what extent can their psychology explain their politics and why one won the power struggle against the other? What difference would it have made if the outcome of the struggle between them had been different? In the chapters that follow, we will pursue many of the same psychological issues in the biographies of turncoats from Communism, radicals from the New Left of the 1960s, and feminists and antifeminists in the 1970s. Although these cases are far apart historically, they raise many of the same psychological issues.

Leon Trotsky

Trotsky was born into a Jewish farming family, which was struggling to raise its modest social status through hard work and prudent investment.[2] He felt neglected by his parents. In his view, they were too busy for their children and "there was no display of tenderness in our family, especially during my early years."[3] This despite the fact that he was apparently their favorite. Max Eastman described him as a child who was "so sweet-tempered and has such a merry disposition that his parents cannot get along without him."[4]

He was closer to his mother than to his father and especially resented his father's persistent efforts to pressure him into studying civil engineering. As a student, he searched for a cause that would allow him to express his need for independence from paternal and academic authority. In the course of this search, he made two dramatic changes in his beliefs. His first commitment was to pure mathematics. At this time he argued vehemently against advocates for radical anti-Tsarist movements. He was such an effective advocate for a life devoted to respectable scholarly pursuits that mothers sought him out in the hope that he could persuade their sons to abandon their socialist visions. The more the socialists argued, the more vehemently he resisted. His dogmatism concealed considerable repressed doubt, however, which broke through in about half a year. He suddenly changed his tune and became a passionate advocate for socialism as defined by the populist *Narodnik* party, which stressed the importance of dramatic acts by revolutionists.

At this time, Marxism struck Trotsky as a sterile economistic doctrine suitable for shopkeepers or academics. He even wrote a bitter anti-Marxist polemic, which was never published. In the course of writing a play about the Marxist-*Narodnik* controversy, however, he found that the Marxist character was emerging as the most attractive. The Marxist emphasis on the economic roots of social change didn't keep the hero from playing a dramatic role. Indeed, his importance was augmented by the conviction that he was an instrument of the inevitable forces of history. Trotsky switched again, becoming a Marxist instead of a *Narodnik*. In later life, Trotsky observed that the Marxist doctrine of determinism was similar to the Calvinist doctrine of predestination. Instead of inspiring fatalism in their followers, both doctrines inspired them to greater activism in the belief that they were acting in harmony with superior forces.

Isaac Deutscher described Trotsky's thinking as follows:

> He is confronted with a new idea to which up to a point he is conditioned to respond; yet he resists at first with stubborn haughtiness; his resistance grows with the attraction and he subdues incipient doubt and hesitation. Then his inner defences crumble, his self-confidence begins to vanish; but he is still too proud or not convinced enough to give any sign of yielding. There is no outward indication yet of the struggle that goes on in his mind. Then, suddenly, the new conviction hardens in him, and, as if in a single moment, overcomes his spirit of contradiction and his vanity. He startles his erstwhile opponents not merely by his complete and disinterested surrender, but by the enthusiasm with which he embraces their cause, and sometimes by the unexpected and far-reaching conclusions which he draws from their arguments.[5]

As a youth, Trotsky had little invested in his beliefs and was able to change them fairly easily. Ideological commitments were enjoyable and even somewhat playful. They gave him a way to express his rebelliousness, which enhanced his feeling of importance. When he became involved with a Southern Russian Workers' Union, however, and was arrested and put into jail, it was quite a shock for him. The air was foul, he had to wear the same underwear for three months, had no soap, and was eaten alive by vermin. Holding up against this oppression strengthened his commitment to his revolutionary beliefs.

After his prison experience, he remained a committed Marxist for life despite tremendous disappointment with developments in Russia after the revolution. By this time he had invested so much of his life in Marxism that it had become more of a commitment script than a protest script for him. It is much easier for a young man with no reputation to change his views than for a man who has endured prison and exile, written books, led a revolutionary army, and become a historical figure.

This does not mean that Trotsky did not make significant changes in his thinking within a general Marxist framework. Before the revolution, he made some dramatic shifts from one faction to another, abandoning *Bolshevism* for *Menshivism* and then returning to *Bolshevism* in time to be Lenin's second in command in the victorious 1917 revolution. As a brilliant and charismatic orator, he played a key role in mobilizing the masses for the revolution. As commander of the Red Army, he exercised enormous power and played a crucial role in establishing the revolutionary regime. When Lenin died in 1924, Trotsky was in a very strong position to compete for the mantle of supreme leader of the revolution.

Oddly enough, Trotsky pulled back from the power struggle, taking refuge in one of a series of illnesses, which were probably at least partly psychosomatic.[6] He seemed to value ideological purity and moral self-righteousness more than either personal power or pragmatic accomplishment. When Stalin, who had no such compunctions, won the political contest, Trotsky was forced into opposition and then into exile.

Unlike British or American admirers of the Soviet Union who managed to remain blissfully unaware of its deficiencies, the exiled Trotsky was exceptionally well informed about the failure of the Bolshevik revolution to accomplish its humanistic goals. A brilliant writer as well as a speaker, he described them eloquently:

> The realities of Soviet life can indeed be hardly reconciled even with the shreds of old theory. Workers are bound to factories, peasants are bound to the collective farms . . . freedom of movement has been completely restricted . . . every citizen is required at an appointed time to cast his ballot for the one and only candidate handpicked by Stalin or his agents. . . . how many have been shot, thrown into jails and concentration camps, or exiled to Siberia, we do not definitely know. But undoubtedly hundreds of party members have shared the fate of millions of nonparty people.[7]

Speaking from an American pragmatist's perspective, Max Eastman commented, "On reading these words from the organizer of the October revolution, one exclaims almost irresistibly:

" 'Surely then, after getting this result, you are not going to do the very same thing over again!' "[8]

Yet that was precisely what he proposed to do. Trotsky was well versed in the Marxist theory that social forces, not personalities, determine the course of history. He was never content with this doctrine, however. As a youth, he had been able to adhere to Marxism only when he convinced himself that it permitted a decisive role for the individual. He continued throughout his life to believe that exceptional individuals could make history. In his *History of the Russian Revolution* he departed from Marxist doctrine to concede that without Lenin's personal intervention the proletarian revolution would not have taken place.[9] When the revolution failed to live up to its promises, he blamed the failure on Stalin's "betrayal" as if the great march of history could be reversed by the perfidy of a single individual. He seemed to believe that if only he could regain power social forces could be redirected and the revolution could be redeemed, not only in Russia but around the world.

Max Eastman, who worked with Trotsky during his exile in Turkey, thought that he was having doubts and might have abandoned Marxism-Leninism if he had lived into the post-war era. In an essay written in 1939, Trotsky wrote:

> If [at the conclusion of the war] the world proletariat should actually prove incapable of fulfilling the mission placed upon it by the course of development, nothing would remain except openly to recognize that the socialist program based on the internal contradictions of capitalist society ended as a utopia.[10]

Giving up on socialist utopianism would have deprived Trotsky's life of much of its meaning. A man who could write that he knew "no *personal* tragedy"[11] despite the murder of his son by Stalinist agents would have found it very difficult to abandon the ideal that made his personal sufferings seem worthwhile. Better to keep the mind clearly focused on the ideological vision than to muddle it with discouraging evidence. As a writer, without the responsibilities of power, he was able to convince millions that he was the true incarnation of the Leninist ideal. Stalin won the struggle for power, but Trotsky won the consolation prize for ideological purity by dying as a martyr at the hands of Stalin's agent.

Joseph Stalin

Stalin was descended from a long line of peasants in Georgia.[12] His father drank and beat him brutally. His mother, who was also abused by her husband, was devoted to her son and wanted him to get an education despite his father's insistence that he should follow him in the trade of shoemaking. The boy was small and physically unimpressive. Two toes were joined together, he was pock-marked from an illness when he was seven, and his left arm was short and weakened because of a childhood accident. He was, however, exceptionally bright and was at the top of his class in school. His father died when he was eleven. One of his friends later reported that "the early death of the father made no impression upon the boy. In the man he was supposed to call father he lost nothing."[13] He had not had time to settle accounts with his father and was left with an enduring feeling of vindictiveness and rebelliousness against authority.

He attended a local church school where his brilliance won him a scholarship to the Tiflis Theological Seminary. His widowed mother could never have afforded to give him a higher education on her earnings as a washerwoman. The seminary was a repressive institution. The students were not allowed to read books or newspapers in the Georgian language, nor could they read literary classics, which might have exposed them to attitudes inconsistent with life as a priest. The students rebelled by reading prohibited literature and dabbling in revolutionary politics. Stalin was particularly impressed by a Georgian novel, *The Patricide,* by Alexander Kazbegi. Kazbegi was a Georgian nationalist who wrote tales of fierce mountain men who resisted Russian conquest. Their chief virtues were toughness toward their enemies and loyalty to their friends. Stalin adopted the name of the hero of *The Patricide,* Koba, as his first pseudonym and retained it into his thirties.

Stalin joined the Social Democratic Party at the age of eighteen and was expelled from the seminary. When the police came after him, he went underground and devoted himself to clandestine activities such as smuggling literature and holding up banks. He was not a gifted writer or orator. To be successful in the revolutionary movement, he had to develop organizational skills. He conformed to party discipline, while expressing his rebelliousness by flouting the authorities and violating the law.

Stalin exemplifies the mentality typical of members of terrorist groups.[14] Terrorists are often young adults who have a history of abuse, which gives them a deficient sense of self-esteem. They tend to split off the deficient parts of themselves and project them onto the establishment. They protect their self-esteem by joining a group of like-minded individuals who believe that it's "us against them." They use ideology as a glue to hold the group together and to define the good guys and the bad guys. Their ideological language is that of black and white, with no room for shades of gray or ambiguity. In terms of group-development theory, the terrorist group is usually dominated by a "fight-flight" assumption.

Although he was a committed member of a terrorist group, Stalin had only a minor role in the revolutions of 1917. He was in exile in Siberia until after the February revolution and was in the background during the October revolution. After the revolution, however, his reliability as a disciplined organization man made him very useful to Lenin as he sought to impose Communist rule on the society. He rapidly accumulated power while avoiding drawing attention to himself. Trotsky and the other Old Bolsheviks underestimated him, since he was not known as a thinker, writer, or orator. Lenin became suspicious of his accumulation of power, however, and even wrote a deathbed testament suggesting that he be removed from the office of Party secretary. However, the document was suppressed when Lenin died prematurely in 1924, and Stalin was the major contestant with Trotsky to be Lenin's successor.

Although there is some historical debate about why Stalin won the power struggle, two reasons stand out. First, he really wanted to win. Much to the despair of his closest supporters, Trotsky made only a halfhearted effort. He missed crucial meetings and refused to confront Stalin openly with Lenin's testament. Second, Stalin advocated a realistic revision of Leninist doctrine. Lenin had assumed that the Russian revolution would be only a prelude to revolutions in the more developed capitalist countries, particularly Germany. Trotsky placed great emphasis on agitating for worldwide revolution. Stalin faced up to the reality that a world revolution was not in the cards and advocated the doctrine of "socialism in one country."

Once he took power, Stalin moved to purge the Trotskyists from the Party. Actually, "Trotskyist" was a label Stalin used to brand anyone who was a threat to him. Claims of sabotage by the "Trotskyist anti-party clique" were used as a convenient scapegoat for all the problems of the revolution. This kind of splitting and scapegoating is typical of ideological movements. Stalin's personality was such that he took to this stage of the Party's development with enthusiasm.

One might argue that Stalin's purges were necessary to maintain ideological discipline. However, he carried the purges much further than necessary for any such purpose. As his power grew, he went beyond purging people from the Party and had them killed. He killed a great many professional army officers, for example, at a time when the country was threatened by attack from Nazi Germany. He killed most of the top leaders who had made the revolution with Lenin, claiming that they were traitors.

These purges went on until Stalin died and were stopped by the Party leaders as soon as he passed away. This makes it clear that the purges were in large part his own personal crusade, not the consequence of organizational dynamics within the Party. Stalin was much more popular with the general public than he was with the Party leaders. Even today, many Russians look back on the 1930s as a "time of great enthusiasm, of national unity and pride, of belief in the leadership, and of a historical mission."[15] Stalin was a father figure. His poster was everywhere. Groups of children were led in thanking Comrade Stalin for their happy childhoods. The Soviet Union was building a glorious future under the guidance of a wise leader who was steadfastly crushing the wreckers who stood in the way. Even many people in concentration camps convinced themselves that Stalin could not possibly have known about the repression that was going on.

People who are under great stress often resort to idealization of a strong father figure as a way of finding strength. Former Yugoslavian Communist Milovan Djilas reports that:

> When the humming of Hitler's planes woke everyone up early one clear spring morning in Belgrade, when bombs started slashing the beautiful and innocent body of the city, with their gray smoke spreading death among the parks, streets, buildings and tree-lined avenues, the vision that came before the eyes of the shocked populace was that of Stalin—fatherly, concerned, and smiling. . . . our people sensed that there is one leader in the world, teacher and father of mankind, who thinks of us and will never forget us. . . . Stalin became our closest and dearest comrade. He commiserates with the suffering of our people, he rejoices over the success of our fighters for freedom, he sits with us as we wait in ambush, he soothes our wounds, he gives courage to our people not to lose faith, he commends us for our bravery and our noble deeds.[16]

Djilas's last sentence recalls the twenty-third Psalm: "The Lord is my shepherd. . . . He maketh me to lie down in green pastures, he leadeth me beside the still waters, he restoreth my soul." This kind of identification with the aggressor is common among authoritarians. The fantasy that the Godlike leader will take care of them gives them an illusion of strength. In addition to providing protection, identifying with the strong man's persecution of enemies provides a vicarious outlet for aggressive feelings. If they receive punishment from the leader or his henchmen, this may help to assuage repressed guilt feelings. This kind of leadership also seems to appeal to people after a revolution, possibly because they feel guilty for having killed the previous leader.

Stalin had an intuitive understanding of the process. When someone asked him why he was so popular, he demonstrated by picking up a chicken and tearing out all its feathers. When he let the chicken go, it responded by huddling up against his legs for warmth.

The process of identification with the aggressor may help to explain Stalin's curious attitude toward Adolph Hitler. Hitler was clearly a threat to the Soviet Union as a nation. He was also the bitter enemy of Communism who had killed thousands of German Communists and destroyed the German Communist Party. Yet Stalin admired him and may even have been sexually attracted to him.[17] His alliance with Germany in 1939 might be justified on the grounds of national interest. But there was no need for Stalin to send German and Austrian Communists leaders who had taken refuge in the Soviet Union back to Germany to be killed.[18] He refused to believe a great many warnings from his own spies and foreign leaders that Germany was preparing to cheat on the treaty and attack Russia. When Germany finally did so, Stalin was so upset he threw a temper tantrum, abandoned his post and went off to his summer house where he was reported to be drunk, depressed, or having a nervous breakdown.[19]

Stalin pulled himself together well enough to lead the war effort. He was not one to give up easily. The Soviet victory, however, came at a greatly increased cost because of his purges of army officers before the war, his failure to accept the information about the pending German attack, and his tendency to trust his judgment over that of professional military officers.

Stalinism and Trotskyism

Both Stalin and Trotsky show the psychological similarities in the protest and authoritarian scripts. Stalin joined a leftist party because it was the toughest movement available to someone of his social class in his society. Had he been a young German in the 1930s, however, he would have been a natural recruit for the Nazi storm troopers. Stalin fits the "authoritarian personality" syndrome as well as any major leader in history.[20] He had tremendous destructive and cynical feelings, was preoccupied with plots against him, valued power and toughness, and even adhered in many ways to conventional values in his personal lifestyle. He was submissive toward Lenin and even showed an inclination to submit to Hitler. He was loyal to the Party as a young recruit, but showed no guilt about killing off most of his closest Party comrades when he had the power to do so. He showed no remorse about policies that killed millions of innocent people.

Trotsky was a much more appealing figure, much more the protestor than the authoritarian. He was able to be a strong leader and send men to their deaths when he believed it to be necessary for military reasons, but at least he felt badly about it. He wrote books debating bourgeois philosophers about the ethics of terrorism.[21] Stalin would never have bothered. As a protestor, Trotsky cared about ideas and ideals even more than he cared about winning power. He attached himself to Lenin long enough to help win the revolution, but when he was on his own in the power struggle with Stalin he clung to his illusions about world revolution and gave up the fight. He spent the rest of his life in a forlorn quest to rebuild a proletarian international. His protest script had prepared him to rally the masses against oppression, but not for the cold-blooded ruthlessness needed to exterminate his own closest friends and comrades.

Stalinists and Trotskyists still exist in the world. The Stalinists are bureaucrats clinging to power in Leninist regimes or citizens frightened by change and longing for a strong leader to restore order and discipline. The Trotskyists are small bands of true believers who view him as "a romantic hero, the man of the Revolution, the creator of the Red Army he led with confidence, skill and distinction—and the victim of a brutal dictatorship that expunged his name from the histories of the country he did so much to create."[22] He symbolizes the protestor who stubbornly clings to ideals in the face of reality. The Iron Law of the Sectarian Left might be: the Trotskyists always lose. Indeed, they need to lose if they are to remain true to their utopian illusions.

If Trotsky had lived into the postwar era he would have had to confront the failure of Marxism-Leninism as a revolutionary ideology. At that point in his life it would have been virtually impossible for him to shift his ideology as he had as a young man, and it would have been hard for a man of his intelligence to maintain his illusions. His life might well have ended with suicide. As it was, in the words of Philip Pomper, "Stalin obligingly played the role of murderous tyrant and provided the tragic ending to Trotsky's career—the only appropriate ending."[23]

Chapter Ten

The God that Failed:
Mourning the Loss of Ideological Belief

And where false ideas are twisted into our minds, it is with difficulty we get fairly disentangled.
> —John Woolman, 1762

Intellectuals in Retreat

In 1939, two outstanding Trotskyist leaders, James Burnham and Max Shachtman, published a blistering denunciation titled: *"Intellectuals in Retreat:* A POLITICAL ANALYSIS OF THE DRIFT OF THE ANTI-STALINIST INTELLECTUALS FROM MARXISM TOWARDS REFORMISM—A CRITIQUE OF SIDNEY HOOK, MAX EASTMAN, EUGENE LYONS, BENJAMIN STOLBERG, CHARLES YALE HARRISON AND OTHER CRITICS OF BOLSHEVISM, WHERE THEY STAND AND WHERE THEY ARE GOING."[1]

Burnham and Shachtman conceded that their subjects were intellectuals of outstanding ability, talent, and moral virtue, which made their apostasy much harder to take than that of many Stalinists. They were all doing quite well as writers for "bourgeois" publications, despite their reluctance to elaborate a clear political line. Burnham and Shachtman denounced their politics as:

> *negative* in the sense that they are always and constantly criticizing and attacking everybody else's politics . . .
> *irresponsible* in the sense that they do not lay their cards on the table . . .
> and *unprincipled* because their specific political actions and positions are not derived from consciously, explicitly recognized principles.

Their criticism was one that is often made of turncoats:

> Our subjects take great pride in believing that they are contributing something "fresh", that they are "reevaluating in the light of new experiences", that they "are not dogmatists who refuse to reexamine their 'basic assumption' ", *etc.* What a pathetic self-deception! None of them has brought to light any new facts, given any new understanding of the present or future. . . . All that they say in their formal program can be found long, long ago in the pages of Kautsky and put far more brilliantly, consistently and *openly.*[2]

Apostates often find themselves in a period of doubt and indecision, having rejected their previous beliefs but not yet feeling ready to identify with a new ideology even though their thinking is clearly leading them in that direction. Later events, however, confirm that Burnham and Shachtman were correct in noting that many of their former colleagues were moving toward support for democratic capitalism, even though they weren't ready to acknowledge that themselves.

What is most fascinating, however, is not the fate of their former colleagues but the fact that Burnham and Shachtman soon moved into apostasy themselves.[3] Burnham made a definitive break with Marxism in a letter of resignation from the Workers' Party on May 21, 1940, three years after "Intellectuals in Retreat" had been published.[4] In a few short years Burnham became one of the "imperialist maggots" he had so vehemently denounced in "Intellectuals in Retreat," finishing his career as an editor for the conservative *National Review*. Shachtman, on the other hand, never renounced the word "socialism" but moved to the far right wing of the movement. He supported the Bay of Pigs invasion and the intervention in Vietnam in the interest of defending the free world, and supported Hubert Humphrey in the Democratic Party primaries in 1972.

The thinking that led up to Burnham's apostasy is well documented in an essay, "Science and Style," which the Socialist Workers' Party published, together with his letter of resignation, as appendices to Trotsky's *In Defense of Marxism*.[5] The Trotskyists wanted these documents published because they proved that Burnham was actually a nonbeliever all along. In "Science and Style" Burnham delivers a devastating attack on the "dialectical logic," which Trotsky resorted to in justifying his defense of the Soviet Union under Stalin.[6] Burnham anticipated C. Wright Mills's conclusion that "the 'dialectical method' is either a mess of platitudes, a way of double-talk, a pretentious obscurantism—or all three."[7]

At first Burnham thought that Trotsky's use of the dialectic was a silly joke. When he realized that Trotsky was serious, he was forced to the conclusion that he was relying on metaphysics to cover over the failure of the real world to conform to his expectations. In defending dialectical materialism, Trotsky went so far as to argue that a fox uses dialectics when it chases a chicken but runs from a wolf (because the wolf is larger than a chicken, and the philosophically sophisticated fox realizes that this quantitative difference has engendered a qualitative change from prey to predator).[8] By this logic, a dialectical fox would run even faster at the sight of a harmless herbivorous cow while having no fear of a petite but poisonous snake.[9] Burnham thought dialectics was of no more use to the socialist strategist than it would be to a fox, and he accused Trotsky of resorting to metaphysical logic because:

> There is little else for you to write about, with every appeal you make to actual events refuted the day after you make it, with each week's developments in the war smashing another pillar of your political position. An argument about dialectics is 100 per cent safe, a century ago or a century hence. Among those lofty generalities, no humble and inconvenient *fact* intrudes.[10]

When he wrote "Science and Style" on February 1, 1940, Burnham was committed to socialism and to Marxism as a science, purged of dialectical mumbo jumbo. He argued that "for me, certainly, 'Marxist politics' means 'scientific politics'; if it did not, then I would reject Marxist politics."[11] Trotsky had warned socialist youth to "beware of the infiltration of bourgeois skepticism into your ranks" and to spend their time reading the Marxist classics.[12] Burnham thought that Trotsky's doctrine of "class truths" was on:

> the road of Plato's Philosopher-Kings, of prophets and Popes and Stalin. For all of them, also, a man must be among the anointed in order to know truth. . . . You issue many warnings to the young comrades of our movement. I add an ominous warning to the list: Beware, beware, comrades of anyone or any doctrine that tells you that any man, or group of men, holds a monopoly on truth, or on the ways of getting truth.[13]

A few months later, in his resignation letter of May 21, Burnham decided Trotsky was right about Marxism and for that reason he could no longer consider himself a Marxist. He recognized that "dialectical materialism though scientifically meaningless, is psychologically and historically an integral part of Marxism."[14] He was embarrassed about abandoning the Workers' Party group, which he had led in splitting from the Socialist Workers' Party and stated that he should have left several years ago but was inhibited by feelings of personal obligation. He also observed that "no man should be so brash as to imagine that he knows clearly the motives and springs of his own actions" and conceded that the whole letter might be an overly elaborate way of saying, "I feel like quitting politics."[15] Nevertheless, he felt that "at every single one of the many tests provided by history, Marxist movements have either failed socialism or betrayed it" and he wanted out.[16]

Burnham offered to leave the party quietly, to allow it to expel him, to take a six-month leave of absence, or even to continue writing for the party press for two months. A few months later he published a best-selling book, *The Managerial Revolution,* which developed themes from the debates within the Trotskyist movement about Stalinism and Nazism for a general audience.[17] His subsequent books, *The Struggle for World Power* and *The Suicide of the West,* were openly anti-Communist.

Sources of Disillusionment

Tens of thousands of Communists and fellow travelers followed the pattern exemplified here by Burnham and Shachtman. A number of them wrote memoirs and autobiographies chronicling their ideological journeys. Perhaps the best known of these books was a collection titled *The God That Failed,* which was edited by British parliamentarian Richard Crossman and included essays by Arthur Koestler, Richard Wright, Louis Fischer, Ignazio Silone, André Gide, and Stephen Spender.[18] These men were all writers and intellectuals who were active in Communist movements. Koestler elaborated his insights in book-length autobiographical volumes, as did writers Max Eastman and Eugene Lyons.[19] Books of this kind continue to be published, including the memoirs of writer Howard Fast published in 1990.[20]

There have also been a number of memoirs by party leaders and activists who were not primarily intellectuals. These included Louis Budenz and Whittaker Chambers, who became involved in anti-Communist movements in the 1950s.[21] Chambers's book caused a tremendous controversy because of his accusations against State Department official Alger Hiss. The writings of Yugoslavian Communist turncoat Milovan Djilas were also very influential, because of his insider status and his personal acquaintance of Stalin and Tito.[22] Dorothy Healey, a leader of the Communist Party in Los Angeles from 1928 to 1973, has recently published her memoirs.[23]

These books had a significant impact on public opinion because they explained the writers' disillusionment with socialism through personal experiences and feelings. Although they differ in details and perspectives, they make many of the same basic points. These will be summarized here.

Utopianism. Most of the apostates had a highly idealized view of socialism and of the Soviet Union, which seemed to be based on their sensitivity to flaws in the Western societies in which they lived. Louis Budenz reports that "knowing some of our ills at home, we began to build a Paradise on the Volga and Vistula and across the Siberian Steppes."[24] This utopian imagery was easier to maintain when the utopia was far away, but many believers made trips to the Soviet Union and managed to see what they expected to see.[25] Often they praised things in the Soviet Union that they hated at home; vegetarians praised slaughter houses and back-to-nature enthusiasts were enthralled by mass production in polluting factories.

As a teenager growing up in a leftist immigrant family in the 1920s, Dorothy Healey disciplined herself to read a little Marx and Engels, but she was inspired by Upton Sinclair, Charles Beard, Henry David Thoreau, and Walt Whitman. In her reading, she responded to "emotional rather than theoretical questions. I was developing a hatred of the brutality of the existing economic system, a hatred of the impersonal degradation of human beings." As a Young Communist League activist in the 1930s, she was totally absorbed in her work in protest movements. She had joined at a time when capitalism seemed to be collapsing, just as the Communists had predicted. They were "inspired by the Soviet example and felt that their success in building a new world was a token of our coming victory."[26] Her selective attention to the flaws of capitalism and the strengths of socialism was typical of true believers at the early stage of the process.

Growing Disillusionment and Repressed Doubt. Eugene Lyons was a young Communist journalist who had the opportunity to be a correspondent in the Soviet Union in the 1920s and 1930s. He took pride in being a radical journalist, superior to the correspondents of the bourgeois press in his commitment to the socialist project. He went to the Soviet Union with a pledge that:

> Whatever happens, I shall never attack the Soviet regime. . . . I knew the bitterness in my own heart against the Emma Goldmans and other "renegades" who had turned against the socialist fatherland. . . . they were white-livered, bourgeois-minded backsliders, namby-pamby liberals, tired radicals, if not actually on the payroll of Wall Street. Did the idiots think that a revolution could be made without terror and bloodshed? Their "objective" reports, their self-righteous horror, their lugubrious pity for the sufferings of the Russians—just transparent masks of their treachery to the cause.[27]

While serving as the United Press correspondent in Stalin's Moscow, however, Lyons was continually confronted with incidents and evidence that contradicted his idealized image of the Soviet Union. The trials of the old Bolsheviks were particularly disturbing, as he became convinced that most if not all of them were innocent and that they were being persecuted by an unjust and sadistic system. These were "my inner conclusions —conclusions some of which I buried far out of sight, because they would have inhibited me in serving the revolution."[28]

Keeping these conclusions buried was difficult when he was confronted with dramatic evidence of the brutal persecution of the peasants during the forced collectivization drive. The sixty-five days between Stalin's launching of the slogan "liquidation of the kulaks as a class," on December 27, 1929, and his rescinding of the order on March 2, 1930, were particularly difficult. Lyons reported that:

> The concentrated terror of the sixty-five days marked a frontier in my thinking and feeling. For two years I had been building an intricate structure of justifications for the Soviet regime. Now, without my willing it, the structure began to disintegrate around me. The color and the strength seemed to have run out of the symbols of the faith for me; the socialist slogans and songs, the brave revolutionary promises, the parades and invocations for a better world, now seemed to me touched with mockery.[29]

His critical thoughts began to find their way into his journalistic reports, but in the main he refrained from criticizing the Soviet regime on the theory, widely held among his colleagues, that "victories must be exaggerated, failures denied, and the vision of a socialist fatherland nurtured at all costs."[30] Even after he returned to New York, he found it difficult to tell his story because of his "desire to 'belong,' not to be a political dog in the manger."[31] Finally he overcame these inhibitions and published an article, titled "To Tell or Not to Tell" in *Harper's* magazine.

Looking back after his apostasy, Lyons recognized that:

> The fact, however, that I pledged myself in advance to silence was proof that doubts gnawed at the core of my faith. The very speed and heat with which I consigned critics of the new Russia to the outer darkness of impotent liberalism and foul renegacy showed that I dreaded their corroding effects upon my untarnished beliefs.[32]

Max Eastman abandoned his belief in Soviet Marxism gradually after a great deal of difficult and conflicted thinking, turning first to Trotskyism and then to a loosely defined radicalism before abandoning the leftist vision altogether. He became a specialist in Soviet politics, translating Trotsky's *History of the Russian Revolution,* and was disillusioned by the purges of the old Bolsheviks. Even more upsetting to his rational mind than the Russian reign of terror was:

> the stupidity with which so many Americans swallowed down the phantasmagorical "confessions" with which its true meaning was concealed from the real world. To me it was sickening to see supposedly intelligent people surrender their good sense to the self-refuting notion that all the known leaders of the October revolution, builders of the Soviet state, had been treacherous and contemptible fiends, except only one, and that one, by a sublimely improbable accident, the very man who had managed to concentrate all power in his hands.[33]

Despite this strong reaction, he clung to his socialist beliefs for many months, at least in his conscious mind, until one day at a cocktail party the hostess suddenly asked him:

> "Aside from these Russian developments, do you still believe in the socialist idea?"
> I said, "No," and I could not have said it with more conviction if I had made the decision months before. My mind had made it, I suppose, but at that moment I threw off the constraining emotions, the conception of self, the position in society, the way of life—the *being a believer* as well as the belief.[34]

Kronstadts. Loss of belief is often a gradual, almost undetectable process. The vague doubts accumulate until they are brought into acute awareness by a particularly troublesome event. The classic example was the repression by the new Soviet government of a revolt by the revolutionary sailors at the Kronstadt naval base in 1921. As Daniel Bell observed:

> Every radical generation, it is said, has its Kronstadt. For some it was the Moscow Trials, for others the Nazi-Soviet Pact, for still others Hungary (the Rajk Trial or 1956), Czechoslovakia (the defenestration of Masaryk in 1948 or the Prague Spring of 1968), the Gulag, Cambodia, Poland (and there will be more to come). My Kronstadt was Kronstadt.[35]

Often the Kronstadt is a minor event that the person happens to experience personally. Ignazio Silone's came at a meeting of the Communist International when the delegates were required to condemn a resolution by Trotsky that none of them had read. Richard Wright was physically thrown out of the Communist ranks in a May Day parade after he had resigned from the Party because it interfered with his artistic development. Arthur Koestler gave a speech in which he stated that no party is infallible and "a harmful truth is better than a useful lie." When the half of the audience who were Communist Party members sat with folded arms while the other half applauded, he decided to resign from the Party.[36] Whittaker Chambers tells of a man who one day took a walk in Moscow and heard screams.[37] After idolizing Stalin, Milovan Djilas met him personally and found him to be a boorish man who thought it of no consequence whether his soldiers raped women as a diversion from the rigors of combat.[38]

More frequently, the Kronstadt people remember is a historical event such as, in the case of Louis Fisher, the Nazi-Soviet pact of 1939, or in the case of Dorothy Healey the invasion of Czechoslovakia in 1968.[39] These historical events, however, may be important primarily because they provide a justification for apostasy. Fisher had doubts for many years, but resisted acknowledging them. He noted that "What counts decisively is the 'Kronstadt.' Until its advent, one may waver emotionally or doubt intellectually or even reject the cause altogether in one's mind and yet refuse to attack it. I had no 'Kronstadt' for many years."[40]

During these years of wavering, Fisher kept balancing his doubts off against the perceived strengths of the Soviet system. The Soviets may have been undemocratic, but they were helping the Spanish Republic and standing up to Hitler. Also, if he announced his "Kronstadt" he would lose many friends and connections in the Soviet Union. Finally, the Nazi-Soviet pact provided such a strong argument that he publicly announced his apostasy. If he had not been ready to do so, however, he could have easily agreed with others who justified it as necessary to defend the Soviet Union. He felt the Nazi-Soviet pact was big enough to justify his public renunciation to himself and to others.

Organizational Conflicts and Splits. When people join an organization with others who share their ideals and commitments, they expect a feeling of enthusiasm, camaraderie, and mutual support. At first, this is often what they find. With time, however, the relationships often go sour. When Louis Budenz first met leading Communist Party members in 1921, he observed that "they were chummy together then, and neither they nor I could guess that in a few short years they would be castigating each other as the spawn of Hell, or its equivalent in Communist jargon. When Reds fall out, throttles are wide open on expletives and execrations."[41]

Living with this kind of conflict was especially difficult for American Communists in the heyday of the Party, because the Party dominated its members' personal and social lives. Dorothy Healey's mother had to fight Party discipline because she insisted on talking with her own son who was a Trotskyist.[42] The Party went so far as to approve marriages, and people got into trouble if their wife was not a member. This interference with personal lives often caused problems even when the Party was cohesive. When a split occurred, personal relationships got crossed and more people found that their lives would be simplified if they distanced themselves from Party and ideological life.

Splits are particularly discouraging for those who find themselves on the losing side. Many of the ninety-five Philadelphia Communists active in the 1930s who were interviewed by Paul Lyons were led to break with the Party as a result of the split between the Fosterites and the Gatesites.[43] This was a classic split between orthodox and reformist factions. When the orthodox faction won, the reformers began to leave the Party. In leaving, many cited Kronstadts such as Stalin's purge trials, Soviet anti-Semitism, or the invasion of Hungary in 1956. Others left because of personal Kronstadts. Philadelphia Communist Al Silverman was shocked when he learned from a friend that American Party "hatchetmen" had killed a North Carolina Party member in Spain during the Civil War. His sin was alleged Trotskyist sympathies.[44] The assassins were confronted about the killing by American Party veterans at a Party meeting and did not deny it. They were elected to leadership posts in the New York Party. Silverman was also given a hard time from the Party when he married a woman who was not a Party member and when he attended a Trotskyist meeting. He was allowed to keep the wife, but had to promise never to attend a Trotskyist meeting again.

Dorothy Healey may have set a record as the longest surviving member of the Gatesite reformist faction. She was a Party leader in Los Angeles where the local Party organization maintained considerable independence from the national organization. She focused as much as possible on local activism and tried to put the Party's problems out of her mind. When a group of friends urged her to leave in 1958, she replied "I'm not gong to let those bastards have the Party." The invasion of Czechoslovakia in 1968 was her Kronstadt in that it was the "beginning of the end of my years of involvement." She was "fed up with the internal bickering and despondent about the possibility of ever making any real change in the Party's outlook." She finally left in 1973 over a minor incident, Party criticism of a book of memoirs by apostate Al Richmond.[45]

Even if people are not strongly drawn to one side or another in a split, or do not care much about the issues being discussed, they often find the internal conflicts frustrating and tiresome. This can lead to a gradual erosion of belief. In his study of apostates among leftist American writers in the 1920s and 1930s, Daniel Aaron found that "It seems to have been boredom that repelled them and killed their zeal, the rituals of meetings where nothing of importance was discussed, the discovery that one's comrades, among the leaders and the rank and file, were ignorant or vulgarly ambitious or unpleasant."[46]

Perhaps because of the anger they engender, open turncoats from political movements are rare. Most people just fade away. After the initial enthusiasm wanes, ideological politics often becomes routinized and dull. If the number of turncoats and dropouts exceeds the number of recruits, an *avant garde* movement can quickly deteriorate into a band of diehards. Irving Howe described the depressing atmosphere in a faltering political movement:

> You feel as if you have been invaded by some mysterious sickness. . . . leaders lose their power to persuade; the bonds of fraternity crack; the very aroma of the movement—the air in the office, the mood at a meeting—turns bad. It's no longer a pleasure to go down to the party headquarters. . . . at meetings everyone seems to be counting the house. For the few to whom it matters, this decline can be agonizing, like a secret, nagging pain.[47]

Louis Budenz remained loyal to the Party despite a number of events that might have been Kronstadts for him. He objected to the Party calling strikes to keep arms from being shipped to Great Britain during the Nazi-Soviet pact. He had grave doubts about the honesty of the referenda in the Baltic republics in which over 90 percent were reported to have voted for incorporation into the Soviet Union. He felt, however, that there were "bigger questions involved," which overshadowed his objections. He finally left just after Pearl Harbor when the Party was newly legitimate because of its support of the war effort. As Party struggles became less urgent, and the persecution less severe, it seemed less necessary to put up with the tiresomeness of internal Party life:

> It was as though I had performed my assignment from the Party and was now intent upon putting my own personal house in order. . . . Perhaps the stifling air of bureaucracy was strangling me and I was seeking to free my soul. One thing I can note as having been of some consequence. That was the general morbidity of so many of my comrades, their furtive unhappiness with life and the unendurable aspect of the years stretching ahead of them. In my capacity as managing editor of the paper, many avowals of moral weariness were given me.[48]

Alternative Ideologies. People's beliefs do not necessarily change when they leave an organization because of internal splits or organizational decline. If they are part of an orthodox faction that loses a power struggle, they may join a purist splinter group. If they are reformists, they may choose another organization that is less dogmatic than the one they are leaving. Al Silverman, Dorothy Healey, and some other Gatesites joined Democratic Socialists of America. They continued to call themselves "socialists," defining the term in a social democratic way. Democratic Socialists of America is a small social democratic organization, which appeals to many alumni of both the old and the new left whose views have moderated but who feel nostalgic about the socialist label.

The most dramatic turncoats are those who adopt a new ideology diametrically opposed to their old one. Louis Budenz returned to the Catholic faith of his youth, largely because he thought it offered an answer to the moral emptiness he found in the Party:

> I read in a Chicago paper the oft-repeated tale of the "fanaticism and boundless energy" of the Communists. . . . I happen to know that in countless cases this endless activity arises from a feverish desire to get away from the deep challenges of life. There was a balm for such moral illnesses, I knew—and it lay in the Catholic Church and its Sacraments.[49]

After deciding consciously to leave the Party, Budenz made preparations. He moved to another community and made a new set of friends. He got in touch with some Church leaders, to make sure he would be welcomed back. His total renunciation of socialist ideology was thus facilitated by having a new faith community to replace it. Whittaker Chambers made similar arrangements and became involved in Quakerism as an alternative. People with an alternative community and support system find it easier to abandon an ideology altogether and may also be encouraged to turn against their former cobelievers as a way of affirming their new faith.

For others, such as James Burnham and Max Eastman, finding employment that did not depend on their former connections facilitated a complete ideological break. For a writer, breaking with a sectarian group may open up new publishing opportunities. Burnham published a successful non-Marxist book and joined the staff of the *National Review*. After a period of uncertainty, Eastman carried his new beliefs to what he thought was their logical conclusion and became a believer in free enterprise and a staff writer for the *Reader's Digest*. Arthur Koestler made a successful career as a writer largely by writing about his own loss of faith.

Ironically, turncoats who move ahead professionally sometimes retain more of the scientific core of their earlier beliefs than true believers who put symbolism ahead of scientific analysis. Arthur Koestler said that:

> Although today I reject the End-justifies-the-Means ethics of Marxism;
> its rigid economic determinism; its dogma of the irreconcilable hostility

between the classes; the rudimentary character of its mass-psychology, and in fact, most of its basic tenets I have nevertheless retained a residue of the Marxian method of approach as a valuable asset. I also still believe that the elimination of Marx and Engels from the history of human thought would leave a gap almost as large as the elimination of Darwin.[50]

Sidney Hook noted that after Max Eastman left Marxism as a political movement, he continued to think as a historical materialist:

> There was a puzzling and unwonted dogmatism about Eastman's shift to an extreme laissez-faire economic and social policy. It had the character of a religious conversion, and it surprised many of his friends and admirers, for whom he had personified, despite his shifting allegiances, something of the eternal rebel. In jettisoning Marx's view that the socialization of production would inevitably lead to a new birth of human freedom, in favor of Hayek's contention that it would necessarily result in human slavery, he seemed unaware that he was still subscribing to the historical materialist dogma that the mode of economic production was the decisive factor in human culture.[51]

Eastman would have replied that he was retaining the valid scientific core from Marxism while reinterpreting it in view of new evidence. Indeed, he wrote a book on this very point.[52] Since he still accepted the Marxist theory that the economic organization of society largely determined political and cultural life, he was forced to the conclusion that the political horrors of Stalinism were inherent in socialism as an economic system. Hook, on the other hand, was able to retain his belief in socialism as a moral ideal by rejecting the core of Marxism as a scientific theory. In his view, socialism failed in the Soviet Union because its leaders betrayed their ideals, not because of anything inherent in socialist economic organization.

Conclusions

Lack of Utilitarian Calculation. Several things one might expect to find are missing from the memoirs of turncoats from Communism. So far as I have been able to find there is no one who sat down and listed the pluses and minuses of Communism and decided that on balance it was not worth it. This sort of utilitarian calculation of "the greatest good for the greatest number" is very difficult because there are too many unknowns. People seem to unconsciously adjust their estimates of the costs and benefits to get the outcome they want.

There is also no one who reports having been persuaded by a speaker, article, or book by anyone on the other side. If anything, pressures from opponents seem to have inhibited people from defecting. Many Communists felt that to defect during the McCarthy period would have been cowardice, giving in under pressure. Perhaps the people who did this did not write books about it. People on the fringes of the movement were certainly scared away. Committed believers, however, seem less inclined to give in under pressure than to defect during the boring periods when no one is paying much attention to what they say or do.

Differences between Protestors and Authoritarians. Another surprising point is the dearth of parallel literature by apostates from the other side. This is particularly true of supporters of Nazi Germany. There is a book called *The Other God That Failed* about Nazi sociologist Hans Freyer who tired of the Nazi regime when he found that his own mail was being opened and when some of his conservative friends were fired from the university where he worked. Freyer went through a process of disillusionment together with "many other German intellectuals who went from identification with the regime through stages of doubt, skepticism, concern, and antipathy before the German defeat in 1945."[53]

Their antipathy, however, was rooted largely in the fact that the Nazi repression went beyond Jews, gypsies, and Communists and began to impact on them. After the war, many Nazi sympathizers disguised their past or went into hiding. Many continue to deny that the Nazi genocides even took place. There is little or no evidence of the kind of crisis of belief that characterized the Communist turncoats.

This is a central difference between protestors and authoritarians in general, as it was between Stalin and Trotsky. Protestors take their ideals seriously and regret what they believe to be the necessity of repressing people in their behalf. Authoritarians have few if any such regrets and even value repression as an end in itself. Authoritarians mourn when their side loses power. Protestors mourn the loss of their illusions when their side wins.

Mourning Ideological Loss. Elisabeth Kübler-Ross describes five stages people go through in accepting the imminence of death: denial, anger, bargaining, depression, and acceptance.[54] Ideological apostates go through similar stages in mourning the death of a cherished belief. Of course, biological death is ultimately undeniable while loss of ideological faith can be denied indefinitely, so the analogy is imperfect. But apostates do begin with nagging doubts, which they deny in their conscious minds. They frequently display displaced anger, directed at apostates who have come out of the closet or at anyone who reminds them of their repressed doubts.

The terminally ill sometimes try to make bargains with God or fate such as promising to do good works if only their life is spared. This "bargaining" process is much more pronounced in the death of an ideological belief. Ideological apostates go through a process of reconceptualizing and redefining their beliefs in the hopes of salvaging them. They in effect promise to bury the most offensive or unsatisfactory of their beliefs if only they can be spared the agony of admitting that they have done so. This process is often much more successful than bargaining with God to escape an illness, but the new watered-down beliefs typically lack the emotional force of the original convictions. They may not be strong enough to prevent the onset of depression as the believer mourns the loss of vigorous emotional conviction even while continuing to deny any fundamental change on the cognitive level.

The depressed stage often lasts for many years, during which many activists simply shy away from political involvement or activity. They think of themselves as "burned out" and needing time for personal growth and replenishment. Making new friends from different social circles and finding meaning in new activities and commitments are important tasks during this period.

Many apostates never fully accept the fact that they have lost faith in their beliefs. They simply go on indefinitely in a more or less depressed state, never admitting the reality of the change. Full acceptance of change requires that one "come out of the closet" and run the risk of embarrassment or rejection by old friends and associates. "Kronstadts" can be a useful part of this process by providing a clear and well-articulated rationale for change. Accepting one's new status as a nonbeliever lifts the burden of repressed doubt and opens up the possibility of making new commitments unhindered by dead weight from the past.

Chapter Eleven

The Sixties: Failure of a Generation?

There is an ongoing struggle today to define the sixties. On one side are conservatives who agree with President Reagan that the Vietnam War was a "noble cause" and the sixties an ignoble decade. On the other are those old associates of mine (Abbie Hoffman comes to mind) who adamantly express no regrets about their activities in those years.

—Tom Hayden, 1988

When Tom Hayden went to Port Huron, Michigan, for the 1962 summer retreat of a tiny group called Students for a Democratic Society (SDS), he had no idea that he would be writing the manifesto of a generation.[1] The *Port Huron Statement* defined the theme for a New Left, which rejected the dogmatism, sectarianism, and elitism that had defeated the left of the previous generation.[2] Filled with the utopian optimism of youth, the young radicals were confident that they would not repeat the mistakes of their elders. They had little patience for slightly older radicals such as Michael Harrington who warned them against being too tolerant of leftist sectarian groups.

The New Left's hopes of avoiding sectarianism lasted less than a decade. In 1969 Students for a Democratic Society was destroyed by sectarian wrangling that made the struggle between the Gatesites and the Fosterites in the American Communist Party look like a high-school debate. By the midseventies the New Left was history and the New Right was on the rise.

Although the sixties were predominately a liberal and radical decade, the conservative Young Americans for Freedom was a product of the same generation.[3] It represented a small minority of the youth of the era but it still exists today, and its ideas are more influential than ever. The leaders of Students for a Democratic Society have been pushed to the fringes of American society, swept with Trotsky into what he derisively called the wastebasket of history. By contrast, many of the conservative youth leaders have matured into positions of real power.[4] All of them have had the satisfaction of seeing their ideas adopted as official state policies.[5]

If we just compared the fate of these two vanguard groups we would have to conclude that the radicals failed and the conservatives succeeded in their historical missions. But the picture is more complex. Many other political tendencies and groups flourished in the 1960s and many have had a lasting impact on American society. The civil rights movement, which began in the fifties, continued throughout the sixties and evolved new militant tendencies preaching black power and separatism. The feminist movement, which largely grew out of the New Left, survived and flourished as a force of its own. The antiwar movement declined after the Vietnam War but revived in the form of the nuclear freeze movement, the movements in support of Central American revolutions, and the movement against the 1991 Gulf War. The indignation many conservatives feel about leftist "political correctness" on university campuses in the nineties shows that the left retains a significant power base in American universities.

The psychological and social factors that led to radicalism in the sixties are undoubtedly still with us, and whatever we can learn from the sixties may help us to avoid repeating many of the mistakes that were made then. Despite a tremendous amount of theorizing, writing, and research, however, the reasons for the explosion of radicalism in the sixties remain controversial and poorly understood. None of the analysts predicted the explosion of the movement before it occurred, and none of them anticipated that it would die down as quickly as it did. Most of the research was quite partisan, either for or against, and the arguments were predictable. The mostly young, leftist social scientists who supported the radical movement heralded it as a prophetic new generation liberated from the psychological hangups of the past. They published a number of scientific studies, which argued that the new radicals were less authoritarian and more empathetic, nurturant, self-aware, and self-actualized than nonradical students.[6] Their studies used objective questionnaires and seemed quite objective and scientific when compared to the polemical writings of the anti–New Left authors who generally offered little more than their own personal feelings and observations.

These usually older, more conservative professors were understandably outraged when their classes were disrupted by unruly radicals.[7] Some of them dismissed the student revolt as an Oedipal rebellion aimed at taking the "alma mater" away from the male faculty. When the students at the University of California at Berkeley rebelled against the University administration, Professor Lewis Feuer argued that they "projected upon the Impersonal Knowledge Factory and the Administration all the traits which would justify their revolt; their fruitless rebellion never reached to the unconscious cause within themselves, the inner, inaccessible Being who tyrannized over and emasculated them."[8]

Unfortunately, Feuer had little to say about the nature of this "inaccessible being." Nor did he explain why this "being" suddenly became so tyrannical in the sixties after being quiescent in the fifties.

The analysis of the New Left as a "liberated generation" went sour very quickly, however, when the leading New Left organizations split apart in sectarian factionalism. The "me generation" replaced the "liberated generation" in the mass media, and cultural critics argued that the two were really the same. A new revisionist analysis of the sixties argued that the New Leftists were motivated by a narcissistic preoccupation with their own need to inflate their egos and express hostility and frustration.[9]

The most rigorous and comprehensive psychological study of New Left radicals supports this contention. Rothman and Lichter administered projective psychological tests to samples of radical activists and found them to be characterized by weakened self-esteem, injured narcissism, and paranoid tendencies.[10] They found that many radicals were motivated by a preoccupation with power, which attracted them to radical ideologies, which answered their doubts and offered clear and unambiguous answers to their problems.

Rothman and his colleagues discounted the earlier questionnaire studies on the grounds that most respondents do not understand themselves well enough to give accurate responses on questionnaires. The validity of projective psychological tests when applied to this (or any) population, however, can also be questioned. Highly educated respondents understand that a projective test is intended to get at their unconscious feelings and thoughts. It may be that people who are more open and "in touch with their feelings" are less inhibited and express feelings and thoughts that are repressed by the apparently healthier subjects.

Ultimately, psychological tests of whatever kind have to be validated with behavioral studies or qualitative interviews of the same population. Rothman and Lichter failed to do this, which forced them to be highly tentative in their conclusions. This chapter uses biographical materials to help fill this gap by looking in some depth at the life histories of important sixties activists. Of course, we do not have a representative sample and our cases are weighted heavily toward the interesting minority of sixties radicals who have become turncoats. We will, therefore, also review some other studies that have used more systematic samples.

Theoretically, this chapter goes beyond the psychological reductionism of both the "liberated generation" and the "culture of narcissism" schools. Neither of these approaches really captures the personalities of the New Left radicals as they are revealed in biographies, nor can either explain the rise and fall of radicalism as a social movement. Whatever the psychological needs of activist youth, there is no reason to believe that they change markedly from one decade to the next. Script theory and the theory of group psychodynamics offer more potential for drawing the links between psychological and sociological phenomena.

Script theory suggests that the collapse of sixties radicalism was the failure of a utopian script that appealed to people with a wide variety of personality traits. This utopian script attracted idealistic young people with a sincere desire to change the world as well as many students who were simply swept up in the enthusiasm of the time.[11] The movement failed because, like most utopians, the New Left radicals lacked a realistic social analysis or an adequate understanding of their own motivations and needs. An understanding of group psychodynamics would have helped them to cope with the inevitable factional, personality, and leadership conflicts involved in building an effective organization.

The New Left leadership was naive in believing that it was exempt from these patterns, which it knew very well from the experiences of the "old left." This kind of naive expectation of a simple and dramatic transformation to an untroubled world is, of course, the hallmark of the utopian script. As the failure of the movements to cope with these problems became apparent, the mass following disappeared, leaving behind a hard core of true believers many of whom may well have been driven by narcissistic and paranoid personality patterns. Fortunately, these true believers failed to win power and were marginalized.

To say that the sixties generation failed is not to say that the individuals who happened to be born into that generation were failures or that they had no impact on society. What failed was a social movement based on the utopian promise of a Liberated Generation, which would bring about a new societal consciousness. That vision was born in Port Huron in 1962 and peaked in 1970 with the publication of Charles Reich's *The Greening of America: How the Youth Revolution Is Trying to Make America Livable.*[12] Ironically, Reich's best-seller appeared just as the youth revolution was consuming itself with sectarian squabbling.

The New Left

Tom Hayden. Tom Hayden grew up in Royal Oak, Michigan, a working-class suburb of Detroit, where he attended the Catholic school in the parish of anti-Communist radio preacher Father Charles Coughlin. His accountant father was a World War II veteran who spent a lot of time drinking at the local American Legion hall before divorcing Tom's mother. His librarian mother was a liberal Catholic who tried to shield him from Coughlin's opinions. He "dealt with the insecurity of being an outsider by becoming a brainy, advanced kid in class, winning spelling contests and reading aloud from Saint Thomas Aquinas to enrapture the nuns in second grade."[13]

He had been named after Thomas Aquinas, but when he went to public high school he made Jewish friends and could not accept the doctrine that they were fated to roast in hell because they had been born into a different religion. Although he was rebellious in high school, he was first exposed to radicalism as a political philosophy as a freshman at the University of Michigan. As a writer for the student newspaper, he covered political activism and visited Berkeley, California, where the student movement was exploding. As a promising young activist he was recruited by Al Haber, an organizer sent out by the League for Industrial Democracy (LID) in New York. The LID was a small educational and propaganda arm of the anti-Communist left. It hoped to build a student affiliate in order to spread the social democratic gospel to a new generation.

The Student League for Industrial Democracy took off beyond the LID's wildest expectations. In doing so it split from its parent and became Students for a Democratic Society. Tom has no idea where he and his friends got the self-confidence to define themselves as the voice of a new generation: "I still don't know where this messianic sense, this belief in being right, this confidence that we could speak for a generation came from. But the time was right, vibrating with potential."[14]

The appeal of this utopian vision to Tom's psyche was strong enough to change his life. It promised purpose and excitement for his life. He had been studying to be a reporter and he was good at it. He had offers from major newspapers, but much to his parents' dismay he passed them by to become a full-time activist. In addition to his writing ability and personal charm, he had a gift for sensing the spirit of the times and the courage to throw caution to the wind. Many of his activist friends remained in graduate school, just to be on the safe side. Tom decided to make a career of radical politics.

Tom's first wife, Casey, was a tall, attractive blonde whose mission in life was to work with the civil rights movement in the south. She gave up working in the south to earn a living as a secretary in Ann Arbor in order to support his activities. Casey and many of the other women in the movement resented the secondary role they were asked to play in leftist organizations. Casey introduced feminism to SDS with a paper she coauthored in 1965 titled "Sex and Caste: A kind of memo from Casey Hayden and Mary King to a number of other women in the peace and freedom movements." Feminist rage exploded in the organization, astonishing the male leaders who were used to being fawned over by adoring female followers.[15] Tom and Casey were divorced, a failure he, in typical New Left fashion, "understood not so much as a personal failure but yet another example of how society dehumanized and atomized us all."[16] Providing this kind of rationale for externalizing personal problems is a central psychological function of protest scripts.

Hayden differs from most protestors in his ability to supplement protest with pragmatic and survivor scripts.[17] He usually manages to be where the action is and to parlay his involvement into a prominent leadership role. When the radical movement was growing, he helped to develop the Economic Research and Action Project of SDS, working as a community organizer in Newark, New Jersey. He was there for the Newark riots and wrote a book defending them.[18] After helping the students at Columbia University to capture the campus Mathematics Building in 1968, he helped to organize the protests at the Democratic Convention in Chicago, which led to a police riot and demolished Hubert Humphrey's chance of defeating Richard Nixon. He was indicted as one of the organizers of the demonstration and stood trial as one of the group that became known as the Chicago Seven. Their convictions were eventually overturned because of the gross misconduct of the judge and the prosecuting attorneys.

From 1969 to 1971, he lived with the Red Family commune in Berkeley where he tried to keep up with the progressive radicalization of the New Left. When SDS split between the Weatherpeople and Progressive Labor factions, he sided with the Weatherpeople considering them "the natural final generation of SDS, the true inheritors of everything that had happened from 1960 on."[19] He founded an International Liberation School, which trained revolutionaries for the forthcoming armed struggle.

His disillusionment with the extremes of New Left radicalism was triggered by the group dynamics of the Red Family commune where he lived. He was what sixties radicals called a "star" or a "male heavy." Like other organizations, radical groups depended on these leaders in the early stages of their development. Ideologically, however, they opposed strong leadership, especially from men, in favor of participatory democracy, feminism, and egalitarianism. As the interpersonal tensions in the Red Family grew, Hayden was scapegoated and subjected to extensive "criticism/

self-criticism" sessions. It got so bad that his own lover, Anne Weills, denounced him for "bourgeois privatism" and "elitism." The final outcome, as Hayden observed in good Freudian terms, was "the ritual killing of the father figure."[20]

Fortunately, the killing was only symbolic. He was humiliated and depressed. He moved to Los Angeles and lived under an assumed name for a period of time while he rethought his extremist views. He became involved in supporting the McGovern campaign in 1972 and met his second wife, actress Jane Fonda, at a peace rally in Ann Arbor, Michigan. He decided to build a political career for himself in California, capitalizing on Fonda's money and fame and his own leadership and organizational skills.

From the start, he had rejected the socialist label, telling Michael Harrington it was a European word, which would cut the movement off from an American audience.[21] In California, he replaced it with something he called Economic Democracy, which is more or less the same as the social democracy of the LID.[22] The leading theorist of economic democracy, Derek Shearer, argues that "no amount of wishful thinking on the part of the left" is going to change socialism's bad name with the American public and suggests that the term Economic Democracy is a useful "euphemism for democratic socialism."[23] His Coalition for Economic Democracy sounded new enough to appeal to many radicals in California, yet was not quite offensive enough to keep him from being elected to the state legislature from Santa Monica. He traveled to Hanoi and supported the Khmer Rouge in Cambodia when they appeared to be progressive anti-imperialists, but recanted his support when their atrocities became known. His marriage to actress Jane Fonda, during her radical phase, added to his celebrity status, but he would probably have had a successful political career in any event.

Abbie Hoffman. Tom Hayden's praise of Abbie Hoffman as an example of a sixties radical who was still true to his beliefs in 1988 was typical. Abbie was everybody's favorite sixties radical who never sold out. It became poignantly ironic when Hoffman took his own life with a massive dose of barbiturates in 1989.[24] Hoffman had suffered from manic-depressive illness for many years but was thought to have the condition under control. He even planned to write a book about it. He coped with his illness while living underground from 1974 to 1980.[25]

Why did he kill himself in 1989, at age fifty-two, when he was safe from legal persecution and was widely admired for his lifelong commitment to his countercultural lifestyle? The press treated him as a cultural icon when he was arrested in 1987, along with former President Carter's daughter, in protests against Central Intelligence Agency recruiting.[26] He received generous speaking fees on college campuses, where the students saw him as a link to a colorful past. He had published several successful books. Why, then, was Abbie so unhappy that he chose to end his life?

Abbie Hoffman was born into a Jewish family in a wooden triple-decker in Worcester, Massachusetts. Although his politics was the epitome of adolescent rebellion—a cult of long hair, shabby clothes, and outrageous behavior—his relationship with his own parents was unexceptional. He "acted up" a lot and was often sent to his room without his dinner, but he had a cache of Devil Dogs and Tootsie Rolls hidden away there. His mother called on his father to spank him, but he learned that dungarees "absorbed all the whammy out of a whipping."27 Growing up during World War II, Abbie was embarrassed that his father was home supporting a family instead of fighting the war.

He was a troublemaker at Classical High School, telling jokes in class, carving things into the desks, smoking in the toilet, and wearing an odd pink-on-pink shirt. He was finally expelled for fighting with a boy who tore his shirt. But his parents got him into another high school where he graduated and went on to Brandeis University. At Brandeis, he studied with humanistic psychologist Abraham Maslow, Marxist philosopher Herbert Marcuse, and several other distinguished leftist intellectuals. He decided on a career in psychology and went to graduate school at Berkeley.

At Berkeley, his rebellious streak naturally attracted him to the radical activism that was breaking out at the time. He participated in what became a historic protest when the House UnAmerican Activities Committee (HUAC) held hearings in San Francisco. He was still a good Jewish boy, however, and when his girlfriend got pregnant, he did the right thing and married her. They moved back east, and he took a job testing patients at a state mental hospital. He knew R. D. Laing and other radical psychologists who claimed that mental illness was a myth and the mentally ill an oppressed minority group, but he had the sense to recognize that many of his patients were "whacked out of their skulls."28

The last thing his patients at the hospital needed or wanted was to be organized into a protest movement. He found his job boring and got turned on to politics again when he went to a meeting that showed the film *Operation Abolition,* which exaggerated and distorted the "Communist" assault on HUAC in which he had participated in San Francisco. He protested during the discussion period and was hired by the American Civil Liberties Union to go around Massachusetts speaking against the film.

From this point on, Abbie found conventional work boring and activism exciting. When politics got dull, he livened it up with dramatic guerilla theater tactics. His most famous action was standing in the gallery of the New York Stock Exchange and throwing money onto the floor. It caused a minor disruption, but "in the minds of millions of teenagers the stock market had just crashed."[29] He and his friend Jerry Rubin organized the Youth International Party (Yippies) and planned creative, attention-grabbing hijinks such as sending marijuana cigarettes anonymously in the mail to establishment media figures. When Jerry was called before HUAC, he showed up stoned, wearing a Revolutionary War uniform and blowing bubbles.[30]

Hoffman's actions were good natured pranks and practical jokes, designed to produce a good time while making a point. For him, they were serious politics as well as fun. He wasn't just blowing off steam, he was making a revolution. His revolution wouldn't be an armed uprising with blood and gore, but a joyous sabotage of the stuffy establishment by young people who refused to follow the rules. He published a book titled *Steal this Book,* which was a practical guide to ripping off the system and living for free.[31] It included things such as wiring pay telephones to make free long distance calls and sitting down in cafeterias and finishing meals other patrons had left half eaten. The book sold well through counterculture channels, although most bookstores wouldn't stock it because of the title.

But making a revolution required more than pranks and petty theft. Hoffman wanted to unite his alienated youth with the traditional protest groups. This meant helping to organize many political actions that were not funny at all, such as the "Days of Rage" at the Democratic Party Convention in Chicago in 1968. As he grew older, the contradiction between youthful exuberance and serious politics became more acute. When the Republicans held their 1972 convention in Miami Beach, Hoffman and Rubin worried that massive disruptions would only help the Republicans to sabotage McGovern's antiwar campaign. They were attacked as revisionists by young orthodox "Zippies" within their own Yippie party. The Zippies wanted to put the Zip back in Yip. They had been hearing about Chicago for four years, and they wanted their turn to vent their rage in the streets. The Zippies also organized other protests that Hoffman and Rubin found objectionable, such as a "Free Arthur Bremer" rally in support of the man who shot George Wallace and left him paralyzed for life. Hoffman's critique of them sounds like a middle-aged man tired of adolescent rebellion: "Their act got heavy handed. They made an enemy of anyone (including me) who did not see things their way. They were too quick to isolate themselves from other groups and the general population. Too willing to accept the smug arrogance provided by a closed cult."[32]

Still, he was their leader and he had to try to keep up with them. When he was charged with involvement in a cocaine deal, he decided to go underground rather than fight what might be a losing battle in court. He might have beaten the charges but his cause wasn't noble, and he had to admit he shouldn't have been involved in the "shenanigans." Going underground was difficult. His manic-depressive illness flared up, but he got some help from a Marxist psychiatrist and eventually settled into a new identity as Barry Freed, an environmental activist in upstate New York.[33] Being underground meant that he had to tone down his lifestyle to avoid attracting attention. He enjoyed the relief from being forced to protect his image in public. The excitement of being underground added a tinge of excitement to the venture, protecting him from boredom.

When he came out of hiding, he had to resume his celebrity identity. Being a celebrity made it difficult for Abbie to make a normal transition to an adult lifestyle. In his autobiography, he tells of a peaceful day when he and his wife were pushing their baby carriage through the park. Two policemen stopped to chat and play with the baby. It was a fine day until they noticed two amateur photographers getting ready to photograph the scene. They couldn't let such a photograph be published. How could they be seen fraternizing with police when their comrades had just been shot at Attica prison? They felt they had to insult the cops in order to quickly drive them away. Abbie felt that "The public image had been saved, but inside I was shattered. The insults were not real. To protect an image I was being forced to be something other than human."[34]

Abbie Hoffman, like Winston Churchill, suffered from a depressive illness, which was relieved when he was intensely involved in a cause. The manic phases of his illness probably helped him to carry his protests far enough beyond the bounds of propriety to make a dramatic impact. He got committed to a role as a celebrity, which made it difficult for him to settle into a mature but modest activist role. As Barry Freed he was able to do this, but as Abbie Hoffman he could not.

Nor could he bring about the youth revolution he had dreamed about. As Abbie Hoffman, he was an oddball that everyone could love because they didn't find him threatening. Back in 1980, Norman Mailer had the sensitivity to observe that "given his life, given his immersion in a profound lack of security, in a set of identity crises that would splat most of us like cantaloupes thrown off a truck, it is prodigious that he is now neither dead nor demented."[35] Despite his antics, Abbie was always in good touch with reality. As long as he could believe that he was making the revolution, he could live with the strain. As Abbie Hoffman, curious relic of a bygone age, he could not.

Jerry Rubin. When Jerry Rubin went to the Republican convention in 1972, the Zippies criticized him for sleeping in a hotel instead of a park. They tried to throw a cake in his face to throw him out of the movement. When he refused to drop out of the leadership, a group of New York Zippies trashed his car. At the age of thirty-two, he was the leader of a national movement. By thirty-four, he was the subject of "where is he now" stories.[36] His girlfriend fell in love with someone else while he was in jail, and he was so depressed that friends slept over out of concern that he would commit suicide. He was sick of media attention and visits from young fans who would examine him carefully for flaws. Instead of trying to carve out a new political role or live up to his media image, Rubin sought help in the personal growth movement. In the sixties he had rejected therapy as "adjusting people to a sick system," believing that "social revolution was the only effective therapy." Now that the revolutionary movement had become the problem, not the solution, he tried one New Age remedy after another. In the five years from 1971 to 1975, he "directly experienced est, gestalt therapy, bioenergetics, rolfing, massage, jogging, health foods, tai chi, Esalen, hypnotism, modern dance, meditation, Silva Mind Control, Arica, acupuncture, sex therapy, Reichian therapy, and More House."[37] These activities filled his days from his 7:00 A.M. jog and his midday yoga session to his evening encounter group.

This odyssey seems to have worked. He abandoned the protest script and became a survivor. He got in touch with his feelings about his parents' deaths and about the people who wanted him to stay frozen in the role of a media icon. He learned that "people need me to fulfill the image of the devil so they can play the antidevil. I am the devil they fear they really are."[38] He also learned that he didn't have to play that game. He cut his hair and embarked on a career as a businessman. Using his celebrity status and skill as a promoter, he made a lot of money with a scheme called "Network America" in which people paid to go to parties where they might meet someone who could help them in their careers. He married, had a daughter, and settled into straight society.

At first Rubin's radical friends were outraged by his betrayal, but by the time of his fiftieth birthday party in 1988 most had forgiven him, and they were glad to celebrate his survival. Politically, Rubin had evolved into a "Bill Bradley Democrat." He felt his unique contribution was that "until me, nobody had really taken off their clothes and screamed out loud, 'It's O.K. to make money!' "[39]

Michael Harrington. At the Port Huron conference of SDS, Michael Harrington acted as the representative of the parent League for Industrial Democracy.[40] When he reviewed the draft of the Port Huron Statement he liked the emphasis on participatory democracy, but he could not accept the attacks on George Meany and the American union movement. He agreed with his mentor, Max Shachtman, that Walter Reuther, not George Meany, was the vanguard of the labor movement. He demanded a stronger critique of Soviet Communism.

In 1962 Harrington was a little too old to be accepted by the young radicals. As Hayden recalled, "There couldn't be a more perfect setup. We were giving birth to some new force in American politics. And Michael, purely by virtue of being older and having other attachments, was being an obstacle in the delivery room."[41]

Harrington recalls it the same way:

> I was thirty-four. I'd been a youth leader for so long that people were joking that I was "the oldest young socialist in America." . . . Now, I'm in this Oedipal situation. Up comes this younger generation. I think that they are ignoring my honest, sincere and absolutely profound advice. And this struck at my self-image. I think that part of my emotional overresponse was there: I interpreted this as an Oedipal assault on the father-figure.[42]

Harrington couldn't lead the New Left generation because his anti-Communism made him reluctant to oppose the Vietnam War. He was suspicious of the aims of the Viet Cong at a time when the New Left accepted them uncritically. He was also a committed socialist ideologue at a time when the New Left was into spontaneity and emotional genuineness. The New Left had to go through its growing pangs before it was ready for Harrington. When the utopianism went sour, Harrington was waiting in the wings to welcome disillusioned New Leftists into the social democratic fold.

Harrington's life centered around a shibboleth,* democratic socialism, which limited him to the fringes of American political life. I use the term shibboleth to refer to Harrington's advocacy of socialism because it was the *word* "socialism," not the content of his beliefs, which was essential to this process. To most people the word "socialism" implies government ownership of the means of production. Harrington rejected this definition. To him, socialism might mean cooperatives or worker ownership of small industries, or it might even mean a capitalist economy with a democratic socialist government such as those in Sweden or Austria.[43]

In his many books, articles, and speeches on the topic he could never make up his mind exactly what kind of socialism he preferred. He made it quite clear, however, that he sided with western democracy against Soviet Communism. Critics claimed that he was too credulous of the democratic aspirations of groups such as the Sandinistas in Nicaragua, but this in itself did not put him outside the fold of respectable American politics.

---

*a phrase, practice, or custom that is symbolic of a particular group, party, or ideological tendency.

Yet, despite the vagueness of the term's meaning and its certainty of being misunderstood by American audiences, he insisted on calling himself a socialist.

Harrington was a powerful orator and prolific writer whose energy, intellect, and political skills could have carried him much further than a university professorship and leadership of a small socialist organization. He worked closely with liberal politicians, and there was nothing in the substance of his beliefs that would have kept him from abandoning the stigma of the socialist label and seeking real political power. Yet he stubbornly clung to what members of his own organization, the Democratic Socialists of America, often referred to as "the S-word." He also insisted on calling himself a Marxist, even though he continually had to defend his interpretation of Marx as a democrat.

Socialism for Harrington was a substitute for religious faith. He was raised in a middle-class Irish Catholic community in St. Louis and was educated by Jesuits at the St. Louis University High School. He rejected the rationalist Christianity he was taught because he thought it was "not only monstrous but a violation of the principle of causality for God to decree the infinite punishment of hell for any finite human act, no matter how terrible it might be. Once I came to that position . . . the rationalist faith the Jesuits had jerry-built for me came tumbling down around my ears."[44]

Harrington was never comfortable with his renunciation of faith, however. Two years later, he returned to the fold after reading existentialist philosophers who argued that faith should be accepted precisely because it is absurd. Deeply moved by human suffering, he joined the Catholic Worker movement and lived among the poor in New York City. He found that, on an intellectual level, he couldn't continue to believe in God but described himself as a "pious apostate, an atheist shocked by the faithlessness of the believers."[45] He began his autobiography with this quote from Nietzsche's *Thus Spake Zarathustra:* "O Zarathustra, you are so pious for you believe with such disbelief. Some God in you drives you to this godlessness. Isn't it your piety itself that no longer permits you to believe in God?"[46]

His piety led him to socialism, which satisfied his need for a faith based on rational, scientific argumentation. He was comfortable in a sectarian socialist youth group where members scoured the writings of Marx, Lenin, and Trotsky in the hope of offering sage advice to the Vietnamese revolutionaries. In later life, he was aware of the irony of a group that had recruited only eighty-three members in its own country offering tactical advice to the leaders of mass revolutionary movements in other countries. He observed that "our Marxist sophistication stood in inverse relation to any possibility of changing the world."[47]

Harrington might have lived out his life in this happy obscurity if success had not rudely intervened. He felt it was his responsibility to bring the suffering of the poor to the attention of the American public and wrote an article for *Commentary* magazine based largely on his observations while working with the Catholic Worker group. A friend got him a contract with MacMillan and a $500 advance. He decided, without giving it much thought, not to mention "socialism" in *The Other America:* "I decided that if I even mentioned the word socialism, I would divert attention from the plight of the poor, evoke all the misconceptions Americans had about the term, and would then have to deal with the myths the word had conjured up."[48]

The strategy worked better than he ever imagined. A few months after the book came out, Dwight MacDonald published a lengthy review in the *New Yorker.* It caught the attention of John Kennedy and became the inspiration for the war on poverty. Harrington was in demand as a lecturer all over the country and found that he could make more money in an evening than a worker might earn in a month of labor. This success was more than he could handle. One Sunday evening in March 1965, he was about to give a speech when he felt faint and had to grip the side of the lectern in order to keep his balance. Soon he was in the midst of a full-fledged anxiety attack. As a sophisticated New York intellectual he knew all about Freud and the unconscious, but this was the first time he was face to face with his repressed feelings. Simple tasks like going to the post office were fraught with anxiety and had to be abandoned if the line was long or there was any other source of frustration. After four years of Freudian psychoanalysis, he concluded that:

> I was the victim of my own success, and the sudden access it offered to the fringes of power, the rewards of money, and the consolations of minor celebrity. . . . I refused to recognize who, or what, I was becoming. Eventually, all the turmoil and transition which my conscious self ignored could no longer be denied. If my rationality would not deal with it, then it would assert itself irrationally as an "it" which took control of my "I".[49]

Never again did Harrington write a book without the "S-word," and never again did he have a best-seller. After a long series of books on political themes, he returned to the topic of religion in *The Politics at God's Funeral* in which he took "democratic socialism as the point of departure in a search for the moral reformation of the Western world."[50] Recognizing that he had a dollop of St. Augustine with his Marx, he knew that the socialist ideal was tarnished and had no illusions about the likelihood of democratic socialism being established in his lifetime.

By remaining true to socialism as a symbol, Harrington maintained his self-image as an idealistic searcher after truth and justice, immune from the temptations of fame and fortune. He carved out a niche for himself in American society and attracted a small band of followers who were equally dedicated to socialism as an ideal, which set them apart from the American mainstream. In avoiding success so as not to compromise his protest script, however, he limited his impact both as a writer and as a political leader.

Defectors from the CIA. Joining the Central Intelligence Agency was a natural thing for a conservative southern white boy in the 1950s, and Philip Agee found the readings from anti-Communist defectors the most interesting part of his training.[51] While stationed in Latin America, however, he gradually came to the conclusion that the CIA was helping to shore up elitist and exploitative regimes. He reversed the imagery he had been taught in his CIA training, demonizing capitalism and idealizing Communism:

> When I joined the CIA, I believed in the need for its existence. After twelve years with the agency I finally understood how much suffering it was causing, that millions of people all over the world had been killed or had had their lives destroyed by the CIA and the institutions it supports.[52]

His first book was a detailed account of dirty deeds he had done in Uruguay and Ecuador. When he went on the lecture circuit people kept asking him why he defected. They would ask, "but where are *you*" in the book? At one meeting he finally blurted out, "Why did I leave the CIA? I fell in love with a woman who thought Che Guevara was the most wonderful man in town."[53]

At first he regretted this impromptu remark, but the crowd loved it, and on rethinking he found that it contained an element of truth. In his first book, he explained his defection in purely ideological terms, composing a letter to CIA director Helms, which portrayed the CIA as the agent of an imperialist capitalist class and the communists as the only hope of the poor and oppressed. He brushed aside the evils of communism, which he had studied at Langley: "Does KGB terror come packaged of necessity with socialism and communism? Perhaps, perhaps not, but for most of the people in Latin America the situation couldn't be much worse— they've got more pressing matters than the opportunity to read dissident writers."[54]

Agee knew all about the purge trials, the forced collectivizations and famines, the slave labor camps, and the mass executions. In his eagerness to denounce American imperialism and retain a simplistic "good guys vs. bad guys" view of the world, he brushed these issues aside with a flippant remark on dissident writers.

The audiences on his speaking tours were not interested in debating ideology. They wanted to learn about the man behind the books. Why, the audiences wanted to know, did Agee reach these conclusions while the vast majority of CIA agents remained loyal? He found it difficult to explain:

> In many ways I was lucky to meet the right people at the right time. ... there was no sudden conversion in a religious sense. Instead I experienced a gradual, step-by-step progression, with both human and political influences constantly at work until I reached the point . . . that I would do whatever was required to put my knowledge and experience at the service of those who needed it.[55]

Agee didn't see himself as unusual. In the 1960s, many people were adopting leftist views. He was different only in his CIA background. Most turncoats feel no need to analyze their changes psychologically. They understand their evolution as a recognition of objective reality and are most eager to expound the facts, which will help others to see the light. David Horowitz's remark, "I got hit in the face with reality,"[56] applies perfectly to Agee, although reality led Horowitz in precisely the opposite direction.

The CIA's psychological staff was asked to analyze Agee's motivations and had access to psychological evaluations done at the time of enlistment. Agee obtained a copy of their report. In it, he is portrayed as a person with a strong drive for success and an exaggerated estimate of his own worth. He joined the agency for opportunistic reasons and may have had a mid-life crisis when he did not achieve as much as he hoped. The analyst thought that:

> the ideological conversion of which the Subject speaks would seem to rest on a rather shallow base. It is probably his rationalization for this self-aggrandizing act. Yet, we do need to take note of the zeal and Messianic fervor of which several observers speak. Feelings of personal inadequacy lead some individuals to overcompensate by developing a Messiah complex, feelings of being a world savior.[57]

The analyst suggested that Agee would "probably find nothing more delightful than engaging in warfare through the headlines" and that the best strategy might be to have an officer appeal to him to avoid endangering friends and former colleagues by exposing their identities.

Agee saw no merit in the analyst's opinion, claiming that he had no desire to do battle with them, but his own accounts do mesh in several ways with the CIA psychologist's analysis. He described himself as opportunistic in joining the CIA, and his attacks on the agency consistently exaggerate its ability to control political events in Latin American societies. In referring to his activities in Ecuador he remarks, "And the arrogance! God how we manipulated that country. . . . Drunk with secret power, that's what I was. Thank god, thank god I quit."[58]

Agee's attack on the agency in a best-selling book made him a celebrity. He traveled the world's "solidarity circuit" denouncing American foreign policy and exposing CIA agents. In his writings, he was strongly critical of the American government for its efforts to suppress his revelations, never stopping to reflect on what would happen to anyone who attempted similar activities in one of the Communist countries. When a law was passed prohibiting the publication of the names of CIA agents, however, he complied and even submitted his writing to the CIA for censorship.[59] He has been living in exile, traveling on Grenadian and Nicaraguan documents until the leftist regimes in those countries were defeated. At last report, he was seeking some way to return to the United States.

Several other CIA agents have written books about their disillusionment with the agency's clandestine activities and its failure to live up to their expectations. During a tour of duty in Vietnam, Ralph McGhee found that the agency was more interested in promoting American policies than in revealing the true extent of Communist penetration of the South Vietnamese government. He came to doubt the agency's:

> intelligence, its personnel, and even its integrity. Furthermore, my simplistic view of communists as the incarnation of evil and the United States as all good was slowly beginning to change. I knew by now that any careful examination of available information . . . would prove that the vast majority of the Vietnamese people were fighting against U.S. troops and for the NLF.[60]

John Stockwell thought the Agency's abandonment of its local agents when Vietnam fell was disgraceful and was frustrated by Henry Kissinger's "no win" policy of making life difficult for Soviet proxy forces in Angola. In his memoir, he alternated between denouncing the morality of American policies and regretting the government's inability to carry them out. His conclusion: "Worst of all, by retaining the CIA we are accepting ourselves as a harsh and ruthless people. It's the wrong game for a great nation.

And the players we've got are losers."[61]

These defectors all seem to have idealized the agency at first, then became disillusioned by their experiences. Victor Marchetti reports that despite being disenchanted and disagreeing with many of the agency's policies he "was still imbued with the mystique of the agency and the intelligence business in general, even retaining a certain affection for both."[62] At first he was unable to speak publicly so he wrote a novel about life in the agency. Finally he published a nonfiction memoir, which he allowed the CIA to censor.

None of the defectors make any detailed comparison of Soviet and American activities or attempt to weigh systematically the costs of CIA activities against its benefits. The immediacy of their own personal experiences overweighs second-hand evidence from books or other people. The most striking characteristic of the CIA defectors is the extent to which they retain a view of the world as polarized between good and evil. All that has changed is that the U.S. has become the enemy and the third world socialist movements have become the victim. Although the authoritarian and protest scripts are superficially opposites, both meet a need for a comprehensive theory of the world as polarized between good and evil forces. When personal experiences undermine a believer's faith in the goodness of his allies, one solution is to recast them in the role of enemies.

Turncoats from the New Left

Norman Podhoretz. Michael Harrington's fear of success contrasts with Norman Podhoretz's voracious pursuit of it. In his book *Making It,* Podhoretz frankly and proudly confesses to seeking fame and fortune rather than literary or scholarly excellence.[63] He argues that most of the other members of the New York literary establishment are equally opportunistic, but they are not honest enough to admit it.

Podhoretz's decision to "make it" coincided roughly with his decision to break with the left. He does not, however, tie the two together. Presumably he might have "made it" equally as well as a leftist instead of as the neoconservative editor of *Commentary* magazine. Instead of examining his own motives, Podhoretz critiqued the flaws in the thinking of prominent leftist writers and smugly defended the superiority of his own thinking. His thinking changed gradually over a period of years, but there was a moment in 1970 when his "growing doubts about radicalism had coalesced and come to a head in a conviction so blazing that it ignited an all-out offensive against the Movement in *Commentary.*"[64]

The strength of his feelings were such that he committed the magazine, beginning in June 1970, to what became a three-year crusade against the left. This one casual reference to a "blazing conviction" is the only remark in his book that gives any recognition to the possibility of an emotional component in his ideological transformation. His literary style, however, reveals a strong emotional force, which is devoted almost exclusively to denouncing or satirizing people who do not agree with him.

While Podhoretz doesn't provide us with a psychologist's analysis of his personality, there are hints scattered through the book that show a striking similarity with CIA defector Philip Agee as portrayed by the CIA psychologist. He confesses that his "noblest" ambitions were based on "the vulgar desire to rise above the class into which I was born," that he was ashamed of his Yiddish speaking mother and eager to betray her in favor of a Christian English teacher, that he "was a man much given to anxiety and disadvantaged in the world of power by a childish desire for everyone to love me and a terror of making enemies," and that narcissism was "an invariable and indispensable element of his very being as a writer."[65]

The fact that he makes these observations about himself shows a degree of self-awareness, which is absent in Agee's work. He is critical of his "brutal insensitivity" in jumping on the anti-Communist bandwagon during the McCarthy era.[66] Podhoretz went through a period of writer's block in the mid-1960s, which may have been an interval of "creative illness" in the Freudian sense.[67] This period of anguish actually produced some of his best writing, but it was resolved by his "blazing" conversion to neoconservatism in 1970. After his conversion his writing became more predictable and ideological.

Eldridge Cleaver. Former Black Panther Eldridge Cleaver is "often described by friends as an opportunist."[68] And not just by his opponents. Fellow turncoats Peter Collier and David Horowitz say that "he is now what he always was—a hustler."[69] Cleaver became disillusioned with socialism and black radicalism during a period of exile in Cuba, Algeria, China, and North Korea. He converted to Christianity and adopted a strongly pro-American, anti-Communist political ideology. His book *Soul on Fire* describes his conversion to Christianity and was intended as a sequel to his best-selling black consciousness volume, *Soul on Ice,* in which he explored the political significance of his history as a rapist of white women (after practicing on black ones).[70] The accusation of opportunism may owe something to the fact that after his conversion to fundamentalist Christianity he tried his hand at designing men's clothing and made a big splash in the media with pants that featured a special pouch to emphasize the male organ.

Cleaver had become a Marxist during the nine years he spent in prison for nonpolitical crimes, a period when he also read great books and became a writer. On his release in 1966 he became involved in the Black Panther party, which was being organized by Huey Newton and Bobby Seale in Oakland, California. After a shootout with the Oakland police in 1968, he fled to Cuba to avoid prosecution. In Cuba he met a black Cuban officer who was disillusioned with the use of black Cubans to fight wars in Africa. In Oakland Cleaver had been "turned on to the ruthless power of Joseph Stalin," but in Havana he was out of power and struck by the absence of human rights and respect for legal procedures. Because of his long involvement with the American legal system, he had come to expect certain rights; if someone was arrested, for example, you knew you would hear from them within forty-eight hours. In Cuba, and later in Algeria, he found that there were no such guarantees. As a guest in these countries, "I carefully promoted their party line back to the United States . . . but inwardly my doubts and dismay were growing."[71]

He finally found legal political asylum in France, where he lived comfortably with his wife and children, enjoying apartments in Paris and on the Riviera. Nevertheless, he felt uprooted and abandoned by his American friends. The Panthers had split and he was on the outs, and no one was willing to help him return to America. He felt a lack of meaning in his life and guilt about depriving his children of an American upbringing. Life was "meaningless, pointless, getting nowhere," and he began to think of suicide.[72] Finally, he had a vision in which Castro, Mao, Marx, and Engels passed in review and dropped out of sight, replaced by the "dazzling, shimmering" image of Jesus Christ. From this point on he was able to sleep peacefully, and he returned to the United States, confident that God would take care of him. He subsequently made new friends who shared his religious worldview, but his conversion in France was not the result of recruitment by any proselytizing group.

Cleaver is a better writer than Philip Agee or Norman Podhoretz. There is none of the flatness of a world peopled by superficial stereotypes. He notes that his conversion to Christianity has "blessed [him] with the opportunity to travel all over the country and share [his] testimony with thousands of people," but there is nothing in the description that would lead a reader to believe that he is insincere.[73] Of course, a talented writer could easily invent a dream scene such as Cleaver's parade of icons. As an admitted rapist with a long criminal career, who learned all the con man's techniques for manipulating the system, Cleaver certainly has the skill to present himself in any way that seems in his best interest.

Cleaver admits to opportunistically promoting a Communist line he didn't believe while a guest in Communist countries, but this is no worse than the compromises many people make in order to survive in difficult circumstances. Jean-Paul Sartre did the same thing after returning to a secure life in France, yet he is not tarred with the label "opportunist." If Cleaver were motivated purely by opportunism, he could easily have turned to secular anti-Communist politics or focused more of his energy on his literary career.

The accusation of opportunism is often used as an excuse not to listen to what someone is saying. A letter in the *New York Times* argues that:

> David Horowitz and Peter Collier are opportunists of the very worst type, and the attempt to legitimize them as "born again" is ludicrous. Particularly revolting is the mental image of Mr. Horowitz "squeezing back tears" at the Vietnam Veterans Memorial. He, and others, of his ilk, shouldn't even be allowed near the place.[74]

This letter, which I have quoted in its entirety, uses anger as a defense against having to respond to any of Horowitz and Collier's ideas. Another writer dismisses the "whole business of born-again anti-Communism [as] an elaborate hoax designed to gain attention for a small group of unrepresentative burnt-out cases."[75]

It seems clear that Cleaver, Horowitz, and Collier are interested in selling books and promoting themselves as celebrities, but this is equally true of Philip Agee and the other CIA defectors who are welcomed by the same people who denounce the leftist defectors. Cleaver's self-promotion is no more opportunistic than Jane Fonda's promotion of exercise tapes or Bobby Seale's attempt to mimic her success with his "Barbeq'n with Bobby" cookbook. Podhoretz's argument that everyone is opportunistic has merit, if we remember that everyone has other motives as well. People who know an individual intimately may be able to judge the balance of selfish and altruistic motives in their personalities, but there is no reliable way to make this judgment about public figures. Let those who have never tried to benefit from their views or affiliations cast the first stone.

Cleaver fits the pattern of a protestor who became disillusioned when his personal experiences conflicted with his idealizations and who resolved the problem by reversing his imagery. He is a survivor who capitalizes on his experiences as best he can, but he shares this trait with many protestors who have remained within their fold.

David Horowitz and Peter Collier. These two turncoats from the New Left have worked so closely together throughout their political lives that they may be treated together, although their family backgrounds naturally differed.[76] Horowitz was raised in a Communist family in New York City, Collier was the son of a California insurance agent. Both were involved in the New Left in northern California, where they were editors of *Ramparts* magazine and worked with the antiwar, People's Park, and Black Panther movements. They recruited a former *Ramparts* bookkeeper, Betty Van Patter, to keep the Panther Party's accounts. When she confronted them with discrepancies in the accounts she was found floating face down in San Francisco Bay. Horowitz and Collier were convinced that the Panthers had killed her. They were shaken by their friends' continued loyalty to the Panthers and demonizing of the police when they had no one but the police to turn to apprehend the killers.

They quietly withdrew from leftist politics and coauthored successful biographies of the Rockefeller, Kennedy, and Ford families. At the beginning they thought of the Rockefellers as leaders of a powerful capitalist ruling class. By the end of the volume they saw them as a family split by personal, ideological, and generational conflicts. Far from ruling the world, the elder Rockefellers couldn't even keep their own children and grandchildren from defecting to radical causes. While writing these books, Collier and Horowitz were quietly rethinking their politics. Horowitz recently noted that it "took me about ten years to rethink all of my thoughts and to look at the world with new eyes."[77] Their transition was complete when they voted for Ronald Reagan in 1984 and announced their conversion publicly in the *Washington Post*.[78]

Collier and Horowitz are unusual not so much for their disillusionment as for their conversion to strident anti-Communism. As Churcher comments, "What shocks their former allies is not the abandonment of the radical cause; it's the 180-degree turnaround. Couldn't they have done the decent thing and settled into apolitical yuppiedom? Or taken up tomato farming, as one leftist critic has suggested?"[79]

In their rhetorical style, Collier and Horowitz are more consistent with their radical past than with their former comrades who have moderated their views. The revolutionary left has replaced American imperialism as their enemy, and its evils and powers are exaggerated. At one speech in Philadelphia, David Horowitz attacked the American Communist Party and its dupes in such an extreme way that he embarrassed even his conservative hosts, several of whom pointed out that the Party was not a serious force in American politics. Collier and Horowitz's critique of the follies and foibles of the New Left is caustic and scathing, but well written and more challenging than the discreet appraisals of Gitlin and Hayden.[80] Their rhetorical excesses, however, make it easy for those who disagree to dismiss their more telling points. In an exchange with Todd Gitlin in Philadelphia, for example, Horowitz referred to radicals burning books in libraries yet was unable to come up with any examples when challenged.

Collier and Horowitz happily acknowledged their own extremism, and provided some justification for it, when they concluded *Destructive Generation* with a quote from Susan Sontag who accused them of "projecting your own Manichean politics onto the world." After she left, they "realized that she was right—we did push things to extremes. But the judgment on us was also a judgment on her and others who understood the political stakes but didn't push things far enough."[81]

The Libertarians: Turncoats from the Right and the Left

Karl Hess was a gifted youngster who claims to have read H. G. Wells's *Outline of History* before he entered kindergarten. He found school boring and oppressive, and he resented the state, which compelled him to be there. In his first year of high school he enrolled in two schools, then informed each of them he was transfering to the other. They never caught on, so he lied about his age and got a job with a radio network. He was exceptionally successful until the network found out about his age and fired him to comply with the regulations of the same oppressive state.

When Hess became interested in politics, he rejected both the Democrats and the Socialists as statist and bureaucratic. He learned a great deal from the disucssions at the Socialist meetings, however, including a hatred of Stalinism. He chose to join the Republicans because "in 1940 the Republican party presented itself as the party that was against centralized power, against militarism and foreign meddling, against Communism; it was for local control, individual liberty and the pioneer spirit. That was my ticket."[82]

Honorably discharged from the army because of health problems, he settled into a career as a conservative journalist and activist. He was one of the founders of the *National Review,* wrote the platform for the Republican convention, which nominated Richard Nixon in 1960, put in a stint in Nixon's White House, then worked as director of special projects for the American Enterprise Institute (AEI). In 1964, he was disappointed when the corporate elite put their money on Lyndon Johnson, and he left the AEI job to become speech writer for Barry Goldwater.

Hess was one of a number of conservative idealists who became disillusioned when anti-Communism caused many leading conservatives to abandon their isolationist and libertarian convictions.[83] They were opposed to the draft on the grounds that it was an unjustifiable enslavement of the free individual by the state. Hess thought that William Buckley and the *National Review* crowd "took over conservatism from the old isolationist-pacifist right and converted it into a military-religious crusade against the Reds. It was a tragedy for it left no political opposition to resist the liberal push toward more and more U.S. intervention around the globe."[84]

As with most turncoats, Hess went through a transitional period of uncertainty and vacillation before definitively changing his views. He took up the welder's trade in the hope of escaping from his doubts by working with his hands, but was drawn back to do some speech writing for conservative congressmen while ghosting columns for Barry Goldwater. After helping Goldwater get back in the Senate in 1968, he discovered that Students for a Democratic Society really articulated his viewpoint. Once inside SDS, he found that everywhere he went he ran into other former Goldwater campaigners.

Hess's conversion was facilitated by Murray Rothbard, another libertarian purist who had discovered that the left was more sympathetic to his antimilitarist, antistatist views.[85] Rothbard published an article titled "Confessions" in *Ramparts* in June 1968. Hess saw the article and called Rothbard. They hit it off and, when two-hour long distance phone calls got too expensive, Hess traveled to Rothbard's for summer weekends where the conversation could flow freely. By the end of the summer of 1968, he was a convinced anarchist even though he was still writing for Goldwater's campaign. This explains remarks Goldwater made that fall drawing attention to communalities between his own thought and certain "anarchistic elements in S.D.S."[86]

Before entering politics, Hess had been assistant to the president of Champion Paper and Fibre Company, and he had spent his life in respectable Republican circles. Now he adjusted his lifestyle to suit his new convictions. In 1969, when young conservatives were all short-haired and cleanly shaven, he boldly appeared to defend his new views at a Young Americans for Freedom (YAF) conference looking like "a nicely balanced mixture of General U.S. Grant and Fidel Castro as he strode to the podium, his knotty black curls bunched behind his ears, a frizzy coal-black beard covering most of his face."[87]

This change in appearance was a political statement that resulted from his disgust at the conservatives claiming that they were for freedom while demanding that the state "get tough" with people they didn't like. This didn't mean just controlling rioters but:

> getting tough on entire ranges of attitudes: clipping long hair, rousting people from parks for carrying concealed guitars, stopping and questioning anyone who doesn't look like a member of the Jaycees, drafting all the n'er-do-wells to straighten them up, ridding our theaters and book stores of "filth" and, always and above all, putting "those" people in their place.[88]

In short, he objected to the authoritarianism of conservatives who claimed to be advocates of freedom. He adopted a pacifist as well as anarchist perspective, arguing that "if Soviet troops did land here? Beautiful. We could, if an anarchistic society, probably have *them* subverted in a fortnight."[89]

Hess lost the debate at the YAF convention, as did libertarian Jerome Tuccille who hoped to build a coalition of antistate partisans from the left and the right. The audience gave a thundering three-minute ovation to anti-Communist Henry Paolucci who argued that the American state was the culmination of Western civilization and that individual freedom could only be granted to those who accepted American traditions. Hess concluded that "Sadly to some, but not to me, it is only on the new Left today that I find serious concern with the principles of anti-statist individualism. . . . The right, my home for so long, has dug in its heels to save the status quo and, unbearably to me, the state itself."[90]

The New Left disappointed Hess and Rothbard when it abandoned its emphasis on participatory democracy for Marxist collectivism. They found their ideal political vehicle in the Libertarian Party, which combined free-market economics and neo-anarchist politics with a belief in personal freedom, which included legalizing drugs and all kinds of sexual behaviors. Hess became a small businessman in West Virginia and continued to live a hippie lifestyle together with his pony-tailed business partner. He edited the *Libertarian Party News* until 1990 when he resigned to write his autobiography.

Rothbard became disgusted with the frivolous and indulgent lifestyle practiced by many Libertarians and split off to publish his own newsletter and work for a merger between his "paleolibertarians" and the "paleoconservatives." He publishes a newsletter in which he attacks the "modal Libertarians" as aging adolescent science-fiction freaks and computer nerds who can't make a living, mooch off their friends, and are turned on by alienating their parents, their neighbors, and the society around them.[91]

Disillusioned by left-wing utopianism and right-wing pragmatism, the libertarians have created their own anarchistic utopianism. They believe that all problems can be solved by simply allowing the free market to do its work free of government intervention. They should be riding high since their views have been largely vindicated by the course of history since the 1960s, yet they have been no more successful organizationally than the leftist protestors. They value ideological purity over political effectiveness and have split into bitter factions. The left libertarians focus on sex, drugs, and lifestyle while the right libertarians are primarily devoted to free-market economics. Both seek to minimize the power of the state and share the pacifists' opposition to militarism except in local self-defense. They share the protestors' anger at the powers-that-be, but they lack their sympathy for the poor and downtrodden.

The Libertarian Party had hopes of becoming a major electoral contender, but its utopian idealism keeps them from making the compromises needed to win elections. The more pragmatic young people tend to leave the Party, moderate their views, and blend in with the Republican establishment. In this and other respects, Libertarianism is very close to Ayn Rand's Objectivism, and many Libertarians came to the Party from Randism. It is the perfect ideology for a hedonist who seeks a rationalization for self-indulgence. If the culture-of-narcissism school were correct about the motivations of the sixties radicals, more of them should have been attracted to Libertarianism. They have not been because, above all else, the protestors need an ideological script that allows them to express their humanistic concern for the oppressed and downtrodden.

Conclusions

This chapter has discussed the lives of a small number of prominent sixties activists who are not necessarily representative of their generation. An interesting where-are-they-now survey by Jack Whalen and Richard Flacks, however, provides information on a more representative sample of sixties radicals.[92] In February of 1970, revolutionary students in Santa Barbara, California, burned down a branch of the Bank of America during riots, which they thought to be the first stages of a general revolution. Whalen and Flacks tracked down a large sample of these "bank burners" to find out what had happened to them in the intervening decades. Their book is a study of disillusionment and gradual readjustment to the failure of an ideological script.

During the riots these students quickly and enthusiastically embraced irrational transformational illusions. They really believed that there was "a shit storm coming" and that soon the entire country would be swept up in a revolutionary conflagration.[93] This kind of collective delusion is common at the early stages of mass movements when the anonymity and contagion of the crowd weakens people's inhibitions and frees them to express emotions, which are normally controlled by their sense of reality.[94]

When the energy of the crowd dies down, awareness of reality inevitably creeps back in. Within a few years even the most militant of the students had "finally realized there wasn't a social revolution going on, and that there wasn't going to be one."[95] They faced up to this fact and made the best adjustment they could. The less radical students abandoned leftist political commitments easily enough and pursued conventional careers. Those with stronger commitments to their ideological scripts often retreated into sectarian groups or alternative communities. These alternatives were short-lived and served only to delay the transition to conventional occupational roles and life within conventional society. Whalen and Flacks conclude that:

> The story we have been telling depicts the gradual individuation and conventionalization of people who, in their youth, were wholeheartedly submerged in a collective effort to break free of conventional identity. . . . although they appeared to be strongly bonded by revolutionary enthusiasm, movement collectivities began to break apart almost as soon as they formed because of their inability to recognize and encompass the personal needs and interests of members. . . . in the 1980s and in their thirties, most former activists were seeking more individualized and settled adult roles rather than continuing to operate in self-conscious opposition to the status quo.[96]

Can we say that these activists were members of a liberated generation? Flacks was a strong proponent of this idea in the sixties, and he still thinks so. He points out that even in middle age the activists continued to be much more liberal and socially concerned than a comparison sample of students who had not participated in the riots. Many continue to be active in community social reform efforts. Their fundamental personality traits and values had not changed, they had simply been forced to tone down their utopianism and reconcile themselves to adult life in a stable society.

Generational studies have always shown that most people remain true to their fundamental belief system for their entire life span.[97] The conventional wisdom may be that people are typically radical in their youth and conservative in middle age, but the reality is that most people just become a little bit more pragmatic and less extreme in their views. Most sixties radicals fit this pattern. Like Michael Harrington, they may continue to call themselves "socialists" if asked, but they mean something more like Sweden than Cuba or China. Very few continue to make radical politics the focus of their lives, as Abbie Hoffman did until his death.

The turncoats we examined in this chapter are interesting exceptions to the general pattern. Most CIA agents did not defect nor did most sixties radicals turn into anti-Communists. These exceptional cases shed light on the psychology of protest and authoritarian scripts. The fact that Philip Agee was able to convert from anti-Communist to Communist apologist without changing his fundamental way of thinking shows that there is a psychological similarity between the two positions. Collier and Horowitz, also, continue to view the world in black-and-white terms, which in many ways are the mirror image of the New Left ideologists they condemn. Dramatic ideological change can be a way of avoiding the lessening of ideological militancy, which is typical of middle age. By taking up a fresh cause, the turncoat is able to rekindle his energy and enthusiasm.

This kind of dramatic transformation of ideological views is difficult emotionally, however, and seems to be undertaken only by people who have a strong need for ideological commitment. Faced with the apparent failure of a cherished belief system, most people simply become less active and try not to think too much about it. Despite the failure of their movements and the general evolution of the world away from socialist ideas, most veterans of the sixties radical movements remain loyal to the *values* that motivated them in the sixties. Socialism continues to appeal to them as an ideal because it expresses a principled concern for the welfare of the people. This principle is important to their value systems even when they recognize that in the real world the masses often seem to do better under capitalism. They are reluctant to abandon socialist values for alternatives such as Libertarianism, which exalt individualism and freedom but provide no vehicle for expressing altruistic values.

Far from being hedonists or narcissists who indulge in each fad as it comes along, the life-history data shows that the majority of sixties radicals retain a lifetime committment to ideals of selflessness and altruism. The failure of the liberated generation was not a lack of good intentions but a weakness for utopian promises and simplistic solutions. The liberated generation failed, not because of the psychopathology of its members, but because they became locked into a utopian script, which was unrealistic and ultimately self-defeating. They simply had no persuasive model for the revolutionary transformation of American society.

The liberated generation failed as utopians, but they were much more successful as protestors. Over the years they have served as gadflies, drawing society's attention to many flaws in the social order such as racism, sexism, excessive militarism, and environmental pollution. The solutions they offered may not have been viable, but at least they kept up the pressure for change. Their failure to win power was a blessing in disguise since they would not have known what to do with it if they had it. As it was, they have been able to retreat from their utopianism more or less gracefully with their values and some of their illusions intact.

Chapter Twelve

Feminists and Antifeminists

Feminists are fond of observing that "the personal is political," and they often use examples from their personal lives to illustrate political points. They are interested in how their own politics are shaped by their personal lives, but they seem hesitant to approach this topic systematically. As yet, there are no serious adult biographies of important feminist leaders such as Betty Friedan. The link between the personal and the political in the lives of feminists must be pieced together by reading between the lines in feminist monographs and by collecting the scraps of biography that are available.

Some may object that a male scholar is poorly prepared to undertake this task. David Bouchier was quite sympathetic to feminism when he began his study of the British feminist movement. Yet he found that his interest was deeply resented by many of the women who expected him to "shoulder the burden of the sins of all mankind."[1] A prominent feminist scholar, "writing on the notepaper of a distinguished university," insisted that "no matter what you do, you can have no real knowledge or understanding. Our knowledge belongs to us."[2]

But if this is true then it must also be true that only men can understand men, and the feminists have not been shy about dissecting the male psyche. In reacting to the feminists I obviously have a male viewpoint, moreover that of a man who was divorced from his feminist first wife and who had all the other experiences discussed in Chapter One. I hope that my observations are interesting; I make no claim that they are disinterested.

Feminists hope that all women who become conscious of the world around them will share their views. The term "women's movement" is often used as a synonym for "feminist movement" as if all women were, or ought to be, feminists. Women such as Phyllis Schlafly who oppose feminism are angrily denounced as traitors to their gender. If this is so, then there are a lot of traitors out there. Surveys show that women are about as likely as men to oppose feminist positions on issues such as abortion or the Equal Rights Amendment.[3] This chapter will explore the factors that lead some women to become feminists and others to become antifeminists. It will also explore the motivations behind different kinds of feminism and antifeminism.

We will try to uncover the link between the personal and the political in the lives of four feminist writers and leaders: Betty Friedan, Kate Millett, Germaine Greer, and Sonia Johnson. Friedan is the founding mother of contemporary feminism and has been highly effective as an activist and reformer as well as a writer and speaker. Millett is radical lesbian feminist who also draws on Marxist perspectives. Greer is a less systematic thinker, but her life and her writings help to clarify the origins of antifeminine feelings among radical feminists. Sonia Johnson organized Mormons for ERA and has written a memoir, which recounts her transition *From Housewife to Heretic*. The lives of these four feminists will be contrasted to the life of antifeminist Phyllis Schlafly, for whom a good biography by a feminist journalist is available. Schlafly exemplifies the life of the *Positive Woman* who relishes femininity, traditional marriage, and the American way of life.

The Feminists: Liberal, Radical, and Socialist

Feminists agree that "the unequal and inferior social status of women is unjust and needs to be changed."[4] Within this broad consensus there are significant ideological differences. In very general terms, feminism can be divided into three ideological tendencies: liberal, socialist, and radical. The liberals take a pragmatic and reformist approach to bringing about changes, while the radicals and socialists favor revolutionary action against men as a class or at least against male capitalists. Of course, many or most feminists incorporate several elements from one or more of these perspectives in their thinking. A feminist professor may sound like a liberal when negotiating with her dean, a radical when teaching a Women's Studies class, and a socialist when marching in Washington against the latest American imperialist outrage. Nevertheless, there are important psychological as well as ideological differences between these three types of feminism.

Liberal feminists support equal rights for women as part of their advocacy of equal rights for all categories of people. Following the ideas of classical liberals such as John Stuart Mill, they believe that feminist goals can best be accomplished through equal rights legislation and democratic reforms without overthrowing the basic order of society. They are eager to join with any men who agree with them in pursuit of their goals. Psychologically, anger at men is not at all necessary to the liberal feminist position, just a concern for fairness and justice. Most women and most men, at least in developed societies, support liberal feminist positions.

The socialist feminists view women's liberation as part of a struggle of oppressed classes and peoples against capitalism. They urge women to form alliances with leftist groups and causes. They are willing to ally with minority, working-class, and leftist men who respect feminist goals, but they are hostile to white businessmen and large corporations. Socialist feminists are motivated by many of the same factors that motivate socialists who are less interested in feminism: utopianism, concern for the poor and exploited in the world, and anger at the defects of the wealthy capitalist societies.

The radical feminists are perhaps the most interesting psychologically, although they are certainly much less numerous and politically influential than the liberal feminists. Radical feminists believe that "the roots of women's oppression are biological" and that women's liberation "requires a biological revolution."[5] In their view, women can only be liberated if they separate from men and organize independently from them. They often view lesbianism as not just an acceptable lifestyle for those who choose it but as politically preferable since it separates women from men. Anger at men is a central theme in radical feminism. I will argue that an element of self-hatred, expressed as anger at femininity, is also present.

To some extent these three ideological tendencies work at cross purposes, since the liberals seek to ameliorate the problems that the radicals and socialists want to use as a basis for revolution. If the liberals open up job opportunities for women, for example, the women may focus on their careers instead of on organizing to overthrow the capitalistic patriarchy. This is not unlike the conflict between revolutionaries and reformists in other social movements, and it has led to typical organizational conflicts and schisms.

Betty Friedan vs. the Radicals

Betty Friedan was born in Peoria, Illinois, in 1921. She was a sickly baby who was not expected to survive infancy. When she did survive, she needed braces for her crooked teeth and glasses for her bad eyes. Her father was a well-to-do jewelry store owner, but there were no other Jewish children in her class in school, and she was ridiculed for her long nose. In her sophomore year in high school she was the only girl left out when the sororities chose new members. When she was depressed she took comfort in her special prayer: "I want a boy who will love me best, and I want a work to do."[6]

At seventeen, she observed, "I have not been well endowed physically, neither with health nor with beauty."[7] In compensation, she was endowed with a sharp mind. She loved books and skipped two grades in school. Her father chided her, saying it didn't look good for a girl to take more than five books out of the library at once. She tried playing dumb in high school, but the only boys who took an interest in her were a few outsiders and social rejects. She decided to make the most of her strengths and go all out for academic achievement.

When her father's business did poorly during the Depression, her parents' marriage suffered. Her mother was a native-born American and looked down on her unschooled immigrant husband. She had no career, was dissatisfied with housekeeping and volunteer work, and vented her frustrations by nagging her husband and children. When Betty graduated from high school she went away to Smith College, determined to make as sharp a break with her and her mother's life in Peoria as possible.

She did very well in college, but turned down a chance to go to Berkeley for graduate work in psychology in the hopes of getting married and finding the "feminine fulfillment which had eluded my mother."[8] She took a job as a labor reporter in New York and met Carl Friedan who, in 1946, had recently returned from the European war and was building a career in advertising and public relations. They were married in 1947, and she had her first child a year later. She took a year's maternity leave, returned to work for a while, then lost her job when they didn't want to give her another year's maternity leave for her second child as promised in her contract. She decided she wasn't getting anywhere in that job anyway and settled into free-lance writing as a career, which was compatible with raising children.

Betty was a homemaker for the five years it took to write *The Feminine Mystique*. She had a contract for the book, but neither her publisher nor her husband thought she would ever finish it. She may have had doubts herself. The summer before she finished, "for some strange reason—maybe a last gasp at denying my seriousness—I dyed my hair blond."[9] Still, she was deeply involved on a project of her own choosing. On the surface it would seem that her childhood prayer for a man to love her and a meaningful lifework had been answered. But, under the surface, she was unhappy. The available biographies on her were written for children and don't give details about her marital problems. We are simply told that her marriage was "stormy from the beginning."[10]

The Feminine Mystique grew out of a survey she did of members of her Smith College class fifteen years after graduation. It is a well-written and solidly researched book, synthesizing literature from psychology, sociology, and anthropology on the role of women in advanced, post-industrial societies. Her argument was that the cultural image of women as sexy, nurturant wives and mothers had deluded educated women into becoming trapped in housewife roles, which were unsatisfying. She certainly felt that way about her own life, and her data showed that many other women felt the same way. The solution was for women to pursue careers on an equal basis with men, while persuading men to share responsibility for child care and housework.

This was certainly a sensible argument, but the publisher didn't expect very many people to be interested and regretted having given her a contract. They printed only three thousand copies for the first edition in 1963, but Betty promoted it effectively and sales took off through word-of-mouth. Tens of thousands of women were excited to find a book that spoke to their lives and articulated their unexpressed feelings. Betty became a celebrity, with invitations to appear on television shows and to lecture around the country.

All this success added to the stress on her marriage. Resentment from other women made her a "leper in my own suburban neighborhood."[11] She and her husband weren't invited to dinner parties, and her children were kicked out of the car pool to dancing classes. They moved back into the city, but Carl didn't like being "Mr. Betty Friedan," and they divorced after twenty-two years of marriage.

The National Organization for Women. Betty threw her energy into organizing to lobby for women's rights. In 1964, Congress had amended the Civil Rights Act, which prohibited racial discrimination, to include discrimination by sex. Many congressmen thought this was a joke, designed to make the act look silly. There seemed little likelihood that the Equal Opportunity Employment Commission would enforce the provision seriously. At a conference on women's issues, Betty Friedan got a small group together in her hotel room to make plans for a new National Organization for Women.* NOW was roughly modeled on the National Association for the Advancement of Colored People in that it was a civil rights organization that accepted membership from anyone (male or female, black or white) who supported women's rights. In addition to agitating for enforcement of the provisions against sex discrimination, NOW drew up a Bill of Rights for Women and advocated for the Equal Rights Amendment.[12]

---

*Many people, including Germaine Greer in *The Female Eunuch,* use "of" instead of "for" apparently on the erroneous assumption that NOW only welcomes women as members.

Thanks to effective and timely leadership by Friedan and others, NOW was enormously successful as an organization, growing from thirty-two members in 1966 to 250,000 by the mid-1980s. It was very effective in its legal and legislative efforts and in mobilizing public opinion in favor of liberated lifestyles. Thanks to pressure from NOW, newspapers were no longer allowed to divide their classified advertisements into men's jobs and women's jobs. Many career opportunities opened up for women, and they had a new legitimacy in negotiating more equitable arrangements with their husbands. The Equal Rights Amendment was revived as a viable issue and almost put into the Constitution. Ironically, protest movements often have a hard time dealing with this much success. Achieving limited but significant success means that there is nothing quite so dramatic left to protest about. It also means acknowledging that success may not have met up to the movement's more utopian expectations. Although the overall impact was positive in advancing NOW's goals, in some ways women's lives may have actually become more difficult because of the changes brought about by feminism. The divorce rate had increased sharply in the sixties, and studies showed that women often fared poorly after divorce in a legal environment, which disparaged alimony and was ineffective in collecting child support.[13]

Perhaps because of its rapid growth, the feminist movement had a bad case of the growing pains, which plague ideological organizations. In the late sixties and early seventies, its activists split into two major factions or tendencies. The first was the reformist feminists, led by Betty Friedan. The second was a combination of radical and socialist feminists who thought the reformists were not militant enough. These women were usually younger than the moderate feminists and were often organized in small, independent "consciousness raising" and action groups. These groups made a principle of excluding men on the grounds that men were the enemy, or at the very least a drag on the movement's militancy.

Many of these younger, more militant feminists had been involved in the civil rights or student movement before switching over to feminism.[14] They brought with them much of the socialist utopianism and confrontational style of sixties radicalism. They were strongly anti-elitist and reprimanded any woman who showed signs of becoming known as a leader or who accepted a position of power in established institutions. Women who violated these norms by achieving success in some area of endeavor were subjected to a process called "trashing," which scapegoated them and excluded them from the collectives. This was similar to the "criticism, self-criticism" sessions the New Left had adopted from Chinese Maoism. Not surprisingly, "the trashing experience led many talented women to cut all ties with women's collectives."[15]

In 1968, a woman named Valerie Solanas shot artist and playwright Andy Warhol twice in the abdomen, claiming she had aimed a little lower. Instead of dismissing her as a person in need of psychiatric care, some radical feminists hailed her as a heroine. The President of the New York Chapter of NOW was Ti-Grace Atkinson, a blond divorcee pursuing a doctorate in philosophy at Columbia University. Atkinson visited Solanas in the mental hospital and smuggled out her revolutionary proclamation, the SCUM Manifesto. It was reprinted in the popular anthology *Sisterhood Is Powerful.* SCUM stands for "Society for Cutting Up Men," and the Manifesto opened with these stirring words:

> Life in this society being, at best, an utter bore and no aspect of society being at all relevant to women, there remains to civic-minded, responsible, thrill-seeking females only to overthrow the government, eliminate the money system, institute complete automation, and destroy the male sex. . . . the male is an incomplete female, a walking abortion, aborted at the gene state. . . .
>
> SCUM will destroy all useless and harmful objects—cars, store windows, "Great Art," etc. . . .
>
> SCUM will couple-bust—barge into mixed (male-female) couples, wherever they are, and bust them up.
>
> SCUM will kill all men who are not in the Men's Auxiliary of SCUM. Men in the Men's Auxiliary are those men who are working diligently to eliminate themselves.[16]

It is tempting to dismiss this Manifesto as good-humored political satire, a kind of feminist parody of the Communist Manifesto. Indeed, that is how Solanas's publisher took it until the shooting.[17] But Andy Warhol spent six and a half hours on the operating table as surgeons repaired damage to his spleen, stomach, liver, esophagus, and lungs.[18] Valerie Solanas's lawyer characterized her in court as "one of the most important spokeswomen of the feminist movement," and two representatives of New York NOW appeared in court to protest that she was being prejudicially treated because she was a woman.[19] In her own book *Amazon Odyssey,* Ti-Grace Atkinson praised the *SCUM Manifesto* as "the most important feminist statement written to date in the English language."[20] Feminist writer Vivian Gornick called it "an extraordinary document, an authentic love-hate child of its time . . . containing within itself the secret knowledge of the victim, the economical insight of the obsessed . . . its quality is visionary."[21] Solanas's supporters held a rally in Greenwich Village with signs such as "Andy Warhol Shot by Valerie Solanas: Plastic Man vs. the Sweet Assassin" and "A Tough Chic with a Bop Cap and a .38 . . . *Valerie is Ours.*"[22]

Actually, Solanas was a twenty-eight-year-old lesbian writer who had played herself in a scene in Warhol's film *I, a Man*. She had showed Warhol a copy of a play she wrote about a man-hating panhandler. The play was called *Up Your Ass,* and Warhol found it "so dirty I suddenly thought she might be working for the police department and that this was some kind of entrapment."[23] He misplaced the copy she had given him and offered her the bit part in his movie to make amends.

At first the courts found Solanas incompetent to stand trial. She was convinced that both Warhol and her publisher were thieves, scheming to steal from her, although the fact was that she had nothing worth stealing.[24] When the court let her out on bail she made threatening phone calls to Warhol demanding that he drop all charges against her, pay her twenty thousand dollars for her manuscripts, put her in more movies, and get her on the Johnny Carson show. If he didn't pay up she "could always do it again."[25] Fortunately for Warhol, she threatened other people also, and the judge decided to lock her up. Ti-Grace Atkinson was outraged that Solanas was not being treated seriously as a political protestor. Eventually, however, Solanas pleaded guilty and was sentenced to up to three years in prison for first-degree assault.

Betty Friedan was appalled when Ti-Grace Atkinson began "to spout theories of an Amazonian army of women, advocating absolute separatism from men." She thought that "Ti-Grace's 'radical chic' had a certain allure for the young women hippies then emigrating to the East Village and San Francisco. But she certainly did put off the women from the cities and suburbs of Middle America who were beginning to identify with the women's movement."[26]

Friedan found herself spending too much time undoing the hostility the radicals aroused. When the National Conference of Christians and Jews held a one-day conference jointly with NOW, Ti-Grace began the meeting with a speech declaring that married women were only dishonest prostitutes. Many women walked out. The radicals increasingly associated feminism with lesbianism, declaring that any woman who was married to a man was "sleeping with the enemy." Betty Friedan feared that lesbian separatists were taking over the movement and went on the warpath against them. The radicals accused her of "using McCarthy scare tactics to 'purge' NOW of what she called the 'lavender menace'."[27]

Kate Millett and Germaine Greer

The psychology of radical feminism can be explored in the lives of the authors of two best-selling works published in 1970, Kate Millett's *Sexual Politics* and Germaine Greer's *The Female Eunuch*.[28] These books were well timed, reaching the market just as the radical trend in the feminist movement was cresting. Millett's book was widely acclaimed as an expression of the "radical rage" of the new feminist movement. Millett called herself a radical lesbian feminist. Nicholas Davidson describes her as "an aggressively dowdy individual, her face obscured behind heavy black eyeglass frames, overweight, and given to wearing nondescript pants suits."[29] She has also published two memoirs, one of which describes her struggle with manic-depressive illness.[30]

Sexual Politics is an attack on heterosexual family life. Millett argues that the family is a patriarchal institution, which functions solely to perpetuate male domination, and that "the care of children, even from the period when their cognitive powers first emerge, is infinitely better left to the best trained practitioners of both sexes who have chosen it as a vocation" than to the harried and unhappy parents. She agrees with Frederick Engels that "the family, as that term is presently understood, must go. . . ."[31]

Anger at men is the overwhelming emotional theme of Millett's book. She uses the word "male" as an epithet, accuses men of treating their wives as "chattels," and denounces male sexuality whether heterosexual or homosexual. Millett uses quotations from pornographic novels to prove that men hate women, then argues that women have internalized men's hateful attitudes toward them. She argues that "women despise both themselves and each other" and insists that most women wish they had been born men, although many of them "repress and deny" this feeling.[32] Millett is outraged that women "entertain, please, gratify, satisfy and flatter men with their sexuality."[33] She views this as evidence of an oppressed class humiliating itself before its oppressor. It never occurs to her that men also entertain, please, gratify, satisfy, and flatter women, or that many couples find heterosexual relationships mutually rewarding.

Germaine Greer, by contrast, is a heterosexual who publicly mentions "the lessons which can be learned from our homosexual brothers and sisters," but who privately says, "I think it is a sin."[34] Her goal is to "humanize the penis, take the steel out of it and make it flesh again."[35] Nevertheless, she also opposes heterosexual family life, arguing that "if women are to effect a significant amelioration in their condition, it seems obvious that they must refuse to marry."[36]

Greer insists that "women have very little idea of how much men hate them." She also claims that the "men themselves do not know the depth of their hatred."[37] For evidence to support this remarkable assertion, Greer cites the statements of men such as admitted rapist Eldridge Cleaver (who, however, claimed to have hated only white women and who has since found Christian love). Greer and Millett both generalize from rapists, pornographers, and abusers to men in general without offering any evidence that most men feel the same way. Common sense suggests that most men have loving feelings for the significant women in their lives such as their mothers, sisters, girlfriends, wives, and daughters. There is no shortage of autobiographical and literary works that examine these relationships in all their complexity and ambiguity. Rather than refute these works, Greer and Millett selectively cite only works that express anger, hatred, and lust.

As the title *The Female Eunuch* suggests, the predominant emotional theme of Greer's book is not so much anger at men as hatred of femininity. She argues that:

> The female's fate is to become deformed and debilitated. . . . Every girl whose upbringing is "normal" . . . is a female faggot. . . . Woman is never genuine at any period of her life. . . . Women cannot love. . . . Women must be frigid. . . . The ignorance and isolation of most women mean that they are incapable of making conversation. . . . Women are always precipitating scenes of violence in pubs and dance halls. . . .[38]

On a personal level, Greer's problems originated in maternal abuse and paternal neglect. "When Mother's frustrations boiled over and she lit into me with anything she could lay her hands on, Daddy would 'keep out of it,' even though he was sitting reading the paper in the next room where the thud of blows was clearly audible." Her mother was obsessed with her own beauty, while Germaine was "big enough and ugly enough to take care of herself." Her mother insisted that her father loved only her, not the children. Whenever Germaine put her arms around her father, "he would grimace and pretend to shudder and put me from him. It was a joke, of course, a tiresome, hurtful, relentless, stupid joke."[39]

Her father's "response to Mother's goading was always the same, silence and distance. 'It takes two to quarrel,' he would say, apparently unaware that I could not go off to my club until the mad dog in the kitchen had stopped foaming at the mouth."[40] The only time Germaine remembers her father intervening was an occasion when her mother had pinned her three-year-old brother to the floor and was pounding his face with her fists.[41] Her father spent several years away at war when she was very small and kept out of the house as much as possible after his return.

It is not difficult to see how her hatred of femininity grew out of her anger at her beautiful but vicious mother, while her resentment of men was rooted in feelings of abandonment by her father. As a middle-aged woman she spent two years traveling the world trying to uncover her father's past, searching for evidence that he might have loved her after all.

Perhaps because of her childhood experiences, Greer is afraid to marry and have children unless they could be raised in some sort of communal arrangement. She recognizes that children would find such an arrangement difficult and might end up as dropouts or schizophrenics, but she doesn't see this as much worse than what happens to children now. Her attempt at marriage lasted only three weeks.[42]

It is hard to believe that Greer's *The Female Eunuch* was the most widely read feminist book of the 1970s. It certainly expressed anger at men. Perhaps more fundamentally, it appealed to some women's need to believe that their own inadequacies could be blamed on men. Greer did not argue that women were inherently deformed or inferior, but that feminine gender roles imposed by male-dominated societies made them so. She argued that there are no fundamental psychological differences between the sexes, although the literature she cited actually argued the opposite.[43] Only after society has been reformed so that both sexes are treated the same will the psychology of the "uncastrated female" be known. Only in a unisex world will women be capable of love or even able to carry on an interesting conversation. It is easy to see how this longing for a unisex world could be rooted in an unconscious resentment at having been born female. In Millett's case this resentment is hardly unconscious, since she insists that all women, presumably including herself, really wish they had been born men.

In *The Loony-Bin Trip,* Millett accuses her closest female relatives, feminist friends, and lesbian lovers of conspiring unnecessarily to lock her up in a mental ward and to force her to take the lithium prescribed for her illness. She understands that they are trying to help her, but believes that they are misguided and argues that her manic behavior should not be regarded as an illness. She runs from state to state, and country to country, mobilizing civil liberties lawyers to keep her out of mental hospitals and joining a movement against the oppression of mental patients. Only during the depressive phase of her illness does she fully accept the need for help.

In this 1990 work, Millett also reveals the ambivalence of her politically motivated lesbian feelings. She berates herself for not being able to feel lust for all her comrades, even those who are so overweight that they need special chairs to sit in meetings. She confesses her love for "cock in its quintessence. . . . the majesty of its maleness opens itself to me and

I love it, revere it." Nonbelievers in Freud's theory of penis envy may be willing to concede that it fits Millett's case rather well.[44] Much the same argument could be made about Greer, who is convinced that "the universal lack of esteem for the female organ becomes a deficiency in women's self-esteem."[45] Millett feels that her heterosexual longings must be ridiculed and "neutralized in ex-husbands or college romances abandoned for the true lesbian path."[46] She is devastated when her husband, whom she married legally only to prevent his deportation, finally asks for a divorce.

The Loony-Bin Trip offers a valuable entree into the mind of a person struggling with manic-depression and paranoid thinking. Millett is a troubled woman who writes convincingly about her inner struggles. The fact that she is writing about these problems on a personal level instead of projecting them onto male/female relationships in general is a healthy sign for her and a useful development for her readers.

Feminism and Family Life

Gloria Steinem and Sonia Johnson. Millett and Greer are admittedly extreme cases, but their books had a broad appeal. Their anger at men is clearly shared by a great many women who do not take it to such extremes. The feminist movement's strongest constituency is among women who, for one reason or another, are unhappy with traditional family life. This unhappiness may be the result of an unhappy childhood, as we have seen in Germaine Greer's case. In many cases, the young feminist identified more with her father than with her mother.

Gloria Steinem, for example, had a mother whose mental illness was a burden on the whole family.[47] Her father needed to travel in his business ventures and was terribly burdened by the need to care for his wife. He would ask, " 'How can I travel and take care of your mother? How can I make a living?' He was right. It was impossible to do both. I did not blame him for leaving once I was old enough to be the bringer of meals and answerer of my mother's questions."[48]

For some years, her father left Gloria alone to care for her dysfunctional mother. Gloria sympathized with her father's frustration at having to care for his wife. She also suspected that her mother's mental problems may have originated in her frustration at having given up her career to get married. She developed a strong survivor script and learned how to support herself through free-lance writing. For years, however, she justified this as a way to make a living until she settled down and got married. She assumed that her real identity would come through marriage. For years she avoided undertaking a major book project, which would have meant committing herself to a long-term career. Becoming a feminist helped her to take her own work seriously, and she resolved to maintain her independence by refusing to marry any of her suitors or to have children.

Steinem's first journalistic coup was an account of her experiences as a "bunny" at a Playboy Club.[49] Once plump and brunette, she is now slender with blonde streaks in her hair. She once wrote that "any woman who spends more than fifteen minutes getting herself ready to face the world is just screwing herself," but it is rumored that she often spends more than an hour on herself.[50] She dresses well and enjoys dating successful and influential men, including John Kenneth Galbraith and Theodore Sorenson. The media found her attractive as a spokesperson for the feminists, and she became a television personality as well as a writer and an organizer. The feminist movement supported her in her decision to put career ahead of marriage and family and gave her many opportunities to speak and write. Her celebrity status, however, interferes with her ambition to do more serious intellectual work.

Unhappy marriages and divorces push many women toward radical feminism. Anger at a sexist or unfaithful husband can easily be generalized to anger at men in general, particularly if one commiserates with friends who are in a similar situation. Sonia Johnson was raised in a traditional Mormon community, where women's role was to serve men. She remembers hanging around for hours watching while her boyfriend fixed his car, just because she wanted his company more than he wanted hers. After marriage, she insisted on working to put him through graduate school. At the time he was actually more feminist than she, insisting that she pursue her own graduate education. He was also selfish and inconsiderate on a personal level, however, working into the night at the computer center without even calling to say he would miss dinner.

Despite her own dissatisfaction with the marriage, she was so trusting that she believed him when he said he wanted to get a divorce as a means of strengthening their relationship by eliminating outdated legal conventions. Only after the divorce came through, with an unfavorable property settlement, did he confess he really wanted to break up. At this point, Sonia noticed that her experience was similar to that of many other women:

> It seems to me that my experience is far and away the most common single divorce experience in the country; one day the head of household gets fed up with all the responsibilities and pressures, not to mention his "used" wife, turns her in for a new model and opts out, often abandoning his children at the same time.[51]

At the same time that her marriage was under stress, Sonia became increasingly angry at the sexism of the Mormon church. She denies that her advocacy for the Equal Rights Amendment, in opposition to the church's position, had anything to do with her marital problems. Certainly the sexism in the church was oppressive for a woman who was deeply involved in religious life. Her anger at the church was real and understandable. Nor can we say that her feminist advocacy was the cause of her marital problems, since her husband agreed with her completely on the ERA and feminism, and many traditional Mormon women are also abandoned by their husbands. Still, it seems clear that on an emotional level the "hoard of anger that amassed inside" her during the years of a sexist marriage contributed to her energy in opposing the Mormon patriarchy.[52] In her memoir she moves back and forth from one topic to the other, clearly seeing them both as part of a pattern.

Sonia's thinking was strongly influenced by Greer's *The Female Eunuch* and by the first chapter of Millett's *Sexual Politics,* which quotes sexist passages in novels by Henry Miller and Norman Mailer. Although she is an intelligent, well-educated woman, she couldn't get through Millett's second chapter, which outlines her basic theory. She was clearly focusing on the antimale anger in the books, not on the logic of the arguments. Interestingly enough, her husband agreed with her. After a session when the Mormon officials used a variety of dishonest and arrogant tactics in their campaign to excommunicate her from the religion, he remarked, "I'm ashamed of men; I'm ashamed of us all. We're all bastards, Sonia. All of us. . . . You're right you know. Men do hate women. They're afraid of women. I saw it."[53] In addition to being justifiably angry at the church leaders, he may also have felt guilty for abandoning his loyal wife.

The combination of marital problems and the sexism in the church was enough to convert Sonia Johnson from a traditional Mormon house-wife to a radical feminist activist. Her only hesitation was that "I haven't even enough courage to stop shaving my legs."[54] Personal and political motivations were clearly intertwined in her life, but it seems likely that the anger at her husband was the most fundamental on an emotional level.

Radical Feminism and Lesbian Separatism. In an article published in a radical feminist journal in 1970, Germaine Greer argued that women have been taught to deprecate and hide their sexual organs as part of a patriarchal plot to turn them into sex objects and allow the male "pork sword" to rule the world. She urged that vaginal deodorants ánd germicides be abolished and advocated that women become experts on female anatomy by carefully studying their own vaginas and comparing them to those of other women. She complained that "Revolutionary woman may join Women's Liberation Groups and curse and scream and fight the cops, but did you ever hear one of them marching the public street with her skirt high crying 'Can you dig it? Cunt is beautiful!' "[55]

The number of women eager to join in this crusade was quite limited. The radicals coined slogans such as "feminism is the theory, lesbianism is the practice" and agitated within NOW to make lesbian rights a major focus of the movement. In 1971, NOW passed a resolution that acknowledged "the oppression of lesbians as a legitimate concern of feminism."[56] This did not mean that lesbians had taken over the organization. A survey showed that only 8 percent of the members were lesbian and 9 percent bisexual. Most members were liberals who supported the resolution on the grounds that lesbians deserved equal rights too, not on the grounds that all feminists should be lesbians.

Many lesbian vanguardists, however, were not satisfied with this and continued to denounce heterosexual women. Anne Koedt reported that:

> If you are a feminist who is not sleeping with a woman you may risk hearing any of the following accusations: "You're oppressing me if you don't sleep with a woman"; "You're not a radical feminist if you don't sleep with women"; or "You don't love women if you don't sleep with them." I have even seen a woman's argument about an entirely different aspect of feminism be dismissed by some lesbians because she was not having sexual relations with women.[57]

In addition to denouncing women who had traditional marriages and families, the radicals denounced women who sought to have successful careers in male-dominated capitalistic societies. This attitude was common among New Left socialists, but it didn't endear the movement to mainstream women. Betty Friedan was dismayed at this self-defeating argument. In a debate with French feminist writer Simone de Beauvoir, Friedan expressed the view that "women should take all the jobs they can get as long as they keep fighting to open the door wider for women and have no illusion that the tokenism takes the place of a real breakthrough." De Beauvoir disagreed, suggesting that in France women who take good jobs "are accused of being 'career women,' 'elitist,' 'privileged.' Those who refuse are better liked."[58]

Joan Didion and the Backlash to Radical Feminism. This radical phase in the women's movement led to a strong backlash, as Friedan had predicted. In 1972, conservative writer Midge Decter published *The New Chastity and Other Arguments Against Women's Liberation,* which attacked the movement as a whole as antisex, antichild, and antifreedom. Decter used the writings of the radical feminists as grist for her mill, arguing that they expressed the true feelings of all feminists including those who projected a more moderate image in public.[59]

But the more important rejection of radical feminism came from non-political women who simply found the assault on femininity irksome and insulting. On July 30, 1972, writer Joan Didion published a scathing attack on the writings of Kate Millett, Germaine Greer, Shulamith Firestone, and other radical and socialist feminist writers in the *New York Times Book Review*. With her novelist's eye for characters, Didion observed that the central character of the feminist writings was:

> a certain dolorous phantasm, an imagined Everywoman with whom the authors seemed to identify all too entirely . . . [who] was everyone's victim but her own. She was persecuted even by her gynecologist . . . she was raped on every date . . . during the fashion for shoes with pointed toes she, like "many women" had her toes amputated. . . . Should she work, she was paid "three to ten times less" than an (always) unqualified man holding the same job. . . . when she traveled alone, [she] faced a choice between humiliation in a restaurant and "eating a doughnut" in her hotel room.[60]

Didion wondered why the poor woman didn't change gynecologists, get another job, or, at the very least, check into a hotel where room service offered more than doughnuts. She conceded that many women are victims of exploitation and sex-role stereotyping, but she insisted that "other women are not; nobody forces women to buy the package."[61]

The bitterness and sarcasm of Didion's reaction to the radical feminists was surprising. She is a gifted writer whose work is often appreciated by feminist critics for its subtle and complex portrayal of female characters. In the 1960s she had published articles showing that almost the only jobs open to educated women in San Francisco were secretarial.[62] She certainly knew that discrimination against women was real and that not all women could escape by becoming famous writers.

What angered Didion was what she saw as the feminists' lack of confidence in themselves, their endless complaining and whining about the problems of the world. During the 1960s she had a difficult struggle with depression, even going for a psychiatric evaluation where she was told that she had a "personality in process of deterioration with abundant signs of failing defenses and increasing inability of the ego to mediate the world of reality and to cope with normal stress."[63]

Rather than accept the diagnosis of herself as sick and needing help, she developed her own theory of self-respect based on discipline and hard work. The psychiatric report had found that she "lives in a world of people moved by strange, conflicted, poorly comprehended, and, above all, devious motivations which commit them inevitably to conflict and failure."[64] She wasn't so sure that was wrong. She published her psychiatric diagnosis in the first chapter of a book of essays and went on to argue that the world of the sixties was in fact inhabited by a lot of people with strange, conflicted, and self-defeating motives.[65] With the support of her husband, she pulled herself together and made a literary virtue of her mental anguish.

Didion's reaction illustrates how a person with a strong survivor script often responds to the protest scripts of the radical and socialist feminists. The protestors saw women as victims and assumed that the only way they could remedy their condition was to unite as a class against their oppressor. As a pragmatist and survivor, Didion was determined to believe that an assertive and intelligent woman could do well by advancing her own interests within the existing system, whatever its flaws.

She thought that socialist feminism was a hopeless effort to revive an "eccentric and quixotic" American Marxism. The working class and the racial minorities had declined the Marxists' invitation to make a proletarian revolution. Then, "at that exact dispirited moment when there seemed no one at all willing to play the proletariat, along came the women's movement and the invention of women as a 'class.' "[66] This looked like another hopeless cause to Didion, and she wanted no part of it.

Many women probably felt much like Joan Didion, since pragmatic and survivor scripts are strongly rooted in American culture. These women certainly wanted equal rights and equal pay for equal work, and they appreciated the gains made by the liberal feminists. There were times when they got angry at sexism, at the men in their lives, or even at men in general. But they weren't interested in giving up on marriage or femininity or in joining a futile revolutionary crusade against men as a class. Feminists were widely viewed as strident, hostile, frustrated people who couldn't enjoy life. Many women said they were all for women's rights but certainly weren't feminists. By the midseventies, radical feminism was becoming less and less popular within the educated population at large, just as it was peaking in the factional struggles within the feminist movement.

Group Dynamics in Feminism

The emergence of radical feminism was part of a familiar process in ideological group dynamics. As we argued in Chapter Five, ideological groups typically begin with strong charismatic leadership. They then split into overdependent and counterdependent factions. The counterdependents typically assert strong ideological views and attack the founding leader for not being strong or militant enough. The rebellion of the radical feminists against founding mother Betty Friedan fits this pattern perfectly. The radicals were intent on sacrificing their founding mother, just as the mythical sons in Freud's mythical *Totem and Taboo* killed their father.

The revolt of the counterdependents is a volatile point in the life of a movement, and several outcomes are possible. The group may split up into several splinter groups. Or, with good leadership and a lot of good will, it may work out norms, which allow everyone to express their feelings and work together in the same organization. Or it may continue to waste most of its energy in internal wrangling, losing sight of its larger objectives. While the feminists had hoped that women would be able to avoid the personality conflicts and ideological wrangling, which had destroyed so many male-led organizations, they found that women are just as vulnerable to these problems as men.

The conflict within NOW reached a crisis point at the 1975 convention in Philadelphia. There was a power struggle between the reformist and radical caucuses, with the radicals seeking to take the organization "out of the mainstream, into the revolution."[67] This revolutionary upsurge was exceptionally poorly timed, coming just when revolutionary euphoria of the sixties was petering out in the society at large. Voting went on for three days and nights with accusations of vote fraud and stolen registration books. Neither side trusted the other so they called in the American Arbitration Association to resolve the election. The radicals won. The founding mother was cast aside.

By a fortunate coincidence, two days after the election, October 27, 1975, was the date of the radicals' national "Alice Doesn't" women's strike. On this day, women across the nation were not supposed to work, shop, cook, or sleep with the enemy. To the radicals, the revolution seemed to be at hand. After all, the *SCUM Manifesto* had promised that women could paralyze the nation simply by withdrawing from the labor force and refusing to shop.

They found out what happens to a movement that loses touch with reality and calls a strike without a strike vote by its supporters. Nothing happened but a few small teach-ins and demonstrations. A few days later, on November 4, voters in New York and New Jersey decisively rejected state Equal Rights Amendments, which had been placed on their ballots. This was a devastating blow to the national ERA movement, since these were liberal states whose legislatures had endorsed the federal amendment without serious debate. The newspapers were filled with headlines such as "Can Feminism Survive" and "Is NOW on the Brink of Then?" A Harris poll showed that 65 percent of the nation's women supported the goals of the women's movement, but only 17 percent believed that "most organizations trying to change women's status in society are helping the cause of women."[68]

Many women left NOW to join organizations such as the Women's Equity Action League, which seeks to "steer clear of divisive issues" and focus on lobbying, education, legal action, and monitoring the performance of government agencies.[69] Betty Friedan published an "Open Letter to the Women's Movement" denouncing the preoccupation with lesbianism and the movement's disregard for the sentiments of mainstream women.[70] Her anger at the radical feminists in the "Open Letter" sounds much like Joan Didion's.

Although the conflicts have become less bitter with time, radical and socialist feminism remain strong within NOW. The continuing influence of socialist thinking in NOW accounts for the organization's decision to oppose the American war with Iraq in 1991. NOW leaders praised the Iraqi constitution for providing for equal rights for women. Apparently, NOW leaders were unaware of recent changes in Iraqi law that placated conservative religious sentiments by restoring medieval, patriarchical laws regarding women. For example, on February 18, 1990, the Iraqi government issued a special decree stating that "any Iraqi who, on grounds of adultery, purposely kills his mother, daughter, sister, maternal or paternal aunt, maternal or paternal niece, maternal or paternal female cousin, shall not be prosecuted."[71]

Unaware of these changes, the NOW leaders argued that Iraq was more democratic than the United States, which does not mention women in its constitution. They drew a strained analogy between their position as women in America and Iraq's position in the Middle East, arguing that "as women, we know something of what it is like to be colonized."[72] Whatever one thinks of the merits of this argument, it clearly moved NOW further out of the American mainstream and closer to the ranks of leftist protest groups motivated by hostility to American society and idealization of its enemies.

Unfortunately for the feminist movement, all of this conflict has been broadcast to the public and given extensive media coverage. The image of feminists as strident man-haters persists and continues to stigmatize the movement. Some socialist feminists have given up. Surprising numbers have converted to orthodox Judaism, which they find gives them a special role as women despite the lack of gender equality.[73] Others are struggling to overcome the movement's isolation from the concerns of its mass constituency. As Ferree and Hess observed, "the New Feminist Movement has found a generally sympathetic audience but has failed to engage the strong commitment of a majority of women, causing considerable soul-searching among feminist leaders."[74]

Phyllis Schlafly and the Antifeminists

Phyllis Schlafly was a happy, healthy baby born into a conservative, Catholic St. Louis home in 1924. She has always been a happy person, or at least her smiling face makes it seem so. Betty Friedan has her doubts: "Phyllis Schlafly is such a fake. She's always smiling. Anyone who smiles that much has got to be a fraud. It's enough to make you want to punch her in the mouth."[75]

The feminists have a lot more than Phyllis's smile to be angry about. She almost single-handedly organized the movement that defeated the Equal Rights Amendment. In many ways she symbolizes the antifeminist woman. A happy housewife and mother of six, she is pleased to publicly acknowledge her husband's role as the final authority and decision maker in her family.[76]

Although Schlafly rejects feminist values and politics, she is a remarkably assertive woman with strong leadership and organizational skills. She has an undergraduate degree from Radcliffe, and she went back to school for a law degree in her spare time after her children were grown. She is married to a successful lawyer who has no problem with her outshining him on the national stage, perhaps because in addition to accepting his authority she flatters him with her often stated belief that marriage "is the best deal for women the world has yet devised."[77]

Schlafly's contentment with her lot in life is based on a strong parental commitment script. Her father was a self-educated engineer/salesman who worked for Westinghouse for twenty-five years. He was let go during the Depression with no pension and had a very difficult time until World War II revived the economy. Despite his personal experiences, her father remained a loyal Republican and a friend of big business throughout the Depression. He continued to passionately believe in the free enterprise system and insisted on accepting responsibility for his own fate instead of blaming the corporation or the capitalist system. He was something of a visionary who worked for years on a design for a rotary engine, which he patented in 1944, but which was never manufactured. Phyllis's mother, who was from a socially prominent family, took the children to Los Angeles to live with an uncle for a year, then returned and got a job as a librarian at the Art Museum to make ends meet.

Phyllis's sister wanted to be a stockbroker, but could only get a job as a secretary even though she had a college degree. When the boss kept hiring younger men into the training program for brokers, she finally left and found another job, never complaining about discrimination. Phyllis claims that she was accepted by Harvard Law School in 1945, although Harvard's policy at that time was not to admit women to the law school.

Despite the obvious evidence of gender discrimination in her and her sister's lives, she insists that anyone can achieve up to their potential if they try hard enough and have a positive attitude.

Schlafly's philosophy of life is similar to popular psychologies that emphasize "the power of positive thinking" and argue that people should accept responsibility for everything that happens to them. These approaches argue that we will be happier and more successful if we believe that we are in complete control of our lives. Schlafly's "Positive Woman starts with the assumption that the world is her oyster." By contrast, the "the women's liberationist is imprisoned by her own negative view of herself and of her place in the world around her."[78]

Betty Friedan may be right that Schlafly's happiness is a fraud. Schlafly believes that "the public display of fear, sorrow, anger, and irritation reveals a lack of self-discipline that should be avoided by the Positive Woman just as much as by the Positive Man."[79] If she were unhappy, we can be assured that she wouldn't let us know about it. Unlike the liberationists, who believe it is a gain when men learn to cry and show their emotions, Schlafly wants women to learn to imitate the men's stoicism.

Schlafly went to a Catholic girls' school where discipline was very strict, and she sat for long hours in class without talking. Christian Morality was a part of the curriculum and was taught as a set of axioms as rigid and certain as those of geometry or chemistry. She excelled in this environment, although her family's financial straits made it difficult for her to keep up with the other girls socially. She found social life frivolous anyway and preferred academic pursuits. Her rebellion was to drop out of the Catholic Women's College where she was expected to go. She found it unchallenging academically, so she gave up her scholarship and worked nights so she could take classes at Washington University. This was during World War II, and her night job was test firing ammunition in a munitions factory. Finally, she won a fellowship to Radcliffe where she received her bachelor's and master's degrees in political science.

She turned down the chance to go to graduate school because it was expensive and she was tired of academics. She worked for the American Enterprise Association in Washington, helping to write speeches for congressmen on the merits of the free enterprise system. Working in Washington reinforced her hostility to the government bureaucracy, and after a year of being a single woman in Washington she returned to St. Louis where she worked in a political campaign and got a job writing a public relations newsletter for a bank.

She met her husband to be, attorney Fred Schlafly, through the bank newsletter. He was a thirty-nine-year-old confirmed bachelor from nearby Alton, Illinois, who believed that "marriage is a fine institution, but I'm not ready for an institution."[80] Phyllis was an attractive young woman of twenty-four, but it was her mind and her politics that attracted him. He first sought her out in response to something she had written in the bank newsletter, thinking that she was a man. They shared an intense commitment to right-wing views very similar to those of the John Birch Society. They married and set up housekeeping in his hometown where they have lived ever since.

Before taking up the ERA issue, Phyllis lost a bid for Congress against a well-established candidate who asked his constituents, "who here thinks my Harvard-educated opponent ought to quit attacking my foreign-aid votes and stay home with her husband and six kids? I don't tell her how to take care of her family. And she shouldn't tell me how to take care of my constituents." She responded that her husband thought a woman's place was in the house—the U.S. House of Representatives.[81]

Despite this sexist attack and her feminist response, which was also used by Bella Abzug in the same year, she denied that she lost either of her two bids for Congress because of her sex. She claimed that as many people voted for her as against her because she was a woman. She lost because she went up against popular incumbents who were not the flaming liberals she would have loved to attack but moderate conservatives in good touch with their constituents.

Her political writings during the pre-ERA period were very much in the right-wing tradition. They portrayed a world in which liberal conspiracies threatened to sell America out to its enemies. Her most serious book, *Kissinger on the Couch,* was coauthored with a retired admiral.[82] They denounced Henry Kissinger and the Council on Foreign Relations as "gravediggers" who were selling out U.S. security in arms control negotiations with the Soviet Union. Despite the title, they did not attempt to analyze Kissinger's unconscious motivations. They simply claimed that he may be a "nut" who has made secret deals with the Kremlin. The conservative *National Review* praised the book's technical data on arms control but panned its "polemical overkill. Kissinger, the villain of the piece, is variously depicted as a loon, a coward, a Svengali, a liar, and a traitor."[83]

She was much more successful with a small paperback, *A Choice Not an Echo,* which she published privately and sold for seventy-five cents. It is really a rather dull book, full of arcane "facts" about the internal politics of Republican Party nominating conventions. Its theme is that the "secret kingmakers" in the Republican Party are conspiring to nominate a dull, me-too candidate who won't contest the Democratic Party's conspiracy to sell the free world out to Communism. Its simplistic rhetoric was just what the Republican right-wing was looking for in 1964. It sold three million copies without any advertising and helped Barry Goldwater to win the California primary. Schlafly promised her readers that "Barry Goldwater is the one Republican who can and will win—because he will campaign on the issues of 1964. He is the one Republican who will not pull his punches to please the kingmakers."[84]

After the Goldwater debacle, the Republican right-wing's credibility was low. As vice president of the National Federation of Republican Women, Schlafly was next in line to be president of the organization. But the Republican Party leadership didn't want a right-winger in that post and she was pushed aside. She tried running for Congress again in 1970, but her efforts to red-bait a popular incumbent backfired.

At this point, Schlafly seized on the Equal Rights Amendment as an issue where she could use her talents and revive a fading career. When the ERA had first passed Congress in 1971, she was involved in her book on Kissinger. At that time a friend asked her to debate a feminist on ERA, but she said, "I'm not interested in ERA. How about a debate on national defense?"[85] But in 1972, when the ERA had almost been ratified by enough states to become part of the Constitution, Schlafly took an interest.

Analyzing the amendment, she concluded that, far from helping women, the ERA would harm them by eliminating laws that protected them, such as the laws which require a husband to support his wife. Older wives, who had dedicated their lives to their husbands and families, could be cast aside and left to support themselves with their own limited earning capacity. Women might be drafted into the armed forces. Women workers could lose protections at work and be forced to work longer hours or lift heavy loads. Homosexuals might be granted equal rights to teach school children.

The feminists denied that the ERA would have such drastic consequences, citing the ERA's simple provision that "equality of rights under the law shall not be denied or abridged by the United States or by any State on account of sex." Schlafly detected a sinister conspiracy behind this seemingly innocuous statement, a conspiracy led by Betty Friedan and her sisters at the National Organization for Women. She pointed to the second article of the amendment, which stated that "the Congress shall have the power to enforce, by appropriate legislation, the provisions of this article." Again a seemingly innocuous provision, but who knows what provisions Congress would enact? Who knows how the Supreme Court would interpret it? When, in 1973, the Supreme Court found a right to abortion in Constitutional provisions, which nowhere mention it, Schlafly's warnings seemed plausible to many people.

Schlafly's home state of Illinois was one of the few nonsouthern states that had not ratified the amendment, and Schlafly led a very effective campaign against ratification. She also spoke across the country and helped to mobilize antiratification movements in other states. Several states rescinded their ratification votes. The liberals argued that states couldn't rescind a ratification vote, but it didn't seem fair that a state legislature could change its mind in one direction and not the other.

In many ways, the radical feminist movement played into Phyllis Schlafly's hands during this period. One leader told *Time Magazine* that "feminism is lesbianism. . . . [it is] only when women don't rely on men to fulfill sexual needs that they are finally free of masculine control." At the International Women's Year conference in 1977, hundreds of lesbians released gas filled balloons with the slogan, "We are Everywhere." National television coverage delighted in buttons and signs with slogans such as "The Pope has Clitoris Envy—He Wears Skirts Doesn't He" and "A Woman Without a Man is Like a Fish Without a Bicycle."[86] The Wages for Housework movement advocated requiring husbands to pay their wives a wage, which would have increased the family's social security tax bill. Some ERA backers publicly linked the amendment to homosexuality and abortion. All of these issues were like red flags to Schlafly's conservative constituency.

Schlafly's essential strategy was to frame the ERA in such a way that people could respond to it according to their ideological scripts. Before Schlafly, the ERA was generally viewed as a noncontroversial statement of women's equal dignity and worth as human beings. Together with the radical feminists who were also eager to express ideological points, Schlafly managed to turn it into a left-vs.-right issue. Schlafly got funds from conservative foundations and rallied support from organizations such as the American Legion, the Daughters of the American Revolution, and the Knights of Columbus, as well as from fundamentalist Protestants and Orthodox Jews. The forces in favor, in addition to feminist groups, were liberal organizations such as the American Civil Liberties Union, the League of Women Voters, and the United Auto Workers.

Women across the country became confused and frightened that their way of life was under assault by antifamily, prohomosexual forces, and all for a symbolic amendment, which would change very little while generating a lot of business for lawyers. When the state equal rights amendments were defeated in New Jersey and New York in 1975, it was clear that Schlafly had won and NOW had lost.

Conclusions

In Betty Friedan, the feminist movement had a leader with a rare combination of utopian vision and practical leadership skills. Her personal experiences and background gave her sensitivity to the frustrations of educated homemakers and the energy to work effectively and tirelessly for change. She knew when to temper her vision with pragmatism. Under her leadership, the movement was highly successful in a remarkably short time. Blessed with such a leader and on the verge of its capstone achievement, the ratification of the Equal Rights Amendment, the movement pushed Friedan and her practical vision aside in favor of self-defeating but emotionally satisfying utopianism and rhetorical posturing. The result was the loss of the ERA and the precipitous decline of feminism's prestige and influence in American society.

When David Bouchier finished his study of the British feminists, he concluded that like many aging radical groups the radical feminists had actually given up in any realistic efforts to change the world. They persisted as a kind of Old Girls' Club for former activists, using their radical views to maintain the boundary between themselves and conventional society. This is essentially the same conclusion Betty Friedan reached about the American lesbian separatists. She thought that, for all their radical rhetoric, they were actually opting out of the struggle. She argued:

> Does it help a woman liberate herself, does she become more equal, when she makes love to a woman instead of a man? I doubt it. I think it just evades the issue. It's something any woman can do without breaking through barriers in the office or school, or threatening those in power. . . . As an expression of sexual preference to each her own. But as a political statement, it's a copout.[87]

The radicalization of the feminist movement played into the hands of authoritarians such as Phyllis Schlafly who would have had a much more difficult time fighting a moderate movement without the rhetorical excesses. It was easy to equate the Equal Rights Amendment with lesbianism and radicalism when many in the feminist movement were making the same connections. When radical feminists such as Ti-Grace Atkinson denounced heterosexual love as a "pathological phenomenon" and announced that "the institution of sexual intercourse is anti-feminist," this made the antifeminists' claim to be defending motherhood and the American family seem plausible.[88]

Psychologically, feminists are inclined to externalize their personal problems while antifeminists are more likely to deny them. This is a typical psychological difference between followers of protest and authoritarian scripts. As Ti-Grace Atkinson observed, "so far, the feminist movement has, primarily, been women coming together to complain."[89] The radical and socialist feminists exaggerate the defects of American society, seeking to blame it for their problems. The antifeminists idealize the strong points of the American system, seeking to strengthen their own egos by identification with it. Both groups feel vulnerable to threats from powerful aggressive forces. This feeling of vulnerability is expressed in a common preoccupation with pornography and in a feeling that male sexuality is dangerous and needs to be carefully controlled.[90] The radical feminists are threatened by men in general, especially if they are "macho" (a Spanish word meaning "masculine, vigorous, robust, or male," but used by feminists as a synonym for "male chauvinist"). The antifeminists feel threatened by liberals, radicals, atheists, subversives, or, indeed, by the feminists themselves.

In moderation, both perspectives can lead to useful insights. It is only when they are pushed to extremes that they lose touch with reality. Extremists such as Millett and Greer are simply wrong when they assert that small children are better raised by professionals in institutions than by their parents or that women must avoid marriage if they are to have equal rights. Extremists such as Schlafly are wrong when they deny that discrimination against women exists or when they claim that the campaign for the Equal Rights Amendment was a massive conspiracy against the American family. These claims may be politically useful in the short run by playing on the fear or anger of their more gullible followers, but in the long run they are bound to cost a movement in credibility and prestige.

Both groups are intolerant of their opposition, viewing them as enemies to be repressed instead of fellow citizens to be negotiated with. Anita Bryant noted this parallel when the liberals tried to repress her for leading a campaign against gay rights in Miami:

> Just twenty-five years ago, many artists and writers in the entertainment industry were blacklisted, prevented from practicing their skills, and denied their livelihoods. In response to this blacklisting, civil libertarians and liberal commentators throughout America raised their voices in protest.
>
> Today, we have come full circle. I have just been notified that the blacklisting of Anita Bryant has begun. I have been blacklisted for exercising the right of a mother to defend her children, and all children, against their being recruited by homosexuals.[91]

Anita Bryant's complaint is disingenuous. She has little concern for the civil liberties of people with whom she disagrees. When she led the campaign to deny civil rights protection to gays in Miami, she did not comment on the parallel between her attacks on gays and those of Fidel Castro in nearby Havana.[92] Castro's repression of homosexuals was presumably based on socialist principles, while Bryant's was defended with quotations from the Bible. Psychologically, however, the process was the same. A hated group was stigmatized and scapegoated for the deficiencies of the society.

Bryant is correct, however, in pointing out that many feminists and leftists try to stifle speech they consider to be sexist, racist, classist, or not "politically correct." Feminists seek to censor books and articles to eliminate "sexist" terminology and to modify school curricula to exclude works that offend them.[93] In this, they parallel the efforts of right-wing guardians of traditional values.

Today, the radical feminists are most visible at elite universities, where they often control the Women's Studies programs.[94] Radical feminist groups can often be detected by their spelling of the word "women" as "womyn" to eliminate the hated syllable "men." Academically, they focus on introducing radical feminist literature and perspectives into the curriculum, particularly in required general education courses.[95] Politically, they often focus on issues of sexual harassment, rape, and sexual abuse. This has made universities more sensitive to these issues, as well as exposing many of the wild goings-on at fraternity parties.[96] Difficult questions are raised, such as whether a woman who gets so drunk at a party that she doesn't know what she is doing can be said to have been raped. Often these events do not qualify as rape by legal definitions, but are so defined by the feminists.

The implicit theme of many of the feminist campaigns is that all heterosexual relationships are suspect. Major campaigns are launched to pass laws against rape in marriage, although the use of these laws in troubled marriages is problematic.[97] Surveys are published that claim most women are raped or abused during their college years. On careful examination, however, it is found that these surveys define rape very loosely, including any situation where the man uses verbal persuasion or where the woman later feels that she really didn't want to have sex.[98] Some feminists argue that as long as men have most of the power in society, women may be victims of rape even if they agree to have sex. In several of the cases radical feminists have cited, the woman involved denied that a rape had occurred and continued to have relations with the man in question.

At Brown University, radical feminists posted lists all over campus of the names of men they considered to be sexual abusers. No evidence was given, and the feminists posted the lists anonymously so that the men would have no opportunity to defend themselves or to take legal action for slander. This action won them a tremendous amount of publicity, much of it, however, focused on their disregard for due process and unwillingness to file criminal charges so that the perpetrators of alleged crimes could be prosecuted.

The feminists' tendency toward extremism and single-minded pre-occupation with a single issue turns off many people who would otherwise be sympathetic with feminist goals. Women like Joan Didion simply do not believe that things are as bad as the radical feminists say, or that rallying women for a revolutionary class war will make things better. This seems to be the majority opinion, even among young college women who would normally be one of the strongest constituencies for the feminist movement. In his study of Rutgers College undergraduates in 1984, for example, anthropologist Michael Moffatt found that:

> most women undergraduates were not especially impressed by feminist or other political critiques of gender inequality. . . . such arguments sounded dated to them. Most of them apparently assumed that there were a few "natural" differences between the sexes: "naturally" girls had to be more careful about sexual danger than guys . . . [but] these natural differences were no big deal compared to the real sexual autonomy they now enjoyed and to their near equality with undergraduate males in most other aspects of their daily lives in college.[99]

These young women believe in equal rights for women. Some of them may have even marched in Washington when it looked as if abortion rights were about to be lost. But they have no fundamental anger toward men as a group or towards the capitalist system, and they do not make feminism a major focus of their lives. They do not intend to stop dating men or to forswear marriage. The large majority of American women applauded America's victory over Iraq, even though Iraq mentions women in its constitution and the United States does not.[100] Indeed, thanks to the impact of the feminist movement, many women served alongside the men in the armed services during that war. To be effective as anything but a refuge for frustrated radicals, the feminist movement must relate to the concerns of the large majority of women who do not share radical or socialist feminist assumptions.

Chapter Thirteen

Linus Pauling:
From Eminent Scientist to True Believer

Linus Pauling's early life was a series of stunning successes.[1] He is the only person ever to have received two unshared Nobel Prizes, one for chemistry and the other for peace. At the peak of his prestige and renown, instead of settling into an elder statesman role, he shocked his friends and admirers by launching a crusade to prove that vitamin C was a cure for the common cold. When the evidence was sketchy and inconclusive, he went on the offensive. He claimed that vitamin C was a panacea, useful as a preventative and treatment for all kinds of diseases, including cancer. His advocacy for "orthomolecular medicine," the use of large doses of vitamins and other natural substances to regulate the body's molecular structure, made him a hero to true believers in megavitamins and other "nuts among the berries."[2] His books on vitamin C were a boon to the owners of "health food" stores who displayed them prominently next to the vitamin racks.

All of this embarrassed Pauling's colleagues in the scientific community. Why should an eminent scientist and elder statesman of the peace movement squander his reputation in this way? Why did he abandon scientific skepticism for superficial hucksterism? Was there some flaw in his character from the beginning, or did his powers deteriorate with age?

Boyhood in Oregon

Oddly enough, Pauling's nutritional hucksterism has roots in his family history. His father was a druggist in the frontier town of Condon, Oregon. Herman Pauling was the only member of his working-class-family group to start a business. He threw himself into it and was a great success with the local residents who were desperately in need of medical services. Word spread that Herman Pauling was as good as any doctor, and he charged no fee for a consultation. He often visited his bedridden customers just to see how they were doing and give them a little tender loving care. All his life Herman was a frustrated physician, with a real concern for public health and a curiosity about the effects of his drugs on his customers.

He was also an aggressive merchandiser, and each weekly issue of the *Condon Globe* carried a new full column Pauling advertisement. One week he offered two coupons, which could be redeemed for ten cents on any purchase. Another ad offered a six-hundred-word description of a blood purifier, six bottles for five dollars. He announced a ten-day sale at the store where "Pauling's Prices Please the People" and continued in the alliterative vein with "Pauling's Pink Pills for Pale People."

In the March 30, 1906, edition of the *Globe,* he offered twenty-five-cent bottles of "Dr. Pfunder's Oregon Blood Purifier." This seemingly miraculous compound of natural herbs, roots, barks, and berries was touted as "an almost certain cure for all diseases arising from derangements of the liver and kidneys, or an impure condition of the blood, such as scrofulous affections, erysipelas, pimples, blotches, boils, salt rheum, ulcers, cold sores, dropsy and dyspepsia," to say nothing of curing rheumatism, biliousness, coated tongues, and bad breath.

Dr. Pfunder's blood purifier, containing only natural ingredients and allegedly carefully analyzed to assure the proper dosage, is an early example of orthomolecular medicine as Linus Pauling later defined it. It purported to treat disease and maintain health by regulating the concentrations in the body of natural substances that are normally present. Indeed, while vitamin C was not isolated chemically until 1933, the berry and grape juices used by Dr. Pfunder might have retained some of it. The parallel between Herman Pauling's claims and those made today by many proprietors of "health food" stores is inescapable.

Linus's father died of a perforated gastric ulcer at the age of thirty-three when Linus was nine years old. His grandfather had died a few days before at the age of fifty-five of a heart attack complicated by nephritis (which was to almost kill Linus at age forty-one). These deaths had a profound effect on Linus's emotional development. Before the deaths he was a well-adjusted, outgoing young lad with good social skills and a flair for attracting attention to himself. He had a secure place in a small, tightly knit community and could look forward to a successful future in whatever profession he chose to pursue. Suddenly he became dependent on a mother who was depressed, suffering from pernicious anemia, and ill prepared for supporting a family.

Linus took his father's and grandfather's deaths stoically. When he overheard a neighbor say, "these poor little children do not know what it means to have a father who is dead," he wanted to correct her, to tell her that he had long since understood fully the meaning of the word "dead." He accepted death as a sad but natural fact. Men were born, they grew up, worked, and, sooner or later, died. He seems not to have thought about the failure of Dr. Pfunder's tonic, or his other potions, to save his father or grandfather.

Linus's mother, Belle, had been deeply in love with her husband and centered her life around him. Linus was a love child, born nine months and one day after their wedding, but she was never as close to him as she was to the two girls who came later. Linus never really allowed himself to express the pain he felt after his grandfather's and father's deaths, perhaps because he knew his mother wasn't strong enough to accept his feelings. His main struggle seems to have been to free himself from his mother's need to be dependent on him.

He avoided close relationships with adults, whether teachers or relatives, and put his energies into hobbies and part-time jobs. He did have close friendships with several boys his own age, who treated him as equals without making excessive demands on him. One of these friends introduced him to chemistry, and he became absorbed with experimenting with chemicals. His early preoccupation with science may have had its origins at least in part in a need to sublimate emotional distress, but he was very good at it and recognized that scientific achievement could be an avenue to professional independence. Whether through death, illness, or insensitivity, adults had let him down. He was determined to make his way on his own.

He insisted on going to Oregon Agricultural College (now Oregon State University) in nearby Corvallis, against his mother's pleading that he work as a machinist to support the family. She relented and found him appropriate housing in Corvallis, but she couldn't help with his expenses. One summer she even spent the money he had earned on his summer job as a paving inspector, forcing him to delay his schooling a year. However, the faculty at OAC recognized his brilliance and offered him an instructorship. They also urged him to go on to graduate school at California Institute of Technology, against the strong urgings of his and his new fiancée's families, who all thought it ridiculous to live on a meager student stipend when he could get any number of well-paying jobs with his undergraduate degree. He had supported himself since he was sixteen, however, and he was in no mood to listen to their advice.

The Chemical Bond

Pauling's career in graduate school was brilliant, and when he received an offer of a fellowship at Berkeley, Cal Tech was so eager to keep him that they arranged a fellowship for him to study in Europe. He and his wife, Ava Helen, left their one-year-old son at home with her mother for the year abroad. There he met the leaders in the new field of quantum mechanics. On his return to the United States, he quickly achieved prominence as a pioneer in applying the principles of quantum mechanics to the structural analysis of complex molecules.

His most significant scientific article was published in 1931, "The Nature of the Chemical Bond: Application of the Results Obtained from the Quantum Mechanics and from a Theory of Paramagnetic Susceptibility to the Structure of Molecules."[3] His many papers after that were largely extensions and applications of the same general principles. His monograph, *The Nature of the Chemical Bond,* summed up this work and has become a scientific classic. It is "one of the most cited publications of all time," having received 15,318 mentions in the *Science Citations Index* between 1945 and 1988.[4]

Nothing in Pauling's later career had the same impact or importance as his youthful accomplishments. He had several important successes, especially in modeling the structure of proteins, but he had an embarrassing failure in 1953 when he published an erroneous triple-helix model of the structure of DNA a few months before James Watson and Francis Crick discovered the correct double-helix structure.[5] Pauling's paper, coauthored with Robert Corey, was presented as a tentative hypothesis, but it was full of errors in elementary college chemistry such that, in Watson's judgment, "if a student had made a similar mistake, he would be thought unfit to benefit from Cal Tech's chemistry faculty" where Pauling was a distinguished professor.[6] Pauling quickly acknowledged that his model was wrong.

Of course, this one mistake didn't destroy Pauling's reputation as a distinguished elder statesman of science. In 1954, he received the Nobel Prize in Chemistry for his "research into the nature of the chemical bond and its application to the structure of complex substances." This recognition was for work done several decades before, which is not unusual for Nobel Prizes. Still, Pauling may have been disappointed by his failure to top off his earlier accomplishments with a dramatic discovery such as the structure of DNA.

Defying Stalinism and McCarthyism

Although Pauling was still able to publish creditable papers in scientific journals, he was in danger of becoming more of a historical figure than a leader of modern chemistry. His valence bond theory was being displaced by molecular orbital theories that didn't depend on his work. At the same time political activities, which he had undertaken casually, in part to please his wife, were bringing him considerable attention. There was even speculation that by giving him the Nobel award in 1954 the Swedes were making more of a political than a scientific statement. By celebrating Pauling, the Swedes were able to assert their neutrality by thumbing their noses at both the American McCarthyists and the Russian Stalinists, for Pauling had alienated the McCarthyists with his liberal politics and the Stalinists with his chemical theories.

Two Soviet chemists had translated *The Nature of the Chemical Bond* into Russian, and it met with a negative reaction from the Soviet chemistry establishment who somehow equated his resonance theory of chemical bonding with philosophical idealism and feared it would lure impressionable young minds away from dialectical materialism. Pauling found this odd since the English Marxist philosopher J. B. S. Haldane had cited the same resonance theory as an example of dialectical materialism in science. In fact, he doubted that anyone really understood both resonance theory and dialectical materialism well enough to say whether or not they have anything to do with each other. He had read neither Marx nor Freud but said he would like to if he ever found the time. He issued an eight-page press release, through the public relations department at Cal Tech, which made the Soviets look foolish for trying to settle scientific questions with political resolutions and majority votes.

For an American, of course, McCarthyists were a more dangerous opponent. In 1948 Pauling had spoken out against the House Un-American Activities Committee's loyalty investigations. He also joined with other distinguished scientists, such as Albert Einstein, Harold Urey, and Leo Szilard, in opposing the development of atomic weapons. He defended California teachers who were fired for refusing to sign loyalty oaths. In the political climate of the 1950s he was attacked as a "red sympathizer," and lecture invitations were withdrawn. Finally, the government denied him a passport to attend scientific meetings in Europe on the grounds that he was "not sufficiently anti-Communist." He signed loyalty oaths and affidavits that he was not and had never been a Communist, but to no avail. Indeed, the lack of a passport may have contributed to his failure to solve the structure of DNA, since he was not able to personally examine the X-ray slides and other materials collected by his English colleagues.

Within a few years, however, Pauling won the confrontation with both the Stalinists and the House Un-American Activities Committee. With the passing of Stalin, the Soviets stopped testing scientific theories against Marxist metaphysics. The American government gradually relented to pressure from eminent scientists all over the world and returned Pauling's passport, at first for travel to specific events and finally for general use. Pauling was vindicated for his persistence in sticking to his convictions, just as he had been when he defied his family to go to graduate school.

When the American government insisted that nuclear testing in the atmosphere was harmless, Pauling organized the collection of eleven thousand signatures from eminent scientists all over the world on a petition denouncing nuclear testing. In 1960, Senator James Eastland subpoenaed Pauling to testify about Communist infiltration in the peace movement. Pauling demanded an open hearing and quickly became the star of the show with his sarcasm and brilliant repartee. Even former President Truman remarked at a luncheon that he understood Pauling had been called before a congressional committee to give testimony about the nature of the red corpuscle. "I suggest," he said drolly, "that Professor Pauling confine his investigations to the white corpuscle." Again, Pauling won the struggle when the committee backed down, and, a few years later, President Kennedy conceded that radioactive fallout was harmful and signed an atmospheric test ban treaty.

For Pauling, recognition came easily through politics. His political ideas were never innovative nor based on original thinking or research. His first political involvement, in 1940, was in support of the Union of Great Britain and the United States, a proposal he took from a book by Clarence Streit that was popular at the time. His opposition to McCarthyism and to nuclear testing, although courageous and effective, were not unusual. He was simply a very effective spokesman for positions that were shared by most of his friends.

The general public admires distinguished scientists and often assumes that their genius carries over into the social science and public policy arenas. The evidence doesn't always support this view. Einstein, for example, spoke and wrote extensively on peace but had nothing original to say and never bothered to read the scholarly literature on the subject. Pauling, also, wrote on war without studying it seriously. When *Life* magazine refused to give him space to reply to an article by Edward Teller, which purported to refute his claims against testing, he was also rejected by other mass magazines. He decided to write a book and dictated it furiously over two four-day weekends. It is an elaboration of his speeches against nuclear fallout combined with a simplistic exhortation that nations should stop fighting each other and settle their differences peacefully. The book, *No*

More War!, was well received by liberal readers despite the lack of original ideas or any serious attempt to grapple with difficult political or moral issues.[7]

Vitamin C and Orthomolecular Medicine

This same pattern of enthusiastic advocacy without original research characterizes Pauling's last and most puzzling crusade. The vitamin C controversy came to Pauling's attention quite accidentally at a time when he seemed to be searching for something new and exciting. He had left the California Institute of Technology at the age of sixty-three and moved to the Center for the Study of Democratic Institutions, a liberal think-tank in Santa Barbara where he had no duties other than participation in rambling tape-recorded discussions with other eminent thinkers. There were no scientific laboratories, and Pauling lacked a focus for his energies. He spent a lot of time on the lecture circuit, and during a speech in New York City he happened to mention that he hoped to live another fifteen or twenty years in order to observe new developments in science and society. He received a letter from biochemist Irwin Stone who happened to have been in the audience and who promised him the chance to live for another fifty years if he would take massive doses of vitamin C.

This suggestion was outrageous enough to capture Pauling's interest. He read some of the published literature on the subject, decided that the medical and pharmaceutical establishments had suppressed a simple treatment that might cut into their revenues, and threw his scientific prestige behind the advocacy for vitamin C as a cold remedy. Pauling's scientific prestige enabled him to publish popular books, which became best-sellers despite the fact that he personally had not done any research on the topic.[8] For his books on vitamin C, Pauling simply looked through the literature for studies that he could interpret as supporting his point of view. His review of the literature was completely one-sided. When a study got positive results, he assumed they would have been even stronger if the research had been done differently. When the results were negative, he assumed that they would have been positive if flaws in the research design had been corrected.

In many cases Pauling went well beyond the conclusions of the scientists who had done the research and who had generally concluded that vitamin C was of little or no value in treating the common cold. When the medical establishment reacted negatively, Pauling escalated his claims, offering vitamin C as a treatment for diseases as varied as cancer, mental illness, viral pneumonia, hepatitis, poliomyelitis, tuberculosis, measles, mumps, chicken pox, viral orchitis, viral meningitis, shingles, fever blisters, cold sores, canker sores, and warts. All these claims were based on theoretical speculation, not scientific evidence.

Pauling also became enthusiastic about the work of a small group of dissident psychiatrists who had been experimenting with nicotinic acid as a treatment for schizophrenia. He published an article in the *American Journal of Psychiatry,* which presented some case histories, theoretical speculations, and related scientific information but offered no statistical evidence of the effectiveness of "orthomolecular" treatment.[9] The American Psychiatric Association (APA) published several review essays, which took Pauling's statements apart, exposed the flaws and gaps in each of them, and left the APA looking like a paragon of scientific virtue, which had found it reluctantly necessary to correct an errant dotard. Richard Wyatt noted that "Pauling raises a question about the significance of differences in percent improvement in one essentially negative study with niacin, adds his own inconclusive data on possible vitamin deficiencies, and quotes questionable studies of ascorbic acid."[10]

Donald Kleen questioned "Pauling's incomprehensible acceptance of very minimum differences that lack statistical significance as solid evidence of therapeutic efficacy."[11]

Pauling insisted that although the studies had not proved that ortho-molecular therapy was effective, neither had they proved that it wasn't. Essentially, he demanded that his opponents prove him wrong (in technical jargon, to prove the null hypothesis). Under the rules of statistical analysis, this is logically impossible. All research with statistical methods has a margin of error and Pauling seemed content to assert that as long as there was any possibility of error in the studies on vitamins and schizophrenia his theories were unrefuted. This argument reveals the essentially ideological nature of his claims; in his view they are not falsifiable by empirical evidence.

Pauling's claims for vitamin C as a treatment for cancer have been more modest than his claims on the common cold or schizophrenia.[12] Here again, his role has been to publicize the work of others, especially that of Scottish physician Ewen Cameron. He does not claim to have a cure for cancer, although he asserts that high doses of vitamin C are likely to prevent cancer and help to prolong the survival time of patients with terminal cancer. He does not advocate vitamin C as an alternative to conventional cancer treatment.

When he was encouraged to retire from an appointment at Stanford University, which was embarrassed by his focus on eccentric health research, Pauling founded the Linus Pauling Institute of Science and Medicine, which raises money directly from the general public. The institute has been plagued with controversy largely because of a conflict with Arthur Robinson, a young chemist who was a close associate of Pauling and left a university position to accept a tenured professorship at the institute. At first Robinson also served as director. The problems arose when Robinson did an experiment with hairless mice and found that the rate of skin cancer was actually increased by a diet heavy in vitamin C. These findings resulted in a split between Pauling and Robinson, which led to a lengthy lawsuit ending with a substantial settlement in Robinson's favor.[13]

Pauling has not been vindicated, at least by the professional community, for his stand on vitamin C and orthomolecular medicine. Among the general public, however, the statistical issues inherent in research in these fields are sufficiently confusing that many people suspect that he might be correct. Even biographers are confused. A recent biography gave up on the attempt to evaluate Pauling's writings on vitamin C, claiming that although Pauling hadn't demonstrated its effectiveness in a double-blind experimental study such as the government requires of any new drug, this didn't matter because experiments may have flaws anyway, and if Pauling's claims can't be proved with the existing statistical tests perhaps they will with new Bayesian statistical techniques, which are still being developed. What are these new Bayesian statistical techniques? In the understanding of the biographer, they are nothing more than "an application of the old 'stochastic' method that Pauling developed so many years ago, which advocates the relevance of intuitive judgment over mere data collection."[14] From a scientific point of view, this is nonsense. Intuition and guesswork are essential for generating new ideas and making discoveries, but these ideas need to be tested against the facts.

Conclusions

Early in life, Pauling decided that the only way to succeed was to doggedly follow his own judgment. He developed a strong commitment script, which may have been modeled on his father and grandfather, but which went completely against his mother's wishes. She was preoccupied with survival as an ailing widow and single mother, and she simply could not understand why he insisted on pursuing his scientific interests when well-paying engineering jobs were available to him.

At first the commitment script served him well. He succeeded brilliantly in his work on the chemical bond and won his confrontations with the Stalinists and the McCarthyists. He defeated Edward Teller and the military on the issue of nuclear fallout. His confidence in his judgment was immense. A strong commitment to a theoretical perspective can help a scientist to make discoveries, but it can also lead to rigidity and closed-mindedness. Pauling managed to keep this tendency under control in his work in chemistry because there was a solid body of factual data, which limited his speculations. When he got the structure of DNA wrong, for example, the evidence was incontrovertible and he accepted it. In his early political conflicts, he had the good fortune to be on the winning side as well as on the side of progress and human rights.

When he moved into fields such as biology and medicine, however, Pauling's overconfidence failed him because there were too few facts to constrain his thinking. As the reviewer of Pauling's biography for *Nature* observed, Pauling ventured into areas where:

> the facts are few and one's choice of hypothesis cannot be much more than speculation. The only proven scientific method then is to construct a quantitative theory, to get more facts and to prove the theory valid. When Pauling drifted away from his detailed physico-chemical background towards biology he had already built his belief in his intuition, but afterwards he had too few facts to support his thinking. He made errors in the structure of DNA and the atomic nucleus and, I believe, in his views on preventive treatment for certain diseases. Often his approach can only be described as a consequence of a reckless wish to be in the picture. The flaw of self-belief, perhaps even a cult of personality, enveloped him.[15]

Pauling, of course, is much too sophisticated a scientist to advance the argument that intuition is superior to hard data. This confusion was entirely the invention of the biographer. When thinking like this is found in the only adult biography as yet available, however, it is easy to understand why the public has difficulty distinguishing between well-supported scientific findings and unsupported speculation. The death of his wife from stomach cancer—which Robinson and others speculated might have been caused by taking megadoses of vitamin C for many years—probably has done more to undermine public confidence in his claims than all the statistical studies.[16] Meanwhile, Pauling has retained the respect of professionals in chemistry who are willing to overlook his eccentricities in old age and honor him for his youthful achievements. In 1984, he received their highest award, the Priestly Medal for contributions to chemistry.

Pauling's advocacy of vitamin C made him a focus of attention and kept him in the center of controversy in his old age. Protesting against the medical establishment gave him a sense of mission and purpose in life, just as protesting against nuclear testing had done. If his enthusiasms have lost him the respect of skeptics and many of his fellow scientists,

304   *Turncoats and True Believers*

they have made him the darling of health faddists and other protestors. His extraordinary self-confidence immunizes him from the fear of looking foolish or from any need to reconsider his views in the light of contradictory evidence.

Chapter Fourteen

Holocaust and Genocide Revisionism: Skepticism as Denial

Natural instincts bid all living beings not merely conquer their enemies, but also destroy them. In former days, it was the victor's prerogative to destroy entire tribes, entire peoples. By doing this gradually and without bloodshed, we demonstrate our humanity. We should remember, too, that we are merely doing unto others as they would have done to us.

—Adolph Hitler

Perhaps the most puzzling of contemporary political writers are the small band of "revisionists" who insist that the Nazi Holocaust never took place. Many people make it a point of principle not to listen to anything they have to say, dismissing them as anti-Semitic charlatans and "pseudo-scholars."[1] Within the Organization of American History, there was a controversy over whether their claims should be evaluated by "well qualified historians" or simply dismissed as anti-Semitic "rubbish."[2] The revisionists insist that they are serious scholars and that the people who refuse to debate them are the ones who are imposing an ideological bias on history.

In an attempt to attract some attention, the revisionist Institute for Historical Review offered a $50,000 prize for proof that the Nazis gassed the Jews.[3] This strategy backfired when a Jewish Holocaust survivor, Mel Mermelstein of Los Angeles, submitted testimonials from other survivors as proof. When the institute rejected his evidence and refused to pay, he took them to court. Faced with the prospect of a trial, the institute settled the case by giving Mermelstein the $50,000 prize plus another $50,000 for the "pain, anguish and suffering" caused by their claim that the Holocaust didn't take place. Press accounts of the settlement, based on a news conference given by Mermelstein's side, claim that the institute was also ordered to admit that the Holocaust was a reality.[4] The institute and its supporters deny that this was part of the agreement and claim that they decided to pay the "nuisance suit" because of the difficulty of defending their case in a hostile political climate.[5] They continue to insist on the correctness of their cause.

Legal action has been taken against revisionists in Canada and in France where laws prohibit publication of false statements that tend to promote racial hatred.[6] In France, a lengthy trial was held and Professor Robert Faurisson of the University of Lyon was convicted of "falsification of history," fined, and given a three-month suspended prison sentence for "racial defamation."[7] Apparently Voltaire's principle, "I disapprove of what you say, but I will defend to the death your right to say it," is better observed in the United States than in his native land.[8] In the Faurisson case, the court actually took testimony from historians and officially ruled that the extermination of Jews was a historical reality.

This raises the difficult issue of whether courts of law should be used to judge historical or scientific controversies and whether freedom of speech should be abridged even in cases that most people find abhorrent or potentially dangerous. This might set a precedent for Stalinist, McCarthyist, or other "politically correct" orthodoxies. New Left writer and eminent linguist Noam Chomsky came to Faurisson's defense on the grounds that "people have the right of freedom and expression whatever their views, that the importance of defending these rights is all the greater when the person expresses views that are abhorrent to virtually everyone (as in this case)."[9]

Surprisingly, there are no serious scholarly critiques of the revisionists' writings by qualified historians available in English (although there is one in German).[10] The scholars ignore them, and groups such as the Anti-Defamation League denounce them, but no one in the English-speaking world has been willing to debate them. This position is based on the assumption that to do so would be to give them credibility, to acknowledge that there are "two sides to every question." Opponents assume that it is better to allow the evidence, readily available in reputable histories of the Holocaust, to speak for itself.

This may be a wise strategy. Reputable scholars are not obliged to waste their time responding to outlandish claims by sectarian groups. From the perspective of political psychology, however, the revisionists raise some interesting questions. Many, if not all, of them appear to honestly believe what they say. Extreme cases of this sort can sometimes provide a clearer picture of psychological processes that are present in a less dramatic form in many others.

This possibility is suggested by the fact that the Holocaust revisionists are not so unique as one might think. Denial of well-established historical facts is a common defense mechanism used to repress facts that contradict the tenets of a strongly held ideological script. The Turkish government and many reputable scholars of Turkish history deny the genocide of Armenians by the Ottoman empire in 1915. Quite recent genocides in Cambodia and Burundi have been denied. Whenever a nation, ethnic group, or political party that a believer considers to be "good" commits an atrocity, it is easier to deny the facts than to admit the reality.

In denying unpleasant historical facts, true believers often make use of techniques borrowed from the skeptical script. Skeptics demand rigorous evidence to support any assertion and insist on questioning beliefs that most people take for granted. It is deceptive, however, to apply rigorous skeptical criteria to only one issue since it implies that this issue is in doubt while others are not. This is the same kind of ideological defense used by social scientists who rigorously criticize the methodology of any study with which they disagree while uncritically accepting the results of studies with which they agree. By selectively focusing their skepticism, true believers are able to pose as rigorous scientists and scholars while actually defending ideological preconceptions.

Holocaust revisionists also rely on semantic argumentation as an ideological defense mechanism. If one analyzes their argument closely, much of it can be reduced to an argument about the meaning of words. What exactly is a holocaust and how does it differ from a genocide or a massacre, if at all? Was the nuclear bombing of Hiroshima and Nagasaki a genocidal act? If the United States government insists that it was done out of military necessity when the evidence shows otherwise, is that an instance of denial of genocidal intent? How about the bombing of Dresden or other German cities? It may be true that the Nazis killed Jews, the revisionists argue, but after all it was wartime and every side killed people. Why, they ask, should this particular killing be singled out and labeled "The Holocaust"? These are important questions, but the revisionists misuse them as rhetorical devices to avoid having to concede that the Nazis deliberately exterminated millions of innocent Jewish people.

Denial of Genocides

A close parallel is often drawn between the Ottoman genocide of their Armenian minority during the First World War and the German genocide of the Jews during the Second World War.[11] Indeed, Adolph Hitler is often misquoted as justifying his extermination of the Jews with the remark that "no one remembers the Armenians." As it happens, he actually used this analogy to justify the extermination of Poles, not Jews, but the basic point of the similarity of the two genocides is valid.[12]

Of course, there are differences as well as similarities between the two events.[13] Many Armenians were actively allied with the invading Russian forces, and some extremist Armenian groups committed atrocities against Turks. There are no known incidents of Jewish atrocities against Germans. Nevertheless, the Ottoman policy of exterminating innocent Armenian men, women, and children was verified by men such as the American ambassador who observed that "When the Turkish authorities gave the orders for these deportations, they were merely giving the death warrant to a whole race; they understood this well, and, in their conversations with me they made no particular attempt to conceal the fact."[14]

When Ambassador Morganthau tried to intervene with the Ottoman Minister of the Interior, he first denied the genocide, then finally admitted it but claimed that there was nothing he could do since "we have already disposed of three quarters of the Armenians; there are none at all left in Bitlis, Van, and Erzerum. The hatred between the Turks and the Armenians is now so intense that we have got to finish with them. If we don't they will plan their revenge."[15]

The extermination of thousands of innocent Armenian men, women, and children was documented in a comprehensive collection edited by a young British historian, Arnold Toynbee.[16] The volume is introduced with classic British understatement, but the eye-witness accounts are vivid and horrifying, as in this record of an interview with an Armenian physician:

> I asked my gendarmes what all the strange little mounds of earth were I saw everywhere, with thousands of dogs prowling round about them.
> "Those are the graves of the infidels!" they answered calmly.
> "Strange, so many graves for such a little village."
> "Oh, you do not understand. Those are the graves of those dogs— those who were brought here first, last August. They all died of thirst."
> "Of thirst? Was there no water left in the Euphrates?"
> "For whole weeks together we were forbidden to let them drink."[17]

Although the massacres of Armenians by Turks in 1915 are as well established historically as any such events can be, there is strong opposition to labeling these events a "genocide." In 1986 Turkish Ambassador to the United States Skr Elekdag denounced the "baselessness of the oft-repeated Armenian claim that their forbearers were the victims of a 'genocide' during the waning days of the Ottoman Empire."[18] When the U.S. Congress was considering a resolution listing the 1915 events as one of a number of genocides, sixty-nine prominent American scholars of Turkish history published an advertisement in the *New York Times* and *Washington Post* claiming that:

As for the charge of "genocide," no signatory of this statement wishes to minimize the scope of Armenian suffering. We are likewise cognizant that it cannot be viewed as separate from the suffering experienced by the Muslim inhabitants of the region. The weight of evidence so far uncovered points in the direction of serious inter-communal warfare (perpetrated by Muslim and Christian irregular forces), complicated by disease, famine, suffering and massacres in Anatolia and adjoining areas during the first World War.[19]

A massive *History of the Ottoman Empire* by two of the signatories of the advertisement blames the Armenians for siding with the Russian invaders, claims that the Turkish government had no choice but to evacuate the Armenians, and insists that "specific instructions were issued for the army to protect the Armenians against nomadic attacks and to provide them with sufficient food and other supplies to meet their needs during the march and after they were settled."[20] The authors, California historians Stanford and Ezel Shaw, dismiss the documents collected by Arnold Toynbee and others as coming from "Entente propaganda mills and Armenian nationalists" and insist that there were only 1.3 million Armenians in the Ottoman empire before the war, not 2.5 million as the Armenian scholars claim. They estimate that "about 200,000 perished as a result not only of the transportation but also of the same conditions of famine, disease, and war action that carried away some 2 million Muslims at the same time."[21]

When one reads the debate between the Shaws and historian Richard Hovannisian, it is easy to give up in despair that historians will ever be able to arrive at the "truth" about events of this nature.[22] Hovannisian accuses the Shaws of relying exclusively on Turkish and supportive foreign sources, while the Shaws accuse Hovannisian of wishing to "perpetuate the biased image of the 'Terrible Turk,' " and they cite long lists of Turkish and foreign sources documenting the misdeeds of the Armenians, some of whom were trying to provoke incidents in order to bring about Western intervention. The Shaws claim that they "do describe how over 90 percent of the Armenian residents of the empire died or fled during and after the war," but insist that "the experience of the Armenians, however terrible it undoubtedly was, was not unique to them" and that the "situation" was not a product of "a conscious effort at extermination."[23] Perhaps the only bottom line on which all can agree is that almost all of the Armenians were killed or driven out of the country, a point that the Shaws mention only incidentally!

The parallels between the denials of the Nazi and Ottoman genocides are striking. Both "revisionist" groups insist that the killings, which they don't entirely deny, must be placed in a broader context and that the ethnic group with which they identify must not be singled out for blame. Both groups deny the *uniqueness* of the killing, arguing that it was part of a more general phenomenon. Both dispute the veracity of eyewitness testimony and interpret the statistics in such a way as to minimize the numbers of people killed. Both tend to blame the victims for their fate. Both focus on the issue of formal government policy, take exculpatory government documents at face value, and argue that there is no documentary proof that the government in power officially ordered the extermination of any group.

Similar denials can be found in other cases. The Burundi government, for example, claims that it killed only those Hutus who were guilty of massacres and of planning genocide against the Tutsi.[24] Leftist writers Noam Chomsky and Edward Herman were finishing a 160-page, heavily footnoted refutation of Western press accounts of the Cambodian genocide when the Hanoi government announced that the Western accounts were true.[25] Instead of abandoning their account, or reexamining the assumptions that caused them to be naive apologists for a regime while it was murdering a quarter of its own citizens, they simply added a comment that:

> it may turn out that the more extreme condemnations were in fact correct. But even if that turns out to be the case, it will in no way alter the conclusions we have reached on the central question addressed here: how the available facts were selected, modified, or sometimes invented to create a certain image offered to the general population.[26]

In their view the fact that the Western press accounts turned out to be a true account of the slaughter of a million people in no way excused the journalists for their haste in rushing to reveal the killing to the world while it was still going on and something might have been done to stop it. Perhaps they should have listened to political pilgrims like Gun Kessle who had "been there" instead of reporting the obviously questionable tales of refugees and anti-Communists.[27] Nor, in Chomsky and Herman's view, should the Cambodians be blamed for the killings since in a further study it "may well be discovered" that it was simply an "understandable response to [the] . . . extreme savagery of a U.S. assault that may in part have been designed to evoke this very response."[28]

Chomsky and Herman spend hundreds of pages in minute criticism of the assumptions and arguments of the Western journalists but are content to document their own key assertions with "mays" and "mights." This is a common tactic in holocaust denial, and it was used by other leftist apologists for the Cambodian revolution.[29] Evidence the true believers wish to deny is held up to exhausting and often impossible standards, which are not applied to evidence that supports their views. In Chomsky and Herman's defense, however, they did have the integrity to concede that they "may" have been wrong. Nor have they continued to pursue the issue.

Denial of the Cambodian genocide was common within the American peace movement. When the Khmer Rouge took power, American Friends Service Committee (AFSC) program coordinator Russell Johnson assured his followers that the Khmer Rouge were "capable and committed" and that there was no reason to fear a "bloodbath." Their first step, he was certain, would be to "rally support from the population at all levels, including those who have hitherto been in opposition."[30] Several AFSC leaders continued to defend the Khmer Rouge regime until the stories of massacres became undeniable. At this point, the AFSC largely discontinued work on Indochina and focused its attention elsewhere.

It is always easier to detect and denounce genocides done by one's enemies than those by one's allies or one's own group. It is easy for Americans to denounce the genocides by the Germans and Japanese, but what of the mass killing of civilian populations by our own air force? The Americans dropped atomic bombs on Hiroshima and Nagasaki, for example, precisely because the lack of military targets in those cities had left them unscathed in previous raids. The American government ignored peace overtures from the Japanese government and refused to consider alternative strategies that might have ended the war with no greater cost in American lives and without bombing civilian cities. After the fact, the "Strange Myth of Half a Million American Lives Saved" was used to justify the killing when there was no credible reason for believing that anywhere near that number of American lives would have been lost by defeating Japan in other ways.[31]

Dropping bombs on innocent civilians is more impersonal than shooting or gassing them, but just as deadly. British Catholic philosopher G. E. M. Anscombe argued that:

> The policy of obliterating cities was adopted by the Allies in the last war; they need not have taken that step, and it was taken largely out of a villainous hatred, and as a corollary to the policy, now universally denigrated, of seeking "unconditional surrender." That policy itself was visibly wicked, and could be and was judged so at the time.[32]

Was the American bombing of Hiroshima and Nagasaki, or of a number of European and Japanese cities with conventional weapons, a case of genocide? Was it a holocaust? If we draw the line too narrowly, we run the risk of excusing events that ought to be condemned. If, on the other hand, we denounce every killing as a genocide and every disaster as a holocaust, the terms will lose their impact.

"Holocaust" or "Genocide": The Semantics of Barbarism

Prior to World War II, there was no word in English or other major international languages to describe the destruction of a nation or ethnic group. The word "genocide" was coined in 1944 by human rights lawyer Raphael Lemkin because there was no word that referred specifically to governmental policies aimed at the extermination of a group.[33] The term was intended to fit the Nazi policies against the Jews and also to fit any other cases that might occur. An international Genocide Convention was passed by the United Nations and ratified by enough nations to become law. Genocide was defined as "acts committed with intent to destroy, in whole or in part, a national, ethnical, racial or religious group."[34]

This would seem to be a simple enough solution to a semantic problem, yet to Holocaust scholars such as Yehuda Bauer, the word "genocide" is inappropriate for describing the Nazi extermination of the Jews. Bauer objects to the word "genocide" because it also applies to many other historical events, while the word "Holocaust" (capitalized) is reserved to apply only to "the total, sacral Nazi act of mass murder of all Jews they could lay hands on."[35] The term "Holocaust" has become so strongly associated with the Nazi killing of the Jews that even authors who dislike it for its archaic religious etymology (referring to sacrifice by fire)[36] find themselves forced to use it.[37]

There is nothing wrong with coining a word to refer to a specific historical event. It is easier to say "The Holocaust" than to say to "the Nazi genocide of the Jews." If, however, the new term is used to assert that "The Holocaust" was a unique historical event unlike all other events, then certain problems are raised. Logically, every historical event has unique aspects as well as aspects in common with other events. As Frankl observes, "every situation is distinguished by its uniqueness."[38] There is nothing unique about being unique. If we focus on the unique aspects of the Holocaust, then it loses its relevance to modern life since by definition no unique event can ever recur. Bauer is aware of this problem but never solves it. He states that "to view it as totally unique is to take it out of history and out of the context of our everyday lives, and that means opening wide the gates for a possible repetition."[39]

Bauer is actually asserting more than the uniqueness, which characterizes every historical event. He is claiming that the Holocaust represents a new category of event, that it had fundamentally different causes than events that he calls genocides, and that different measures need to be taken to avoid a recurrence. He even draws a medical analogy: "you don't treat cholera and cancer with the same medication, you differentiate between deadly diseases."[40] He argues that "we should properly use the term 'Holocaust' to describe the policy of total physical annihilation of a nation or people. To date, this has happened once, to the Jews under Nazism."[41]

Sadly, this claim of historical uniqueness does not hold up very well when checked against the historical record. Genocide historian Leo Kuper finds that "in the colonization of North and South America, the West Indies, Australia and Tasmania, many native peoples were wiped out, sometimes as a result of wars and massacres, or of disease and ecological change, at other times by deliberate policies of extermination."[42]

Of course, each of these cases also has its historical uniqueness. The Tasmanians, for example, were mostly killed by English ex-convict settlers who hunted the men for sport, killing or castrating them, and kept the women chained to logs to use as sex objects.[43] Exterminating them was never a formally announced "policy" of the British Crown, but it could easily be argued that Government Order 166, issued on August 27, 1830, which organized a military force to drive the natives to inhospitable regions was intended as a "final solution to the Native problem." The colonists understood that grants of land would be available to those who succeeded in eradicating "nests of pests." The entire Tasmanian ethnic group was annihilated, and it seems arbitrary and racist to refuse to apply the term holocaust to such an event merely because they were dark-skinned people living on a remote island.

Even before the arrival of Europeans, there were genocides committed by one native people against another. The Caribbean island now called Grenada was occupied by the dovish Arawak Indians for centuries until they were invaded by Carib war canoes. The hawkish Carib killed, tortured, and ate all the men, keeping the women as wife-slaves.[44] This created perhaps the only society where the women spoke a different language from the men, perhaps cutting down on "marital" discord. Since the women raised the children it seems that the Arawak language eventually won out.

The Carib master race spread from island to island until they dominated much of the sea, which now bears their name, gradually exterminating the peaceful Arawak. Their custom was to keep their prisoners tied to a hammock for five days without food, then to burn them with hot brands, cut pieces of their flesh out, and shoot them with arrows to see if they would cringe.[45] Then they roasted and ate them, saving the fat to flavor their food until the next battle.

At least this is the orthodox version of Caribbean history. The revisionists denounce this account as a fable or myth, going so far as to deny that the Caribs even existed as a distinct culture.[46] One claims that "there were not two races in the Antilles, but only one with peaceful and sweet customs."[47] Others concede that war parties did raid neighboring communities to steal women and occasionally even engaged in a little ritual cannibalism, but they claim that these practices were greatly exaggerated by Western colonialists as a justification for their own enslaving of the natives. The stereotype of the warlike Carib, however, is not purely a colonialist invention but is also believed by the Arawak people.[48]

Much of the evidence anthropologists rely on comes from stories told to the first European missionaries and settlers by the Arawak. Verifying these stories in any definitive way would seem to be impossible. Certainly there were no written records or photographs. The revisionist scholars, who are Spanish-speaking residents of Caribbean countries, choose not to believe stories that English-speaking anthropologists find credible.

Even in the Nazi case, many people contest the claim that the genocide of the Jews was unique. Other groups such as Gypsies, homosexuals, and "asocials" were subjected to extermination policies quite similar to those imposed on Jews. As one Gypsy camp survivor remarked, "our smoke went up together in the chimneys."[49] In the most definitive historical account of the destruction of the European Jews, Raul Hilberg observes that "the Germans, however, did not draw the line with the destruction of Jewry. . . . the Jews were only the first victims of the German bureaucracy; they were only the first caught in its path. . . . the choice was not confined to the Jews."[50]

Even the distinction of being "first" is contested. Frank Rector argues that the order to exterminate homosexuals began with the killing of SA Chief Ernst Rohm in 1934, five years before the extermination of Jews was ordered. He is indignant at the use of the word "Holocaust" to refer only to Jews and insists that "the truth is that the plight of the gays was exactly that of the Jews."[51] Hilberg is aghast at this claim, arguing that "in no sense may it be claimed that [homosexuals] were being 'exterminated,' and any attempt to consider them, along with the Jews, as victims of the Holocaust is a travesty."[52] Hilberg, the most eminent historian of the Jewish Holocaust, must be considered a revisionist with regard to the Homosexual Holocaust.

Semantics are important in all ideological debates since words are used for their emotional as well as their literal meaning. Some clarity and objectivity can be obtained by the careful use of language. The term "genocide" has the advantage of a clear and specific meaning, defined in international law. It refers to government policies intended to exterminate a group and should be used with that specific meaning and not as a generic term equivalent to "massacre" or "cultural oppression."

Semantics need not always follow legal definitions. It is generally accepted today to use the word genocide to apply to attempts to exterminate groups not mentioned specifically in the Genocide Convention, such as homosexuals, political party members, or social classes. Pol Pot's attempt to exterminate the Cambodian middle class qualifies as a genocide even though they are not a distinct religious or ethnic group. Of course, genocides took place before the word was coined or before the Genocide Convention was ratified. The question of the appropriate use of the term genocide is distinct from the question of legal guilt. The application of the word "genocide" to a historical event implies the *intent to exterminate* a group, and it can legitimately be contested by people who deny that *intent* without denying that massacres or extrajudicial executions took place.

The phrase "The Holocaust," capitalized, is generally used as a synonym for the phrase "the Nazi genocide of the Jews," although it sometimes refers to Nazi genocides in general. The word "holocaust" is also used more generally to refer to terrible disasters of whatever origin, as evidenced by the expression "nuclear holocaust." As a term, holocaust is more literary but less precise and more ambiguous than genocide. Bauer's contention that "genocide" and "holocaust" are two separate "diseases" does not hold up very well historically nor is it consistent with how the words are generally used.

Denial of the Jewish Holocaust

With these historical and semantic prologues, we are better prepared to examine the Holocaust revisionists. The first thing we must ask is, what are these people actually saying? One of the hallmarks of an ideological argument is a big gap between what the rhetoric implies and what the books or articles actually say when they are examined in detail. This is characteristic of much of the Holocaust revisionist literature. Northwestern University engineering professor Arthur Butz titles his book, which is the best-known and most substantial of the revisionist texts, *The Hoax of the Twentieth Century*. From the title, he would appear to be saying that the Holocaust was nothing more than a fraud invented by propagandists. He accepts responsibility for the title and defends it against criticism in one of the appendices added to later editions.

The text of Butz's book, however, makes no effort to prove that a hoax existed by documenting deliberate falsification or conspiracy. He simply assumes that people who looked at the evidence and reached a different conclusion than he did must have been perpetrating a deliberate fraud. Nor, surprisingly, does he even deny that mass killing of Jews took place. He says that he has "no reason to quarrel" with Paul Rassinier, who "accepts the reality of about a million Jewish *victims of Nazi policies,* while rejecting the claims of *extermination.*"[53] Dying as a "victim of Nazi policy" is not any better than being "exterminated." Since this is a book that many more people have heard about than read, the impression is given that Butz has argued that the whole Holocaust story is a hoax. Butz clearly intends to give that impression even though he offers nothing but innuendo to support it.

This is all that was claimed by the first of the influential revisionist writers, Paul Rassinier, a French pacifist and socialist who participated in passive resistance against the Nazis during World War II, including helping to smuggle Jewish refugees into Switzerland.[54] He was arrested by the Gestapo in 1943 and incarcerated at Buchenwald and Dora for the duration.

In the camps, Rassinier was angered at the role played by some Communist prisoners who cooperated with the Gestapo and came to blame them as much as the Nazis for much of what happened. After the war, he became angry about certain accounts by former prisoners that had factual inaccuracies, including the claim that there were gas chambers at Buchenwald. Rassinier did not accept these factual inaccuracies as simple errors, common in eyewitness accounts of all events, but denounced them as deliberate falsifications. He also thought that the numbers of Jewish dead published by Jewish historians and authorities were exaggerated. He undertook his own reanalysis of the statistics in two sources and came up with two estimates of his own: 1,589,492 and 987,592.

Although these numbers are much lower than the best available estimates, all reputable sources concede that many unprovable assumptions are required to make an estimate and no precise figure is available.[55] Even if we accepted Rassinier's lowest figure instead of Hilberg's best estimate of 5,100,000, however, it would still be a monstrous crime against humanity. It is difficult, therefore, to infer Rossinier's motivation from his writings or any available personal information. He seems to have thought of himself as a crusader for truth, perhaps offended by Jewish spokespersons who he perceived as exaggerating Jewish suffering and minimizing the suffering and contributions of people such as himself.

Butz had no personal experience with the Nazis, but is upset with the way the Holocaust "myth" or "hoax" (he uses both terms) is used to justify support for Israeli policies. He argues that it isn't fair to make the Arabs pay for whatever the Germans may have done to the Jews and finds it unfair that Israel welcomes all Jews regardless of whether they or their families had any contact with the Nazis.[56] He doesn't make explicitly anti-Jewish, as distinct from anti-Zionist, remarks in the book, but anti-Jewish feelings can readily be inferred from the fact that he occasionally implies that the fact that a statement was made by a Jewish author or a Jewish organization is sufficient cause for discounting it. Little information is available about him personally or his motivations.

But what of the substance of his argument, not about the "hoax" but about the alleged exaggerations and misinterpretations? His book is often considered to be the authoritative reference work of the "revisionist" school. How would it compare with an authoritative work on the other side such as that of Raul Hilberg? At first glance, these both appear to be well-documented scholarly treatises with abundant references and footnotes, although Butz relies much more heavily on secondary sources. Both authors clearly have strong feelings about their subjects, yet attempt to write in a scholarly and objective style. In some cases, both authors rely on the same sources and documents in reaching opposite conclusions. Butz, for example, quotes the following Nazi document, which he accepts as genuine:

> Under proper direction the Jews should now in the course of the final solution, be brought to the East in a suitable way for use as labor. In big labor gangs, with separation of the sexes, the Jews capable of work are brought to these areas and employed in road-building, in which task undoubtedly a great part will fall out through natural diminution.
>
> The remnant that finally is able to survive all this—since this is undoubtedly the part with the strongest resistance—must be given treatment accordingly, since these people, representing a natural selection, are to be regarded as the germ cell of a new Jewish development, if they are allowed to go free. (See the experience of history.)
>
> In the program of the practical execution of the final solution, Europe is combed through from the West to the East.[57]

Remarkably, Butz cites this document as evidence *against* the thesis that the Nazis intended to exterminate the Jews. Butz denies that the phrase "the final solution" was a code word for the extermination of the Jews, insisting that it referred to a plan to move the Jews from Germany to eastern Europe. He further comments that:

> it may astonish the reader that the documents we have reviewed, which constitute very strong evidence that no extermination program existed, are not passed over in silence by the bearers of the extermination legend, but are thrust boldly into our faces as evidence that an extermination program did exist.[58]

I am sure most readers will be astonished, as I am, at Butz's interpretation of this document. Butz's belief in his thesis is so strong that even statements that plainly state a genocidal intent—how else do you keep the "germ cell" of a group from "developing"—are seen as saying just the opposite. If Butz didn't really believe what he was saying, it is hard to see why he would include documents of this sort. He is completely insensitive to the monstrous evil of the policies described in the quotation. He is simply unable to empathize with Jewish people or with people who object to exterminating them. He expresses no indignation against the Nazis for enslaving Jews and working them to death, but great indignation against the historians who dare to call this policy genocide.

Although Butz's book appears to be scholarly in form, it differs from Hilberg's or other works by reputable historians because Butz does not attempt to reconstruct, from primary sources, the fate of Europe's Jews. He simply offers a critique of the supposed "hoax" committed by the establishment historians. This kind of critique is often used by ideologically motivated authors who find it easier to find flaws in the opposition than to construct a thorough argument themselves. It is the same technique used by Chomsky and Herman, who devote endless pages to criticizing the journalistic accounts of the Cambodian holocaust instead of trying to make the best possible judgment about what was actually happening in Cambodia. With this kind of abuse of skeptical principles, doubt can be cast on almost anything, at least in the minds of those who are eager to deny an unpleasant reality.

Given this format, Butz is not forced to weigh the evidence on all sides as closely as possible and then come up with his own best estimate of what happened.[59] He claims that he could not do this since he didn't have access to the necessary documents. Instead, he focuses on whatever weaknesses he can find in the arguments of the legitimate historians, assuming that any mistakes they may have made were a result of a deliberate conspiracy instead of understandable human error.

The logic of the revisionists' argumentation is remarkably similar to that of the "creation scientists," who deny the scientific evidence of human evolution. The creation scientists eschew original scientific research, but devote themselves to searching for errors and inconsistencies in the work of legitimate scientists. Back in the 1920s and 1930s, creationist Harry Rimmer made a standing offer of a $1,000 prize for anyone who could prove that evolution had taken place. None of the evidence published by reputable scientists ever proved satisfactory to Rimmer or to creationists who have followed him.[60]

Another emphasis in the revisionist writings is to point out that other people did evil things. They published books showing, for example, that the Soviets and not the Nazis were responsible for the Katyn massacre in Poland. This point was always conceded by Western historians and today the Russian government has accepted it. The revisionists are strongly anti-Communist and claim that Stalin was much worse than Hitler. In effect, they imply that Hitler's policies were justified by the necessity of fighting Stalin, although they seldom if ever make such an explicit statement.

Jan Myrdal's Revisionism

As we have seen, this same kind of argumentation is relied upon by the pro-Turkish historians, and it can be found in work by leftist writers who denounce the evils of capitalism while ignoring or minimizing the horrors of socialism. The Swedish leftist writer Jan Myrdal, for example, tends to agree "with those Germans who protest at the fact that it is the Germans . . . in the twentieth century that have been portrayed as being the epitome of racism."[61] He thinks that what the Germans did in Europe is no worse than what the British did in India, and, what's more, the English seemed to enjoy the killing while the German officers considered it an unpleasant duty. He quotes from a book by an officer of the British Royal Artillery who reminisces about the joys of military life in the nineteenth century, when it was more fashionable to celebrate the joys of killing than it is today:

> Hark to that cheer—a wild Tally-ho! What! is this, then, fox-hunting? No—but not unlike it, only more madly and terribly exciting even than that—it is man-hunting my friend! and that cheer proclaims that we have "found." Hard! to that quick volley which follows it, with death in its every note! See here and there a flying Sepoy, and here and there a dust-stained, still warm corpse. . . . see that soldier fiercely plunging down his bayonet into some object at his feet—see, is it not red as he uplifts it for another blow? Raise yourself in your stirrups and look down and behold that living thing, above which the steel is flashing so mercilessly: is it a dog, or some venomous and loathsome reptile? No—but a human being.[62]

Myrdal estimates that perhaps a million to three and a half million people died in the Great Bengal Famine of 1943, which was completely unnecessary and unjustified even in military terms.

The son of the distinguished Swedish social democrats Gunnar and Alva Myrdal, Jan Myrdal is deeply alienated from Swedish and European society in general. In *Confessions of a Disloyal European* he decries the racism and anti-Semitism in neutral Sweden during and after World War II and the hypocrisy with which Swedish publishers refused to publish his autobiographical or political writings for fear they would embarrass his politically prominent parents. The Swedish cultural establishment is small and closely knit, and the liberal and bourgeois publishers joined the socialist ones in ignoring his manuscripts. Many years later, when some of his early writings were published to critical acclaim, editors apologized at cocktail parties saying, "I am sorry. I had that manuscript to read many years ago. But as everybody said you were impossible, I never read it."[63]

Jan Myrdal never forgave the editors for the ten years in which he had only "the most impressive collection of refusals in the country to show as proof of my existence." What the editors demanded of him was that he should "deny myself completely, deny what I had seen and what I had experienced and what I had thought." Although he realized that this was complicated by "family considerations" in his case, he refused to reduce it to an "enlarged Oedipus story." He rarely saw his parents and never discussed his publication problems with them. He assumes they had no active role in suppressing his writings, but he never asked them.[64] His inability to discuss with his parents this problem, which forced him to "deny himself completely," indicates that he had real family problems as well as legitimate complaints against the cultural establishment.

Myrdal adopted an ideological script in which the evil, exploitative Europeans were responsible for the suffering of the third-world poor. Oddly enough, this view had been advocated by his father in an influential book in 1956, but his father abandoned it for a view that placed the primary responsibility for third-world poverty on the third-world countries themselves.[65]

Finding no outlet for his writings in Europe, Jan Myrdal left for several years of travel and writing in Asia. Although he regarded Stalinism in the Soviet Union as just as bad as the worst of the European regimes, he became enthusiastic about Mao's regime, which was carrying out many of the same policies. In his first book on China, he acknowledged that Mao's Great Leap Forward caused a famine, but he never fully acknowledged the fact this single famine killed twenty-five to thirty million people, more than in all the famines in postindependence India, which he totaled up meticulously.[66] He defended the Maoist Cultural revolution as "profound and rational," even as he described the use of forced labor and the war on private plots and traditional peasant practices, which other Scandinavian Marxist scholars denounced as a Stalinist assault on the peasantry.[67]

In a book on India, Myrdal insisted that the only hope was the Maoist Naxalite movement, and he quoted, approvingly, his girlfriend, photographer Gun Kessle, who defended the Pol Pot regime in Kampuchea:

Just what was it that Pol Pot did that was so unforgivable? Was it the killing? It might seem that way. But it isn't. Those atrocity tales are not credible. I know. I was in Kampuchea both before the war and during the Democratic Kampuchea period. Of course there was killing—as in all wars and revolutions—but the incidence was not especially or unusually high.[68]

Kessle was convinced by the regime's claims that all it was doing was sending the urban folk to the country to raise food. She thought that the objections of these urbanites were nothing more than class prejudice against manual work. The fact that gifted, sensitive, and humanistic observers such as Kessle and Myrdal became apologists for genocide shows how easy it is to deny unpleasant realities about an idealized object. The greatest irony is that their alienation from Swedish society, rooted in their personal experiences, led them to idealize regimes that by any objective measure cannot come close to Sweden in human rights, freedom, or in the economic welfare of their least advantaged citizens.

Confessions of a Holocaust Revisionist

Holocaust revisionists very seldom write about their personal motivations or experiences. An exception is Bradley R. Smith, who has published his own book *Confessions of a Holocaust Revisionist*.[69] His book is sold by the Institute for Historical Review, and he was employed as editor of their newsletter, but he is not a researcher or Holocaust "expert." The book offers frank insights into the motivations and thinking of a naive individual who was recruited into the revisionist movement.

Smith introduces himself as a fifty-seven-year-old, five-foot-ten, 240-pound high-school graduate and unpublished writer who worked at "many odd and boring jobs." As a writer, he went even longer than Jan Myrdal without publication:

It has been pointed out to me that I have been writing for 35 years without making a dime from it and now I am taking money to write for anti-semitic racists. I will never be able to disprove these charges. . . . It's true I don't have any other source of income. . . . I have always written what I wanted and how I wanted. I never got paid for it. I still write what I want and now I get paid for some of it. Everybody needs an income, even me.[70]

Smith was introduced to revisionism when someone handed him a copy of a pamphlet by Robert Faurisson, *The "Problem of the Gas Chambers."* The pamphlet points out that early writers about the Holocaust claimed that there were gas chambers in camps in Germany, while it is now acknowledged that there were not. It raises questions about the existence of gas chambers in Auschwitz and other camps in Poland. Disproving the existence of gas chambers is a frequent revisionist theme. Eyewitness accounts are dismissed as fabrications, and the use of Zyklon B gas is explained as a public-health measure to control typhus.[71]

Although he denies the gas chambers or a genocidal intent on the part of the Nazis, Smith does not deny that the "German-Jewish scenario in Eastern Europe" was a "cruel and ugly affair." Nor does he deny that there was a Holocaust: "A thousand-year-old Jewish culture in Eastern Europe was destroyed in three or four years. It doesn't offend me if someone wants to say that was a Holocaust. I got interested in the Holocaust business when I discovered that there's a taboo against questioning what's been written about it."[72]

Smith's "interest" became a compulsion. His mind was "crazily preoccupied" with Butz's book to the point where there were days when he could "hardly think about my job." The compulsion was so strong that it even drove him to the library to check out some of Butz's references. Butz says he experienced a "rude awakening" when he read pages 567–71 of the 1961 edition of Raul Hilberg's book on the *Destruction of the European Jews.* Smith got the book out hoping to have the same experience. He read the five pages several times and "was not rudely awakened." In those pages, Hilberg relied on two witnesses's statements that almost all the Zyklon B gas at Auschwitz was used for killing people, not lice. Smith thought that was not a lot of documentation for a key claim, but he didn't think it proved Hilberg a fraud either. What offended him was Hilberg's refusal to answer Butz:

> Hilberg had published his book in 1961. Now Butz had replied to it. The ball was in Hilberg's court, but he didn't want to play. Why not? More than that, nobody else had responded to Butz either. . . . Hilberg had the support and respect of every historian in America but he was unwilling to respond to his one critic, Butz. . . . Butz had done the fair thing. He had published his book. He had called the Hilbergs of the world to account. He had called a spade a spade. Hilberg and the intellectuals had refused to answer Butz. They were doing the craven thing.[73]

Smith's revisionism is based on a populist anti-elitism, particularly a resentment of the intellectuals who ignored his writing for thirty-five years.

He is not consciously anti-Semitic and points out that his first wife was Jewish and that he read at her son's bar mitzvah, "which took place on the green lawns at our house where two young rabbis played guitars and sang for us." Nevertheless, he is resentful of Jews who refuse to talk to him and claim that the Holocaust is a parochial Jewish affair. He insists that "I do not find myself less human than someone that believes the gas chamber stories, less human than Holocaust experts, less human than Jewish survivors." Smith has no understanding of historiography and is quick to attribute errors or weaknesses in the arguments of the Holocaust historians to a deliberate conspiracy. The proof of this, in his eyes, is the unwillingness to respond to the revisionist books and the fact that people "refuse on principle to speak to us."[74]

For Smith, revisionism provides an opportunity to build his self-esteem by externalizing his self-doubts onto the omissions and errors of the establishment. The revisionists respect him, publish his writings and share his feelings of persecution. Indeed, the main attraction of the revisionists for him is the fact that they are a persecuted group. If Hilberg or some other expert had written a detailed criticism of Butz's book, Smith would have had no idea who was right and would probably have been bored by the whole thing.

Conclusions

Denial of genocide is part of a set of defense mechanisms used to preserve an idealized image of an ally and a demonized image of an enemy. The Nazi Holocaust revisionists fit a general pattern of denial of genocidal behavior. They use the same arguments as other genocide deniers: re-estimating statistics, questioning the motives of witnesses, pointing out that other people did evil things, pouncing on errors or exaggerations in the arguments of their opponents, quibbling over terminology, and so on.

Leftists such as Jan Myrdal, Noam Chomsky, and Edward Herman, however, usually back off when confronted with overwhelming evidence. Even if they never actually concede that they were wrong, they at least drop the subject. In addition to having greater intellectual integrity, they are utopians and protestors who are driven by a vision of a world without exploitation and strife. They are profoundly disappointed when the groups they have idealized turn out to be mass murderers. The Holocaust revisionists, by contrast, are prototypical hawkish authoritarians who "exalt the inevitability of conflict, deny their sense of guilt and develop a defensive pride in their freedom from all scruples."[75] They are unshaken by evidence of the most unspeakable atrocities because this only confirms their "tough-minded" view of the world as a place where only the strong survive.

The leftist genocide deniers are often introspective and self-critical, and some even publish insightful autobiographies. The Nazi Holocaust revisionists seldom publish autobiographies or make themselves available to biographers, probably because to do so would threaten their externalization of their aggressive feelings. With the exception of Bradley Smith's naive account, the only autobiography of a revisionist I have been able to find is a blatantly anti-Semitic tract filled with sentences such as, "with the contempt they feel for Aryans, whom they regard—*not without justification*—as a vastly inferior race, stupid and easily manipulated . . . the Jews at once instructed their hirelings to spread the audacious lie that Hitler had advocated the use of the Big Lie."[76] Written by Revilo P. Oliver, a Professor of Classics at the University of Illinois for thirty-two years, the book scarcely conceals a vicious self-hatred. The author is full of contempt for his own "Aryan" race for being so stupid as to fall for the tricks of the Jews, who he believes to be secretly behind every unfortunate development in the world.

The Holocaust revisionists are unique in being organized as a group with a publishing house and annual conferences for the exclusive purpose of denying a genocide. The other revisionists, including the Turkish and other nationalist groups, prefer to avoid the topic as much as possible. They resort to defense mechanisms only when they are confronted by critics. The Holocaust revisionists focus on the Holocaust issue because they believe it to be more effective than openly advocating for their anti-Semitic and pro-Nazi views. Although the Institute for Historical Review limits itself to "scholarly" activities, it is linked organizationally and financially with anti-Semitic individuals and organizations who pursue other tactics.[77] Anyone who purchases literature from them is placed on mailing lists offering anti-Semitic literature and Nazi memorabilia from these related organizations. Their "scholarly" conferences are closed to people who do not agree with them. In order to register, one must give references known to the organization who can vouch for one's acceptability. An open-minded skeptical organization would be eager to encourage participation from scholars who were critical of their views.

Proving genocide legally is difficult since it includes the dimension of *intent*. It is much easier to prove that killing has taken place than to prove an intention on the part of a government to exterminate a group. Since the adoption of the Genocide Convention, no nation has been prosecuted under it despite numerous mass exterminations, which would seem to qualify such as those in Cambodia and Burundi.[78] The failure to enforce the convention largely reflects the weakness of international institutions, but the difficulty of proving intent is also a problem. Independent organizations such as Amnesty International, which are not limited by legal or political constraints, find it more effective to condemn governments for their deeds than to get bogged down in debating their intentions.

The issue of intent is also a key focus of much of the denial of historical genocides. No one denies that hundreds of thousands, if not millions, of innocent Jews, Armenians, Gypsies, and Hutu were killed. What is contested is the intent to destroy the group in question. Even in the case of Adolph Hitler, where numerous quotes can be found stating an intent to exterminate the Jews, the revisionists argue that this was mere rhetorical excess and that his "real" intent was to use them as slave laborers or resettle them outside of Europe. Somehow this is thought to be exculpatory.

Proving genocidal intent may not be of great importance from a legal or humanitarian point of view. International law clearly prohibits the killing of civilians or prisoners of war (without due legal process), and it is easier to prove that a government is murdering people than to prove that it has a genocidal intent.[79] These provisions also cover killings on political grounds, such as the massacre of Communists in Indonesia, or on grounds of social class, such as the extermination of middle-class Cambodians, neither of which are covered by the Genocide Convention. Bombing of civilian targets is also prohibited by the international rules of war, and much of the bombing of cities during World War II must be condemned as morally wrong and in violation of the law and ethics of war, although it does not qualify as genocidal in that it was not intended to exterminate a group.

As with many ideological issues, much of the debate about holocausts and genocides revolves around semantic issues. Quibbling about words is used to avoid and deny realities. Attempts to define the Holocaust of the Jews as something fundamentally different from other historical genocides can play into this kind of semantic gamesmanship and alienate people who do not deny what happened to the Jews but who feel their own group is being slighted. Genocide is clearly defined in international law as an attempt to exterminate a group, and if we use any reasonable standards for making historical or legal judgments there are no grounds for doubting that Hitler intended to exterminate the Jews. He stated that this was his intention, and, more importantly, he succeeded in exterminating several million innocent Jewish civilians. Hitler also intended to exterminate several other groups, including Communists, homosexuals, and Gypsies and to enslave others such as the Poles. The fact that we don't know precisely how many died or exactly how all of them were killed is of no importance. No amount of nitpicking details or criticizing the critics can obscure either the intent or the crime itself.

Chapter Fifteen

Fidel Castro and the Cuban Revolution: Aging Narcissism and Unyielding Leninism

For more than thirty years Cuba has been an island of Marxism-Leninism thumbing its nose at the imperialist colossus just ninety miles from its shores. In the sixties, radicals delighted at the Cubans' success in doing what they could only fantasize about. Rightists feared that the Cuban revolution was a portent of a red tide sweeping over Latin America. Today Cuba's persistence as a museum of pure Communism evokes more misgivings than daydreams. Will history absolve Fidel Castro, or will he be remembered as one more example of how much better off humanity would have been if the Marxists had understood the world better before trying to change it?

For more than thirty years Cuban society has been shaped by a single personality. Fidel Castro's personal leadership was decisive in the 1959 revolution, and he has exercised virtually absolute power ever since. Dominance by a charismatic leader is, of course, typical of Leninist regimes. But Castro was younger than Lenin, Mao, Ho Chi Minh, or Tito when he took power as a thirty-two-year-old guerrilla leader, and his period of uncontested rule has been longer. It is my thesis that the uniqueness of Cuban society since 1959 cannot be understood without an analysis of Fidel Castro as a personality.

Fidel's Childhood

Fidel Castro's father was a Spanish immigrant who was thought to have been an officer who was deported to Spain when Cuba won its independence but who returned to the land of opportunity to become a wealthy landowner.[1] Fidel was illegitimate. His mother was the family's maid when she became pregnant with the first of Fidel's two older siblings, and bore his father four legitimate children after the father finally married her so that the children could be enrolled in a Catholic school.

Illegitimacy was a considerable stigma in their moralistic Catholic community and may explain why Fidel and his out-of-wedlock siblings were sent away to boarding school. His father was a strong man who was sometimes tyrannical but "did not crush the individuality and initiative of his children when they challenged him."[2] His parents, who were largely illiterate, were eager for him to be well-educated and socially mobile.

Fidel retained considerable anger toward his father, which was unresolved when his father died while Fidel was in college. He was pulled out of a meeting when a telegram came telling of his father's death. He simply put the telegram in his pocket, said, "please do not tell the others," and went back to the meeting, never to mention the death again. As late as 1965, Fidel told an interviewer that his father was a wealthy landowner who exploited peasants, paid no taxes, and played politics for money.[3]

His father bought Fidel a new Ford to drive to the University of Havana in 1946, where he decided to study law because people told him he talked a lot and ought to be a lawyer. After he took power and assumed responsibility for managing Cuban society, he said he wished he had studied something else, but his legal training did help him to prepare the "History Will Absolve Me" speech, which established him as a charismatic figure.[4] Fidel generally wore a dark blue suit and tie, which contrasted with the informal tropical attire favored by Havana students. He was tall, handsome, and an excellent speaker who was viewed as a little bit crazy because of his grandiose ambitions. Student politics was a serious and dangerous game in Havana. The student groups were linked with national parties and movements, and disputes were often resolved with assassinations and gun battles.

Fidel tried to function as a loner, but joined the Ortodoxo Party when it became too dangerous to be on his own. The Party espoused values such as nationalism, anti-imperialism, socialism, economic independence, political liberty, and social justice. Fidel considered joining the Communists, but found them too sectarian and dogmatic. They didn't allow much latitude for a rebellious, dashing young activist. He later joked that he would have joined the Communists if he could have been Stalin.[5]

Fidel as a Revolutionary Leader

Fidel's first major leadership role was to organize a protest when some drunken American sailors were observed urinating on a statue of Cuban founding father José Martí. The protestors succeeded in winning an apology from the U.S. Ambassador, who disgraced himself, however, by forgetting Martí's name when he delivered it. Fidel also joined a group that was training to overthrow Dominican Republic dictator Rafael Trujillo, but that mission was cut off by the Cuban and American governments after the group spent months training in the heat on a remote island.

Never again did Fidel allow himself to be put in a position where anyone else would be in command of his operations. The attack on the Moncada garrison, which established him as a public figure in Cuba, was organized by him independently of any political party. It was an audacious, almost suicidal, attack, which could have succeeded only if the defenders were incredibly incompetent. Most of the attackers were killed, and Fidel escaped only by the good fortune that one of the officers leading the group that apprehended him recognized him from the University and talked the men out of killing him. Biographer Peter Bourne thinks that "Fidel was driven at this moment not by ideology, but by the romantic perception of himself as the reincarnation of three men, José Martí, Antonio Guiteras, and Eddy Chibás, and it was their actions as national heroes as much as their political theory with which he primarily identified."[6] Bourne believes Fidel may have been upset by marital and career problems at the time, and he may have felt ready to pay with his life for the recognition and honor the attack would bring him. In any event, one must agree with Bourne that "whether interpreted as an extraordinary act of patriotism or a drastic effort to deal with personal emotional needs, Fidel's decision to launch the Moncada attack was a true gamble with life and death and history."[7]

Suicidal imagery is an important part of Fidel's thinking and of Cuban political culture. Castro once told a reporter that "if I had time I would have killed myself."[8] In a key speech as a young revolutionary, Fidel quoted a line from the national anthem that reads, "To live in chains is to live sunk in shame and dishonor. To die for the fatherland is to live!"[9] When hiding in the cane fields after landing in Cuba on the yacht Granma, Fidel slept with his rifle barrel against his throat, his fingers on the trigger, and the safety off, dramatically telling his comrades, "I shall not be taken alive by the soldiers of tyranny while asleep! If I am found, I'll just squeeze the trigger and die."[10] Even as a mature leader, biographer Tad Szulc notes that "Castro tends to court death," with foolhardy acts such as traveling to Mexico on a high-speed boat to test the Yanqui boats patrolling for arms going to Nicaragua.[11]

Castro is clearly a master in appealing to the Cuban national psyche, and it is difficult to distinguish posturing from personal feelings in his pronouncements. Some biographers believe that Cuba's national hero, José Martí, deliberately sought a martyr's death.[12] Fidel clearly portrays himself as Martí's successor. Despite his "victory or death" pronouncements, Fidel allowed himself to be captured instead of fighting to the end in the Moncada attack. He concealed his identity to avoid being killed. He seems to enjoy taking risks, however, even when they are foolish, such as disembarking from a plane as a young man making a stopover in the Dominican Republic to see whether the officials would recognize him as a member of a group that had conspired to overthrow the regime.[13]

In 1953 the Cuban Communist Party denounced the Moncada attack as "adventurist, false and sterile" and as "a putschist method peculiar to all bourgeois political factions."[14] Indeed, there are interesting tactical parallels between the Moncada assault in 1953 and Adolph Hitler's "Beer Hall Putsch" in 1923 (see Chapter Seven). Both actions were foolhardy from a tactical point of view but served the strategic purpose of establishing their leaders as heroes willing to risk their lives while others only talked. Both leaders mesmerized courtroom audiences with their personal charisma in speeches that led up to the same dramatic conclusion. Only the rhetoric differs:

> Hitler: You may declare us guilty a thousand times, but the Goddess who presides over the Eternal Court of History will with a smile tear in pieces the charge. . . for she declares us guiltless.[15]

> Castro: I come to the close of my defense plea but I will not end it as lawyers usually do—asking that the accused be freed. . . . *Sentence me. I don't mind. History will absolve me.*[16]

Of course, Fidel didn't quote from Hitler or Mussolini in his speech, although he had studied them carefully. In high school, Fidel came under the influence of a priest who was an admirer of Franco's Spain, and who tutored him in Falangist thinking.[17] Biographer Georgie Anne Geyer found that as a youth in the 1930s Fidel's "heroes were Hitler, Mussolini and Primo de Rivera, the Spanish Falangist. He used to walk around with a Spanish copy of *Mein Kampf* under his arm, and he had maps on his wall showing the victories of the Axis across Europe."[18] Nor did he quote from Marx or Lenin, although he later claimed that he had acquired "a Marxist-Leninist ideology, a quite well-developed revolutionary ideology" as a university student.[19] It is not clear what this means. While contemporary Cuban spokespersons insist that *History Will Absolve Me* is in essence a Marxist work, the quotations in it are from religious figures such as John of Salisbury, Thomas Aquinas, and Martin Luther and democratic theorists such as Montesquieu, Rousseau, and Locke.[20]

Even after coming out of the closet as a Marxist-Leninist in 1962, Fidel described himself and his followers as "sentimental Marxists, emotional Marxists," whose experiences led them to "discover all the truths which the Marxist doctrine contained." As late as 1967 one of his top officials remarked that "even today Fidel is not a Communist," by which he seemed to mean that Fidel was not a systematic or consistent Marxist thinker.[21] Fidel was clearly anticapitalist in his sentiments, even if his knowledge of and commitment to abstract doctrine may be in doubt.

The reason it is so difficult to pin down exactly what Fidel thought at different points in his life is that he redefines and reinterprets his past to suit the image he wants to portray at a given point in time. It is also clear that he deliberately lied about his views, particularly in speeches made in the United States when he explicitly denounced Communism as repressive and denied that the Cuban revolution was based on class struggle or that it intended to end private property.[22] In lying, Fidel was following José Martí's advice to conceal one's goals since to "proclaim them as what they are would raise difficulties too great to be able to reach them in the end."[23] As Fidel put it, "much guile and smiles for everyone . . . defend our points of view without creating problems. There will be ample time later to squash all the cockroaches together."[24] A few years later he found the time to "squash the cockroaches" by purging, jailing, or exiling the revolutionary comrades who opposed the imposition of a Leninist state.

History Will Absolve Me is the classic document of the Cuban Revolution. The text was smuggled out of prison in secret writing. It gave a full account of the Moncada assault and admitted everything the court had charged. It provided detailed documentation of the poverty in which most Cubans lived, in contrast to the lavish lifestyle of millionaires. It proposed five revolutionary laws aimed at returning to the 1940 constitution, confiscating the supposedly ill-gotten gains of the rich, and distributing wealth more equitably.

This memoir is an excellent example of the use of archetypal imagery portraying reality as a struggle between good and evil leading to a dramatic transformation to an idyllic state. This imagery is found in many millenarian political and religious movements. Historian James Billington claims that on an unconscious level European revolutionary ideologies are modeled on Christian mythology in which "the present was hell, and revolution a collective purgatory leading to a future earthly paradise."[25] Castro had been educated in Catholic schools, so it is not surprising that

History Will Absolve Me follows the Christian story so well. Indeed, this may have been quite conscious in Fidel's mind; the speech drew an explicit analogy between Dante's Inferno and Batista's Cuba.[26] Billington suggests that the whole structure of the speech is modeled on the Christian story. He claims that Castro:

> represented his own original revolutionary assault on the Moncada barracks as a kind of Incarnation. The subsequent torture and martyrdom of his virile fellow revolutionaries was the Passion and Crucifixion; and Castro's trial by Batista was Christ before Pilate. The Cuban people were promised corporate Resurrection, and their revolutionary apostles Pentecostal power. The coming revolution would fulfill all the Law (the five "revolutionary laws" of the Moncada raiders) and the Prophets (José Martí).[27]

The parallel between Fidel and Christ was not lost on the Cuban population. Szulc observes that:

> The deification of Fidel Castro became a phenomenon in Cuba in the aftermath of his victory. . . . *Bohemia* magazine published an immensely controversial portrait of the thirty-one-year-old Maximum Leader with a Christlike halo subtly drawn around his bearded countenance. . . . every five minutes, at every intersection of the highway, women stopped him, the old women kissed him, telling him he was greater than Jesus Christ.[28]

Luis Conte Agüero reports that photographs of Marx, Lenin, and Castro were substituted for religious images in many churches and that Brazilian deputy Everardo Magalhães, who was in Cuba at the time, later published a photo he took of a resplendent image of Castro substituting for one of Christ.[29]

People were responding to Fidel in terms of the Christian imagery that was established in Cuban culture. One could make an equally plausible argument that Castro's speech was modeled on the *Communist Manifesto,* which also combined a dramatic polarization between good and evil and visions of revolutionary transformation with quite moderate demands for social reforms.[30] Rather than mimicking a particular story or historical document, Fidel Castro enunciated in his own way the emotions that underlie all revolutionary and millenarian movements: frustration with existing reality, externalization of self-doubt and dissatisfaction onto enemy objects, and visions of transformation to an idyllic state.

Wolfenstein argues that men become revolutionaries because they have unresolved conflicts with their fathers.[31] Conflicts of this kind are, of course, very common, but it must be conceded that Castro fits the theory well. He had deep-seated resentment against his father, related in some way to the stigma he suffered because of his illegitimacy. He was sent away to boarding schools and never seems to have confronted his father about his feelings.

Fidel also fits the portrait of the "revolutionary ascetic" as described by Mazlish.[32] Although Fidel has had an active sex life, he completely subordinates personal life, including sex, to political demands. During an uprising in Bogotá in 1948, Fidel was part of a group that stopped a car that turned out to be driven by a man who was taking two prostitutes to have sex. He responded incredulously, "Can you imagine, the city burning, the war erupting, and this man driving around Bogotá with two prostitutes."[33] As a young husband, Fidel left his wife alone most evenings while he attended political meetings. At the time, the Communist newspaper *Hoy* ridiculed him as "Chaste Fidel" (*Casto Fidel* in Spanish).[34] A friend who knew him all his life described him as a man with "no tenderness for anybody, not even for his wife."[35] A phenomenally hard worker, he fits Mazlish's model of an ascetic leader who channels much of his energy into his cause.

Fidel's asceticism may be more image than reality, however, if we are to believe the accounts of insiders who have defected from the regime. José Luis Llovio-Menéndez reports that:

> In absolute contrast to the spare, self-abnegating life of virtue Che preached and practiced, Fidel maintained several residences. He spent lavishly on himself and gave away as gifts luxury houses, cars, and such expensive items as waterproof Rolexes, the preeminent emblem of personal power in the early years of the revolution. He indulged his every whim, ate well, and was known in leadership circles for his womanizing. Not surprisingly, everybody [in the revolutionary elite] followed the leader.[36]

Castro is attended by orderlies, who rush over to tuck his pants in his boots whenever they fall out, and he keeps the air conditioning turned down so cold that he freezes his associates in order to be comfortable in his perfectly tailored olive-green campaign uniforms.[37] He throws lavish parties where as many as a thousand guests are fed steak and lobster. He travels everywhere in a motorcade of Mercedes Benz limousines. This lifestyle, however it compares to other heads of government, contrasts sharply with his rhetoric of self-abnegation.

Fidel also fits Mazlish's model of the revolutionary leader as a narcissist who displaces his self-love into abstractions. A narcissist is a person whose exaggerated self-love masks a deeper insecurity. Biographers and commentators have often described Fidel Castro in this way. One notes his "childish temper tantrums, his paranoia, his abnormal fits of anger, his insane jealousy directed toward any person who might stand out or might begin to win the people's love or admiration."[38] A close friend from his university days, now estranged, observes that "in him there is a grave fear, the fear of humiliation, the fear of his offenses, the fear of the very crowd which adores him, even fear of this stage of adoration."[39]

Fidel's personal insecurity is revealed by his extreme sensitivity to criticism. Conte Agüero reports that "Castro cannot resist a polemic. He doesn't discuss, he gives monologues. He pronounces, he doesn't listen. If any of his entourage dares to voice the slightest criticism he pounds angrily on the table and utters a mountain of obscenities."[40] Castro's dehumanizing epithets for his enemies have become part of the Cuban vernacular: "worms, lackeys, ruffians, mercenaries, traitors to the fatherland, sons of bitches, sissies, homosexuals, social plague, rabble, etc."[41] These terms serve to dehumanize the regime's opponents, making them suitable targets for externalization of angry and hostile feelings. They can then be scapegoated or punished for the regime's internal problems.

Castro's insecurities are also revealed in minor incidents that are sometimes observed by foreign visitors. For example, he was so upset when a ten-year-old boy won his cap in a bet he had insisted on making in a Ping-Pong game that he practiced for months for a return match. Then, when he won, he sent a driver to the boy's home to retrieve the cap.[42] He stormed out in anger when the wife of a friend suggested a different way of cooking some meat he had brought as a gift. When a foreign scholar asked him who told him he was wrong when he was wrong, he replied, "I do not need criticism. I am my own best critic."[43] He told television interviewer Barbara Walters, "what we say is always the truth. . . . we will never allow someone to try to test our realities or to refute our truths."[44]

One of history's most powerful orators, he nevertheless suffers stage fright before speaking in Revolution Square and finds his stride only when he feels a positive response from the audience.[45] He is reputed to be shy with women and tends to establish a dependent mother-son relationship with the one he is closest to, seeking and demanding her approval for all that he does.[46]

Fidel broke with his wife when she accepted financial support from family members who were in the government while he was in jail after the Moncada attack. Later, he schemed to take their son away from her, even though he was unable to raise the boy himself because of his plans to go into the mountains as a guerrilla fighter. He felt at a loss after losing his wife, and once broke into tears in a friend's dining room, crying out, "I am alone, I am alone; I know that tomorrow, when I have power, many women will approach me and offer themselves to me, but this will not be sincere. What a brute I have been! What a brute I have been!"[47]

Fidel thought his fantasies had come true, in the heady days just after the revolutionaries seized power, when a pretty girl approached him with talk of love. He was bitterly disappointed when, on taking her to a hotel room, he found she intended only to give him a lecture on Christian love. He complained, "what you preach is impractical and utopian. . . . we are in a revolution, not paradise. . . . I thought you came to speak to me of a more substantial and accessible love."[48]

Fidel's personal insecurity is compensated for by his exalted public image. As a presidential assistant in the Carter White House, and as an assistant secretary-general with the United Nations, psychiatrist Peter Bourne made frequent trips to Cuba, met with Fidel, and conducted hundreds of interviews with supporters and opponents of the regime. His analysis of Fidel meshes perfectly with Mazlish's description of the revolutionary ascetic:

> Mazlish: Narcissists . . . do not become revolutionary leaders unless they are also able to displace their self-love onto an abstraction with which they then totally identify. Thus it is the Revolution, the People, Humanity, or Virtue which the leader glorifies and extols; only "accidentally" does he happen to embody it.[49]

> Bourne: Fidel is like de Gaulle when he said, "I am France." There is a fusion in Fidel's mind between his own ego and the national identity. What he sees as good for himself he inevitably sees as good for Cuba. He knows that most Cubans are willing to accept this view. His need to thrust himself on the world stage with an impact outrageously disproportionate to Cuba's tiny size is an acceptable overcompensation for the generations of humiliation and denigration of the national spirit that Cubans feel they suffered at the hands of other nations.[50]

In Mazlish's view, the revolutionary leader serves as an ego-ideal for his followers. By identifying with him, they are able to externalize needs for self-assertion, which they have not been able to actualize due to personal deficiencies and/or social conditions. The revolutionary leader is extremely sensitive to his followers, yet he is able to avoid having his own emotions shaped by them. Castro fits this model perfectly. He is famous for his ability to hold the audience's attention for very long speeches in which he receives thunderous applause and support for his ideas, the record being nine hours.[51] Fidel's rapport with his audience during one speech was carefully observed by José Luis Llovio-Menéndez:

No sooner did he begin than I felt a strange, profound sense of connection between the huge mass of people and their *Líder Máximo*. Fidel stood before them, fully conscious of his magnetism. He controlled every movement and modulated his voice to perfection, manipulating the crowd as he chose. . . . I could *feel* him emphasize just the right word and then repeat that emphasis. Then, for dramatic effect, there would be a void, silence. That intense, brilliant gaze was directed from time to time at his entourage, seeking the approval that was never denied. . . . Minutes, hours went by with the people in a trance. After several hours Fidel closed his speech at midafternoon with the standard "*¡Patria o Muerte!*"— "Fatherland or Death!"—"*¡Venceremos!*"—"We Shall Vanquish!"[52]

Vamik Volkan classifies narcissistic leaders into two types: reparative and destructive.[53] The reparative narcissistic leader idealizes his followers and has a generally beneficial impact on a society that has suffered injuries to its self-esteem. The destructive narcissist demonizes outsiders and encourages hostile and aggressive tendencies among his followers. Volkan cites Kemal Atatürk as an example of the first and Adolph Hitler as the second. The Armenians, however, might argue that Volkan's Turkish patriotism caused him to be too generous to Atatürk. The distinction is somewhat artificial since the same leader can change from one type into the other.

Fidel Castro's leadership exhibits reparative narcissism in his glorification of Cuba and destructive narcissism in his demonization of the United States and capitalism in general.[54] Narcissistic leadership of either type induces collective regression among the followers as they become dependent on the leader.[55] This tendency, also, can be observed in Cuba, and much of the opposition can be explained by the frustration many people feel in living in a society that limits the individual autonomy needed for personal growth.

Cuba as a Narcissistic Society

One consequence of dependence on a narcissistic leader is that the nation itself becomes an object of narcissistic perception. Achievements are exaggerated and exalted, while deficiencies are denied, excused as temporary failings or remnants of the past that will soon be overcome, or externalized on the Yanqui imperialists or on shirkers, bureaucrats, and technocrats within Cuba. Llovio-Menéndez, a defector who held several high positions in the Cuban regime, reports one occasion on which Fidel explicitly instructed his followers in the technique of scapegoating the United States for the country's failures: "The people must be taught infinite hatred for the Yanquis, who are responsible for all our misfortunes. So whether it's true or not, whether it can be proven or not, the Yanquis will always be responsible for any mishap we may suffer. The people will always respond to this argument."[56]

The leading Cuban newspaper, *Granma,* is a primary vehicle for this propaganda, and over the years it has "become more and more shrill, and the portrayal of a simplified battle between good and evil has become more pronounced" as Cuba's problems have worsened.[57] The United States and its allies are portrayed as "greedy, corrupt, crime-ridden, disease-infested, and drug-plagued societies" while Cuba and its allies are "moral, forthright, healthy and progressive societies standing at the cutting edge of all . . . advances in the world."[58] Blatant distortions are used, as when Cuba's massive foreign debt was blamed on the low world price of sugar, despite the fact that almost all of Cuba's sugar was bought by the Soviet bloc countries at four times the world price, or when General Jaruzelski's declaration of martial law was presented as being imposed in a climate of social calm and unity.

The case of the "ten million tons" harvest illustrates the nature of this process. After abandoning his attempt to rapidly industrialize Cuba in the 1960s, Fidel got the idea of setting a target of a ten-million-ton sugar crop in 1970. When Fidel gets an enthusiasm, it is very difficult for members of his entourage to be critics or naysayers. Sugar Minister Lt. Orlando Borrego, however, finally got up his courage to tell Fidel all the reasons why it couldn't be done. Fidel was outraged and told the nation that "we'll make our ten million, and it's the people who are going to produce them despite the skeptics, in whose ranks we find the man who until this very moment had been sugar minister."[59] He pledged that "our country's honor is pledged to this. Our country's prestige. This goal will be attained because it is a challenge to the tenacity and iron will of our people."[60]

The country's resources were marshalled in an extraordinary way, including vast amounts of "voluntary" labor, which inevitably cut into the productivity of the rest of the economy. Everyone's aspirations were focused on this goal, which demanded great sacrifices, but it promised to bring the affluence that had been promised but not achieved during the revolution's first decade. In the end, the Sugar Minister turned out to have known his business, and it became undeniable that the goal would not be reached. Fidel waited for a propitious moment to admit this to the people, and jumped at the opportunity when a small group of anti-Communist exiles kidnapped a Cuban fishing boat. He mobilized a mass patriotic rally and claimed a victory when the U.S. forces returned the fishermen. Once the crowd was worked up in a patriotic frenzy, he claimed that the enemy was hoping that the country would fail to make its ten-million-tons goal and be so demoralized that they could attack. He then conceded, "I must tell you frankly . . . we have had difficulties. Are we going to blame somebody for this? No! Are we going to blame the imperialists? No! A revolutionary people doesn't have to go around blaming anybody for its difficulties. . . . I can tell you that we won't reach the ten-million-ton mark."[61]

This was a complete switch from Fidel's usual practice of blaming the imperialists for all Cuba's difficulties. He admitted that "our ignorance of the sugar industry contributed to our not realizing in time, discovering in time, seeing in time the variety of problems."[62] His next step was to offer his own resignation during a mass rally, successfully counting on the crowd to demand that he stay. Blaming the Yanquis for the failure of the sugar harvest clearly wouldn't have worked; the people were too intimately involved with it and understood it too well. Castro had the sense to realize this and was able to change the line to one that depended entirely on the people's emotional identification with him as a leader.

No one else in the system could possibly have made such an announcement. No Cuban journalist would have dared write an article analyzing the flaws in the ten-million-tons goal, even though this was the major focus of the nation's energies. Everything depends on the supreme leader's ability to select an appropriate line for everyone else to follow.

Another example of Fidel's role in setting the line was the Soviet invasion of Czechoslovakia in 1968. At the time, there was considerable sentiment even within the leadership against the invasion of a small country by a big power. As they awaited Fidel's speech, one Vice Minister said, "He'll really give it to them!" Another exclaimed, "The Soviets are as imperialist as the Yanquis!"[63] They all expected Fidel to get even with the Russians for backing down in the missile crisis and cutting Cuba's petroleum supplies. When Fidel took the opposite line, reluctantly supporting the Warsaw Pact invasion, the leaders had no choice but to celebrate Fidel's superior insight in detecting the long hand of the CIA and the Pentagon in the Prague developments. The Cuban press, of course, parroted Fidel's analysis.

Reporting the propaganda of the leader as brilliant truth is typical of the press in Leninist countries. What is surprising in the Cuban case is the extent to which this simplistic and grandiose self-promotion has been successful among people outside Cuba who are much more skeptical of the propaganda of other Leninist states. A study prepared for Ronald Reagan's Commerce Department claimed that "Cuba has succeeded in almost totally eliminating illiteracy" and that its "health care system rivals that of most developed nations."[64] Biographer Tad Szulc, who is highly critical of Castro's leadership and Cuban politics, nevertheless credits the revolution with "immeasurably improving the human condition of millions of Cubans."[65]

When someone uses the word "immeasurably," it is sometimes a clue that he hasn't had time to examine the data thoroughly, since most things are at least roughly measurable. Moreover, statistics can always be quoted out of context to "illustrate" a point. For example, one might cite the fact that life expectancy in Cuba increased from 55.8 years in 1950–55 to 74.2 years in 1984.[66] This was a measurable improvement. Castro fills his speeches with facts such as these, and long lists of them can be found in the writings of apologists for the revolution.[67]

To evaluate a statistic, it needs to be put into a historical and comparative context. What were the trends in life-expectancy statistics in Cuba before the revolution? How did the trends after the revolution compare to what might reasonably have been expected without one? The record shows that life expectancy in Cuba was improving steadily before the revolution and that the improvement after the revolution was at almost precisely the same rate as the improvement before it.[68] The improvements in life expectancy in Cuba since the revolution have been closely paralleled by improvements in Panama and Costa Rica, two countries that are similar to Cuba in their level of development.[69]

Health care is the area in which Cuba's progress has been the strongest, but other indicators of improvement in the human condition are not as impressive. In education, for example, Cuba's progress since the revolution has been roughly comparable to that of Costa Rica, Panama, Chile, or Jamaica. Mexico, which was far behind Cuba in the 1950s, has made much stronger gains than Cuba.[70] But these gains are not perceived in the same way either in Mexico or in the international community. Sergio Diaz-Briquets suggests that this difference in perception is because:

> these countries view achievements as a matter of course in their socio-economic development; while meritorious they are to be expected. Revolutionary Cuba, on the other hand, may feel it is necessary to announce what it has done in order to justify its radical policies. Uncritical acceptance of officially inspired historical distortions and inflated claims of achievements, particularly by many foreign observers ideologically partial to the revolution, likewise contributes to this state of affairs.[71]

Another reason for Cuba's inflated image in health and education may be the occasional publication of intentionally falsified statistics. Fidel has been particularly proud of Cuba's progress in lowering infant mortality, but demographers have found inconsistencies in the data used to calculate Cuban infant mortality statistics in certain years.[72] These inconsistencies may be within the normal margins of error expected in all statistical efforts, yet they tend to distort the results in ways that make Cuba look better. There is also a tendency to redefine categories in such a way as to obscure negative trends—for example, by reporting mortality data only for ages sixteen and under in certain years, which makes it impossible to check the figures for infants. These occasional lapses contrast with the generally high quality of Cuban demographic statistics, which makes them more suspicious.

Worms, Rats, and Sycophants

Opponents to Cuban Communism can be roughly divided into three categories. The earliest opponents were individuals who never favored building a Leninist system in Cuba. Many of these people supported the overthrow of the Batista dictatorship and felt betrayed when Castro reneged on his pledges to hold elections. Many of them left Cuba in the early 1960s. The Castroists generally refer to them as *gusanos,* a Spanish word for worms, which has become the colloquial term for exiles. Some of the early opponents expressed their opposition more openly or even fought against the imposition of Communism. Many of these were killed or jailed by the Castro government.

The second broad category of opponents includes people who were initially supportive of Cuban socialism, but became disillusioned over the years. In his speech at the closing of the First National Congress on Education and Culture in 1971, Fidel Castro compared intellectuals who abandoned socialism to rats abandoning a sinking ship:

> While capitalist Europe declines more and more and nobody knows where it will go in its fall, like a sinking ship . . . And with the ship in this tempestuous sea of history the intellectual rats will also sink. When I speak on intellectual rats, of course, I don't mean all of them. No: they are a minority there, too! But I mean the rats that try to make their miserable role as passengers on ships sinking in the tempestuous sea of history into something of great importance.[73]

Of course, the ship the intellectual "rats" were abandoning was socialist Cuba, not capitalist Europe. In these remarks Castro is projecting his (Cuba's) repressed problems onto others in a fashion typical of a destructive narcissistic personality.

The third kind of opposition, or quasi-opposition, is more subtle but probably much more widespread. These are the sycophants or, to continue with zoological metaphors, the fawns, who give lip service to the official ideology while privately doubting or rejecting it. Carlos Montaner recounts an incident: "Once, while leaving a televion station, Major Faustino Pérez, a resistance hero punished by Fidel, became hysterical, took hold of Fidel by the lapels, and half in repentance and half in anger asked him for another opportunity to be loyal. Castro placed his hands on Pérez's shoulders, looked at him intently, and gave him a second chance."[74]

One can imagine the emotional stress engendered as "people in Leninist systems suffer the daily humiliations of fawning before the powerful and dissembling in front of their children" in order to obtain jobs, housing, travel documents, schooling for their children, medical care, food, and so on.[75] Many people find it easier to live with this if they repress or deny their feelings of shame and humiliation. Their unconscious feelings can be inferred, however, from behaviors such as shirking work, engaging in corruption, avoiding participation in political activities or voluntary labor, telling jokes critical of the regime, and so on.[76]

The fact that this kind of opposition is difficult to verify or measure does not make it any less important. Tad Szulc reports that Castro "is furious over the immense rate of absenteeism among Cuban workers, low productivity, shoddy quality of industrial goods, and the shocking waste of materials and resources in industrial plants, farms, and government offices."[77] This passive, even unconscious, opposition from "fawns" accounts for much of the economic weakness of Leninist societies, as well as for the way in which support for seemingly popular regimes may collapse suddenly when the authorities seem weak or vulnerable. Of course, Castro cannot denounce the poor work habits of the Cuban workers without abandoning a key element in his reparative narcissism. Instead, he blames it on managers or technocrats who lack sufficient commitment to Leninist ideals.

Perhaps the best known of the "worms" is Armando Valladares, whose book *Against All Hope* is a vivid description of the life of one of the *plantados* (intransigents) in Cuba's prison system.[78] The *plantados* are prisoners who refuse to make any compromise with the system's rehabilitation programs and consequently suffer long terms of imprisonment under especially severe imprisonment. Valladares reports, for example, that for several months the only bath he received was a daily dousing with a bucket of urine and feces. He went on long hunger strikes, which, combined with the poor prison food, led him to develop a case of nutritional flaccid paraplegia, forcing him into a wheelchair. As Valladares tells the story, his steadfastness during his twenty-two years in prison was motivated by the great value he placed on the integrity of his value system:

there are things one cannot compromise or change—one's deepest con- victions and ethical values, those principles which, like pillars, sustain a person's self-respect. If a single one of them developed a crack, started to give way, a person's life's edifice could come crashing down about his ears. I felt, when I looked at my situation, that to waver, as my jailers obviously wanted me to do, was to put the internal structures of my life in danger. Still, I did vacillate, and I doubted; but then I prayed to God, and He, whom I never doubted, showed me the right path again—my rationalizations suddenly looked flimsy and transparent, and I began again with new reserves of faith and hope.[79]

Valladares insists that he was punished for his opposition to Castro's campaign to impose a Communist system on the island. Specifically, he says he was arrested for refusing to place a sign saying, "If Fidel is a Communist, then put me on the list. He's got the right idea" on his desk. The Cuban government has questioned the veracity of his account, claiming that he wasn't really paralyzed as badly as he claimed he was (they don't deny the paralysis altogether). They also claim that he was a police agent under the Batista regime and that he was arrested for terrorist activities.[80]

Another prominent "worm" is Huber Matos, a revolutionary *coman- dante* who claims he was imprisoned for twenty years because he wrote Fidel a letter warning him that Communists were taking over the revolu- tion. In the same document in which he denies Valladares's claims, Fidel states that "Huber Matos was not arrested for his ideas. Huber Matos organized a revolt in Camaguey, he was on the verge of provoking a bloody battle."[81] Matos was one of a number of revolutionists who be- lieved Castro's promises about democracy and freedom and opposed the establishment of a Leninist system.

Another disillusioned revolutionary was Luis Conte Agüero, who was a close friend of Fidel's during his student years. Many of Fidel's most important letters during his imprisonment were sent to Conte Agüero, who believed his claims of devotion to democratic values. Conte Agüero went into exile when Fidel betrayed these principles and has written several critical books.[82] His *Fidel Castro: Psiquiatría y Política* is a vicious char- acter assassination.[83] He equates Fidel with Satan, claims that he "sweats like a mule, although they call him The Horse," and dismisses him as "pathetic and psychopathological."[84] Despite this intense hostility, his book is full of psychological detail, which fits well with the more objective psychological appraisals. One cannot help but wonder, however, why the author failed to detect these fundamental personality flaws sooner, since he was such a close personal friend.

The "rat" who most provoked Fidel's wrath in 1971 was poet Heberto

Padilla, the most prominent of a number of writers who became disillusioned with the restraints on literary freedom in Cuba.[85] In the first few years after the revolution, there was a flowering of literary expression among writers who were generally supportive of the revolution, but this inevitably led to the accusation that certain writers were not truly loyal to the socialist revolution. Fidel Castro finally stepped in and tried to draw a line that would permit a degree of free expression without permitting outright anti-revolutionary thought. In response to the question, "What are the rights of the revolutionary and nonrevolutionary writers and artists?," Castro answered, "Within the Revolution, Everything; against the Revolution, no rights."[86] While this policy was applauded by the writers who naturally believed that they were within the revolution, the obvious question was who was going to decide what was within the revolution and what wasn't. In 1968 Heberto Padilla was awarded a prize by an international jury in a Cuban literary contest for a book of poems that the Cuban authorities believed to be excessively critical. At the next year's literary conference, which was judged solely by Cuban referees, the government announced the principle that "Cuban writers and artists have the same responsibilities as our soldiers. . . . he who does not [fulfill his duty] regardless of his position, will receive the most severe revolutionary punishment for his fault."[87]

The First National Congress on Education and Culture, held in 1971, established the principle that:

> In the field of ideological struggle there is no room for palliatives or half measures. The only alternative is a clear-cut, uncompromising stand. There is room only for ideological coexistence with the spiritual creation of the revolutionary peoples with socialist culture, with the forms of expression of Marxist-Leninist ideology. . . .
>
> Cultural institutions cannot serve as a platform for false intellectuals who try to make snobbery, extravagant conduct, homosexuality and other social aberrations into expressions of revolutionary art.
>
> We condemn the false Latin American writers who, after the first successes obtained with works that still expressed the drama of those nations, broke their links with the countries where they were born and took refuge in the capitals of the rotten and decadent societies of Western Europe and the United States to become agents of the metropolitan imperialist culture.
>
> In Paris, London, Rome, West Berlin and New York, these hypocrites find the best terrain for their ambiguities, vacillation and misery generated by the cultural colonialism which they accept and support. All they will receive from the revolutionary peoples is the contempt which the traitor and deserter merits.[88]

This passage captures the intense feeling of narcissistic injury, which is at the root of a totalitarian mindset that is terrified by a volume of critical poetry. This is the same mindset that reviewed the "fashions, customs, and extravagant behavior" among Cuban young people and concluded that:

> although it is true that certain forms of extravagant behavior, exhibitionism, etc., should not constitute a focus of attention for the Revolution, since they are limited to minority and generally marginal groups, yet the necessity of maintaining the monolithic ideological unity of our people and the struggle against all forms of deviation among our young make it imperative to implement a series of measures for their eradication.[89]

Fidel Castro was delighted with the Congress, claiming that "the debates in the commissions were very far ranging, opinions were expressed with absolute frankness and freedom," yet "when it came to revolutionary matters, when it came to political matters, there was only one attitude, a firm, solid, unambiguous monolithic attitude (APPLAUSE)."[90]

In this environment, it is not surprising that Heberto Padilla ended up in jail where he was pressured to sign a statement admitting his faults. No *plantado*, he decided to give in and typed up a thirty-page confession admitting that he had "deviated from the correct opinion."[91] The policeman who had interrogated him seemed convinced that "repression had triumphed, where effusive submission to orders had transformed us into docile marionettes for the satisfaction of the Comandante."[92] Padilla, on the other hand, correctly anticipated that intellectuals outside Cuba would be outraged by the Stalinist spectacle of an intellectual being forced to confess ideological sins in order to get out of prison. Octavio Paz's statement was typical of the reaction among Latin American intellectuals:

> In order to cleanse the reputation of its directorate, supposedly stained by a few books and articles which cast doubt upon their competence, the Cubans oblige one of their critics to declare himself an accomplice of abject and ultimately insignificant politico-literary intrigues. All this would be grotesque were it not yet another symptom of the fact that the fatal process is already on the way in Cuba, a process which turns the revolutionary party into a bureaucratic caste and its leader into a Caesar.[93]

Padilla worked as a translator for several years and was finally released from Cuba in 1981, carrying a copy of the manuscript for a novel that has since outraged the Cubans, *Heroes Are Grazing in My Garden,* in his luggage. He had been living in New York City when Batista was overthrown, and when he received the news, he "leapt out of bed, threw some cold water on my face, and opened the windows. As the biting air filled the room, suddenly I felt a joy I had never felt before."[94] After spending twenty years in Leninist societies, including jobs representing Cuban institutions in Moscow, Prague, Budapest, and Warsaw, Padilla returned to New York feeling:

> strangely empty. Not only am I incapable of taking any slogan seriously, but I feel betrayed by many intellectuals who, I once thought, were our sages. . . . the theoretical model proposed by Marx and Engels seems to me now a fatal determinism, as repugnant as the Absolute Ideal of Hegel. . . . The 19th-century socialist utopias now seem to me precursors of the forced-labor camps. . . . Their works seem to me now like luxuriant verbal constructions, no less distant from reality than those of the socialist thinkers Georg Lukács, Herbert Marcuse and Theodor Adorno: empty Scholasticism. Communism is no longer the exemplary challenge of our epoch. Rather, it is the ugly summation of everything that has been and is.[95]

The sycophants, by contrast, worry less about their illusions and more about making the best of their situation. José Luis Llovio-Menéndez was a high-ranking official of the Cuban government for ten years, and he offers an insider's view of *La Dolce Vita* Havana style. Llovio-Menéndez was a supporter of the revolution before it turned Communist and became disillusioned early when, as an emigré in Paris, he found that high-ranking Cuban diplomats visiting the city were more interested in buying up expensive perfume to "to win over the *compañeros* wives" and visiting expensive nightclubs and restaurants than they were in visiting working-class cafes or museums.[96] He says he returned to Cuba with his wealthy French wife because he wanted to help an uncle who was in prison. He knew Fidel well and thought that he was only pretending to be an ascetic while living luxuriously. Fidel was entranced by the luxurious new Mercedes Benz Llovio-Menéndez had brought with him, for example, and ordered himself one just like it.

Of course, an individual can move from "fawn" to "rat" very quickly when the opportunity presents itself. Manuel Sánchez Pérez was Vice-Minister of Economic Planning through the 1970s and began as an enthusiastic supporter of the socialist project. During the mid-1970s, he began to have doubts about the efficiency of the system of central planning. He tried proposing liberalizing methods, but these were rebuffed because they were viewed as imposing elements of free enterprise. He decided that the top leadership of the country had no interest in change of this sort because it went against their ideological commitment to anticapitalism. The Mariel boat lift—when twenty thousand people left Cuba in fifteen days—was the incident that crystallized his growing belief that the Cuban system was fatally flawed. He continued to work within the system until the opportunity presented itself to go into exile in Spain.[97]

The most striking incident of sycophancy was the discovery that many of the most prestigious members of the Cuban elite were involved in drug smuggling. Arnaldo Ochoa was one of only five "Heros of the Republic" because of his revolutionary exploits, which "always seemed larger, more romantic, than any reality" to Sandra Levinson, coeditor of the newsletter of the Center for Cuban Studies in New York and a longtime Cuba advocate.[98] When Ochoa was arrested with thirteen other Cuban leaders on June 12, 1989, "myth, legend and reality received a crushing blow," in Levinson's view. Why did they do it? Apparently they got tired of being revolutionary heroes and wanted to make some money. Ochoa offered no defense for his deeds, claiming only that "there came a point in my military life when I felt weary."[99] In response to insistent questioning about his motivations (he never denied his guilt), Ochoa was at a loss for words:

> Well, I can tell you, consternated as I am now, it isn't easy to say why I did it, right? That's the truth, right? I didn't act rashly, I acted irresponsibly. And, well, there's no doubt I assumed powers and rights I didn't have, no? And, well, I think there are things in life that for many reasons make a man change. Also, acting independently has a bit to do with it.[100]

The prosecutor finally concluded that "Ochoa was tired of public service, he got bored of living for a cause, he got fed up with fighting and working for others, he got tired of the peoples' liberation struggle; and he decided, fully aware and in a calculated manner, to live his other life, a life that was completely centered around himself."[101]

This incident contributes to what seems to be a growing perception that the Cuban elite is corrupt. Sandra Levinson did some interviews with Cubans who made remarks such as the following from a fifty-five-year-old housewife: "everyone knows that lots of bigwigs, like Diocles [Torralbes, ex-minister of transportation] live too well. An indoor swimming pool—imagine! When there are people in Old Havana who have no water sometimes three days in a row." A forty-five-year-old writer commented: "Carlos Rafael [Rodríguez] once said that one of the things he felt worst about when all the revelations about Stalin came out was that Stalin had proved true everything the enemy had said. That's how I feel: one of the worst things about all this is that this little group makes all the U.S. has accused us of seem true."

While it is difficult to measure, it seems likely that fawning over official leaders is the predominant mentality in Cuba and other late Leninist societies. It probably has as much to do with the crisis of productivity in these societies as the technical economic factors. On a basic, fundamental level, people simply don't want to make the system work. It might be possible to assess this kind of attitudinal trend with sophisticated survey methods or with projective tests or depth interviews, but this has not been done in Cuba or any Leninist state and may not be done before the species becomes extinct.

The best evidence we have is the accounts of sensitive observers who have lived in Cuba for long periods of time and have the literary skills to describe the mentality. Early in this century, Cuban cartoonists used the character "Liborio" to symbolize the common man, who "continually suffered political disillusionment and the social consequences of corrupt politicians."[102] While Liborio does not appear in the Communist press, Llovio-Menéndez claims that he has just been pushed underground, and he describes life under Communism as follows:

Liborio will go to any lengths to attend any assembly that he's told to or any productive work that is organized. And he will even go further to be there always in the crowd on the Plaza de la Revolución to listen to Fidel. He will shout "*¡Patria o Muerte! ¡Venceremos!*" without stopping to think what the slogan means; he will scream "Down with the Yanquis!" although at bottom he might have preferred to go and live in the United States a long time ago; he will frantically applaud when he is told that his quota of sugar or coffee will be reduced, although the measure breaks his heart; he will volunteer to fight in the name of proletarian internationalism, although in reality what happens in other countries doesn't matter to him very much; he will let himself be talked to about problems and hear them analyzed minutely through a paternalistic lens as if he were retarded; he will listen without protest to one excuse after another, one promise after another; he will allow them to postpone his prosperity until 1990, until 2000, until the time of his grandchildren or his great-grandchildren. . . .

When Liborio returns home after the long speech, exhausted by so much applauding and hoarse with so much shouting, he will ask himself: "But what does he really think? How far does he plan to take us?" In a whisper he will unburden himself to his wife, if he trusts her and doesn't plan to divorce, and he will blame himself for being so docile. But then, as he looks at his sleeping children, he will forgive himself because he understands that for the moment there is nothing else he can do. The next day he will get up again very early to go to work, he will wash his face and shave, and before he leaves the house he will put on a convincing expression.[103]

If this account seems like nothing more than the wishful thinking of a prominent "rat," we can find the much the same analysis in the writings of Fidel himself:

> It was starting to go to pot. . . . the peasants were also getting corrupted. . . . we offered examples of enterprises that sold their materials and charged the prices of finished jobs . . . enterprises that tried to become profitable by theft, swindles, swindling one another. What kind of socialism were we going to build along those lines? What kind of ideology was that? And I want to know whether these methods weren't leading us to a system worse than capitalism . . . that almost universal chaos in which anyone grabbed anything he could, whether it be a crane or a truck. These things were becoming habitual and generalized.[104]

Failed Theories and Broken Promises

A central feature of Fidel's thinking, and of Leninist discourse in general, is splitting the world into good and evil forces. In the Latin American context, this often means blaming Latin America's poverty on the United States. This view was very popular at the time of the Cuban revolution, when it was given academic respectability in the form of "dependency theory."[105] This thesis was most forcefully expressed by André Gunder Frank, whose "development of underdevelopment" thesis asserted that poverty and underdevelopment in Latin America had been caused by the colonial powers and that the only way for these nations to develop was to break out of the world capitalist system.[106] Leading economists encouraged Latin American countries to use protectionist measures to help their economies break out of dependency.[107]

These theories are appealing to people who sympathize with the world's poor and criticize those who live in luxury while others starve. Fidel Castro evokes these feelings masterfully in his speeches and books. He illustrates his points with carefully selected examples to show how the prices of carefully selected items have gone up over the years. For example, he is fond of quoting how many tons of sugar are needed to purchase an item such as a construction crane or a soft ice cream machine.[108] These examples sound convincing, but they depend on the logical flaw of selecting the illustrations that fit the thesis while ignoring those that do not. It would be just as easy to choose examples to illustrate the opposite point. Imagine, for example, how much more computing power a ton of sugar can buy today than in 1960.

To answer questions about the validity of dependency theory accurately, one must look at rigorous quantitative studies. If Castro were to look at recent statistical studies, he would find that they have not supported his presuppositions.[109] In fact, on average, the trends in international prices have been more positive for the third-world countries than for the wealthy countries.[110]

The most successful third-world countries have been those that emphasized export promotion strategies, often in collaboration with multinational corporations. Reviews of the literature on dependency note that "dependency arguments failed to anticipate the recent course of events" and suggest that in the modern world "the least enviable position may not be 'dependency,' but the lack of it."[111] Even those writers who still find value in dependency theory are quick in "rejecting the dogmatic simplistic version of dependency, often worded in the core-periphery language."[112] As one of the few remaining exponents of precisely these dogmatic and simplistic views, Fidel Castro has become more and more of an anachronism, a relic of a bygone era when anti-imperialist rhetoric seemed more in touch with reality.

While Castro has remained true to the theories, he has not been able to force the Cuban economy to perform as expected, especially in the last decade. While before 1980, annual growth rates between 3 percent and 5 percent were common, since 1980 the Cuban economy has stagnated, and by 1987 it was shrinking.[113] The Cuban economy is highly inefficient, highly dependent on foreign sponsors, and burdened with excessive debt to the capitalist countries. Its annual subsidy from the Soviet Union, until 1991, represented about one-third of the gross national product. The economy's only strong point is in income redistribution, with significantly less inequality than other Latin American countries.[114]

While Cuba's economic crisis is similar to that of other Communist economies in the last decade, Castro's response has not been to move toward market-oriented economics, but to attempt to purify and "rectify" Cuban socialism.[115] He has blamed the economy's failures on "bureaucrats" and "technocrats" who mimicked capitalist ways by relying on material incentives to maximize production, and he urged a return to voluntary labor and moral incentives, relying on Che Guevara's writings as his guide to economic theory.[116] The Russians have informed Cuba that it must pay world-market prices for goods such as oil and machinery, and Castro has been warning the people to be "prepared for exceptional measures," which might include moving large numbers of people out of the cities to farm and forage for wood.[117] As Russian oil deliveries lag and foreign exchange is unavailable to purchase oil at world-market prices, the government is urging a return to draft animals instead of machinery for farm work.[118] An experimental zone has been created in the municipality of San Cristóbal where people are trying to live off the land as if they were participants in a wilderness survival training program.[119]

It is difficult to judge the amount of dissatisfaction with a regime that is still announcing austerity measures after three decades in power. Amnesty International reported that at least sixty government critics were arrested during 1989, including many members of "the growing number of unofficial groups involved in civil and political rights."[120] In this climate, people are not always free to express their feelings publicly, especially to foreigners or reporters. In one Havana store, however, a woman told an American reporter that "we should be living at the rhythm of the rest of the world, but we have been condemned to live for 31 years a completely limited existence."[121] Hero of the revolution Yanez Pelletier has joined the tiny human rights movement, and he predicts that "next year is going to be a terrible year for Cuba, not only is the internal situation deteriorating, but the external situation is getting worse too."[122] No wonder "Socialism or Death" became a leading slogan in 1990, reviving the suicidal imagery of Fidel's youth.[123]

There is every reason to expect that isolating the nation as much as possible from the world economy will be at least as unsuccessful in the future as it has been in the past. Cuba's hard currency reserves are almost exhausted, and its seven-billion-dollar debt makes it impossible to borrow money to help in the transition away from dependency on Soviet aid. Indeed, the current "rectification" campaign, although presented as a quest for a purer socialism, can also be seen as an austerity program meeting the demands that the International Monetary Fund typically imposes on nations that are unable to pay their debts.[124]

After thirty years of opposition to dependency, Cuba remains largely dependent on sugar exports for foreign exchange. It has not developed an export-oriented industrial sector comparable to those of many Latin American countries, but has recently begun to seek foreign exchange through an aggressive promotion of foreign tourism. In the modern world, successful industrialization requires close links with the world economy, and Cuba's commitment to dependency theories has retarded its development in this area.

Conclusions

A whole generation of Cubans has lived in a state of psychological dependency on a father figure who is the one person free to act on his own behalf, to make his own mistakes, to think for himself without fear of recrimination. Cubans who could not accept this have been forced into exile or imprisonment. As a result, Cuba has become a narcissistic society, in love with a glorified self-image, which masks its feelings of inferiority. This depends fundamentally on scapegoating the United States for the nation's obvious poverty and oppressiveness, while giving Castro and Communism full credit for its accomplishments.

This pattern is not unusual for a Communist country. Although many people perceive Cuba as different from other Leninist societies, the differences are more superficial than substantive. Political power is monopolized by a single party, which justifies its rule with an official state ideology to which everyone is required to give allegiance. People who disagree with the fundamental dogmas of the regime are marginalized, exiled, shot, or jailed, sometimes for very long prison terms. The economy is centrally commanded by an elite, which has privileged access to housing, food, and luxuries. This group is usually referred to by an Afro-Cuban term, *los marimbes,* but it means the same thing as the Russian word *nomenklatura.*[125] People not in the elite receive assurances of employment, education, medical care, and basic sustenance in exchange for surrendering political, intellectual, and economic freedoms.

To move beyond this system, a Leninist country needs to go through some version of the usual stages of group development. This means that the leader has to be overthrown or at least neutralized in some way. Factional disagreement must be tolerated, and the country must give up blaming the United States for its problems. Only then will it be able to motivate its people to find viable solutions to its problems.

It is very difficult for a revolutionary society to make this kind of change when the original charismatic leader is still in power. Since 1989, when most Leninist societies abandoned their narcissistic illusions and began to work on real reform, Cuba has been adamant in defending its rigid Leninist model. Beginning in 1986, even before the crisis of Leninism in Europe became generally known, Fidel found it necessary to rally his nation once again to rectify the failures of Leninism.[126] He blamed the regime's failure on "corruption" within the cadres and promised to purify them. He claimed that:

> we have reacted in time so that the Party members will not be corrupted, the Party will not be corrupted, the people will not be corrupted, the young people will not be corrupted and above all our working class will not be corrupted. I'm not falling into wishful thinking: I'm expressing what we have been seeing in this rectification process.[127]

The arrest of several other top Cuban leaders for drug smuggling, three years after the rectification campaign began, shows that Fidel's thinking was more wishful than he believed. International support for the regime has crumbled, not just financially, but also ideologically. Outside of the few remaining hard line, Leninist states, advocates for Marxism-Leninism are scarcer than prohibitionists, single taxers, or antivivisectionists. Those who are trying to save or recreate a "socialist" ideal almost universally reject the Leninist model. This lack of prestige in Latin America and Europe for their no longer revolutionary model is profoundly threatening to the Cuban ego.

A little narcissism is a healthy thing, especially in youth, but an adult has to distinguish between romance and reality. In old age, narcissistic nostalgia can be charming, but only if it is not allowed to interfere with progress. At times, Castro seems ready to retire and let the nation get on with its development. In a recent interview he compared his role to that of Spain's nonelected King and opined that he would like to retire and become "just like everybody else. . . . diplomats can retire, everyone can retire. The only ones who can't retire are the revolutionaries."[128]

Ironically, United States foreign policy is a major force reinforcing Cuba's narcissistic illusions. As anti-Castro Cuban Llovio-Menéndez argues:

> Washington should seriously consider ending the embargo and granting Cuba diplomatic recognition. The embargo has been a myth; through intermediary nations Cuba has access to nearly all the U.S. technology it can afford. Furthermore, a lifting of the blockade would rob Fidel of his favorite alibi for Cuba's economic failure. It's true that U.S.-Cuban trade would open to him a source of hard currency, but it would also open Cuba to ideological penetration. As Fidel's experience in welcoming the exile Cuban Community has shown, the people's revolutionary consciousness remains quite vulnerable to the subversive influence of consumerism.[129]

The lifting of the "blockade" would give Fidel a face-saving victory and raise tremendous expectations of material and political improvement among the population, expectations that cannot be realized by a Leninist command economy and one-party dictatorship. The embargo feeds the *Fidelista's* narcissistic image of Cuba as important and threatening, and it reinforces their splitting of the world into good and evil forces. Without this external threat, the Cuban people would find it easier to abandon their dependency on a leader whose narcissism has lost its lustre.

Chapter Sixteen

Bush and Gorbachev: Visions of the Future or a Future without Vision?

George Bush and Mikhail Gorbachev are in some ways puzzling figures. Neither has much personal charisma. Their early life histories did not show outstanding promise. Yet both emerged as powerful leaders who made a major impact on history. Together they set the stage for a "new world order," which is likely to shape the future for a long time to come.

Bush and Gorbachev are both pragmatists who excel at playing the political game within the rules of their respective societies. Their success came about because both the Soviet and the American systems had evolved to a point where they needed lackluster, pragmatic leadership. This is easy to understand in the American case because pragmatic leadership is appropriate in a mature, stable society that is not experiencing significant pressures for dramatic social change.

It is much more surprising in the Soviet case. Soviet society had serious contradictions, and there was a need for a charismatic leader who could take control and find dramatic solutions for the nation's problems. When Gorbachev took office, however, power was still firmly in the hands of a Communist Party known for stagnant, authoritarian leadership. He won power by working his way up in this Party organization, and we must look to organizational dynamics for much of the explanation of what came to be known in the west as the "Gorbachev phenomenon."

The Enigma of Mikhail Gorbachev

If there are "Great Men" who make history, Mikhail Gorbachev would seem to qualify. Yet even the most insightful of his biographers, Gail Sheehy, is at a loss to understand how this most opportunistic and trustworthy of Party autocrats was transformed into *The Man Who Changed the World.*[1] As one reviewer of Sheehy's book observed:

Our Man Who Changed the World is variously described as a hypocrite, a chameleon, a liar, an opportunist who groveled and pandered his way to power, and a heavyhanded Party hack unwilling to part with his own luxuries, which include five dachas or so and a limitless budget to keep Raisa, the "trained Marxist philosopher," in furs, Parisian finery, and a comfy Zil limousine of her very own.[2]

Other biographers mine the same scanty store of facts about Gorbachev's personal life but offer no solution to the enigma.[3] To be sure, they can readily explain why change was necessary. The Soviet Union was an increasingly urban society in crisis, unable to compete economically with the West and burdened with a rigid and despotic political system. New generations were eagerly awaiting the passing of the Politburo gerontocracy. But the world abounds with nations in enduring societal crises where power remains clutched firmly in the grip of the old guard. Before Gorbachev took the helm in 1985, no one anticipated that the gerontocracy would appoint a new leader with a mandate to transform the system. With hindsight it is easy to criticize him for not moving quickly enough, but when he became General Secretary in 1985 no one imagined that he could move as quickly as he did. As recently as 1984, Samuel Huntington expressed the consensus of the experts when he stated that "the likelihood of democratic development in Eastern Europe is virtually nil."[4]

Insights from Psychobiography. What can psychobiography contribute to solving the enigma? The available details about Gorbachev's childhood on a farm in the North Caucasus suggest that his early experiences were more typical than unusual for his generation. His was, however, a generation cursed to live in "interesting times." His paternal grandfather was one of the *kulaks* (successful peasants) arrested and deported during the collectivization drives. His maternal grandfather accommodated to the system and became the chairman of a collective farm. Mikhail had to take on many adult responsibilities as early as eleven years of age because his father was in the army during the war. If his father's absence left him with an unresolved Oedipal complex, as Wolfenstein's theory of the revolutionary personality would suggest, he kept it well hidden.[5] He lived through five months of German occupation, making whatever concessions to authority were necessary to survive.

Like many of his compatriots, Gorbachev emerged from these experiences with a strong survivor script.[6] He knew that life was risky and unfair and that only the careful and clever were likely to survive. In some ways, Gorbachev fits Mazlish's model of the "revolutionary ascetic."[7] He was a grimly ascetic young man, abstaining from alcohol and spending long hours with his books while others partied. He had a strong need for achievement and the discipline to focus his energies on long-term goals. He did not, however, display the narcissism or love of abstract principles found in many revolutionary leaders. He was a bland and unassuming young man, not much noticed by his contemporaries. He knew how to keep out of trouble.

The Communist Party was the best chance at social mobility for a poor rural youth, and he became a dedicated Komsomol (Communist Party youth group) member at fourteen. He worked hard in school, receiving a silver (but not a gold) medal for good grades. As a Komsomol activist, he set a good example for other youth by volunteering enthusiastically to help out with the harvest. He made sure his efforts were noticed by the right people and was rewarded with a Red Banner of Labor award. This award and strong recommendations from local officials won him admission to Moscow University, not in physics as he had hoped, but in the law school.

In law school, Gorbachev roomed with a Czechoslovakian student, Zdenek Mlynar, who was later active in the Prague spring.[8] Reports of Gorbachev's political behavior as a student are contradictory. He had his rebellious moments, including one when he publicly criticized a teacher who bored everyone by reading Stalin's latest book aloud from cover to cover. This was a daring thing to do at the height of Stalin's personality cult, but Gorbachev persuaded the authorities that he was a dedicated Communist who objected only to the professor's pedantic and uninspiring way of spreading the truth.[9] The professor was replaced, and Gorbachev moved ahead.

He indulged in freewheeling bull sessions with selected friends in the privacy of his dorm room. They were intelligent enough to see through the simplistic stereotyping of Stalinist propaganda. Mikhail was especially irritated by a Soviet film that showed happy peasants from his home region celebrating around tables of food. He knew better. There was little food, and the farmers worked only because of strict discipline. But he was very careful to express his critical thoughts only when they could be constructive. He was not above demanding that other students be expelled from the Komsomol for offenses such as telling political jokes. One student remembers him mimicking Stalin's style in a Komsomol meeting, and not in jest. Mlynar insists that Gorbachev took Communist doctrine seriously:

> Our political discussions were very open. He was one of the few who
> talked about politics. The others were just not interested. I knew that
> he was a convinced ideological Communist and that we shared the
> conviction that Communism was the way of the future. He was never
> cynical. He was reformist by nature.[10]

More worldly students, from well-educated urban families, might mouth
the slogans while concealing their cynicism. Gorbachev, however, was a
true believer who insisted that the deficiencies of the system could and
must be corrected. He could not easily stomach the cynics who dismissed
the doctrine sarcastically or the sycophants who parroted it emptily.

There is little in Gorbachev's childhood, youth, or career before 1985
that makes him stand out from hundreds of other faceless Soviet *apparat-
chiks.* He may have been cleverer and harder working and more sincere
than most, but he was in every way the organization man. Throughout
his career, Gorbachev excelled primarily in the ability to make himself
useful to powerful people who were in a position to help him. He was
keenly attuned to the factional conflicts within the Party hierarchy and
formed his alliances carefully while doing his best not to alienate anyone.
He spent twenty years as Party boss in a region that included a popular
elite resort, and he used this position to build friendships with the movers
and shakers of the Soviet system. Finally, these connections enabled him
to move back to Moscow, enter the Politburo, and build a strong position
to compete for the top job as the feeble gerontocrats died off.

Insights from Group Psychology. If Gorbachev was the Organization
Man par excellence, then the answer to the enigma may be found in the
psychodynamics of the Communist Party as an organization. As we saw
in Chapter Five, studies of group development have found that groups
go through developmental stages and that they use social defense mechanisms analogous to those used by individuals. These group processes help
to explain the enigma of Gorbachev.

Like all revolutionary regimes, the Soviet regime began with power
and legitimacy concentrated in a strong charismatic leader. Lenin died
prematurely, leading to the power struggle between Stalin and Trotsky
(Chapter Nine). With the exception of Khrushchev's removal from power
in 1964, Soviet leaders have remained inviolate until their death from natural
causes. Factional struggle has been covert and severely restricted since Stalin
repressed Trotsky's faction. Dependence on the "personality cult" of the
leader has been reestablished as a social defense mechanism with each
new supreme leader.

In terms of the Stages of Group Development (Table Three in Chapter
Five), Lenin's early death forced the Communist Party to move rapidly

from a primitive to a transitional stage of development. The factional splits and power struggles were especially severe, and Stalin established a regime that depended heavily on ideological dogmatism as a social defense. When he died, factional struggle reemerged. Khrushchev's attempt to move the Party to a more mature level of development was aborted by the orthodox faction because they felt that the country was doing well enough with an authoritarian, centrally administered system.

This failure to develop led to a long period of stagnation, with aging leaders and an increasingly corrupt Party apparatus. During this time, however, Soviet leaders became increasingly aware of the failure of the country to keep up with the more dynamic Western nations. In 1978, S. F. Kissin was able to demonstrate that Marxist orthodoxy had declined steadily in official Party policy statements during the years since World War II.[11] Many Party leaders understood that messianic prophecies of the collapse of capitalism, which seemed to make sense in the thirties, were out of touch with the realities of the postwar era. Ideological dogmatism was so firmly established as a social defense mechanism, however, that they could not openly acknowledge their doubts.

Official Party documents gave formal obeisance to the old theories, while tacitly acknowledging changing realities. For example, the 1961 program of the Communist Party of the Soviet Union gave lip service to Lenin's analysis of the increasing decay of capitalism, but at the same time did "not rule out the growth of capitalist economy at particular times and in particular countries" and made plans for peaceful coexistence with capitalist societies. The Party's preeminent goal was the prevention of nuclear war "by the present generation." Nothing in the document suggested that the authors expected the collapse of capitalism during their lifetimes.[12]

In the midsixties, the term "state-monopoly capitalism" was resurrected from the Leninist corpus and used in Party documents to apply to a stable and enduring form of capitalism. Western European Communist parties developed the policies known as "eurocommunism," which were, for all practical purposes, social democratic. Instead of aiming to "smash the capitalist state machine," Communist parties were urged to strive for gradual reform through parliamentary means. By the eighties, specialists were reporting that:

> Emigrés from the Soviet Union have been reporting for at least the last generation now that virtually nobody in that country truly believed in Marxism-Leninism any longer, and that this was nowhere more true than in the Soviet elite, which continued to mouth Marxist slogans out of sheer cynicism.[13]

While this statement may be exaggerated, it is clear that Gorbachev's policies of *perestroika* and *glasnost* articulated long-standing trends in elite Soviet thinking. They appeared to be a bolt out of the blue because no top leader before Gorbachev had stated them publicly before. By articulating his belief in the need for radical change, Gorbachev prompted what social psychologists call a "risky-shift phenomenon" in the Party.[14] His forthright leadership broke the taboo on questioning Leninist orthodoxy. Ideological dogmatism lost most of its potency as a defense mechanism. He made it possible for the Party to openly take steps it had been frightened to take before. A brief period of euphoria set in, before the enormity of the problems, which had previously been denied, became fully apparent.

Understandably, many observers were skeptical of this change. Medvedev expected a continuation of the old pattern, asserting that "the eventual emergence of Gorbachev's own 'cult of personality' is inevitable."[15] This prediction was out of touch with the Party's level of development. It needed to move beyond dependence on a charismatic leader to a modern form of organization in which alternative policies could be openly debated. In fact, Gorbachev enjoyed only a brief "honeymoon" period similar to that given to American presidents, a sign that the Communist Party had moved well beyond the primitive stage of group development. His popularity declined steadily as he failed to resolve the nation's economic problems, yet he did not resort to scapegoating minority groups or dissenters.

Of course, there remained a significant orthodox faction in the Party, some of whom were apparently sincere believers. The orthodox and revisionist factions were most often associated with the names of Yegor Ligachev and Boris Yeltsin. These two men typify the orthodox and revisionist personalities as psychological types. Ligachev is a "confirmed teetotaler" who "is regarded as a puritan in his personal life—as a man who detests divorce and lack of self-discipline." Yeltsin is brash and rebellious. His trademark is "outbursts of blunt personal criticism."[16] Both of these men were brought into the Politburo by Gorbachev, whose goal seemed to be to help the Party develop the ability to routinize factional conflict. He was eager to focus the Party's energies on the urgent task of restructuring the economy.

Gorbachev was able to keep the lid on these factional conflicts until August of 1991, when a group of orthodox leaders attempted to seize power in a military coup. Gorbachev was sequestered in his vacation home, and Boris Yeltsin quickly took the lead of the democratic forces. The coup leaders apparently thought that Gorbachev could be manipulated into supporting them, but he refused to do so. Without the President's stamp of approval, the plotters had only very limited support within the military and the security forces. The democrats were able to successfully resist the coup and bring Gorbachev back into office. This left the reformists in a much stronger position, enabling Yeltsin to take over the predominant leadership role.

Gorbachev's strategy of balancing off the two wings of the Party collapsed when the hard-liners were defeated in their coup attempt. The hard-liners had lost their legitimacy and credibility. At this point, Gorbachev had no option but to abandon his attempt to sustain the Communist Party of the Soviet Union as a viable organization. Without the Party or the support of the armed forces, there was nothing to hold the Soviet Union together, and he was reluctantly forced to accept the "dismembering" of the country and "disuniting" of the state he had struggled to preserve. He took comfort in having saved the country from the "shackles of the bureaucratic command system, doomed to cater to ideology and suffer and carry the onerous burden of the arms race" and remained convinced that "the democratic reform that we launched in the spring of 1985 was historically correct."[17]

Conclusion. The enigma of Gorbachev's transmogrification from party hack to prime mover disappears when he is understood as an other-directed man who is acutely sensitive to the social defenses current in elite Party circles. As a student, he internalized the ideological dogmatism of the Stalin era, making the beliefs his own. As a mature leader, he internalized the increasing rationality and task orientation of the Party elite. He was selected as General Secretary in 1985 because the progressive faction in the Politburo felt the need for a leader who could help them face up to the task of responding to the crisis of the nation's institutions. He took to the task with enthusiasm. In his speeches to the Party, he repeatedly stressed the urgency of the problems:

> the rates of economic development in our country had decreased and reached a critical point, but even those rates, it has now become clear, were achieved in large measure on an unhealthy basis, making use of opportunistic factors. I am referring to trade in petroleum on the world market at the high prices in effect at that time and to the totally unjustified step-up in the sale of alcoholic beverages. If we remove the influence of these factors from the economic growth indices, the result is that we had no increase in the absolute growth of the national income over virtually four five-year plans, and it even began to decrease in the early 1980s. . . .
>
> This effort was seriously impeded by the personality cult, by the command-administrative system of management that came about in the 1930s, by bureaucratic, dogmatic and voluntaristic distortions, by high-handedness, and, in the late 1970s and early 1980s, by the lack of initiative and retardation phenomena that led to stagnation.[18]

Despite the urgency of the crisis, however, Gorbachev did not act as a revolutionary with a mandate to sweep the old system and its leaders into the dustbin of history. He described the crisis of the system in precise dystopian fashion, but he did not offer a vision of the future except in vague terms, which allowed people to project their own hopes into his remarks. Nor did he offer himself as a transformational object. He built no personality cult. Instead he acted to routinize factional conflict and leadership succession. He tried to steer a middle course between the orthodox, who were reluctant to give up the command system, and the radicals, who wanted to abandon it completely for a market economy. In all of these ways, he acted as a leader intent on helping the Communist Party to mature as an organization.

Gorbachev's leadership was probably the best that could have been hoped for in the 1980s. It was certainly much more progressive than anyone expected at the time. He had to work within the limits of Communist Party tolerance or he would never have come to power. His doctrines of *glasnost* (openness) and *perestroika* (restructuring) were vague enough to be acceptable to the Party elite, yet offered a promise of transformation.

As time went on, his vague promises of economic restructuring were not enough to resolve the economic crisis. Gorbachev was unable to break out of his Party role decisively enough to challenge the fundamental privileges and dogmas of the elite. As Russian writer Viktor Yerofeyev concluded, "Gorbachev was a true instrument of fate. . . . He had enough faith in Communism to be named its head, but enough doubts about it to destroy it. If he had seen everything clearly, he would not have changed Russia."[19]

George Bush: A Vision of the Future?

George Bush has not been an easy target for biographers.[20] To be sure, his exploits as a naval pilot during World War II, when he was shot down and rescued by a submarine, make a good adventure story. But the rest of his life is too trite and wholesome to make the best-seller list. When one author began a biography, a sympathetic friend commiserated, "the publisher asked you to write 60,000 words about George Bush? What will you find to say after you've copied his resumé?"[21]

Like Woodrow Wilson, George grew up in the shadow of a powerful father. Prescott Bush was tall and handsome with a strong chin and imposing eyebrows, a perfect hero for an Ayn Rand novel. He commuted from stately Greenwich, Connecticut, to Manhattan every day to make a good living as an investment banker, then returned to sit on community and charitable boards in the evenings. He read the children a lesson from the Bible every morning before breakfast and took them to church on Sunday.

Fortunately, unlike Wilson's father, Prescott Bush was fulfilled with his own life and gave his children the space they needed to develop independently. They spent more time with their mother who encouraged them to compete at sports and strove to keep them from being too self-satisfied. George recalls one time when, as an adolescent, he complained that his tennis game was off. She told him, "you don't have a game."[22] George shared a room with Prescott, Jr., who was two years older. They were very close, refusing their parents' effort to give them separate rooms. Growing up in a large family, including a younger sister and two younger brothers, helped George develop skills in getting along with others. He was always popular, always eager to share his toys. The family sometimes jokingly called him "have half" because of an occasion when he insisted that his older brother "have half" of his first toy that wasn't a hand-me-down, a pedal car. His brother had already driven off in the thing, however, and George may have been worried that Pres would take more than half. On his report card, George got his best grades in the category, "claims no more than his fair share of time and attention." For years, the family teased him about his excellence in "claims no more."

Bush developed two strong character traits from his childhood experiences: a drive to win and a need to be liked. Competitive sports are the ideal outlet for these two traits, and Bush has loved them all his life. He makes the best of his talents and was captain of a strong baseball team at Yale, although he wasn't the best player. He loves tennis and horseshoes, but he will play almost any competitive game. One neighbor from his Texas days observed that:

> When I'd drop into the Bushes' house in Midland after work, George would pounce on me for a game of tiddlywinks. He'd sit me down on the carpet and pop those little things into an old-fashioned-size glass until he'd wump me; which he did soundly every time. Only then would I be allowed to get up and have supper.[23]

One is reminded of Fidel Castro becoming upset when a boy beat him at Ping-Pong, but Bush never had Castro's narcissistic insecurity. As a child, there was never any question of his being loved and respected. He accepts losing graciously, as the patrician gentleman he was raised to be, and simply tries harder next time. He went off to Texas to make his fortune in the oil business instead of using his father's connections in the New York financial community, but he didn't have to rebel against his father to do it. His father understood his need to be his own man and wished him well.

The American free-enterprise economic system and two-party political system are ready-made for a man who loves to compete within well-defined rules and in a congenial atmosphere. Bush did well enough as a salesman and entrepreneur in the oil industry, but he found his real challenge in politics. He succeeded in being elected to Congress from Houston as a Republican and could have kept the seat indefinitely. But he couldn't resist the chance to try for the Senate, especially since the liberal Democratic Senator Ralph Yarborough looked vulnerable. Unfortunately, Yarborough was so vulnerable that he lost the Democratic primary to Lloyd Bentsen, a more conservative Democrat who defeated Bush in the general election. Running as a Republican in Texas gave Bush a considerable handicap.

When Bush gave up his Congressional seat to run against Yarborough, president Nixon promised him a high appointive position if he lost. He made him Ambassador to the United Nations. Bush was popular with the diplomats, learning their names, meeting their wives, and giving a lot of successful parties. He nevertheless lost a bitter fight to keep Taiwan in the United Nations, along with the Beijing government, and many third-world delegates danced in the aisle to celebrate their victory over the United States. Ever the gentleman, Bush escorted the Taiwanese to their limousine and welcomed the Communist Chinese delegates graciously when they arrived. He was never one to stew over setbacks. When a local magazine rated Bush as one of the "ten most overrated men" in New York, he good-humoredly held a party for the ten of them. Bush left the United Nations when Nixon needed his diplomatic skills in the role of chairman of the Republican National Committee. He remained loyal to Nixon until the Watergate tapes made his guilt undeniable, then he wrote Nixon a letter advising him to resign. Coming out of Watergate with clean hands, he went on to stints as Ambassador to China and Director of the Central Intelligence Agency. He added lines to his resumé, building his reputation as a moderate Republican who could be counted on to follow instructions enthusiastically. His hope was that his popularity with Republican Party activists, and his reputation as a tireless team player, would win him an invitation to run as vice president. His biggest disappointment was when Gerald Ford chose Nelson Rockefeller instead.

When Bush launched his own presidential campaign in 1980, he was outclassed as a campaigner by Ronald Reagan. The biggest blow was in the New Hampshire primary, when Reagan dramatically seized the microphone from an organizer who wanted to include all the Republican candidates at a debate. As an actor, Reagan recognized the scene as one where he had to appear strong and decisive. Bush was trying to be a nice guy and work something out. Bush has little charisma or brilliance as an orator. His voice is a bit high-pitched and can get squeaky. Nobody hates him, but nobody finds him exciting either. Reagan found him useful as a moderate to balance his ticket, forgiving him for having labeled Reagan's economic proposals "voodoo economics" in the New Hampshire primary. It is the only memorable phrase Bush ever coined, and he has regretted it ever since.

Bush was not generally expected to be a highly popular president. Many people thought that he was a good number-two man but that he had no ideas of his own. In a book that tried to assess the character of all the 1988 presidential candidates, pop psychologist Gail Sheehy concluded that:

> In sum, what we have in George Bush is a person whose most consistent characteristic is the effort to avoid confrontation, to evade taking chances so he cannot be blamed for things that go wrong. . . . If George Bush cannot bear to offend people, if he hasn't got the outer strength to pursue a lonely course, if he feels wholly comfortable only when being liked, might he not, as a president, become paralyzed?[24]

To which Bush might reply, "tell it to Saddam Hussein." Sheehy wasn't the only person to underestimate Bush. In the 1988 campaign, he struggled to overcome an image as a "wimp," which he finally shed when he proved his toughness by lashing into anchorman Dan Rather during a television interview. He also chose a boyish running mate so the public would have someone else to ridicule. Throughout the campaign, Bush was also criticized for a lack of "vision." He had no ready answer to this charge and was reported to be mystified about what he called, "this vision thing." Despite these problems, however, Bush won handily against a lackluster Democratic candidate.

Given all his supposed limitations, how can we explain Bush's success both in winning the presidency and in maintaining unprecedented popularity after the election? First of all, the image of him as a wimp was really just "a series of cultural stereotypes," not a reflection of his actual character.[25] He is a wealthy Easterner with an Ivy League background, a weak voice, and an unimpressive stage presence. These traits led people to see him as weak, especially in contrast to Ronald Reagan's well-staged cowboy image. But he has always had confidence in his own judgment and the courage to follow it. He was, after all, a bomber pilot when Reagan was making war movies. He could have followed his father's advice to stay in college and wait to see whether he would be drafted. He didn't have to make his own fortune in the oil business. He has also been steadfast in his religious commitments and in his dedication to family life, values that Reagan preached more than he practiced. After Reagan, perhaps the country was ready for a man whose substance was stronger than his posturing.

As a congressman in 1968, Bush supported a controversial fair housing bill, despite strong opposition from his constituents. When he returned to his district, he was met with boos and catcalls at a public rally where one speaker claimed that the bill would lead to "government control of private property, the Communists' number one goal." Bush responded by reminding the crowd that black servicemen were fighting in Vietnam and argued that "somehow it seems fundamental that a man should not have a door slammed in his face because he is a Negro."[26] Bush's sincerity appealed to the crowd's better nature, and he received a standing ovation at the end.

To be sure, this is the only occasion when Bush is known to have risked his career by standing on principle. He switched to a more conservative position on civil rights to win Nixon's endorsement for his Senate race, and he consented to using the menacing picture of a black murderer in his television advertisements in 1988. He is fundamentally a pragmatist who does whatever is necessary to win, but he does have the strength to stand on his convictions when he chooses to do so. He may lack the ability of a Trotsky or a Reagan to internalize and articulate a crowd's feelings, but that leaves him free to follow his own logic.

The strength of Bush's leadership was most clearly demonstrated in the G lf War. Although it was not apparent to the public at the time, both the Chairman of the Joint Chiefs of Staff, Colin Powell, and the Chief of the Command responsible for the Middle East, Norman Schwarzkopf, were very reluctant to commit the United States to driving the Iraqis out of Kuwait. Schwarzkopf told Bush in March 1991 that it would be eight to twelve months before they could be ready for an offensive campaign. The only intelligence expert who had correctly predicted that the Iraqis would actually invade Kuwait, Walter Lang, insisted that the Iraqi army would fight vigorously and would only be dislodged with a heavy loss of American lives. The polls showed that public support was eroding, and prominent Democratic senators spoke out against escalating the war.[27]

Instead of becoming paralyzed or passing the buck to someone else, as Sheehy's analysis had anticipated, Bush made a firm decision and stuck with it. He went with the Air Force's optimistic projections of the effectiveness of bombing and with the advice of foreign leaders who thought the Iraqis would crumble. Always the team leader, he knew that the military would rally around his plan once he gave them their orders and the resources to do the job. And he let them glory in the success of his policies, never holding a grudge against officers who had expressed reservations.

Bush is happy to be the leader of a winning team, he doesn't have to be the prima donna. He was fortunate that his estimation of the Iraqi response turned out to be correct, but, even if his strategy had turned out to be the disaster many predicted, he would have put to rest any concern that he was indecisive.

Like Gorbachev, Bush was able to make the transition from a loyal subordinate to an assertive leader. Unlike Fidel Castro, Saddam Hussein, or other narcissistic leaders, he doesn't have a psychological need to be number one all the time. He wanted desperately to defeat Reagan in the primaries in 1980, but he swallowed his ambitions and stayed quietly in the background for eight years. He was a good number-two man when those were the cards history dealt him, but he was in the game to win.

Bush and Gorbachev have both been accused of lacking a vision of the future, yet it seems likely that the future will include many more leaders like them. Voters in the West might prefer leaders with a bit more sparkle than George Bush, but they seem fundamentally satisfied with pragmatic leadership. Gorbachev's audacious nonviolent revolution from the top shows that pragmatic leadership can accomplish remarkable things even when a social system is in crisis. The Russians may prefer a leader with a more stirring utopian vision, but they would be poorly served by a person without the skepticism to accurately assess unpleasant realities and the pragmatic sense to manage them. The challenge for the next Soviet and American leaders will be to more persuasively articulate the joys of pragmatism.

Chapter Seventeen

Conclusions

If we choose to regard everything we see and do within the frame-work of the new physics, then we can say that, to some extent, reality construction is what we do every instant of our conscious lives. We accomplish this construction by choosing among the many alternatives increasingly offered to our minds. Thus, at the quantum level of reality, when we choose to "see" what we see, reality becomes both paradoxical and sensible at the same time. Our acts of observation are what we experience as the everyday world.
—Fred Alan Wolfe

Some Personal Observations

When I started working on this book, I was troubled by my own ideological disillusionment and the suicide of my friend Albert Szymanski. I was curious to learn how others had dealt with similar experiences. Writing a book was an opportunity for personal catharsis and growth, and the book developed and changed shape as my interests expanded. It is naturally easier to understand people whose life course parallels one's own. As a turncoat myself, I found it easier to understand Jerry Rubin's need for growth and change than Abbie Hoffman's stubborn devotion to the causes of the sixties. I could sympathize with socialists who denied or apologized for the barbarism of Stalin's Russia, Mao's China, or Fidel's Cuba, because I had shared some of their illusions. But I was mystified at how anyone could deny that the Nazi Holocaust had taken place.

As a perennial supporter of lost causes, I found myself more fascinated with the losers than with the winners in ideological contests. My wife, patiently reading draft after draft of my chapters, suggested that I write more about people who were successful in using their ideological scripts. So I read about people who made a real impact on the world and tried to figure out what made them successful. I began to see ideological development as a growth process, not just for individual people, but for organizations and even for societies as a whole.

Social scientists have always known that their research is shaped by their personal feelings and concerns, but they viewed this as a weakness to be overcome. Today a few of us are beginning to see personal emotional involvement as a positive feature of our work.[1] In a sense this is analogous to the quantum revolution when physicists had to accept the fact that the process of observation inevitably shapes that which is observed. I would not want to push this analogy too far; social scientists write for people like themselves, and their influence on their readers is quite different from that of a physicist manipulating subatomic wave-particles. But I make no apologies for bringing a personal dimension to my work.

In the preceeding chapters I have been as objective as possible in summarizing factual material. There are copious endnotes for the benefit of anyone who wants to check my arguments against the source material. But it is obvious that another writer might have read the same biographies and autobiographies and interpreted them differently. What I have written is the result of the interaction between my own feelings, concerns, and perspectives and the lives of the subjects.

In these conclusions, I do not pretend to offer a definitive analysis of the people whose lives I have examined. Their lives are, of course, richer and more complex than my analyses. Instead, I have simply shared some of the most important things that I feel have learned from them.

One point that surprised me is the ubiquitousness and seductiveness of utopian thinking. This is most dangerous when it is buried in purportedly scientific and rational doctrines such as Marxism or Objectivism. It is also hidden in scientific reports such as archeological accounts of the ancient Maya, Margaret Mead's fieldwork in Samoa, and the works of contemporary feminist anthropologists. In all these cases, one has to do a bit of careful analysis to detect the utopian elements, which are nevertheless at the core of the doctrine's emotional appeal. The fictional utopias of Bellamy and Donnelly are a refreshing contrast in their open and explicit statement of their utopianism.

Much utopian thinking relies on people's unconscious eagerness to assume that if things are bad in the world as it exists now, then there must be a much better alternative just around the corner. Perhaps people need this illusion to keep them going or to ward off depression, but it can lead them to accept pernicious doctrines, which offer false hopes at best, murderous catastrophes at worst. The key to avoiding this trap is to focus on the short-term steps one is asked to take in the interest of a distant utopia.

Utopias ask their followers to commit their lives to ends that are distant and uncertain. Avoiding ideological commitment of any kind is one way to avoid the utopian trap, but at the cost of giving up the hope of being more than a passive observer blown to and fro by the winds of history.

One puzzle that I believe this research has helped me to answer is why left-wing protestors often end up behaving so much like right-wing authoritarians, despite the diametrically opposite nature of their goals. Political psychologists have long been puzzled by the phenomenon of "left-wing authoritarianism," which seems to be a contradiction in terms.[2] Leftist protestors are usually compassionate people who empathize deeply with the suffering of others, while authoritarians, such as the Nazis and their apologists, have only hatred and disdain for society's victims. Despite this difference in their *feelings,* protestors and authoritarians have a great deal in common in the way they *think* about the political world. In both ideological scripts, the world is polarized between good and evil forces. Both are so sure of the correctness of their views that they are tempted to suppress people who get in their way. Both are prone to deny information that goes against their preconceptions. This similarity in ideological scripts has led protestors to repeat many of the worst sins of the authoritarians.

Most generally, I have been struck again and again by the tremendous power of emotional forces in the public lives of even the most brilliant thinkers and leaders. Few human beings can rival Bertrand Russell for intellectual power and commitment to rational thought, yet his personal and political life was driven by emotional forces, which he was unable to understand or control. If great thinkers and leaders such as Russell, Wilson, Comte, Mill, Marx, Trotsky, Gandhi, Boulding, and Pauling were unable to master the emotional factors that drove them, what can we expect from the Ayn Rands and Ignatius Donnellys of the world, to say nothing of the Hitlers, Stalins, Castros, and Saddam Husseins? If people can deny the Nazi Holocaust, follow Jim Jones in mass suicide, or persuade themselves that the road to revolution in America is to attack heterosexual marriage or preach the virtues of selfishness, who can doubt the power of emotion to overcome rational thought?

Of course, people can free themselves of at least some of their ideological illusions, as we have seen in the cases of turncoats such as Russell, Eastman, Koestler, Einstein, Rubin, Collier, and Horowitz. One of my hopes for this book is that it will help some readers to complete the process of mourning for ideological scripts that no longer suit them. I don't expect to reach people who are still at the stage of angry denial, but readers who have struggled to redefine unsatisfactory beliefs, or who may be depressed about the failure of the world to live up to their hopes, may take some comfort in knowing that others have gone through the same travail and that it can be viewed as part of a growth process. Knowing this may help them to mature into skeptical and pragmatic views instead of simply exchanging one utopian illusion or oversimplified protest script for another.

This kind of ideological growth can be a real benefit to the individual, but for society as a whole it seems to me that the best hope is in the social dynamics that enable groups and even entire societies to advance to the point where skepticism and pragmatism are able to prevail over the more primitive forms of ideological thinking. Leaders such as Bush and Gorbachev are far from the most brilliant thinkers covered in this book, nor are they particularly introspective or sensitive to psychological matters. Yet, they were able to come to power because their parties and societies had developed to the point where lackluster, pragmatic leadership was the order of the day.

The Future of Ideology

Predicting the future is a risky business. At the beginning of the twentieth century, most people thought that Marxism had passed its prime. Only a handful of true believers expected its adherents to take power in major societies. In the early 1960s, a group of writers on the "End of Ideology" argued that ideological conflicts were largely a thing of the past.[3] They thought that everyone who mattered agreed that the fundamental institutions of the advanced capitalist societies were sound. In the language of script theory, they expected pragmatism and skepticism to be the wave of the future. Their pronouncement of the End of Ideology, however, was immediately negated by the explosion of ideological movements now remembered as "the sixties."

As we approach the end of the century, history seems to be repeating itself. Marxism is once again in eclipse. It appears that the End of Ideology theorists were premature visionaries instead of false prophets. Scientific skepticism is firmly entrenched in the school systems and responsible mass media, despite rearguard actions by fundamentalists, creationists, and the like. The Cold War is over, and the struggle between hawks and doves seems increasingly irrelevant. Multi-party democracy and free-market economics are the wave of the future in eastern as well as western Europe, and advocates of other systems are fighting defensive rearguard actions.

A large degree of consensus has emerged on many social issues, with a few noteworthy exceptions such as abortion, capital punishment, and gun control. These remaining issues provide an outlet for those who choose to commit their lives to a struggle for good against evil, but most people would much prefer to find some kind of pragmatic compromise to make the issues go away.

Sociologically, it is hard to identify major contradictions that will provide the impetus for massive social changes in the developed countries. In the past, revolutions have usually come in the aftermath of major wars, and the risk of war between the major world powers seems remote. Many people have found plausibility in Francis Fukuyama's argument that History, in the Hegelian sense of epoch-making conflict between important ideas, is over.[4] If this is true, then utopian, authoritarian, and protest movements may seem increasingly archaic and unnecessary.

From the perspective of mass psychology, however, there is reason to suspect that this new End of History may be as ephemeral as the End of Ideology was. Ideological politics serves important emotional needs for many people who find comfort and meaning in a vision of the world as heroic struggles between evil empires and righteous utopias. The boring, routinized, pragmatic politics of modern societies cannot meet these needs. Socialism is rapidly losing its remaining appeal, even among Western intellectuals. Socialist sociologist Erik Wright observes that today, "many radicals believe that classlessness is a utopian fantasy, unachievable even in principle."[5]

Many protestors are searching for another issue to take socialism's place as a believable utopian vision. In announcing his recognition of the failure of the socialist project, for example, economist Robert Heilbroner expresses a somewhat forlorn hope that environmentalism will replace socialism as the antithesis to capitalism.[6] It is hard, however, to envision "environmentalism" as an alternative means of organizing society. Others place their hopes in feminist or minority revolutions, but it is hard to see these movements succeeding as anything other than pressure groups for equal rights within existing social relations. Without a believable vision of an alternative future, utopian and revolutionary movements cannot get off the ground.[7]

I am well aware of the poor record of social scientists in predicting the future. It may be that some new utopian vision now gestating in the mind of an unfulfilled novelist or frustrated journalist will sweep the world in the decades to come, completely upsetting the trends that we observe at this time. Nevertheless, it seems timorous to end this section without a prediction, so I will venture to forecast that pragmatism and skepticism will continue to reign supreme at least in the developed societies. People with needs for utopianism will find it in New Age cults or in religious fundamentalism. Those with a need for a moralistic crusade will join religious sects or single-issue movements such as the extremist wings of the right-to-life, the environmentalist, or the antiwar movement. Racist and homophobic groups will continue to provide an outlet for externaling some people's rage, but I expect that these groups will remain permanently marginalized, because I think the Western establishment will be able to manage affairs well enough to avoid world wars, catastrophic depressions, or systemic social breakdowns. If they fail to do so, the major threat is likely to come from charismatic leaders who offer themselves as transformational objects with little or no commitment to specific policies or ideological visions, such as Alberto Fujimori in Peru, Fernando Collor de Mello in Brazil, or Ross Perot in the United States.

The future of the third-world and communist, or formerly communist, countries is likely to be much more unstable. Religious fundamentalism and ethnic nationalism are clearly ascendant in many areas. Communist true believers may hold on for as long as a decade or two in a few countries. In the long run, however, there seems to be no viable alternative except the hard transition to Western-style market economies. The relative success of the countries that have taken this route is too impressive to ignore. Managing this transition will require a lot of pragmatism, perhaps tinged with utopian rhetoric and/or authoritarian controls.

If the developed societies have evolved beyond the age of ideology, the challenge will be to find leaders who can temper their pragmatism and skepticism with enough creativity and charisma to generate enthusiasm for necessary changes. The people we have met in this book were wrong about a great many things. Some of them were evil, others were foolish. Others were well intentioned but made mistakes that caused enormous human suffering. But the best of them cared deeply about making the world a better place. The challenge for the future is to sustain this kind of energy and vitality without carrying it to extremes that are destructive or self-defeating.

Notes

Chapter 1.   Confessions of a Turncoat and
Remembrance of a True Believer

1. Richard Reeves, "A Reporter at Large," *New Yorker,* 14 September 1981, 113–14.

2. Abraham Hoffman, "Jewish Student Militancy in the Great Depression: The Roosevelt High School Blowouts of 1931," *Newsletter of the Southern California Jewish Historical Society.* Hoffman states incorrectly that Victor was sent to a disciplinary high school.

3. Aldous Huxley, *Ends and Means* (London: Chatto & Windus, 1937), 118.

4. Burton Clark, *The Distinguished College: Antioch, Reed, and Swarthmore* (New York: Aldine, 1970). "Red diaper babies" means children raised by leftist parents.

5. Ted Goertzel, "Albert Szymanski: A Personal and Political Memoir," *Critical Sociology* 15 (1988): 139–44.

6. Verna Szymanski to author, 10 January 1992.

7. This, and subsequent information on Albert Szymanski's student experiences, is from his FBI file.

8. Fred Pincus and Howard Ehrlich, "The New University Conference: A Study of Former Members," *Critical Sociology* 15 (1988): 145–47.

9. Alfred McClung Lee, "Sociology for Whom?" *American Sociological Review* 41 (1976): 925–36.

10. I am thinking particularly of the work of Nicos Poulantzas as compared to that of Talcott Parsons. This work has been devastatingly critiqued by Axel Van den Berg in *The Immanent Utopia: From Marxism on the State to the State of Marxism* (Princeton: Princeton University Press, 1988). I don't intend to give an analysis here, but just to report my feeling of disillusionment with the best work being produced by leading Marxist sociologists. Some were using abstract formulations such as "contradictory locations in class relations" to obscure the fact that class analysis really didn't explain much about contemporary society. Others were retreating into historical schema that claimed to explain the evolution of capitalism into the world system centuries ago but had little or nothing to say about contemporary society or the future.

11. G. E. M. Anscombe, "War and Murder," in *Nuclear Weapons and Christian Conscience,* ed. Anscombe et al. (London: Merlin Press, 1965).

12. Boris Kagarlitsky, *The Thinking Reed* (New York: Verso, 1988).

13. William Hinton, *The Great Reversal* (New York: Monthly Review, 1990).

Chapter 2. Ideologies as Life Scripts

1. Douglas Collins, *Sartre as Biographer* (Cambridge, Mass.: Harvard University Press, 1980), 5.

2. Kenneth Boulding, *Three Faces of Power* (Newbury Park, Calif.: SAGE, 1990), 24.

3. Silvan Tomkins, "Script Theory," in *The Emergence of Personality,* ed. Joel Aronoff, A. I. Rabin, and Robert Zucker (New York: Springer Publishing Company, 1987). Rae Carlson, "Exemplary Lives: The Uses of Psychobiography for Theory Development," *Journal of Personality* 56 (1988): 105–138. Of course, other theorists such as Irving Goffman and Eric Berne have developed similar perspectives. Tomkins's script theory does not assume that people are *consciously* following scripts, playing games, or managing impressions, nor does it exclude this possibility.

4. When we are born, we experience the world as a flow of unstructured and undefined sensations. We make sense of these experiences by associating them with our feelings. Our memories consist of scenes with people, objects, and the associated feelings. We notice that some scenes are repeated and that some people and objects are associated with good feelings and others with bad feelings. When we encounter a scene that we seem to have seen before, we understand it as a repetition of the previous situation, and we remember how we responded then. We repeat the behaviors that seemed to work and avoid those that did not. We also learn by modeling the behavior of our parents and other role models in similar situations. Our most important memories of scenes and the ways to respond to them can be called our life scripts. For a more systematic treatment *see* Roger Schank and Robert Abelson, *Scripts, Plans, Goals, and Understanding* (Hillside, N.J.: Erlbaum, 1977), 144–49. Schank and Abelson refer to ideological scripts as "life themes" and recognize that they are essential to their theory of mind, but can offer no explanation of them from their cybernetic perspective.

5. The concept of ideological script is developed in Silvan Tomkins, "Left and Right: A Basic Dimension of Ideology and Personality," in *The Study of Lives,* ed. Robert White (New York: Atherton, 1963). In this essay Tomkins uses the phrase "ideo-affective posture," which he later replaced with "ideological script." His concept of "left" and "right" corresponds roughly to what I call protest and authoritarian scripts or what Thomas Sowell, *A Conflict of Visions* (New York: William Morrow, 1987), calls "unconstrained" and "constrained" visions.

6. Tomkins, "Left and Right," 388.

7. Kenneth Boulding, *The Meaning of the Twentieth Century* (New York: Harper & Row, 1964), 159.

8. Ibid., 161–62.

9. Carl Jung, *Psychological Types* (New York: Harcourt, Brace, 1920).

10. Robert Browning, *Men and Women* (1855). Quoted in John Bartlett, *Familiar Quotations* (Boston: Little Brown, 1955), 570b.

11. From the first canto of *Deutschland, ein Wintermächen* in S. F. Kissin, *Farewell to Revolution: Marxist Philosophy in the Modern World* (New York: St. Martin's, 1978), 5. Heine was a follower of Henri Saint-Simon for a part of his life.

12. Tomkins, "Script Theory," uses the term "nuclear script" to refer to the people I call survivors and shows how this script encompasses their personal and vocational life

as well as their politics.

13. Heraclitus. Quoted in Bartlett, *Familiar Quotations,* 12a.

14. Oliver Wendell Holmes, *The Path of Law* (1897). Quoted in Bartlett, *Familiar Quotations,* 709a.

15. Peter Goldmark, quoted in Gail Sheehy, *The Man Who Changed the World: The Lives of Mikhail S. Gorbachev* (New York: Harper Collins, 1990), 173.

16. Shakespeare, *Hamlet,* act I, sc. 3, line 75.

17. Gerald White Johnson, *Baltimore Sun,* September 1940. Quoted in Bartlett, *Familiar Quotations,* 956a.

18. Carl Schurz, Anti-Imperialistic Conference, Chicago, 17 October 1899. He continued, "When right, to be kept right; when wrong, to be put right," in an attempt to refute the usual meaning of the slogan.

19. A slogan used at the end of Fidel Castro's speeches. *Patria o Muerte* means "Fatherland or Death." *Venceremos* is usually translated as "We Shall Overcome," which evokes the nonviolent American civil rights movement, but is perhaps better translated as "We Shall Triumph."

20. Isaiah, 2: 4.

21. Virgil, *Eclogues,* X, line 69.

22. The concept of the "authoritarian personality" was introduced by T. W. Adorno, E. Frenkel-Brunswik, D. J. Levinson, and R. N. Sanford, *The Authoritarian Personality* (New York: Harper & Row, 1950). The concept stimulated a tremendous amount of research, which ended in a state of conceptual confusion. Many researchers concluded that authoritarianism is a worldview or set of political attitudes, not a personality type. This is similar to thinking of it as an ideological script. *See* Howard Gabennesch, "Authoritarianism as World View," *American Journal of Sociology* 77 (1972): 857–75. Most of the psychological measures that attempt to measure authoritarianism actually ask about political opinions, not personality in the usual psychological sense. My own scale (Ted Goertzel, "Authoritarianism of Personality and Political Attitudes," *Journal of Social Psychology,* 127 [1987]: 7–18) is an exception.

23. Daniel Rancour-Laferriere, *The Mind of Stalin* (Ann Arbor, Mich.: Ardis, 1988), 51. The concept of identification with the aggressor was developed by Anna Freud in *The Ego and the Mechanisms of Defense* (New York: International Universities Press, 1946).

24. Bruce Mazlish, *The Revolutionary Ascetic* (New York: Basic Books, 1976). Victor Wolfenstein, *The Revolutionary Personality* (Princeton: Princeton University Press, 1967).

25. Karl Marx, *The Eighteenth Brumaire* (New York: International, 1963), 124.

26. *Progressive,* February 1991: 10.

27. Karen Horney, *Our Inner Conflicts* (New York: Norton, 1945), 116.

28. Quoted by Paul Hockenos, "East Left Meets West Left Amid Democratic Chaos," *In These Times,* 12 December 1990: 11.

29. Hockenos, "East Left Meets West Left," 11.

30. Cited in John Stuart Mill, *Auguste Comte and Positivism* (Ann Arbor: University of Michigan Press, 1961), 6.

31. Friedrich Nietzsche, *Beyond Good and Evil* (Chicago: Gateway, 1955), 19.

32. Peter Rossi, "No Good Applied Social Research Goes Unpunished," *Society* 25 (1): 73–79 (November 1987).

33. Michael Fumento, *The Myth of Heterosexual AIDS* (New York: Basic Books, 1990).

34. Thomas Babington (Lord Macaulay), *On Lord Bacon* (1837). Quoted in Bartlett, *Familiar Quotations,* 492b.

35. A traditional proverb which can be found in John Ray, *English Proverbs,* 1670. Also appears in Bernard Shaw's *Maxims for Revolutionists. See* Bartlett, *Familiar Quotations,* 715a.

36. *See* Erik Erikson, "The Eight Ages of Man," *Childhood and Society* (New York: Norton, 1950), for a general overview of life-cycle stages. In terms of his neo-Freudian terminology we would suggest that utopian-dystopian scripts correspond to the oral sensory stage, the survivor and commitment scripts to the muscular-anal and locomotor-genital stages, the hawk and dove scripts to the latency stage, the protest and authoritarian scripts to the adolescent stage, and the skeptical and pragmatic scripts to the adult stages. Of course, as Erikson points out, the issues of each life-cycle stage persist throughout the life span.

37. Karl Marx, *The German Ideology* (New York: International Publishers, 1947). Raymond Aron, *The Opium of the Intellectuals* (Garden City, N.Y.: Doubleday, 1957). Talcott Parsons, "An Approach to the Sociology of Knowledge," in *Transactions of the Fourth Congress of Sociology* (Milan: International Sociological Association, 1959). Raymond Boudon, *L'idéologie: L'origine des idées reçues* (Paris: Fayard, 1986), reviewed by Jeffrey Herf in *Contemporary Sociology* 18 (March 1989): 291–95.

38. V. I. Lenin, *What Is to Be Done?* (Moscow: Foreign Languages Publishing House, 1957). Louis Althusser, *For Marx* (London: Allen Lane, 1969). Edward Shils, "The Concept and Function of Ideology," *The International Encyclopedia of the Social Sciences,* 7 (1968): 66–76. Clifford Geertz, "Ideology as a Cultural System," in *Ideology and Discontent,* ed. David Apter (New York: Free Press). Karl Mannheim, *Ideology and Utopia* (New York: Harcourt, 1954).

39. Leon Trotsky, *Their Morals and Ours* (1938; reprint, New York: Pathfinder, 1969), 36.

40. John Dewey, "Means and Ends," in *Their Morals and Ours* (1938; reprint, New York: Pathfinder, 1969), 52–53.

41. Bertrand Russell, "Voltaire's Influence on Me," *Studies on Voltaire* 6 (1958): 161.

42. Jerome Tuccille, *It Usually Begins with Ayn Rand* (San Francisco, Cobden Press, 1971).

43. Nathaniel Branden, *Judgment Day* (Boston: Houghton Mifflin, 1989), 18, 19.

44. Arthur Koestler, *Arrow in the Blue: An Autobiography* (New York: Macmillan, 1952), 259.

45. Quoted in Morris Stein, *Stimulating Creativity* (New York: Academic Press, 1974), 21.

46. Mari Matsuda, "Public Response to Racist Speech: Considering the Victim's Story," *Michigan Law Review* 87 (August 1989): 2320–81. *See also* Steven Helle, "A New-Century First Amendment," *In These Times,* 26 June 1991.

47. Kitty Muggeridge and Ruth Adam, *Beatrice Webb: A Life* (New York: Knopf, 1968), 42.

48. Phyllis Schlafly, *The Power of the Positive Woman* (New Rochelle, N.Y.: Arlington House, 1977), 50.

49. William Gamson, "The Political Culture of the Arab-Israeli Conflict," *Conflict Management and Peace Science* 5 (1981): 79–93.

50. Quoted in *New Republic,* 18 February 1991, 39.

51. Sigmund Freud, *The Future of an Illusion* (New York: Norton, 1961), 32.

52. Irving Howe, "Thinking About Socialism," *Dissent* 31 (1985): 509–25.

53. Sidney Hook, *Out of Step* (New York: Harper & Row, 1987), 596.

54. Ibid., 599–600.

55. Hannah Ahrendt, "Ideologie und Terror," *Offener Horizont* (Munich: R. Piper and Co., 1954), 30.

56. James McRandle, *The Track of the Wolf* (Evanston, Ill.: Northwestern University Press, 1965), 125.

57. Ayn Rand, *For the New Intellectual: The Philosophy of Ayn Rand* (New York: Random House, 1961), 152–53.

58. Nathaniel Branden, *The Psychology of Self-Esteem* (New York: Bantam Books, 1971), 235.

59. Branden, *Judgment Day,* 417–18.

60. Heinz Brandt, *The Search for a Third Way* (Garden City, N.Y.: Doubleday, 1970), 58.

61. Max Eastman, *Love and Revolution* (New York: Random House, 1964), 229.

62. Arthur Koestler in *The God That Failed,* ed. Richard Crossman (New York: Macmillan, 1949), 59–60.

63. Michael Gold, *Daily Worker* 16 February 1934, quoted in Daniel Aaron, *Writers on the Left* (New York: Octagon Books, 1974), 319.

64. Sonia Johnson, *From Housewife to Heretic* (Garden City, N.Y.: Doubleday, 1981), 198.

65. Suzanne Steinmetz, "The Battered Husband Syndrome," *Victimology* 2 (1978): 505. A critique and Steinmetz's reply appear in *Victimology* 2 (1978): 680–85.

66. Murray Straus, "The National Family Violence Surveys," in *Physical Violence in American Families,* ed. Murray Straus and Richard Gelles (New Brunswick, N.J.: Transaction, 1990), 11.

67. Jeffrey Masson, *Final Analysis: The Making and Unmaking of a Psychologist* (Reading, Mass.: Addison-Wesley, 1990), 153.

68. Dinesh D'Souza, *Illiberal Education: The Politics of Race and Sex on Campus* (New York: Free Press, 1991). *Also see* Jerry Adler, et al., "Taking Offense: Is This the New Enlightenment on Campus or the New McCarthyism?," *Newsweek,* 24 December 1990, 48–53; John Taylor, "Are You Politically Correct?," *New York,* 21 January 1991, 32–41; Eugene Genovese, "Heresy, Yes—Sensitivity, No: An Argument for Counterterrorism in the Academy," *New Republic,* 15 April 1991, 30–35; Vann Woodward, "Freedom and the Universities," *New York Review of Books,* 18 July 1991, 32–37; 18 February 1991 issue of *New Republic.*

69. D'Souza, *Illiberal Education.* David Bryden, "It Ain't What they Teach, It's the Way that they Teach It," *Public Interest* 103 (Spring 1991): 38–53.

70. D'Souza, *Illiberal Education,* 196.

71. Ibid., 195.

72. Genovese, "Heresy, Yes—Sensitivity, No" (see n. 67), 30.

73. D'Souza, *Illiberal Education,* 217.

74. Ibid., 202.

75. Ibid., 203.

76. Ibid.

77. Ibid., 142.

78. Ibid., 147.

79. Ibid., 239.

80. Ibid., 220.

81. Ibid., 150.

82. Wini Breines and Linda Gordon, "Review Essay: The New Scholarship on Family Violence," *Signs* 8 (1983): 492–93.

83. Straus, "National Family Violence Surveys," 12–13.

84. George Smith, *Atheism, Ayn Rand, and Other Heresies* (Buffalo, N.Y.: Prometheus Books, 1990), 35–50.

85. Lynda Davies, "The Institution as an 'Ideological System'; How Morals Maketh Organization," *Systems Practice* 2 (1989): 300.

86. Comments by Morton G. Wenger on a draft submitted to the journal *Humanity and Society,* August 1990.

Chapter 3. Survival and Commitment: Bertrand Russell and Woodrow Wilson

1. Bertrand Russell, *The Autobiography of Bertrand Russell: 1872–1914* (Boston: Little Brown, 1967), 3.

2. Ibid.

3. Bertrand Russell, *Human Society in Ethics and Politics* (London: Allen & Unwin, 1954), 25.

4. Ibid 220–21.

5. Bertrand Russell, "Democracy and Revolution," *Liberator* 3 (May 10–13, 1920): 11–13.

6. Russell, *Autobiography,* vol. II, 141–42.

7. Max Eastman, *Great Companions* (New York: Farrar, Straus, and Cudahy, 1959), 200.

8. Bertrand Russell, *The Practice and Theory of Bolshevism* (New York: Simon and Schuster, 1964), 70.

9. Paul Hollander, *Political Pilgrims* (New York: Oxford University Press, 1981).

10. Max Eastman, *Love and Revolution* (New York: Random House, 1964), 203.

11. Russell, *Autobiography,* vol. II, 158.

12. Ibid., 36.

13. Ronald Clark, *The Life of Bertrand Russell* (New York: Knopf, 1976). Paul Johnson, *Intellectuals* (New York: Harper & Row, 1988).

14. Johnson, *Intellectuals* (see n. 13), 208.

15. *Listener,* 29 May 1959, cited in ibid., 207.

16. Bertrand Russell, "Appeal to the American Conscience," Bertrand Russell Peace Foundation, London, n.d.

17. Sidney Hook, *Philosophy and Public Policy* (Carbondale: Southern Illinois University Press, 1980), 208.

18. Clark, *The Life of Bertrand Russell.*

19. Hook, *Philosophy and Public Policy.* Norman Thomas, "Open Letter to Bertrand Russell, *New Leader,* 7 January 1957.

20. Bertrand Russell, *Marriage and Morals* (London: Allen & Unwin, 1930), 72, 83.

21. Russell, *Autobiography,* vol. II, 156.

22. Andrew Brink, "Bertrand Russell's Conversion of 1901 or the Benefits of a Creative Illness," *Russell: The Journal of the Bertrand Russell Archives* 4 (1984): 83–99. This article is incorporated in Andrew Brink, *Bertrand Russell: The Psychobiography of a Moralist* (Atlantic Highlands, N.J.: Humanities Press International, 1989), which provides a comprehensive psychobiographical analysis of Russell.

23. Russell, *Autobiography,* vol. I, 230.

24. Harry Guntrip, "Sigmund Freud and Bertrand Russell," *Contemporary Psychoanalysis* 9 (1973): 276.

25. Russell, *Autobiography,* vol. I, 146.

26. Edmund Wilson, *The Shores of Light* (New York: Farrar, Straus and Young, 1952), 322.

27. Arthur Link, *Wilson: The Road to the White House* (Princeton: Princeton University Press, 1947), 90–91.

28. Wilson quoted in ibid., 54.

29. Ibid., 84.

30. Ibid., 76.

31. For example, compare "A Credo" of 6 August 1907 (*Papers of Woodrow Wilson,* vol. 17, 335–38) with "A Speech Accepting the Democratic Gubernatorial Nomination" of 15 September 1910 (*Papers of Woodrow Wilson,* vol. 21, 91–94).

32. Link, *Wilson,* 307.

33. Sigmund Freud and William Bullitt, *Thomas Woodrow Wilson: A Psychological Study* (Boston: Houghton Mifflin, 1966), 163.

34. Ibid., 113.

35. Ibid., 243.

36. David Lloyd George, *Memoirs of the Peace Conference,* vol. I (New Haven: Yale University Press, 1939), 140–42.

37. For an overview *see* Thomas Bailey, *Woodrow Wilson and the Lost Peace* (Chicago: Quadrangle, 1944).

38. Freud and Bullitt, *Thomas Woodrow Wilson.*

39. Arthur Link, "The Case for Woodrow Wilson," *Harper's Magazine,* April 1967, 93.

40. Henry Cabot Lodge, *The Senate and the League of Nations* (New York: Scribner's, 1925), 226.

41. Freud and Bullitt, *Thomas Woodrow Wilson.* Freud and Bullitt delayed publication of their book until Wilson and his wife were deceased.

42. Erik Erikson, *Life History and the Historical Moment* (New York: W. W. Norton, 1975), 81–97. Silas Warner, "Fourteen Wilsonian Points for Freud and Bullitt," *Journal of the American Academy of Psychoanalysis,* 16 (1988): 479–89.

43. Freud and Bullitt, *Thomas Woodrow Wilson,* x.

44. Ibid., 36.

45. Cushing Stout, "Review Essay," *History and Theory* 13 (1974): 322.

46. Edwin Weinstein, James Anderson, and Arthur Link, "Woodrow Wilson's Political Personality: A Reappraisal," *Political Science Quarterly* 93 (1978): 585–98.

47. Alexander L. George and Juliette L. George, *Woodrow Wilson and Colonel House: A Personality Study* (New York: Dover, 1964).

48. Freud and Bullitt, *Thomas Woodrow Wilson,* 29.

49. "Leaders of Men," *Papers of Woodrow Wilson,* vol. 21, 134–35.

50. *See* photographs in Joseph Bongiorno, "Woodrow Wilson Revisited: The Prepolitical Years," in *The Leader: Psychohistorical Essays,* ed. C. Strozer, D. Offer, and P. Gay (New York: Plenum, 1985).

51. Ibid., 151.

52. "A Crime of Trusts Is Individual," *Papers of Woodrow Wilson,* vol. I, 660.

53. Bongiorno, "Woodrow Wilson Revisited," 145.

54. Alexander George, "Power as a Compensatory Value for Political Leaders," *Journal of Social Issues* 24 (1968): 30.

55. Edwin Weinstein, *Woodrow Wilson: A Medical and Psychological Biography* (Princeton: Princeton University Press), 1981.

56. M. F. Marmour, "Wilson, Strokes, and Zebras," *New England Journal of Medicine* 62, (3): 9–20 (16 August 1982). Jerrold Post, "Woodrow Wilson Re-examined: The Mind-Body Controversy Redux and Other Disputations," *Political Psychology* 4 (1983): 289–306. For an extensive bibliography *see* Arthur Link, ed., *The Papers of Woodrow Wilson*, vol. 54 (Princeton: Princeton University Press, 1986), ix–x. The editors of the *Papers* no longer take a position on the issue.

57. P. G. Aaron, Scott Phillips, and Steen Larsen, "Specific Reading Disability in Historically Famous Persons," *Journal of Learning Disabilities* 21 (1988): 523–38.

58. Bongiorno, "Woodrow Wilson Revisited," 137.

59. Victor Wolfenstein, *The Revolutionary Personality: Lenin, Trotsky and Gandhi.* (Princeton: Princeton University Press, 1967). Bruce Mazlish, *The Revolutionary Ascetic* (New York: Basic, 1976).

60. Quoted in George and George, *Woodrow Wilson and Colonial House*, 291.

61. Bertrand Russell and Patricia Russell, *The Amberly Papers* (London: Hogarth Press, 1937).

62. Weinstein, *Woodrow Wilson.*

Chapter 4. The Dynamics of Skepticism: Auguste Comte and John Stuart Mill

1. Thomas Whittaker, *Reason: A Philosophical Essay with Historical Illustrations* (Cambridge: University Press, 1934). John Stuart Mill, *Auguste Comte and Positivism* (Ann Arbor: University of Michigan Press, 1961).

2. *See* Arline Standley, *Auguste Comte* (Boston, Twayne, 1981), for a biography and comprehensive bibliography. George Dumas, *Psychologie de Deux Messies Positivistes* (Paris: Alcan, 1905), is most useful from a pschological point of view. Henri Gouhier, *La Vie d'Auguste Comte* (Paris: Gallimard, 1931) is also helpful particularly for his childhood.

3. Henri Gouhier, *La Jeunesse d'Auguste Comte*, vol. I (Paris: Vrin, 1933), 32.

4. Ibid., 38.

5. Auguste Comte, *Course de Philosophie Positive* (Paris: Schleicher, 1908), viii.

6. *See* Dumas, *Psychologie de Deux Messies Positivistes* (see n. 2), for a psychiatric account.

7. Ibid., 139, quoting from Esquirol's *Mémoire sur la Manie*, published in 1818.

8. Gouhier, *La Jeunesse d'Auguste Comte*, 40.

9. Dumas, *Psychologie de Deux Messies Positivistes*, 313.

10. Comte, *Course de Philosophie Positive*, vi.

11. Dumas, *Psychologie de Deux Messies Positivistes*, p. 158. (Mes misérables ennemis, outre l'espoir de me réduire à l'indigence, ont aussi, je le sais, confusément tendu toujours à déterminer, par le concours de leurs attaques avec mes propres travaux, quelque terrible et irréparable retour du fatal épisode de 1826, raconté dans ma préface; mais leur abominable espoir sera, je ose l'affirmer, toujour complètement illusoire, grâce à la constant discipline que j'exercice sur mes émotions et sur ma conduite.)

12. *See* W. M. Simon, *European Positivism in the Nineteenth Century* (Ithaca, N.Y.: Cornell University Press, 1963), 90–93 for a summary of historical appraisals.

13. Isaiah Berlin, *Historical Inevitability* (London: Oxford University Press, 1954), 3–4.

14. James Martineau and Louis Dimier, quoted in Simon, *European Positivism in the Nineteenth Century,* 91.

15. Simon, *European Positivism in the Nineteenth Century,* 265.

16. Ibid., 267.

17. Russell Middleton, "A Reappraisal of Comte's Position in the Development of Sociology," *Sociology and Social Research* 44 (1960): 178–84.

18. Pierre van den Berghe, "Why Most Sociologists Don't (and Won't) Think Evolutionarily," *Sociological Forum* 5 (1990): 179.

19. Ibid., 183–84.

20. Shulamit Reinharz, *Becoming a Social Scientist: From Survey Research and Participant Observation to Experiential Analysis* (San Francisco: Jossey-Bass, 1979).

21. Barbara Laslett, "Unfeeling Knowledge: Emotion and Objectivity in the History of Sociology," *Sociological Forum* 5 (1990): 413–34.

22. John Stuart Mill, *Autobiography* (New York: Liberal Arts Press, 1957), 3–4.

23. Mill, *The Early Draft of John Stuart Mill's Autobiography,* ed. Jack Stillinger (Urbana: University of Illinois Press, 1961), 181–84.

24. George Sabine, *A History of Political Theory* (New York: Holt, Rinehart and Winston, 1961), 708, 696.

25. Ibid., 699.

26. Victor Wolfenstein, *The Revolutionary Personality* (Princeton: Princeton University Press, 1971).

27. Bruce Mazlish, *The Revolutionary Ascetic* (New York: Basic Books, 1976).

28. Mill, *Autobiography,* 147.

29. Michael Packe, *The Life of John Stuart Mill* (London: Seckar & Warburg, 1970), 286.

30. Bruce Mazlish, *James and John Stuart Mill* (New York: Basic, 1975), 330.

31. Peter Glassman, *J. S. Mill: The Evolution of a Genius* (Gainesville: University of Florida Press, 1985), 22.

32. Howard Wolf, "British Fathers and Sons, 1773–1913: From Filial Submissiveness to Creativity," *Psychoanalytic Review* 52 (1965): 53–70.

33. Mill, *Autobiography,* 44.

34. Ibid., 71, 73.

35. Ibid., 74.

36. Ibid., 86.

37. Ibid., 91.

38. A. W. Levi, "The 'Mental Crisis' of John Stuart Mill," *Psychoanalytic Review* 32 (1945): 98.

39. Mill, *Early Draft,* 184–85.

40. Mill, *Autobiography,* 144.

41. *See* Whittaker, "Comte and Mill," 42–43 for a philosophical analysis of this logic.

42. Mill, *Auguste Comte and Positivism,* 60–63. Standley, *Auguste Comte,* 90–91.

43. Mill, op cit., p. 62.

44. Standley, *Auguste Comte,* 91.

45. John Stuart Mill, *Principles of Political Economy* (London: Longmans, Green, 1909), 208.

46. Iris Mueller, *John Stuart Mill and French Thought* (Urbana: University of Illinois Press, 1956), 113.

47. Mill, *The Subjection of Women,* in *John Stuart Mill: A Selection of His Works,* ed. by John Robson (New York: Odyssey, 1966), 369.

48. Mary Baker Eddy, *Science and Health* (Boston: First Church of Christ, Scientist, 1971), 232–33.

49. Comte, *Synthèse Subjective*, quoted in Mill, *Auguste Comte and Positivism*, 192.

50. Mueller, *John Stuart Mill and French Thought*, 131.

Chapter 5. The Ideological Group

1. Leon Trotsky, *My Life* (New York: Pathfinder Press, 1970), 295.

2. Herbert Blumer, "Collective Behavior," in *Principles of Sociology*, ed. Alfred McClung Lee (New York: Barnes & Noble, 1959). Ralph Turner and Lewis Killian, *Collective Behavior* (Englewood Cliffs, N.J.: Prentice-Hall, 1987).

3. Charles Ashbach and Victor Schermer, *Object Relations, the Self, and the Group* (London: Routledge & Kegan Paul, 1987). Larry Hirschhorn, *The Workplace Within* (Cambridge, Mass.: MIT Press, 1988).

4. Warren Bennis and Herbert Shepard, "A Theory of Group Development," *Human Relations* 9 (1956): 415–37.

5. Hirschhorn, *The Workplace Within* (see n. 3). Wilfred Bion, *Experiences in Groups* (New York: Basic Books, 1959).

6. Karen Horney, *Neuroses and Human Growth* (New York: Norton, 1950), 18–22.

7. Ibid.

8. Bion, *Experiences in Groups* (see n. 5).

9. Crane Brinton, *The Anatomy of Revolution* (New York: Vintage, 1963).

10. Anthony Payne, Paul Sutton, and Tony Thorndike, *Grenada: Revolution and Invasion* (New York: St. Martin's Press, 1984). Latin American Bureau, *Grenada: Whose Freedom* (London: Latin American Bureau, 1984). Michael Ledeen and Herbert Romerstein, eds., "Grenada Documents: An Overview and Selection," U.S. Department of State and Department of Defense, September 1984.

11. Latin American Bureau, *Grenada: Whose Freedom*, 20.

12. Ibid., 29.

13. Ibid., 119, quoting speech given by Castro in Havana on 14 November 1983.

14. Ledeen and Romerstein, "Grenada Documents" (see n. 10), 1–6.

15. Ibid., 26.

16. Ibid., excerpts reprinted in Latin American Bureau, *Grenada: Whose Freedom*.

17. *Extraordinary Meeting of the Central Committee NJM, 14–16, 17 September 1983* in Ledeen and Romerstein, "Grenada Documents," 4. Subsequent quotes from this document.

18. Ibid., 15, remarks of Comrade Liam Jones.

19. Ibid.

20. Ibid.

21. Bion, *Experiences in Groups*.

22. *Extraordinary Meeting of the Central Committee NJM*.

23. Quoted in Latin American Bureau, *Grenada: Whose Freedom*, 69.

24. Ibid., 70.

25. Ibid., 72.

26. Payne, Sutton, and Thorndike, *Grenada: Revolution and Invasion*, 136.

27. Latin American Bureau, *Grenada: Whose Freedom*, 57.

28. Payne, Sutton, and Thorndike, *Grenada: Revolution and Invasion*, 178.

29. Ibid., 143.

30. Ibid.

31. A. W. Singham, *The Hero and the Crowd in a Colonial Polity* (New Haven: Yale University Press, 1968).

32. Sigmund Freud, *Group Psychology and the Analysis of the Ego* (London: Hogarth, 1922), 90.

33. Joan Haslip, *The Sultan* (New York: Holt, Rinehart and Winston, 1958), 156, 289.

34. Vamik Volkan and Norman Itzkowitz, *The Immortal Atatürk: A Psychobiography* (Chicago: University of Chicago Press, 1984); Vamik Volkan, "Narcissistic Personality Organization and 'Reparative' Leadership," *International Journal of Group Psychotherapy* 30 (1980): 131–252.

35. Victor Wolfenstein, *The Revolutionary Personality: Lenin, Trotsky, Gandhi* (Princeton, N.J.: Princeton University Press, 1967).

36. Ibid., 167–68.

37. M. K. Gandhi, *Autobiography* (Boston: Beacon Press, 1957), 30–31, quoted in ibid., 86.

38. Ernst Fischer, *An Opposing Man* (New York: Liveright, 1974), 38.

39. Ibid., 38.

40. Bruce Mazlish, *The Revolutionary Ascetic: Evolution of a Political Type* (New York: Basic, 1976).

41. Ibid., 23.

42. Philip Pomper, *Lenin, Trotsky and Stalin: The Intelligentsia and Power* (New York: Columbia University Press, 1989).

43. Richard Grenier, "Jane Fonda & Other Political Thinkers," *Commentary* 67 (June 1979): 67–70.

44. Marshall Kilduff and Ron Javers, *The Suicide Cult* (New York: Bantam Books, 1978).

45. Ibid., 11.

46. Phil Kerns with Doug Wead, *People's Temple, People's Tomb* (Plainfield, N.J.: Logos, 1979).

47. Ibid., 268.

48. Kilduff and Javers, *The Suicide Cult*, 102.

49. Gairdner B. Moment, "From Utopia to Dystopia: The Jonestown Tragedy," in *Utopias: The American Experience*, ed. G. B. Moment and O. F. Kraushaar (Metuchen, N.J.: Scarecrow, 1980).

50. Ibid., 216.

51. Kerns, *People's Temple, People's Tomb*, 193.

52. Ibid.

53. Ibid., 194.

54. Marianne Horney Eckhardt, "Organizational Schisms in American Psychoanalysis," in *American Psychoanalysis: Origins and Development*, ed. Jacques Quen and Eric Carlson (New York: Brunner/Mazel, 1978), 141.

55. Ibid., 145. For more details on these splits *see* Susan Quinn, *A Mind of Her Own: The Life of Karen Horney* (New York: Summit, 1987).

56. Eckhardt, "Organizational Schisms in American Psychoanalysis," 159.

57. Christopher Manes, *Green Rage* (Boston: Little, Brown, 1990), 131.

58. John Judis, "The War at Home," *In These Times*, 14 March 1990, 12–13.

59. This is usually by men, but women are not immune. *See*, for example, the account of abuses by Karen Horney in Quinn, *A Mind of Her Own* (see n. 50), 377–78.

60. Todd Gitlin, *The Sixties: Years of Hope, Days of Rage* (New York: Bantam Books,

1987), 108, 371.

61. Sigmund Freud, *Group Psychology and the Analysis of the Ego.*

62. Bennis and Shepard, "A Theory of Group Development," 424.

63. Vladimir Lenin, *"Left-wing" Communism: An Infantile Disorder,* New York: International Publishers, 1940. James West, "Lenin on Petty-Bourgeois Radicalism," *Political Affairs* 49 (May 1970): 22.

64. *See* John Horton, "Left Wing Communism: A Reply to Lenin," in *The Unknown Dimension,* ed. Dick Howard (New York: Basic Books, 1972), for an analysis of the historical origins of Lenin's concept of petit bourgeois politics.

65. Dorothy Healey to Democratic Socialists of America group in Philadelphia, 4 November 1990.

66. Dorothy Healey and Maurice Isserman, *Dorothy Healey Remembers* (New York: Oxford University Press, 1990), 247–48.

Chapter 6. The Utopians

1. For religious millenarians *see* Norman Cohn, *The Pursuit of Millennium* (New York: Oxford University Press, 1970). For a history of political millenarianism *see* James H. Billington, *Fire in the Minds of Men: Origins of the Revolutionary Faith* (New York: Basic Books, 1980).

2. C. J. Jung, *Archetypes of the Collective Unconscious* (Princeton: Princeton University Press, 1959). Anthony Stevens, *Archetypes* (New York: Quill, 1983).

3. Stevens, *Archetypes* (see n. 2), 139.

4. D. W. Winnicott, *The Maturational Process and the Facilitating Environment* (London: The Hogarth Press, 1965).

5. Lloyd deMause, *Foundations of Psychohistory* (New York: Creative Roots, 1982), 244–332.

6. Christopher Bollas, "The Transformational Object," in *The British School of Psychoanalysis,* ed. Gregorio Kohon (New Haven: Yale University Press, 1986). Originally published in *International Journal of Psychoanalysis* 54 (1973): 195–201.

7. Ibid., 98.

8. *See* Krishnan Kumar, *Utopia and Anti-Utopia in Modern Times* (Oxford: Basil Blackwell, 1987), for descriptions of these and other utopias.

9. Martin Ridge, *Ignatius Donnelly* (Chicago: University of Chicago Press, 1962), 4.

10. Ibid., 92.

11. Ibid., 195.

12. Quoted in Phyllis Young Forsyth, *Atlantis: The Making of a Myth* (Montreal: McGill-Queen's University Press, 1980), 28.

13. Kenneth Feder, *Frauds, Myths and Mysteries: Science and Pseudoscience in Archeology* (Mountain View, Calif.: Mayfield, 1990), 113.

14. L. S. de Camp, *Lost Continents: The Atlantis Theme in History, Science and Literature* (New York: Brazilier, 1970).

15. Forsyth, *Atlantis,* and Feder, *Frauds, Myths and Mysteries.*

16. Marvin Harris, *The Rise of Anthropological Theory* (New York: Thomas Crowell, 1968).

17. R. Jackson Wilson, "Experience and Utopia: The Making of Edward Bellamy's *Looking Backward,*" *Journal of American Studies* 11(1): 45–60 (April 1977).

18. Arthur E. Morgan, *Edward Bellamy* (New York: Columbia University Press,

1944), ix.

19. Franklin Rosemont, "Bellamy's Radicalism Reclaimed," in *Looking Backward: 1988-1888: Essays on Edward Bellamy,* ed. Daphne Patai (Amherst, Mass.: University of Massachusetts Press, 1988).

20. *See* the essays and annotated biography in Patai, *Looking Backward: 1988-1888,* and the biographies by Morgan, *Edward Bellamy,* and Sylvia Bowman, *Edward Bellamy* (Boston: Twayne Publishers, 1986).

21. Morgan, *Edward Bellamy,* 50.

22. Ibid., 53.

23. Edward Bellamy, *Selected Writings on Religion and Society,* ed. and with an introduction by Joseph Schiffman (Westport, Conn.: Greenwood Press, 1955). The introduction summarizes the origins of Bellamy's religious ideas.

24. Lee Cullen Khanna, "The Text as Tactic: *Looking Backward* and the Power of the World," in Patai, *Looking Backward: 1988-1888.*

25. H. P. Peebles, "The Utopias of the Past Compared with the Theories of Bellamy," *Overland Monthly,* 2d ser., XV, no. 90 (June 1890), 574.

26. Edward Bellamy, *Looking Backward* (New York: Grosset & Dunlap, 1917), 128.

27. For example, Garcilaso de la Vega, *Historia General del Peru* (1617; reprint Buenos Aires: Amecé Editares, 1944).

28. Rosemont, "Bellamy's Radicalism Reclaimed."

29. Bellamy, *Looking Backward,* 208.

30. Arthur Lipow, *Authoritarian Socialism in America: Edward Bellamy and the Nationalist Movement* (Berkeley: University of California Press, 1982).

31. Khanna, "The Text as Tactic."

32. Bellamy, article in *Nationalist,* December 1889, quoted in Morgan, *Edward Bellamy,* 253.

33. Patai, *Looking Backward: 1988-1888,* 13.

34. Comments by Mr. Abbot Clark, California Theosophist, in Morgan, *Edward Bellamy,* 268.

35. Bowman, *Edward Bellamy* (see n. 20), 121.

36. Sylvia Bowman, *Edward Bellamy Abroad: An American Prophet's Influence* (New York: Twayne, 1962), as well as Rosemont, "Bellamy's Radicalism Reclaimed."

37. Ridge, *Ignatius Donnelly,* 337.

38. Ibid., 401.

39. *See* James Baker, *Ayn Rand* (Boston: Twayne, 1987), for a comprehensive bibliography of works on Rand. *Also see* Barbara Branden, *The Passion of Ayn Rand* (Garden City N.Y.: Doubleday, 1986), and Nathaniel Branden, *Judgment Day: My Years with Ayn Rand* (Boston: Houghton Mifflin, 1989).

40. Baker, *Ayn Rand,* 95.

41. Ibid., 57.

42. Galt's speech and Rand's other key philosophical writings can be found in Ayn Rand, *For the New Intellectual* (New York: Random House, 1981).

43. *See* Jerome Tuccille, *It Usually Begins with Ayn Rand* (San Francisco: Cobden, 1971), for a hilarious satirical account of life in the Objectivist and libertarian movements. Another apostate's account is Sidney Greenberg, *Ayn Rand and Alienation* (San Francisco: Bridgeberg, 1977).

44. Nathaniel Branden, *Judgment Day,* (see n. 39).

45. Ibid., 139. Nora Ephron, "A Strange Kind of Simplicity," *New York Times Book Review,* 5 May 1968, 42–43.

46. Ibid., 18.
47. Nathaniel Branden, *Judgment Day,* 171.
48. Tuccille, *It Usually Begins with Ayn Rand,* 20.
49. Murray Rothbard, *The Sociology of the Ayn Rand Cult* (Port Townsend, Wash.: Liberty Publishing, 1987).
50. Nathaniel Branden, *Judgment Day,* 255.
51. Wallace Matson, "Rand on Concepts," in *The Philosophic Thought of Ayn Pand,* ed. Douglas Den Uyl and Douglas Rasmussen (Urbana, Ill.: University of Illinois Press, 1984), 36.
52. Ayn Rand, *Philosophy: Who Needs It?* (Indianapolis: Bobbs Merrill, 1982), 131.
53. Tuccille, *It Usually Begins with Ayn Rand.*
54. Ibid., 16.
55. Ibid., 32.
56. Ibid., 31. Murray Rothbard, "My Break With Branden and the Ayn Rand Cult," *Liberty* September 1989, 27–32. Rothbard says that Tuccille's book is a "perceptive" but "imaginative reconstruction" of his break with the cult.
57. Murray Rothbard, "Why Paleo?" *Rothbard-Rockwell Report,* May 1990, 4.
58. Barbara Branden, *The Passion of Ayn Rand,* 383.
59. Nathaniel Branden, *Judgment Day,* 405.
60. George Smith, *Atheism, Ayn Rand, and Other Heresies* (Buffalo, N.Y.: Prometheus Books, 1991), 31.
61. Albert Ellis, *Is Objectivism a Religion?* (New York: Lyle Stuart, 1968), 9.
62. Nathaniel Branden, *Judgment Day,* 369–70.
63. Ellis, *Is Objectivism a Religion?,* 175–77.
64. *See* Nathaniel Branden's best-selling *The Psychology of Self-Esteem* (New York: Bantam, 1969).
65. Smith, *Atheism, Ayn Rand, and Other Heresies,* 193–211.
66. Murray Rothbard, *The Essential Ludwig von Mises* (Auburn, Ala.: The Ludwig von Mises Institute of Auburn University, 1980).
67. G. D. H. Cole, *Socialist Thought: The Forerunners* (London: MacMillan, 1955).
68. Kumar, *Utopia and Anti-Utopia,* 92.
69. Karl Marx, *Contribution to the Critique of Political Economy,* (1911; reprint New York: International Publishers, 1970), 11.
70. Karl Marx and Friedrich Engels, *The German Ideology* (New York: International Publishers, 1947), 22.
71. *See* Kumar, *Utopia and Anti-Utopia,* 49–68 for a review of Marxist utopian writings. Lenin's *State and Revolution* simply rephrases the few paragraphs from *The Critique of the Gotha Program.*
72. Friedrich Engels, *Socialism: Utopian and Scientific,* quoted in Kumar, *Utopia and Anti-Utopia,* 56.
73. August Bebel, *Woman Under Socialism* (New York: Socialist Literature Company, 1910). A paperback edition was published by Schocken Books in 1971, and an abridged edition with the title *Society of the Future* was published by Progress Publishers in Moscow in 1971.
74. Ibid., 1910 ed., 470–71.
75. Ibid., 374.
76. Ibid., 371.
77. August Bebel, *My Life* (New York: Howard Fertig, 1973).
78. Ibid., 435.

79. Ibid., 436.

80. V. I. Lenin, *State and Revolution* (New York: International, 1932), 75.

81. Ibid., 366.

82. *See* Jerrold Seigel, *Marx's Fate: The Shape of a Life* (Princeton: Princeton University Press, 1978), for a psychological analysis of Marx's life with comprehensive references.

83. David Felix, *Marx as Politician* (Carbondale, Ill.: Southern Illinois University Press, 1983), 3.

84. Karl Marx, *Writings of the Young Marx on Philosophy and Society* (New York: Anchor, 1967), 49.

85. Ibid., 46, 47.

86. Seigel, *Marx's Fate*, 60.

87. Marx, *Writings of the Young Marx*, 46.

88. Ibid., 64.

89. Ibid., 36.

90. Charles Fourier, *The Utopian Vision of Charles Fourier* (Boston: Beacon Press, 1971), 277. For an overview and bibliography on Fourier, *see* M. C. Spencer, *Charles Fourier* (Boston: Twayne Publishers, 1981).

91. Seigel, *Marx's Fate*, 384.

92. Ibid., 385.

93. Ibid., 289.

94. Ibid., 232.

95. Wilhelm Liebknecht, "Reminiscences of Marx," in *Marx and Engels Through the Eyes of Their Contemporaries* (Moscow: Progress Publishers, 1978), 63.

96. Yvonne Kapp, *Eleanor Marx* (New York: Pantheon, 1976). *Also see* Rae Carlson, "Exemplary Lives," *Journal of Personality* 56 (1988): 104–138.

97. Feder, *Frauds, Myths and Mysteries*, v.

98. F. Harrold and R. Eve, eds., *Cult Archeology and Creationism* (Iowa City: University of Iowa Press, 1987).

99. Lewis Spence, *The History of Atlantis* (New York: Bell, 1968), 2.

100. Helena Blavatsky, *An Abridgement of the Secret Doctrine* (London: Theosophical Publishing House, 1966).

101. Edgar Cayce, *Edgar Cayce on Atlantis* (New York: Hawthorne Books, 1968), 158–59.

102. J. Alcock, "Channeling: Brief History and Contemporary Content," *Skeptical Inquirer* 13 (1989): 380–84.

103. Jose Argüelles, *The Mayan Factor* (Santa Fe, N.M.: Bear, 1987). David O'Reilly, "Taking the Cosmic Pulse," *Philadelphia Inquirer*, 14 August 1987, sec. D, 1.

104. E. H. Thompson, "Archeological Research in the Yucatan," *Proceedings of the American Antiquarian Society*, n. s. 8: 248. Cited in Marshall J. Becker, *Theories of Ancient Maya Social Structure* (Greele, Colo.: University of Northern Colorado, 1979).

105. *See* Becker, *Theories of Ancient Maya Social Structure* (see n. 104), for an analysis of the various editions of this book.

106. *See* Norman Hammond, *Ancient Maya Civilization* (New Brunswick: Rutgers University Press, 1982), for an overview of the evidence.

107. Evan Vogt, "Some Aspects of Zincantan Settlement Patterns," *Estudios de Cultura Maya* 1 (1961): 143.

108. Becker, *Theories of Ancient Maya Social Structure*, 36.

109. Ibid., 40.

110. Ibid., quoting M. D. Coe.

111. Friedrich Engels, *The Origin of the Family, Private Property and the State* (New York: International, 1972).

112. Janet Sayers, Mary Evans, and Nanneke Redclift, *Engels Revisited* (London: Tavistock, 1987).

113. Marija Gimbutas, *The Gods and Goddesses of Old Europe* (Berkeley, Calif.: University of California Press, 1982). Marija Gimbutas, *The Language of the Goddess* (San Francisco: Harper & Row, 1989). Peter Steinfels, "Idyllic Theory of Goddesses Creates Storm," *New York Times*, 13 February 1990, sec. C, 1.

114. Riane Eisler, *The Chalice and the Blade* (New York: Harper & Row, 1988). Elinor Gadon, *The Once and Future Goddess* (New York: Harper & Row, 1989).

115. Bernard Wailes, quoted in Steinfels, "Idyllic Theory of Goddesses Creates Storm" (see n. 113).

116. Steinfels, "Idyllic Theory of Goddesses Creates Storm" (see n. 113).

117. Carol Ochs, *Behind the Sex of God* (Boston: Beacon, 1977).

118. All references from Steinfels, "Idyllic Theory of Goddesses Creates Storm."

119. Derek Freeman, *Margaret Mead and Samoa: The Making and Unmaking of an Anthropological Myth* (Cambridge, Mass.: Harvard University Press, 1983).

120. Margaret Mead, *Coming of Age in Samoa* (1928; reprint, New York: William Morrow, 1961), second page of preface (no pagination).

121. Lowell Holmes, *Quest for the Real Samoa* (South Hadley, Mass.: Bergin & Garvey, 1987).

122. Mead, *Coming of Age in Samoa*, 89.

123. Albert Wendt, "Three Faces of Samoa: Mead's, Freeman's and Wendt's," *Pacific Island Monthly*, April 1983, 14. Quoted in Holmes, *Quest for the Real Samoa*, 139.

124. *See* the quotes in Freeman, *Margaret Mead and Samoa*, chapter 7.

125. Ibid., 98, quoting Bertrand Russell, *Marriage and Morals* (London: Allen & Unwin, 1958), 107.

126. Ron Westrum, David Smith, and Davis Stupple, "Little Green Men and All That," *Society*, January 1984, 37.

127. C. G. Jung, *Flying Saucers: A Modern Myth of Things Seen in the Skies* (London: Routledge and Kegan Paul, 1959), 128–45.

128. David Jacobs, *The UFO Controversy in America* (Bloomington: Indiana University Press, 1975).

129. Allen Hynek, *The UFO Experience: A Scientific Inquiry* (New York: Ballantine, 1972).

130. Westrum, Swift, and Stupple, "Little Green Men and All That."

131. Ralph Turner and Lewis Killian, *Collective Behavior* (Englewood Cliffs, N.J.: Prentice-Hall, 1987).

132. Jung, *Flying Saucers*, 13.

133. Ibid. Jung, *Archetypes of the Collective Unconscious* (Princeton: Princeton University Press, 1959).

134. Jung, *Flying Saucers*, 140.

135. Alvin Lawson, "Perinatal Imagery in UFO Abduction Reports," *Journal of Psychohistory* 12: 211–39.

136. Carl Sagan, *Broca's Brain* (New York: Random House, 1977). C. B. Becker, "The Failure of Saganomics: Why Birth Models Cannot Explain Near-Death Phenomena," *Anabiosis* 2 (1982): 102–109. Susan Blackmore, "Out of the Body?" in *Not Necessarily the New Age*, ed. Robert Basil (Buffalo, N.Y.: Prometheus Books, 1988).

137. Gerald O'Neill, *The High Frontier* (New York: Morrow, 1977).

138. Gerard O'Neill, "The Colonization of Space," *Physics Today,* September 1974, 32–40.

139. Flora Lewis, "Triumph's Challenge," *New York Times,* op-ed, 29 May 1990.

140. Paul Csonka, "Space Colonization: An Invitation to Disaster?" *Futurist,* October 1977, 285–90.

141. Bellamy, *Looking Backward,* 334.

142. V. I. Lenin, "What the 'Friends of the People' Are and How They Fight the Social-Democrats," *Collected Works,* vol. I (Moscow: Progress, 1960), 298.

143. Vladimir Pozner, *Illusions* (New York: Atlantic Monthly Press, 1990), 137.

144. Marx, *Writings of the Young Marx,* 38.

145. Tuccille, *It Usually Begins with Ayn Rand,* 14–15.

146. Kitty Muggeridge and Ruth Adam, *Beatrice Webb: A Life* (New York: Knopf, 1968), 147.

147. Sidney Webb and Beatrice Webb, *Soviet Communism: A New Civilization?* (New York: Scribner's, 1936). The question mark was dropped in later editions.

148. Malcolm Muggeridge, *Winter in Moscow* (London: Eyre & Spottiswoode, 1934).

149. S. J. Taylor, *Stalin's Apologist* (New York: Oxford University Press, 1990), 206.

150. Margaret Cole, *Beatrice Webb* (New York: Harcourt, Brace, 1946), 198.

Chapter 7. The Hawks

1. Television interview, 28 January 1991, broadcast by Cable News Network.

2. Sam Kean, *Faces of the Enemy* (San Francisco: Harper and Row, 1986). An outstanding video with the same title, which was broadcast on public television stations, is available. For a more historical and analytic study of enemy archetypes *see* Anthony Stevens, *Archetypes* (New York: Quill, 1983), chapter 12.

3. F. W. Nietzsche, *Thus Spoke Zarathustra,* First Part, "On the Friend," and "On the Way of the Creator."

4. *Standard Edition of the Psychological Works of Sigmund Freud,* vol. 4 (London: Hogarth, 1966), 483.

5. Vamik Volkan, "The Need to Have Enemies and Allies," *Political Psychology* 6: 219–47, 1985 and *The Need to Have Enemies and Allies* (Northvale, N.J.: Jason Aronson, 1988).

6. This pattern may not be a universal developmental stage as Freudians assert; *see* Daniel Coleman, "New Research Overturns a Milestone of Infancy," *New York Times,* 6 June 1989.

7. Jay Rothman, "Developing Pre-Negotiation Theory and Practice" (Jerusalem: Leonard Davis Institute, 1989). Harold Saunders, "We Need a Larger Theory of Negotiation: The Importance of Pre-negotiation Phases," *Negotiation Journal* 1(3), 1985.

8. *Granma Weekly Review,* 17 June 1984, 1.

9. Herbert Kelman, "The Political Psychology of the Israeli-Palestinian Conflict," *Political Psychology* 8 (1987): 359.

10. Daniel Bar-Tal, "Delegitimizing Relations Between Israeli Jews and Palestinians," in *Arab-Jewish Relations in Israel,* ed. John Hofman (Bristol, Ind.: Wyndam-Hall, 1988).

11. Theodore Roosevelt, *The Strenuous Life* (New York: Century, 1900), 20.

12. Georg Hegel, *Phenomenology of the Mind* (New York: Macmillan, 1949), 474.

13. Elizabeth Stanton, *History of Woman Suffrage,* vol. II (Rochester, N.Y.: Charles Mann, 1882), 351–52.

14. Ted Goertzel, "The Gender-Gap: Sex, Family Income and Political Opinions in the Early 1980s," *Journal of Political and Military Sociology* 11 (1983): 209–222.

15. William Broyles, "Why Men Love War," *Esquire* 102 (November 1984): 55.

16. Ibid., 62.

17. Ted Goertzel, "Public Opinion on Military Spending: 1939–1985," *Journal of Political and Military Sociology* 15 (1987): 61–72.

18. A. J. P. Taylor quoted by Robert Waite, *The Psychopathic God: Adolph Hitler* (New York: Basic Books, 1977), xiv. For Taylor's views and the debate concerning them *see* his *The Origins of the Second World War* (New York: Atheneum, 1966) *The Origins of the Second World War Reconsidered,* ed. Gordon Martel (Boston: Allen & Unwin, 1986).

19. Waite, *The Psychopathic God,* gives a very comprehensive summary and bibliography of psychohistorical analyses of Hitler.

20. *See* Waite, *The Psychopathic God,* and Bradley Smith, *Adolph Hitler: His Family, Childhood & Youth* (Stanford, Calif.: Hoover Institution, 1967).

21. *See* Waite, *The Psychopathic God,* and Gertrud Kurth, "The Jew and Adolph Hitler," *Psychoanalytic Quarterly* 16 (1947): 11–42.

22. Adolf Hitler, *Mein Kampf* (Boston: Houghton Mifflin, 1943), 42–44. Waite, *The Psychopathic God,* 162.

23. Waite, *The Psychopathic God,* 126–31.

24. Hitler, *Mein Kampf,* 9.

25. Waite, *The Psychopathic God,* 186. *Also see* Kurth, "The Jew and Adolph Hitler."

26. Hitler, *Mein Kampf,* 52.

27. Ibid., 190.

28. Ibid., 40.

29. Ibid., 42, 43.

30. Robert Proctor, *Racial Hygiene: Medicine Under the Nazis* (Cambridge: Harvard University Press, 1988).

31. Admiral von Hintze, quoted in Waite, *The Psychopathic God,* 211.

32. Ibid., 212.

33. Hitler, *Mein Kampf,* 62ff.

34. Ibid., 300.

35. Ibid., 63.

36. Ibid., 182.

37. Winston Churchill, *The Gathering Storm* (Boston: Houghton Mifflin, 1948), 55–56.

38. Kurt Hahn, quoted in Martin Gilbert, *The Roots of Appeasement* (London: Weidenfeld and Nicolson, 1966), 146.

39. Desmond Seward, *Napoleon and Hitler: A Comparative Biography* (New York: Viking, 1989), 192.

40. Sarah Churchill, *A Thread in the Tapestry* (London: Deutsch, 1967), 17.

41. Robert James, *Churchill: A Study in Failure, 1900–1939* (New York: World, 1970), 373.

42. Randolph Churchill, *Winston Churchill: Volume I, Youth* (Boston: Houghton Mifflin, 1966), 43.

43. C. M. W. Moran, *Churchill: Taken from the Diaries of Lord Moran* (Boston: Houghton Mifflin, 1966), 830.

44. Anthony Storr, "The Man," *Churchill Revised,* ed. A. J. P. Taylor (New York: Dial, 1968), 250.

45. A. J. P. Taylor, "The Statesman," in *Churchill Revised* (see n. 44).

46. Martin Gilbert, *The Roots of Appeasement* (London: Weidenfeld and Nicolson, 1966), ix.

47. Ibid.

48. Winston Churchill, *Great Contemporaries* (1937; reprint, Chicago: University of Chicago Press, 1973), 265.

49. Lord Moran, *Churchill,* 832–33.

50. Edward Mortimer, "The Thief of Baghdad," *New York Review of Books,* 27 September 1990, 8–14.

51. Efraim Karsh and Inari Rautsi, *Saddam Hussein: A Political Biography* (New York: The Free Press, 1991), 267–68. Other sources include Judith Miller and Laurie Mylroie, *Saddam Hussein and the Crisis in the Gulf* (New York: Random House, 1990). Samir al-Khalil, *Republic of Fear* New York: Pantheon, 1990). Fuad Matar, *Saddam Hussein: The Man, the Cause and the Future* (London: Third World Centre, 1981). Jerrold Post, "Saddam Hussein of Iraq: A Political Psychology Profile," *Political Psychology* 12 (1991): 279–91.

52. Mortimer, "The Thief of Baghdad," 12.

53. Excerpts published in the *Hamburger Rundschau,* 22 February 1991, 1–6. See *Newsweek,* 4 March 1991, 6.

54. Karsh and Rautsi, *Saddam Hussein: A Political Biography,* 268.

55. al-Kahlil, *Republic of Fear* (see n. 50), 169.

56. Ibid., xv; Karsh and Ratusi, *Saddam Hussein: A Political Biography,* 42.

57. Karsh and Rautsi, *Saddam Hussein: A Political Biography,* 125.

58. Post, "Saddam Hussein of Iraq," 285.

59. Karsh and Rautsi, *Saddam Hussein: A Political Biography,* 35.

60. *See* Matar, *Saddam Hussein: The Man, the Cause and the Future,* for an adulatory biography, Miller and Mylroie, *Saddam Hussein and the Crisis in the Gulf,* for a skeptical one (see n. 50).

61. Miller and Mylroie, *Saddam Hussein and the Crisis in the Gulf,* 30.

62. Karsh and Rautsi, *Saddam Hussein: A Political Biography,* 39.

63. *See* al-Khalil, *Republic of Fear,* Appendix I, for details.

64. Matar, *Saddam Hussein: The Man, the Cause and the Future,* 56.

65. al-Khalil, *Republic of Fear,* 272.

66. Karsh and Rautsi, *Saddam Hussein: A Political Biography,* 136.

67. Matar, *Saddam Hussein: The Man, the Cause and the Future,* 14.

68. Karsh and Rautsi, *Saddam Hussein: A Political Biography,* 96.

69. The Iraqi-released partial transcript of this interview is in the *New York Times,* 23 September 1990, sec. 1, 19.

70. Karsh and Rautsi, *Saddam Hussein: A Political Biography,* 216.

71. Waite, *The Psychopathic God,* 397–99.

72. Moran, *Churchill,* 832.

73. Ralph White, "Why Aggressors Lose," *Political Psychology* 11 (1990): 227–42.

Chapter 8. The Doves

1. Quoted in P. Carbanne, *Pablo Picasso: His Life and Times* (New York: Harrow, 1977), 408.

2. Ibid., 409.

3. S. Johnson, *Dictionary of the English Language* (New York: AMS Press, 1964),

no pagination.

4. Stuart Alsop and Charles Bartlett, "In Time of Crisis," *Saturday Evening Post,* 94 (8 December 1962): 16–20. Anthony Howard, "Washington and Whitehall," *Listener* 76 (21 July 1966): 75, 76, 93.

5. Jeffrey Klugman, "Hawks and Doves," *Political Psychology* 6 (1985): 573–89.

6. R. E. Money-Kyrle, *Psychoanalysis and Politics* (Westport, Conn.: Greenwood Press, 1973), 92. For a similar psychoanalytic interpretation *see* Franco Fornari, *The Psychoanalysis of War* (Garden City, N.Y.: Anchor, 1974).

7. Alexander Amerisov, *Soviet American Review* 4 (nos. 11 and 12), November/ December 1989.

8. Klugman, "Hawks and Doves."

9. Mohandas Gandhi, *An Autobiography: The Story of My Experiments with Truth* (Boston: Beacon, 1957). Hyman Muslin and Prakash Desai, "The Transformations in the Self of Mahatma Gandhi," in *The Leader: Psychohistorical Essays,* ed. Charles Strozier and Daniel Offer (New York: Plenum Press, 1985). Victor Wolfenstein, *The Revolutionary Personality* (Princeton: Princeton University Press, 1971). Erik Erikson, *Gandhi's Truth* (New York: Norton, 1969).

10. Gandhi, *An Autobiography,* 30–31.

11. Wolfenstein, *The Revolutionary Personality,* 87.

12. Gandhi, *An Autobiography,* 89.

13. Unto Tähtinen, *Ahisma: Non-Violence in the Indian Tradition* (London: Rider, 1976).

14. Marvin Rintala, "Chronicler of a Generation: Vera Brittain's Testament," *Journal of Political and Military Sociology* 12 (1984): 23–36.

15. Vera Brittain, *Testament of Experience* (New York: Macmillan, 1957), 135–36.

16. Ibid., 163.

17. Ibid., 168.

18. Max Weber, "Politics as a Vocation," in *From Max Weber: Essays in Sociology,* ed. Hans Gerth and C. W. Mills (New York: Oxford University Press, 1958).

19. Ibid., 126–27.

20. Ibid., 170.

21. Ibid., 177.

22. Albert Nathan and Henry Norden, eds., *Einstein on Peace* (New York: Simon and Schuster, 1960), 94.

23. Ibid., 141.

24. Ibid., 235.

25. Ibid., 229.

26. Peter Brock, *Twentieth-Century Pacifist* (New York: Van Nostrand, 1970), 129.

27. Nathan and Norden, *Einstein on Peace,* 229.

28. *See* Elise Boulding, "The Pacifist as Citizen," *Friends Journal,* November 1989, 13–17 for various definitions of the word "pacifist," including Einstein's revised definition.

29. Nathan and Norden, *Einstein on Peace,* 188.

30. Ibid.

31. Jo Ann Ooiman Robinson, *Abraham Went Out: A Biography of A. J. Muste* (Philadelphia: Temple University Press, 1981). Nat Hentoff, *Peace Agitator: The Story of A. J. Muste* (New York: Macmillan, 1963).

32. A. J. Muste, *The Essays of A. J. Muste* (New York: Bobbs-Merrill, 1967), 45–46.

33. Robinson, *Abraham Went Out,* 23.

34. Ibid., 8.

35. Ibid., 18.
36. Ibid., 21.
37. Ibid., 26.
38. Ibid., 45.
39. Muste, *The Essays of A. J. Muste,* 135.
40. Ibid., 209.
41. Robinson, *Abraham Went Out,* 63.
42. A. J. Muste, *Non-Violence in an Aggressive World* (New York: Harper & Grothers, 1940), 45, 139.
43. Milton Mayer, "The Christer," *Fellowship,* January 1952, 1.
44. Guenter Lewy, *Peace and Revolution: The Moral Crisis of American Pacifism,* (Grand Rapids, Mich.: Eerdmans, 1988), 23.
45. A. J. Muste, *The World Task of Pacifism* (Wallingford, Pa.: Pendle Hill Pamphlet, 1941), no. 13, 27. Quoted in Lewy, *Peace and Revolution,* 22.
46. Muste, "Communism and Civil Liberties," *Fellowship,* October 1949, 10. Quoted in Lewy, *Peace and Revolution,* 19.
47. Lewy, *Peace and Revolution,* 20.
48. In James Finn, ed., *Protest: Pacifism and Politics* (New York: Random House, 1967), 200–201.
49. Kenneth Boulding to author, 26 August 1991.
50. Kenneth Boulding, "A Bibliographical Autobiography," *Banca Nazionale del Lavoro Quarterly Review* 171 (December 1989): 368.
51. Cynthia Kerman, *Creative Tension: The Life and Thought of Kenneth Boulding* (Ann Arbor: University of Michigan Press, 1974), especially Chapter Six.
52. Ibid., 114, 301.
53. Ibid., 130.
54. Ibid., 129.
55. Boulding to author, 26 August 1991.
56. Kerman, *Creative Tension,* 292.
57. T. W. Adorno, E. Frenkel-Brunswik, D. J. Levinson, and R. N. Sanford, *The Authoritarian Personality* (New York: Harper & Row, 1950).
58. Kenneth Boulding, *Three Faces of Power* (Newbury Park, Calif.: SAGE, 1990), 12.
59. Vivian Wilson, *Bibliography of Published Works by Kenneth Boulding* (Boulder, Colo.: Colorado Associated University Press, 1985), iv.
60. Kenneth Boulding, "A Pacifist View of History," *Fellowship,* March 1939, 11.
61. Ibid., 119.
62. Ibid.
63. American Friends Service Committee, *Speak Truth to Power* (Philadelphia: AFSC, 1955), iv.
64. Kenneth Boulding, *The Meaning of the Twentieth Century* (New York: Harper & Row, 1964), 161–62. *See* Chapter Two of this book.
65. Lewy, *Peace and Revolution,* 55.
66. *See* references in Lewy, *Peace and Revolution,* and Jack Powelson, *Facing Social Revolution* and *Dialogue with Friends* (Boulder, Colo.: Horizon Society Publications, 1987 and 1988).
67. Lewy, *Peace and Revolution,* 118–19.
68. *Fellowship,* September 1973, 2, 23. Quoted in Lewy, *Peace and Revolution,* 136–37.
69. Joan Baez, *And a Voice to Sing With* (New York: New American Library, 1987), 273–81.

70. Open letter, *New York Times*, 30 May 1979.

71. Lewy, *Peace and Revolution*, 138–40. Robert Lindsey, "Peace Activists Attack Vietnam on Rights," *New York Times*, 1 June 1979, sec. A, 8.

72. Baez, *And a Voice to Sing With*, 276.

73. *New York Times*, 24 June 1979.

74. Baez, *And a Voice to Sing With*, 281.

75. Richard and Margaret Braungart, "Political Career Patterns of Radical Activists in the 1960s and 1970s: Some Historical Comparisons," *Sociological Focus* 13 (1980): 247.

76. Amnesty International, *Iraq/Occupied Kuwait: Human Rights Violations Since August 2, 1990* (New York: Amnesty International USA, 1990). Jean Sasson, *The Rape of Kuwait* (New York: Knightsbridge, 1991), 67–68.

77. Michael Walzer, "Perplexed," *New Republic*, 28 January 1991, 14.

78. Jane Gross, "The Vietnam Generation Surveys Its Certainty," *New York Times*, 15 January 1991.

79. Tony Horwitz, *Wall Street Journal*, 6 November 1990. Subsequent quotes from this story.

80. Dan Beam, "A Peace Camp Sprouts on Front Line," *Philadelphia Inquirer*, 30 December 1990, quote from Tamara Smith of Missoula, Montana.

81. Interview with Agnes Bauerlein in Moorestown, N.J., 4 March 1991.

82. Recorded from a Cable News Network broadcast as translated by CNN.

83. *See*, for example, Noam Chomsky, "U.S. Gulf Policy," *Open Magazine Pamphlet Series* (Westfield N.J., 1991).

84. John Judis, "How the Peace Movement Missed the Boat on the Persian Gulf," *In These Times*, 27 February 1991, 3.

85. Monica Moorhead, quoted in Joel Bliefuss, "The First Stone," *In These Times*, 16 December 1990.

86. Marcel Boisot, "Esquisse d'une Psychologie du Pacifisme," *Defense Nationale*, 39 (November 1983): 63–74.

87. Hentoff, *Peace Agitator* (see n. 31), 193–96.

88. Richard Gregg, *The Power of Nonviolence* (New York: Schocken Books, 1966), 83.

89. Sigmund Freud, "Why War?" in *War*, ed. Leon Bramson and George Goethals (New York: Basic Books, 1974), 79.

Chapter 9. Protestors and Authoritarians: Trotsky and Stalin

1. Walter Laqueur, *Stalin: The Glasnost Revelations* (New York: Scribner's, 1990).

2. Leon Trotsky, *My Life* (New York: Pathfinder Press, 1954). Philip Pomper, *Lenin, Trotsky and Stalin: The Intelligentsia and Power* (New York: Columbia University Press, 1989). Victor Wolfenstein, *The Revolutionary Personality* (Princeton: Princeton University Press, 1971).

3. Trotsky, *My Life*, 17.

4. Max Eastman, *Leon Trotsky* (1925; reprint, New York: AMS Press, 1978), 2.

5. Isaac Deutscher, *The Prophet Armed* (New York: Oxford University Press, 1955), 22–23.

6. Pomper, *Lenin, Trotsky and Stalin*, 400.

7. Max Eastman, *Marxism: Is It Science?* (New York: Norton, 1940), 281.

8. Ibid.

9. Leon Trotsky, *History of the Russian Revolution* (New York: Simon and Shuster, 1937).

10. Cited in Max Eastman, *Reflections on the Failure of Socialism* (New York: Grossett & Dunlap, 1955), 39.

11. Trotsky, *My Life,* 582.

12. Pomper, *Lenin, Trotsky and Stalin.* Robert Tucker, *Stalin as Revolutionary* (New York: Norton, 1973). Daniel Rancour-Lafferiere, *The Mind of Stalin* (Ann Arbor, Mich.: Ardis, 1988).

13. Quoted by Tucker, *Stalin as Revolutionary,* 73, from Iremaschwili, *Stalin und die Tragôdie Georgiens* (Berlin: Verfasser, 1932), 12.

14. Jerrold Post, "Rewarding Fire with Fire: Effects of Retaliation on Terrorist Group Dynamics," *Terrorism* 10 (1987): 23–36.

15. Walter Laqueur, *Stalin: The Glasnost Revelations* (New York: Scribner's, 1990), 245.

16. Milovan Djilas, *Parts of a Lifetime* (New York: Harcourt, Brace, Jovanovich, 1975), 303.

17. Rancour-Lafferiere, *The Mind of Stalin.*

18. Laqueur, *Stalin,* 207.

19. Rancour-Lafferiere, *The Mind of Stalin,* 112.

20. T. W. Adorno, E. Frenkel-Brunswik, D. J. Levinson, and R. N. Sanford, *The Authoritarian Personality* (New York: Harper & Row, 1950).

21. Leon Trotsky, *Their Morals and Ours* (1942, reprint, New York: Pathfinder, 1969).

22. Albert Glotzer, *Trotsky: Memoir and Critique* (Buffalo, N.Y.: Prometheus Books, 1989), 318.

23. Pomper, *Lenin, Trotsky and Stalin,* 408.

Chapter 10. The God that Failed:
Mourning the Loss of Ideological Belief

1. James Burnham and Max Shachtman, "Intellectuals in Retreat," *New International* 5 (January 1937): 4–22.

2. Ibid.

3. Alan Wald, *The New York Intellectuals* (Chapel Hill: University of North Carolina Press, 1987). George Novack and Joseph Hansen, in Leon Trotsky, *In Defense of Marxism* (New York: Pathfinder Press, 1973), vii–xxii.

4. James Burnham, "Letter of Resignation," in Leon Trotsky, *In Defense of Marxism,* 207–211.

5. Trotsky, *In Defense of Marxism* (see n. 3), 187–213.

6. *See* S. F. Kissin, *Farewell to Revolution* (New York: St. Martin's Press, 1978), 100–59, for a thorough critique of dialectical logic.

7. C. Wright Mills, *The Marxists* (New York: Dell, 1962), 130.

8. Trotsky, *In Defense of Marxism,* 84.

9. Kissin, *Farewell to Revolution,* 133–40.

10. Trotsky, *In Defense of Marxism,* 189–90.

11. Ibid., 197.

12. Ibid., 77.

13. Ibid., 198.

14. Ibid., 207.

15. Ibid., 210.

16. Ibid.

17. It was alleged that Burnham plagiarized this book from the Italian Trotskyist, anti-Semitic, pro-fascist author Bruno Rizzi. However, it seems more accurate to say that both were part of an ongoing debate with Trotsky and reached similar conclusions on some (but not all) issues. *See* Adam Westoby's introduction to Bruno Rizzi, *The Bureaucratization of the World* (London: Tavistock, 1985).

18. Richard Crossman, ed., *The God that Failed* (New York: Harper, 1945).

19. Arthur Koestler, *Arrow in the Blue: An Autobiography* (New York: MacMillan, 1952) and *The Invisible Writing* (New York: Macmillan, 1954). Max Eastman, *Love and Revolution* (New York: Random House, 1964).

20. Howard Fast, *Being Red: A Memoir* (Boston: Houghton Mifflin, 1990).

21. Louis Budenz, *This Is My Story* (New York: McGraw Hill, 1947). Whittaker Chambers, *Witness* (New York: Random House, 1952).

22. Milovan Djilas, *Parts of a Lifetime* (New York: Harcourt, Brace, Jovanovich, 1975).

23. Dorothy Healey and Maurice Isserman, *Dorothy Healey Remembers* (New York: Oxford University Press, 1990).

24. Budenz, *This Is My Story,* 167.

25. Paul Hollander, *Political Pilgrims* (New York: Oxford University Press, 1981).

26. Healey and Isserman, *Dorothy Healey Remembers,* 26, 33.

27. Eugene Lyons, "To Tell or Not to Tell," *Harper's Monthly Magazine* 171 (June 1935): 98.

28. Eugene Lyons, *Assignment in Utopia* (New York: Harcourt, Brace and Company, 1937), 132.

29. Ibid., 291.

30. Ibid., 292.

31. Ibid., 631.

32. Lyons, "To Tell or Not to Tell."

33. Eastman, *Love and Revolution,* (see n. 19), 624.

34. Ibid., 631.

35. Daniel Bell, "First Love and Early Sorrows," *Partisan Review* 48 (1981): 533–34.

36. Arthur Koestler in *The God that Failed,* ed. Crossman (see n. 18), 72–73.

37. Chambers, *Witness* (see n. 21), 14.

38. Milovan Djilas, *Conversations with Stalin* (New York: Harcourt, Brace, World, 1962), 110.

39. Louis Fisher in *The God That Failed,* ed. Crossman (see n. 18), 221. Healey and Isserman, *Dorothy Healey Remembers,* 235.

40. Fisher in *The God That Failed,* 204.

41. Budenz, *This Is My Story,* 85.

42. Healey and Isserman, *Dorothy Healey Remembers,* 62.

43. Paul Lyons, *Philadelphia Communists: 1936–1956* (Philadelphia: Temple University Press, 1982).

44. Al Silverman, interview with author, January 9, 1990. Silverman is one of the men interviewed by Lyons.

45. Healey and Isserman, *Dorothy Healey Remembers,* 150, 235, 242. Al Richmond, *A Long View from the Left* (Boston: Houghton Mifflin, 1973).

46. Daniel Aaron, *Writers on the Left* (New York: Octagon Books, 1974), 309–310.

47. Irving Howe, *A Margin of Hope* (New York: Harcourt Brace Jovanovich, 1982), 31.

48. Budenz, *This Is My Story*, 231.

49. Ibid.

50. Koestler, *Arrow in the Blue*, 235.

51. Sidney Hook, *Out of Step* (New York: Harper & Row, 1987), 141.

52. Max Eastman, *Marxism: Is It Science?* (New York: Norton, 1940).

53. Jerry Muller, *The Other God that Failed* (Princeton, N.J.: Princeton University Press, 1987), 267.

54. Elisabeth Kübler-Ross, *On Death and Dying* (New York: Macmillan, 1969).

Chapter 11. The Sixties: Failure of a Generation?

1. Thomas Hayden, *Reunion* (New York: Random House, 1988). Todd Gitlin, *The Sixties: Years of Hope, Days of Rage* (New York: Bantam Books, 1987).

2. Students for a Democratic Society, "The Port Huron Statement," *Socialist Revolution* 93/94 (1987): 106–40, (originally published by SDS in 1962).

3. Lee Edwards, *Rebels with a Cause* (Washington, D.C.: Young Americans for Freedom, 1968).

4. Margaret Braungart and Richard Braungart, "The Life-course Development of Left- and Right-Wing Youth Activist Leaders from the 1960s," *Political Psychology* 11 (1990): 243–82.

5. Ibid. Jack Whalen and Richard Flacks, *Beyond the Barricades* (Philadelphia: Temple University Press, 1989). James Roberts, *The Conservative Decade* (Westport, Conn.: Arlington House, 1980).

6. Richard Flacks, "The Liberated Generation: An Exploration of the Roots of Student Unrest," *Journal of Social Issues* 23 (1967): 35–61. Charles Hampden-Turner, *Radical Man* (New York: Doubleday, 1971). For an overview of this literature see Ted Goertzel, *Political Society* (Chicago: Rand McNally, 1976).

7. *See* several essays in John Bunzel, ed., *Political Passages* (New York: The Free Press, 1988).

8. Lewis Feuer, *The Conflict of Generations* (New York: Basic, 1969), 467.

9. Christopher Lasch, *The Culture of Narcissism* (New York: Norton, 1978).

10. Stanley Rothman and Robert Lichter, *Roots of Radicalism: Jews, Christians and the New Left* (New York: Oxford University Press, 1982). They relied primarily on the Thematic Apperception Test.

11. Milton Mankoff and Richard Flacks, "The Changing Social Base of the American Student Movement," *Annals* 395 (May 1971): 54–67.

12. Charles Reich, *The Greening of America; How the Youth Revolution Is Trying to Make America Livable* (New York: Random House, 1970). Large portions of this best-selling book first appeared in the *New Yorker*.

13. James Miller, *Democracy Is in the Streets* (New York: Simon and Schuster, 1987), 43.

14. Hayden, *Reunion*, 74.

15. Gitlin, *The Sixties*, chapter 16.

16. Hayden, *Reunion*, 108.

17. John Bunzel, *New Force on the Left: Tom Hayden and the Campaign Against Corporate America* (Stanford, Calif.: Hoover Institution Press, 1983), provides

documentation of the turns in Hayden's career.

18. Tom Hayden, *Rebellion in Newark* (New York: Vintage Books, 1967).

19. Tim Findley, "Tom Hayden: Rolling Stone Interview, Part 2," *Rolling Stone,* 9 November 1972, 29.

20. Tom Krotkin, "Tom Hayden's Manifest Destiny," *Esquire,* May 1980, 44.

21. Miller, *Democracy Is in the Streets,* 54.

22. Tom Hayden, *The American Future* (Boston: South End Press, 1980).

23. Quoted by Bunzel, *Political Passages,* 45, from John Judis, "Sometimes a Great Notion," *In These Times,* 9 May 1979, 14, and Justin Raimondo, "Inside the CED," *Reason,* February 1982, 19.

24. Some friends deny that he could have killed himself, but the coroner's reports seem conclusive. *See* the *New York Times* and *Philadelphia Inquirer* of 19 April 1989. *Also see* obituaries in the *Inquirer* on April 13 and the *Times* on April 14.

25. Abbie Hoffman, *Soon to be a Major Motion Picture* (New York: Perigree, 1980), 294.

26. *See,* for example, Matthew Wald, "Hoffman: A Radical for All Ages," *New York Times,* 1 February 1987.

27. Ibid., 5.

28. Ibid., 47.

29. Ibid., 102.

30. Gitlin, *The Sixties,* 233.

31. Large parts of it are reprinted in *The Best of Abbie Hoffman,* ed. Daniel Simon (New York: Four Walls Eight Windows, 1989).

32. Hoffman, *Soon to Be a Major Motion Picture,* 278.

33. *See* Simon, *The Best of Abbie Hoffman* (see n. 31), chapter 53.

34. Hoffman, *Soon to Be a Major Motion Picture,* 270.

35. Norman Mailer in Hoffman, *Soon to Be a Major Motion Picture,* xiv.

36. Jerry Rubin, *Growing (UP) at Thirty-Seven* (New York: M. Evans, 1976).

37. Ibid., 39, 20.

38. Ibid., 98.

39. Douglas Martin, "Jerry Rubin is 50 (Yes, 50) Years Old," *New York Times,* 16 July 1988.

40. Miller, *Democracy Is in the Streets.* Gitlin, *The Sixties.* Michael Harrington, *Fragments of the Century* (New York: Saturday Review, 1973).

41. Miller, *Democracy Is in the Streets,* 115.

42. Ibid.

43. Michael Harrington, *Socialism: Past and Future* (New York: Arcade, 1989).

44. Michael Harrington, *Fragments of the Century* (New York: Saturday Review, 1973), 17.

45. Ibid., 3.

46. Ibid.

47. Ibid., 62.

48. Ibid., 179.

49. Ibid., 169–70.

50. Michael Harrington, *The Politics at God's Funeral* (New York: Holt, Rinehart and Winston, 1983), 210.

51. Philip Agee, *Inside the Company: CIA Diary* (New York: Stonehill, 1975), 34.

52. Ibid., 8.

53. Philip Agee, *On the Run* (Secaucus, N.J.: Lyle Stuart, 1987), 11.

54. Agee, *Inside the Company,* 504.
55. Agee, *On the Run,* 32.
56. David Horowitz, interview on WWDB talk radio, Philadelphia: 17 April 1989.
57. Agee, *On the Run,* 44.
58. Ibid., 251.
59. Ibid., 371.
60. Ralph McGhee, *Deadly Deceits* (New York: Sheridan Square, 1983), 147.
61. John Stockwell, *In Search of Enemies* (New York: Norton, 1978), 254.
62. Victor Marchetti and John Marks, *The CIA and the Cult of Intelligence* (New York: Knopf, 1974), xii.
63. Norman Podhoretz, *Making It* (New York: Random House, 1967).
64. Norman Podhoretz, *Breaking Ranks: A Political Memoir* (New York: Harper & Row, 1979), 302–303.
65. Podhoretz, *Making It,* 67, 14, 300, 146.
66. Ibid., 291.
67. Henri Ellenberger, "La Malade Créatrice," *Dialogue: Canadian Philosophical Review* 3 (1964): 25–41. Henri Ellenberger, *The Discovery of the Unconscious* (New York: Basic Books, 1970).
68. Richard Braungart and Margaret Braungart, "Political Career Patterns of Radical Activists in the 1960s and 1970s: Some Historical Comparisons," *Sociological Focus* 13 (1980): 245.
69. Peter Collier and David Horowitz, *Destructive Generation* (New York: Summit Books, 1989), 262.
70. Eldridge Cleaver, *Soul on Ice* (New York: McGraw Hill, 1968). Eldridge Cleaver, *Soul on Fire* (Waco, Tex.: Word Books, 1978).
71. Cleaver, *Soul on Fire,* 105.
72. Ibid., 211.
73. Ibid., 231–32.
74. Letter by George Sargent 3d, *New York Times Magazine,* 13 August 1989.
75. Letter by Michael Klare, *New York Times Magazine,* 13 August 1989.
76. Peter Collier, "Looking Backward: Memories of the Sixties Left," and David Horowitz, "Letter to a Political Friend: On Being Totalitarian in America," in *Political Passages,* ed. John Bunzel (New York: The Free Press, 1988).
77. Horowitz, interview on WWDB talk radio.
78. Peter Collier and David Horowitz, "Lefties for Reagan," *Washington Post Magazine,* 17 March 1985.
79. Sharon Churcher, "Radical Transformations," *New York Times Magazine,* 16 July 1989.
80. Peter Collier and David Horowitz, *Destructive Generation* (New York: Summit Books, 1989). Peter Collier and David Horowitz, *Second Thoughts: Former Radicals Look Back at the Sixties* (Lanham, Md.: Madison Books, 1989). *See* Gitlin, *The Sixties,* and Hayden, *Reunion.*
81. Collier and Horowitz, *Destructive Generation,* 338.
82. James Boyd, "From Far Right to Far Left—and Farther—with Karl Hess," *New York Times Magazine,* 6 December 1970, 154.
83. Jerome Tuccille, *It Usually Begins with Ayn Rand* (San Francisco: Cobden Press, 1984).
84. Ibid., 156.
85. Ibid.

86. Ibid., 81.
87. Ibid., 86.
88. Karl Hess, "The Death of Politics," *Playboy,* 17 March 1969, 103.
89. Karl Hess, "In Defense of Hess," *New Guard,* 9 April 1969, 15–16.
90. Ibid.
91. Murray Rothbard, "Why Paleo?" *Rothbard-Rockwell Report,* May 1990.
92. Jack Whalen and Richard Flacks, *Beyond the Barricades* (Philadelphia: Temple University Press, 1989).
93. Ibid., 68, 69.
94. Ralph Turner and Lewis Killian, *Collective Behavior* (Englewood Cliffs, N.J.: Prentice-Hall, 1987).
95. A student quoted in Whalen and Flacks, *Beyond the Barricades,* 116.
96. Ibid., 247.
97. Richard Braungart and Margaret Braungart, "Life Course and Generational Politics," *Annual Review of Sociology* 12 (1986): 205–231.

Chapter 12. Feminists and Antifeminists

1. David Bouchier, *The Feminist Challenge* (New York: Schocken, 1984), 155–56.
2. David Bouchier, "The Sociologist as Anti-Partisan: A Dilemma of Knowledge and Academic Power," in *Research in Social Movements, Conflicts and Change,* vol. 9, ed. Kurt Lang and Gladys Engel (Greenwich, Conn.: Jai Press, 1986), 11–12.
3. Ted Goertzel, "The Gender-Gap: Sex, Family Income and Political Opinions in the Early 1980s," *Journal of Political and Military Sociology* 11 (1983): 209–22.
4. Alison Jaggar, "Political Philosophies of Women's Liberation," in *Feminism and Philosophy,* ed. Mary Vetterling-Braggin (Totowa, N.J.: Littlefield, Adams, 1977), 5. Jagger distinguishes between Marxist and socialist feminists, but these are close enough to be combined for our purposes.
5. Ibid., 13. *Also see* Alice Echols, *Daring to be Bad: Radical Feminism in America, 1967–1975,* (Minneapolis: University of Minnesota Press, 1989).
6. Milton Meltzer, *Betty Friedan* (New York: Viking Kestrel, 1985), 2. As of this writing, there are no adult biographies of Friedan, but this children's biography gives the basic facts about her childhood.
7. Ibid.
8. Betty Friedan, *It Changed My Life* (New York: Random House, 1976), 7.
9. Ibid., 18.
10. Meltzer, *Betty Friedan,* 44.
11. Friedan, *It Changed My Life,* 58.
12. *See* Jo Freeman, *The Politics of Women's Liberation* (New York: David McKay, 1975), for the history of NOW and the feminist movement.
13. Friedan, *It Changed My Life,* 317–28.
14. Myra Marx Ferree and Beth Hess, *Controversy and Coalition: The New Feminist Movement* (Boston: Twayne, 1985). Freeman, *The Politics of Women's Liberation.* Sara Evans, *Personal Politics* (New York: Vintage, 1980).
15. Feree and Hess, *Controversy and Coalition,* 65.
16. Valerie Solanis, "Excerpts from the SCUM (Society for Cutting Up Men) Manifesto," in *Sisterhood Is Powerful,* ed. Robin Morgan (New York: Random House, 1970), 514–19.

17. Maurice Girodias, "Publisher's Preface" to Valerie Solanas, *SCUM Manifesto* (New York: Olympia, 1968), xi.

18. John Leonard, "The Return of Andy Warhol," *New York Times Magazine*, 10 November 1968, 32.

19. Marylin Bender, "Valeria Solanis a Heroine to Feminists," *New York Times*, 14 June 1968, 52. (Her first name is sometimes reported as Valeria, her last name as Solanas.)

20. Ti-Grace Atkinson, *Amazon Odyssey* (New York: Links Books, 1974), 107.

21. Vivian Gornick, in Solanas, *SCUM Manifesto*, xv.

22. Leonard, "The Return of Andy Warhol."

23. Andy Warhol, *POPism: The Warhol '60s* (New York: Harper & Row, 1980), 271.

24. Girodias, in *SCUM Manifesto*, x.

25. Warhol, *POPism*, 286.

26. Friedan, *It Changed My Life*, 109.

27. Freeman, *The Politics of Women's Liberation*, 99.

28. Kate Millett, *Sexual Politics* (Garden City, N.Y.: Doubleday, 1970). Germaine Greer, *The Female Eunuch* (New York: McGraw Hill, 1970). *See* Nicholas Davidson, *The Failure of Feminism* (Buffalo, N.Y.: Prometheus Books, 1988), for an excellent critique of these works and of feminism in general.

29. Davidson, *The Failure of Feminism* (see n. 27), 18.

30. Kate Millett, *Flying* (New York: Knopf, 1974). Kate Millett, *The Loony-Bin Trip* (New York: Simon and Schuster, 1990).

31. Millett, *Sexual Politics*, 126–27.

32. Ibid., 55–56. These conclusions are buttressed by citations to sociological studies. Millett, however, exaggerates the findings.

33. Ibid., 57.

34. David Plante, *Difficult Women* (New York: Atheneum, 1983), 164.

35. Greer, *The Female Eunuch*, 315.

36. Ibid., 317.

37. Ibid., 245, 247.

38. Davidson, *The Failure of Feminism*, 28, selected from Greer, *The Female Eunuch*, 1972 Bantam Books edition, 65, 74, 108, 148, 208, 303, 336.

39. Germaine Greer, *Daddy We Hardly Knew You* (New York: Knopf, 1990), 12, 113, 21, 110, 2.

40. Ibid., 12.

41. Greer, *The Female Eunuch*, 286–87.

42. Plante, *Difficult Women*, 160.

43. She relied primarily on Eleanor Maccoby, *The Development of Sex Differences* (Stanford, Calif.: Stanford University Press, 1966). *Also see* Maccoby's *The Psychology of Sex Differences* (Stanford, Calif.: Stanford University Press, 1974).

44. A point made by Davidson, *The Failure of Feminism*, 22, on the basis of her earlier books.

45. Greer, *The Female Eunuch*, 256.

46. Kate Millett, *The Loony-Bin Trip* (see n. 29), 127.

47. Sondra Henry and Emily Taitz, *One Woman's Power* (Minneapolis: Dillon, 1987). Gloria Steinem, *Outrageous Acts and Everyday Rebellions* (New York: Holt, Reinhart and Winston, 1983).

48. Steinem, *Outrageous Acts and Everyday Rebellions* (see n. 46), 133.

49. Reprinted in ibid., 29–69.

50. Leonard Levitt, "She," *Esquire,* October 1971, 87–89.

51. Sonia Johnson, *From Housewife to Heretic* (Garden City, N.Y.: Doubleday, 1981), 185–86.

52. Ibid., 211.

53. Ibid., 286.

54. Ibid., 355.

55. Germaine Greer, *The Mad Woman's Underclothes: Essays & Occasional Writings* (New York: Atlantic Monthly Press, 1986), 37. Reprinted from *Female Energy Oz,* May 1970.

56. Freeman, *The Politics of Women's Liberation,* 99.

57. Anne Koedt, "Lesbianism and Feminism," *Women: A Journal of Liberation,* 3 (1972): 33.

58. Friedan, *It Changed My Life,* 309.

59. Midge Decter, *The New Chastity and Other Arguments Against Women's Liberation* (New York: Coward, McCann & Geoghegan, 1972).

60. Joan Didion, "The Women's Movement," *New York Times Book Review,* 30 July 1973, 2. Reprinted in Didion's *The White Album* (New York: Simon & Shuster, 1979).

61. Ibid.

62. Joan Didion, "San Francisco Job Hunt," *Mademoiselle,* September 1960, 128–29. *See* Katherine Usher Henderson, *Joan Didion* (New York: Unger, 1981), 129–31, and Mark Royden Winchell, *Joan Didion* (Boston: Twayne, 1989).

63. Joan Didion, *The White Album* (New York: Simon and Shuster, 1979), 14. *See* Henderson, *Joan Didion* (see n. 62), chapter 6.

64. Joan Didion, "On Self Respect," in *Slouching Toward Bethlehem* (New York: Farrar, Straus & Giroux, 1968).

65. Didion, *The White Album,* 14.

66. Ibid., 109.

67. Friedan, *It Changed My Life,* part V.

68. Ibid., 378.

69. Ferree and Hess, *Controversy and Coalition,* 55.

70. Friedan, *It Changed My Life,* section V.

71. Efraim Karsh and Inari Rautsi, *Saddam Hussein: A Political Biography* (New York: The Free Press, 1991), 94. Citing *Guardian* (London), 19 April 1990.

72. Beth Corbin, Jennifer Goldberg, and Sarah Springer, "NOW Critical of Bush's Middle East Meddling," *National NOW Times,* March/April 1991, 1, 2, 17.

73. Renee Kaufman, "Patriarchal Women: A Case Study of Newly Orthodox Jewish Women," paper presented at the 1989 meetings of the Eastern Sociological Society.

74. Ferree and Hess, *Controversy and Coalition,* 138.

75. Carol Felsenthal, *The Sweetheart of the Silent Majority: The Biography of Phyllis Schlafly* (Garden City, N.Y.: Doubleday, 1981), 10.

76. Phyllis Schlafly, *The Power of the Positive Woman* (New Rochelle, N.Y.: Arlington House, 1977), 50.

77. Felsenthal, *The Sweetheart of the Silent Majority,* 83.

78. Schlafly, *The Power of the Positive Woman,* 11.

79. Ibid., 18.

80. Felsenthal, *The Sweetheart of the Silent Majority,* 87.

81. Ibid., 203–204.

82. Phyllis Schlafly and Chester Ward, *Kissinger on the Couch* (New Rochelle, N.Y.: Arlington House, 1975).

83. Quoted in Felsenthal, *The Sweetheart of the Silent Majority*, 224.

84. Phyllis Schlafly, *A Choice Not an Echo* (Alton, Ill.: Pere Marquette Press, 1964), 80.

85. Felsenthal, *The Sweetheart of the Silent Majority*, 240.

86. Ibid., 290.

87. Friedan, *It Changed My Life*, 374.

88. Atkinson, *Amazon Odyssey*, 43, 86.

89. Ibid., 90.

90. *See* Davidson, *The Failure of Feminism*, for a discussion of feminist attacks on pornography.

91. Anita Bryant, *The Anita Bryant Story* (Old Tappan, N.J.: Revell, 1977), 61.

92. William Gaboury, "Human Rights and Social Justice in Cuba," in *Ideology and Independence in the Americas*, ed. April Knutson (Minneapolis: MEP Publications, 1989), 205–208.

93. William Henry, "Upside Down in the Groves of Academe," *Time*, 1 April 1991, 66–68.

94. Philip Weiss, "The Second Revolution: Sexual Politics on Campus," *Harpers*, April 1991, 58–72.

95. David Bryden, "It Ain't What They Teach, It's the Way That They Teach It," *Public Interest*, 103 (Spring 1991): 38–53.

96. Peggy Sanday, *Fraternity Gang Rape* (New York: New York University Press, 1990).

97. *See* Davidson, *The Failure of Feminism*, for a discussion of these issues.

98. Neil Gilbert, "The Phantom Epidemic of Sexual Assault," *Public Interest* 103 (Spring 1991): 54–65.

99. Michael Moffatt, *Coming of Age in New Jersey* (New Brunswick, N.J.: Rutgers University Press, 1989), 48–49.

100. Support for the American victory was so high that pollsters did not bother breaking it down by gender. A *Times* poll on February 24, 1991, found only 19 percent believing the United States should have waited longer to see if bombing worked before beginning the ground war (Michael Kagay, "Public Shows Support for Land War," *New York Times*, 26 February 1991). Even if all 19 percent had been women, which was certainly not the case, they would still be a minority. Other *Times* polls showed overwhelming support for President Bush's handling of the war from all groups in the population ("America's Views of the War with Iraq: Assessing the President's Response," *New York Times*, 4 March 1991). Before the war began, most women (53 percent) preferred to wait for the embargo to work, while most men (53 percent) favored starting military action (Michael Oreskes, "Poll Finds Americans Divided on Sanctions or Force in Gulf," *New York Times*, 14 December 1990). For a British survey analysis with more detailed gender breakdowns *see* Martin Shaw and Roy Carr-Hill, "Public Opinion, Media and Violence," *Centre for Security Studies*, University of Hull, 1991.

Chapter 13. Linus Pauling: From Eminent Scientist to True Believer

1. Ted Goertzel, Mildred Goertzel, and Victor Goertzel, "Linus Pauling: The Scientist as Crusader," *Antioch Review* 38 (1980): 371–82. Anthony Serafini, *Linus Pauling: A*

Man and His Science (New York: Paragon House, 1988). This section is also based on unpublished material collected by Mildred and Victor Goertzel.

2. Ronald Deutsch, *The New Nuts Among the Berries: How Nutrition Nonsense Captured America* (Palo Alto, Calif.: Bull Publishing, 1977).

3. Rich Alexander, ed., *Structural Chemistry and Molecular Medicine* (San Francisco: W. H. Freeman, 1968). This festschrift volume reprints Pauling's article in an appendix.

4. Eugene Garfield, "Linus Pauling: An Appreciation of a World Citizen-Scientist and Citation Laureate," *Current Contents,* 21 August 1989, 9.

5. Horace Judson, *The Eighth Day of Creation* (New York: Simon and Schuster, 1979), 156–58.

6. Ibid., 161.

7. Linus Pauling, *No More War!* (New York: Dodd Mead, 1954).

8. Linus Pauling, *Vitamin C and the Common Cold* (San Francisco: W. H. Freeman, 1970). Linus Pauling, *Vitamin C, The Common Cold, and the Flu* (San Francisco, W. H. Freeman, 1970).

9. *See* Linus Pauling, "On the Orthomolecular Environment of the Mind: Orthomolecular Theory," *American Journal of Psychiatry* 131 (1974): 1251–57.

10. Richard Wyatt, "Comments," *American Journal of Psychiatry,* 131 (1974): 1261.

11. Donald Kleen, "Comments," *American Journal of Psychiatry,* 131 (1974): 1263–64.

12. Ewan Cameron and Linus Pauling, *Cancer and Vitamin C* (Menlo Park, Calif.: Linus Pauling Institute of Science and Medicine, 1979).

13. Arthur Robinson, "Letter to the editor," *Antioch Review* 39 (1981): 385.

14. Serafini, *Linus Pauling* (see n. 1), 278. Technically, the term "stochastic" simply means the study of random processes and applies to statistical methods of all kinds. Serafini, however, uses it in Pauling's special sense as referring to "a sophisticated and educated guessing" (page 79). In the literature on medical research, Bayesian statistical approaches have been applied to the ethical problems involved in assigning patients to different treatment groups. These ethical problems do not arise in the study of vitamin C and the common cold since the disease is self-limiting and not life-threatening. In any event, none of this is relevant to the analysis of data once it has been collected. *See* Kenneth Schaffner, "Ethical Problems in Clinical Trials," *Journal of Medicine and Philosophy* 11 (1986): 297–315, and D. G. Clayton, "Ethically Optimized Designs," *British Journal of Clinical Pharmacology* 13 (1982): 469–80.

15. R. J. P. Williams, "The Political Scientist," *Nature* 342 (9 November 1989): 235–36.

16. Arthur Robinson, interview with John Grauerholz, *Economics,* 28 August 1984, cited by Serafini, *Linus Pauling,* 262.

Chapter 14. Holocaust and Genocide Revisionism:
Skepticism as Denial

1. Gill Seidel, *The Holocaust Denial: Antisemitism, Racism & the New Right* (London: Beyond the Pale Collective, 1986), 72. *Also see* Anti-Defamation League of B'nai B'rith, *Holocaust "Revisionism,"* New York, 1989.

2. Lucy Dawidowicz, "Lies About the Holocaust," *Commentary* 70 (December 1980): 37.

3. Anti-Defamation League, *Holocaust "Revisonism"* (see n. 1). Frank Tompkins, "$50,000 Offered for Proof Nazis Gassed Jews," *Spotlight,* 14 September 1979, 14–17.

4. *See* press accounts in the *New York Times, Washington Post, Philadelphia Inquirer,* and *Los Angeles Times,* 25 July 1985.

5. T. B. Spector, "IHR Settles 'Nuisance Suit,' " *Spotlight,* 5 August 1985.

6. Anti-Defamation League, *Holocaust "Revisionism."*

7. Ibid. Seidel, *The Holocaust Denial.* Nadine Fresco, "The Denial of the Dead," *Dissent* 28 (Fall 1981): 467–83 (longer version in *Les Temps Modernes,* June 1980). Pierre Vidal-Naquet, "A Paper Eichman?" *Democracy* 1 (1981): 70–96.

8. This sentence is usually attributed to Voltaire, but was first used by S. G. Tallentyre (Beatrice Hall) in paraphrasing Voltaire in *The Friends of Voltaire,* according to John Bartlett, *Familiar Quotations.*

9. Noam Chomsky, "All Denials of Free Speech Undercut a Democratic Society," *Journal of Historical Review* 7 (1986): 123–27.

10. Ino Arndt and Wolfgang Scheffler, "Organisierter Massenmord an Juden in Nationalsozialistischen Vernichtungslagern," Vierteljahrshefte für Zeitgeschichte, 24 Jahrgang, 1976, Heft 2, 105–135. For an English summary *see* Bradley F. Smith, "Two Alibies for the Inhumanities," *German Studies Review* 1 (1978): 327–34.

11. Leo Kuper, *Genocide: Its Politics and Use in the Twentieth Century* (New Haven: Yale University Press, 1981), 105–119. Richard Hovannisian, *Armenia on the Road to Independence* (Berkeley: University of California Press, 1967). Richard Hovannisian, "The Armenian Genocide and Patterns of Denial," in *The Armenian Genocide in Perspective,* ed. Hovannisian (New Brunswick: Transaction Books, 1986).

12. Heath W. Lowry, "The U.S. Congress & Adolf Hitler on the Armenians," in Assembly of Turkish American Associations, *Armenian Allegations: Myth and Reality* (Washington, D.C., 1987).

13. Hovannisian, *Armenia on the Road to Independence* (see n. 11). Kuper, *Genocide.*

14. Henry Morgenthau, *The Ambassador's Story* (Garden City, N.Y.: Doubleday, 1926), 309.

15. Ibid., 337–38.

16. Arnold Toynbee, ed., *The Treatment of Armenians in the Ottoman Empire: 1915–16,* preface by Viscount Brice (London: His Majesty's Stationery Office, 1916).

17. Ibid., 563. Quoted in Kuper, *Genocide,* 101.

18. Assembly of Turkish American Associations, *Armenian Allegations* (see n. 12), vi.

19. *New York Times* and *Washington Post,* 19 May 1985; Association of Turkish American Associations, *Armenian Allegations,* 109.

20. Stanford Shaw and Ezel Kural Shaw, *History of the Ottoman Empire and Modern Turkey* (Cambridge: Cambridge University Press, 1977), 315.

21. Ibid., 316.

22. "Forum: The Armenian Question," *International Journal of Middle East Studies,* 9 (1978): 379–400.

23. Ibid., 394, 399.

24. Kuper, *Genocide,* 115.

25. Peter Collier and David Horowitz, *Destructive Generation* (New York: Summit, 1989), 230.

26. Noam Chomsky and Edward Herman, *After the Cataclysm* (Boston: South End, 1979), 293.

27. See Jan Myrdal, *India Waits* (Madras, India: Sangam Books, 1980), discussed below.

28. Ibid., 291.

29. For example, George Hildebrand, *Cambodia: Starvation and Revolution* (New York: Monthly Review Press, 1977) and Michael Vickery, *Cambodia: 1975–1982* (Boston: South End Press, 1984). For a critique *see* Ervin Staub, *The Roots of Evil* (Cambridge: Cambridge University Press, 1989).

30. *Peacework,* April 1975, 9. Quoted in Guenter Lewy, *Peace & Revolution: The Moral Crisis of American Pacifism* (Grand Rapids, Mich.: William Eerdmans Publishing Company, 1988), 141.

31. Rufus Miles, "Hiroshima: The Strange Myth of Half a Million American Lives Saved," *International Security,* Fall 1985, 120–40.

32. G. E. M. Anscombe, "War and Murder," in *Nuclear Weapons and Christian Conscience,* ed. Anscombe, et al. (London: Merlin Press, 1965).

33. Kuper, *Genocide.* Raphael Lemkin, *Axis Rule in Occupied Europe* (Washington: Carnegie Endowment for International Peace, 1944), 78. Raphael Lemkin, "Genocide as a Crime under International Law" *American Journal of International Law* 51 (1947): 145–71. James Martin, *The Man Who Invented "Genocide"* (Torrance, Calif.: Institute for Historical Review, 1984).

34. Kuper, *Genocide,* 210.

35. Yehuda Bauer, *The Holocaust in Historical Perspective* (Seattle: University of Washington Press, 1978), 30–49. Bauer objects to the term "genocide" because it is sometimes used to refer to acts of "cultural genocide," which are short of physical extermination. As defined legally in the United Nations Convention on Genocide, the term refers to "acts committed with intent to destroy, in whole or in part, a national, ethnical, racial, or religious group." It is limited to policies aimed at physically exterminating a group and does not include attempts to suppress a group's language, religion, or culture, which are sometimes referred to as "ethnocide." It does not apply to political or sexual preference groups. As formally defined in international law, the term "genocide" applies perfectly to the Nazi policies against the Jews. *See* Kuper, *Genocide.*

36. Uriel Tal, "On the Study of the Holocaust and Genocide," *Yad Vashem Studies* 13 (1979): 7–52.

37. Seidel, *The Holocaust Denial,* 1.

38. Viktor Frankl, *Man's Search for Meaning* (Boston: Beacon, 1962), 77.

39. Bauer, "Against Mystification," 38.

40. Peter Steinfels, "Auschwitz Revisionism: An Israeli Scholar's Case," *New York Times,* 12 November 1989, sec. E, 5.

41. Bauer, "Against Mystification," 38.

42. Kuper, *Genocide,* 15.

43. David Davies, *The Last of the Tasmanians* (New York: Barnes & Noble, 1974).

44. George Brizan, *Grenada: Island of Conflict from Amerindans to People's Revolution* (London: Zed, 1984).

45. Irving Rouse, "The Arawak" and "The Carib," in *Handbook of South American Indians,* ed. Julian Steward, vol. 4 (New York: Cooper Square, 1963), 565.

46. Jalil Sued Badillo, *Los Caribes: Realidad o Fabula* (Rio Pedras, P.R.: Editora Antillana, 1978).

47. Juan Ignacio de Armas, *La Fabula de los Caribes* (Madrid, 1920), quoted by Badillo, *Los Caribes,* 3. Translated by this author.

48. Lee Drummond, "On Being Carib," in *Carib-Speaking Indians: Culture, Society & Language,* ed. Ellen Basso (Tucson: University of Arizona Press, 1977).

49. Debra Kaufman, "Gypsies Ponder Who Counts," *In These Times,* 6 June 1990, 19–20.

50. Raul Hilberg, *The Destruction of the European Jews* (New York: Holmes & Meier, 1985), vol. III, 999.

51. Frank Rector, *The Nazi Extermination of Homosexuals* (New York: Stein and Day, 1981), 123.

52. Ibid., 140, quoting a letter to *Village Voice* responding to a 10 December 1979 article.

53. Arthur Butz, *The Hoax of the Twentieth Century* (Torrance, Calif.: Institute for Historical Review, 1976), 17.

54. Paul Rassinier. *Debunking the Genocide Myth* (Torrance, Calif.: Institute for Historical Review, 1978).

55. Hilberg, *The Destruction of the European Jews,* 1,202, observes that "most of the published estimates have hovered between five and six million. . . . the numbers are extrapolated from the available, sometimes fragmentary reports of German agencies, satellite authorities, and Jewish councils, or they are refined from comparisons of prewar and postwar statistics. . . . the raw data are seldom self-explanatory. . . . their interpretation often requires the use of voluminous background materials that have to be analyzed in turn. Assumptions may therefore be piled on assumptions, and margins of error may be wider than they seem. Under these circumstances, exactness is impossible."

56. Butz, *The Hoax of the Twentieth Century,* 249.

57. Ibid., 211.

58. Ibid., 214.

59. There is one revisionist book that attempted to do this, *The Dissolution of Eastern European Jewry* by Walter Sanning (Torrance, Calif.: Institute for Historical Review, 1983). Butz contributed a preface in which he criticized the author for not being tentative enough about his conclusions. Even after all his criticisms of other population estimates, Sanning admits that several hundred thousand European Jews are unaccounted for.

60. Raymond Eve and Francis Harold, *The Creationism Movement in Modern America* (Boston: Twayne Publishers, 1991), 52.

61. Jan Myrdal, *India Waits* (Madras, India: Sangam Books, 1980), 111.

62. Ibid., quoting from Lieutenant Vivian Dering Majendie, *Up Among the Pandies,* published in 1859 (no page number or publication information given).

63. Jan Myrdal, *Confessions of a Disloyal European* (New York: Random House, 1968), 184.

64. Ibid., 184, 186.

65. Gunnar Myrdal, *An International Economy* (New York: Harper, 1956). Guenter Lewy, *Peace and Revolution* (Grand Rapids, Mich.: Eerdmans, 1988), 127.

66. See Jan Myrdal, *Report from a Chinese Village* (New York: Signet, 1966), xxxiv, fn 6. Basic Ashton, et al., "Famine in China, 1958–1961," *Population and Development Review* 10 (1984): 613–45. Edward Friedman, "Maoism and the Liberation of the Poor," *World Politics* 39 (1987): 408–28. Myrdal, *India Waits.*

67. Jan Myrdal, *Return to a Chinese Village* (New York: Pantheon, 1984), 149. K. E. Brodsgaard, "State, Party, and Economy in the Transition to Socialism in China," *Bulletin of Concerned Asian Scholars* 18 (January–March, 1986): 46–55.

68. Myrdal, *Indian Waits,* 162.

69. Bradley R. Smith, *Confessions of a Holocaust Revisionist* (Los Angeles: Prima Facie, 1987).

70. Ibid., 75.

71. Robert Faurisson, *The "Problem of the Gas Chambers"* (Costa Mesa, Calif.: Institute for Historical Review), *also* reprinted in Smith, *Confessions of a Holocaust Revisionist.*

72. Smith, *Confessions of a Holocaust Revisionist,* 68, 8.

73. Ibid., 79, 81, 82.

74. Ibid., 37, 117, 37.

75. R. E. Money-Kyrle, *Psychoanalysis and Politics* (Westport, Conn.: Greenwood Press, 1973), 92.

76. Revilo P. Oliver, *America's Decline: The Education of a Conservative* (London: Londinium Press, 1982). Emphasis in the original.

77. Anti-Defamation League, *Holocaust "Revisionism"* (see n. 1).

78. Kuper, *Genocide.*

79. Ted Goertzel, "The Ethics of Terrorism and Revolution," *Terrorism: An International Journal* 11 (1988): 1–12.

Chapter 15. Fidel Castro and the Cuban Revolution: Aging Narcissism and Unyielding Leninism

1. Peter Bourne, *Fidel: A Biography of Fidel Castro* (New York: Dodd, Mead & Co., 1986), reports the story of Angel Castro's military background as fact while Tad Szulc, *Fidel: A Critical Portrait* (New York: William Morrow, 1986), reports that while Castro has told this story on several occasions it is probably inaccurate since two of his sisters say they never heard of his military past. The story is confirmed by Georgie Anne Geyer, "Castro: The 'Knowable' Dictator," in *The Cuban Revolution at Thirty* (Washington, D.C.: Cuban American National Foundation, 1989).

2. Bourne, *Fidel: A Biography,* 17.

3. Ibid., 131, 17.

4. Ibid., 309.

5. Ibid., 56.

6. Ibid., 76.

7. Ibid., 89.

8. Luis Conte Agüero, *Fidel Castro: Psiquiatría y Política* (México: Editorial Jus, 1968), 14.

9. Szulc, *Fidel: A Critical Portrait* (see n. 1), 223.

10. Ibid., 32.

11. Ibid., 44.

12. Ibid., 92.

13. Ibid., 171.

14. Ibid., 290.

15. Norman Baynes, ed., *The Speeches of Adolph Hitler,* vol. I (New York: Howard Fertig, 1969), 87.

16. Fidel Castro, *History Will Absolve Me* (New York: Fair Play for Cuba Committee, 1961), 78–79.

17. Gene Vier, "Analyzing Fidel," *Human Behavior* 4(7): 67 (July 1977).

18. Geyer, "Castro" (see n. 1), 41. Georgie Geyer, *Guerrilla Prince: The Untold Story of Fidel Castro* (Boston: Little Brown, 1991), 42.

19. Frei Betto, *Fidel and Religion: Talks with Frei Betto* (Havana: Publications Office of the Council of State, 1987), 147.

20. Zaira Rodríguez Ugidos, "Valuation and Objectivity in *History Will Absolve Me,*" in *Ideology and Independence in the Americas,* ed. April Ane Knutson (Minneapolis: MEP

Publications, 1989).

21. Edward Gonzalez, *Cuba under Castro: The Limits of Charisma* (Boston: Houghton Mifflin Co., 1974), 146.

22. Ibid., 46, 70. Jorge Edwards, *Persona Non Grata* (London: Bodley Head, 1976).

23. Szulc, *Fidel: A Critical Portrait*, 227.

24. Gonzalez, *Cuba Under Castro*, 46.

25. James H. Billington, *Fire in the Minds of Men: Origins of the Revolutionary Faith* (New York: Basic Books, 1980), 8.

26. Castro, *History Will Absolve Me*, 49.

27. Billington, *Fire in the Minds of Men*, 9.

28. Szulc, *Fidel: A Critical Portrait*, 470.

29. Conte Agüero, *Fidel Castro*, 101.

30. Bruce Mazlish, *The Meaning of Karl Marx* (New York: Oxford University Press, 1984), analyzes Karl Marx's thinking as a "secular religion."

31. Victor Wolfenstein, *The Revolutionary Personality: Lenin, Trotsky, Gandhi* (Princeton, N.J.: Princeton University Press, 1967).

32. Bruce Mazlish, *The Revolutionary Ascetic: Evolution of a Political Type* (New York: Basic, 1976).

33. Szulc, *Fidel: A Critical Portrait*, 180.

34. Conte Agüero, *Fidel Castro*, 27.

35. Szulc, *Fidel: A Critical Portrait*, 115.

36. José Luis Llovio-Menéndez, *Insider: My Hidden Life as a Revolutionary in Cuba* (New York: Bantam, 1988), 128.

37. Szulc, *Fidel: A Critical Portrait*, 81.

38. Carlos Alberto Montaner, *Fidel Castro and the Cuban Revolution* (New Brunswick, N.J.: Transaction Publishers, 1989), 20.

39. Conte Agüero, *Fidel Castro*, 15 ("En él hay un grave miedo, el miedo a la humilliación, el miedo a sus culpas, el miedo a la propria multitud que lo endiosó; miedo incluse en esta etapa de endiosamiento.")

40. Ibid., 64. ("Castro no puede resistir una polémica. Jamás discute; monologa. No concede la oportunidad de ripostar. Sentencia, no escucha. Si alguno de sus alzacolas se atreve a hacer la menor insinuación, golpea colérico en la mesa, y profiere un montón de obscenidades.")

41. Ibid., 17 ("gusanos, lacayos, esbirros, mercenarios"); Juan Vivés, *Los Amos de Cuba* (Buenos Aires: Emecé Editores, 1982), 211–212 ("gusanos, traidores a la Patria, hijos de perra, mercenarios, prematuros, homosexuales, plaga social, gentuza").

42. Llovio-Menéndez, *Insider*, 418.

43. Edward Friedman, conversation with author.

44. Paul Watzlawick, *Münchhausen's Pigtail* (New York: W. W. Norton, 1990), 210.

45. Szulc, *Fidel: A Critical Portarit*, 40. Castro told the magazine *Bohemia*, "I confess . . . I suffer from stage fright when I speak in Revolution Square. . . . It is not at all easy for me."

46. Conte Agüero, *Fidel Castro*, 25.

47. Ibid., 22.

48. Ibid., 27–28.

49. Mazlish, *The Meaning of Karl Marx*, 23.

50. Bourne, *Fidel: A Biography*, 304.

51. Szulc, *Fidel: A Critical Portrait*, 39.

52. Llovio-Menéndez, *Insider*, 40. The word "venceremos" at the end of Fidel's

speeches is usually translated as "we shall overcome," which evokes the American civil rights movement. Llovio-Menéndez's translation is, however, consistent with Spanish-English dictionaries, which translate *vencer* as to conquer, subdue, defeat, or overpower, as well as to prevail upon, persuade, tolerate or bear with patience. Both "vanquish" and "overcome" can be translated into Spanish as "vencer."

53. Vamik Volkan, "Narcissistic Personality Organization and 'Reparative' Leadership," *International Journal of Group Psychotherapy* 30 (1980): 131–52.

54. Edward Gonzalez and David Ronfeldt, *Castro, Cuba and the World* (Santa Monica, Calif: Rand Corporation, 1986), refer to these two themes in Fidel's personality as "hubris" and "nemesis."

55. Wilfred Abse and Richard Ulman, "Charismatic Political Leadership and Collective Regression," in *Psychopathology and Political Leadership,* ed. Robert Robins (New Orleans: Tulane University Press, 1977), 35–52.

56. Llovio-Menéndez, *Insider,* 213.

57. Kevin Greene, "The World According to Granma," in *The Selling of Fidel Castro,* ed. William Ruff (New Brunswick, N.J.: Transaction Books, 1987).

58. Ibid., 41.

59. Llovio-Menéndez, *Insider,* 241.

60. Ibid., 740.

61. Ibid., 249.

62. Ibid., 250.

63. Ibid., 227.

64. Lawrence Theriot, "Cuba Faces the Realities of the 1980s," Office of East-West Policy and Planning, Commerce Department, quoted in *New York Times,* 4 April 1982.

65. Szulc, *Fidel: A Critical Portrait,* 36.

66. Sergio Diaz-Briquets, "How to Figure Out Cuba: Development, Ideology and Mortality," *Caribbean Review,* 15(2): 11 (Spring 1986).

67. For example, William Gaboury, "The Status of Human Rights and Social Justice in Cuba," in *Ideology and Independence in the Americas,* ed. April Ane Knutson (Minneapolis, MEP Publications, 1989).

68. Diaz-Briquets, "How to Figure Out Cuba," 11. For the entire period from 1900 to 1984, life expectancy rose from 33.2 to 74.2 years. The correlation of life expectancy with year for this entire period is .986, indicating a very steady year by year improvement both before and after the revolution.

69. Ibid.

70. Ibid., 8.

71. Ibid., 8.

72. Nicholas Eberstadt, "Did Fidel Fudge the Figures?" *Caribbean Review* 15(2): 6–38 (Spring 1986). Kenneth Hill, "An Evaluation of Cuban Demographic Statistics: 1938–80," in *Fertility Determinants in Cuba,* ed. Paul Hollerbach and Sergio Dias-Briquets (Washington, D.C.: National Academy Press, 1983).

73. Fidel Castro, "Speech at Closing of the First National Congress on Education and Culture," *Granma Weekly Review,* 9 May 1971.

74. Montaner, *Fidel Castro and the Cuban Revolution,* 21.

75. Edward Friedman, "Permanent Technological Revolution and China's Tortuous Path to Democratizing Leninism," in *Reform and Reaction in Post-Mao China,* ed. Richard Baum (New York: Routledge, 1991), 163.

76. Cuban American National Foundation, "Chistes: Political Humor in Cuba," (Washington, 1989).

77. Szulc, *Fidel: A Critical Portrait*, 652.

78. Armando Vallardes, *Against All Hope* (New York: Knopf, 1986).

79. Ibid., 270.

80. *Valladares, a Terrorist as U.S. Ambassador in Geneva* supplement to *Granma Weekly Review*, 6 March 1988, including a long interview with Fidel Castro, a confidential U.S. State Department document on the case, and other articles. On the basis of the best information available to it, Amnesty International officially classified Valladares as a Prisoner of Conscience, which means they were convinced he had not used or advocated violence.

81. *Granma Weekly Review*, 6 March 1988.

82. Luis Conte Agüero, *Fidel Castro: Vida y Obra* (Havana: Editorial Lex, 1959); *Los Dos Rostros de Fidel Castro* (Mexico: Editorial Jus, 1960); *Cartes del Presidio* (Havana: Editorial Lex, 1959).

83. Conte Agüero, *Fidel Castro: Psiquiatria y Política*.

84. Ibid., 13, 67, 75.

85. Lourdes Casal, "Literature and Society," in *Revolutionary Change in Cuba*, ed. Carmelo Mesa-Lago (Pittsburgh: University of Pittsburgh Press, 1971).

86. Fidel Castro, "Palabras a los Intelectuales," in *Obras Escogidas, Tomo I (1953–1962)* (Madrid: Editorial Fundamentos, 1976), 147.

87. Nicolás Guillén, "Speech Delivered at the Awarding of Prizes to Winners of the Annual Literature Contest," *Granma Weekly Review*, 7 December 1969.

88. First National Congress on Education and Culture, *Granma Weekly Review*, 9 May 1971.

89. Ibid.

90. Ibid.

91. Heberto Padilla, *Self-Portrait of the Other* (New York: Farrar, Straus & Giroux, 1990), 156.

92. Ibid., 180.

93. Ibid., 181–82.

94. Ibid., 5.

95. Heberto Padilla, "After 20 Cuban Years," *New York Times*, op-ed, 17 September 1981.

96. Llovio-Menéndez, *Insider*, 37.

97. Luciano Bivar, *Cuba Num Retrato Sem Retoques* (Rio de Janeiro: Barrister's, 1986).

98. Sandra Levinson, "Dateline Havana: The Drug Scandal," *Cuba Update*, Fall 1989, 7. Subsequent quotes from this publication.

99. Ibid., 9.

100. *Granma Weekly Review*, 16 July 1989, 4.

101. Juan Escalona Reguera, "Excerpts from the Summation," *Cuba Update*, Fall 1989, 61.

102. Llovio-Menéndez, *Insider*, 282.

103. Ibid., 292.

104. Fidel Castro, "Speech to the 3rd Congress of the Communist Party of Cuba," 2 December 1986, quoted in *Granma Weekly Review*, 14 December 1986, 8.

105. Paul Baran, *The Political Economy of Growth* (New York: Monthly Review Press, 1957). For an incisive and rigorous critique of this literature in view of recent statistical studies, *see* Bela Balassa, "Dependency and Trade Orientation," *World Economy* 8 (1986): 259–73. For more sympathetic accounts *see* Alejandro Portes and A. Douglas

410   Turncoats and True Believers

Kincaid, "Sociology and Development in the 1990s: Critical Challenges and Empirical Trends," *Sociological Forum* 4 (1989): 479–503, and Gary Gereffi, "Rethinking Development Theory: Insights from East Asia and Latin America," *Sociological Forum* 4 (1989): 505–34.

106. André Gunder Frank, *Capitalism and Underdevelopment in Latin America* (New York: Monthly Review Press, 1967) and *Latin America: Underdevelopment or Revolution* (New York: Monthly Review Press, 1970).

107. Raúl Prebish, *The Economic Development of Latin America and its Principal Problems* (Lake Success, N.Y.: United Nations Department of Economic Affairs, 1950).

108. Fidel Castro, "Speech to the 3rd Congress of the Communist Party of Cuba," 2 December 1986, English translation in *Granma Weekly Review*, 13 December 1987, 10–16. Fidel Castro, *The World Economic and Social Crisis* (Havana: Publishing Council of the Council of State, 1983), 62.

109. Irving Kravis and Robert Lipsey, "Prices and Terms of Trade for Developed Country Exports of Manufactured Goods," *The Economics of Relative Prices,* ed. Béla Csikós-Nagy (New York: St. Martin's Press, 1984). Michael Michaely, *Trade, Income Levels and Dependence* (Amsterdam: North-Holland, 1985).

110. Balassa, "Dependency and Trade Orientation" (see n. 105), 264.

111. Portes and Kincaid, "Sociology and Development in the 1900s" (see n. 105), 479, 495.

112. Manuel Castells and Roberto Laserna, "The New Dependency: Technological Change and Socioeconomic Restructuring in Latin America," *Sociological Forum* 4 (1989): 535–60.

113. *See* references in Michael Mazarr, "Prospects for Revolution in Post-Castro Cuba," *Journal of Interamerican Studies and World Affairs,* 31(4): 61–90 (1989), and C. Mesa-Lago, "Cuba's Centrally Planned Economy: An Equity Tradeoff for Growth," in *Cuban Communism*, sixth ed., ed. Irving L. Horowitz (New Brunswick, N.J.: Transaction Books, 1987). Of course, there are many difficulties in measuring economic output in Leninist economies where much of the growth may be in products of questionable quality or value. Jorge F. Pérez-López, *Measuring Cuban Economic Performance* (Austin: University of Texas Press, 1987) arrives at estimates for the Cuban economy that are about half as large as the official statistics or the estimates of Claes Brundenius, *Revolutionary Cuba: The Challenge of Growth with Equity* (Boulder, Colo.: Westview, 1984).

114. Mesa-Lago, "Cuba's Centrally Planned Economy" (see n. 113).

115. Fidel Castro, *In Defense of Socialism*, ed. Mary-Alice Waters (New York: Pathfinder, 1989).

116. Fidel Castro, "Speech Marking the 20th Anniversary of the Death of Major Ernesto Che Guevara," Pinar del Rio, Cuba, 8 October 1987; translation in *Granma Weekly Review*, English edition, 18 October 1987, 4–6.

117. Howard French, "Castro, Standing Firm Against the Tide, Is Bracing Cuba for Harder Times," *New York Times,* 26 July 1990, sec. A, 6.

118. Mimi Whitefield, "Facing Oil Troubles, Cuba Mandates Steps to Curb Use of Energy," *Philadelphia Inquirer,* 30 August 1990, 11A.

119. French, "Castro, Standing Firm Against the Tide."

120. Amnesty International USA, "Annual Report Summary 1990," 8–9.
121. Ibid.
122. Ibid.,

123. Susan Eckstein, "Crisis in Cuban Socialism—*Perestroika* Marxist Style," paper presented at the 1990 meetings of the American Sociological Association. Abstracted in

Sociological Abstracts, supplement 163, August 1990, abstract # 90S24110.

124. Ibid.

125. Llovio-Menéndez, *Insider*, 278.

126. Castro, *In Defense of Socialism.*

127. Ibid.

128. Eugene Robinson, "Castro: Let World Change, Cuba Will Stay the Course," *Washington Post*, 17 March 1990, sec. A, 21.

129. Llovio-Menéndez, *Insider*, 423.

Chapter 16. Bush and Gorbachev: Visions of the Future or a Future without Vision?

1. Gail Sheehy, *The Man Who Changed the World* (New York: HarperCollins, 1990).

2. Matthew Scully, "A Soviet Life," *National Review,* 11 February 1991, 49–50.

3. Dusko Doder and Louise Branson, *Gorbachev: Heretic in the Kremlin* (New York: Viking, 1990). Zhores Medvedev, *Gorbachev* (New York: Norton, 1986). Donald Morrison, ed., *Mikhail S. Gorbachev: An Intimate Biography* (New York: Time Books, 1988). Dev Muraka, *Gorbachev: The Limits of Power* (London: Hutchinson, 1988). Ilya Zemtsov and John Farrar, *Gorbachev: The Man and the System* (New Brunswick, N.J.: Transaction, 1989).

4. Samuel Huntington, "Will More Countries Become Democratic?" *Political Science Quarterly* 99 (1984): 217.

5. Victor Wolfenstein, *The Revolutionary Personality* (Princeton, N.J.: Princeton University Press, 1971).

6. Alexander Zinoviev, *Homo Sovieticus* (Boston: Atlantic Monthly, 1985).

7. Bruce Mazlish, *The Revolutionary Ascetic* (New York: Basic Books, 1976).

8. Zdenek Mlynar, "Il Mio Compagno di Studi Mikhail Gorbachov," *L'Unita* [Milan], 9 April 1985, 9. Summarized in Morrison, *Mikhail S. Gorbachev*, (see n. 3).

9. Morrison, *Mikhail S. Gorbachev,* (see n. 3), 65.

10. Ibid., 69.

11. S. F. Kissin, *Farewell to Revolution: Marxist Philosophy and the Modern World* (New York: St. Martin's, 1978).

12. Ibid., 217.

13. Francis Fukuyama, "The End of History?" *National Interest* 16 (1989): 12.

14. J. A. F. Stoner, "Risky and Cautious Shifts in Group Decisions: The Influence of Widely Held Values," *Journal of Experimental Social Psychology* 4 (1968): 442–59.

15. Zhores Medvedev, *Gorbachev* (New York: Norton, 1986), 246.

16. Baruch Hazan, *Gorbachev and His Enemies* (Boulder, Colo.: Westview, 1990), 83. *Also see* John Morrison, *Boris Yeltsin: From Bolshevik to Democrat* (New York: Dutton, 1991).

17. "Text of Gorbachev's Farewell Address," *New York Times,* 26 December 1991.

18. Mikhail Gorbachev, "Provide an Ideology of Renewal for Revolutionary Restructuring," *Current Digest of the Soviet Press* 60 (7): 3–18 (1988).

19. Viktor Yerofeyev, *New York Times,* 16 December 1991, sec. A, 8.

20. For an overview from a psychobiographical perspective *see* Paul Elovitz and Glen Jeansonne, "George Bush: From Wimp to President," in *Politics and Psychology*, ed. Joan Offerman-Zuckerberg (New York: Plenum, 1991), 99–116.

21. Fitzhugh Green, *George Bush: An Intimate Portrait* (New York: Hippocrene, 1989), 216.

22. Ibid., 15.

23. John Ashmun, quoted in ibid., 89.

24. Gail Sheehy, *Character: America's Search for Leadership* (New York: Morrow, 1988), 186–87.

25. Elovitz and Jeansonne, "George Bush" (see n. 19).

26. George Bush with Victor Gold, *Looking Forward: An Autobiography* (New York: Doubleday, 1987), 92–93.

27. Bob Woodward, *The Commanders* (New York: Simon & Schuster, 1991), 303, 359–60, 325.

Chapter 17. Conclusions

1. Shulamit Reinharz, *On Becoming a Social Scientist: From Survey Research and Participant Observation to Experiential Analysis* (San Francisco: Jossey-Bass, 1979). For an outstanding example of the insights that can result from this approach, *see* Larry Hirschhorn, *The Workplace Within* (Cambridge, Mass.: The MIT Press, 1988).

2. William Stone, "The Myth of Left-Wing Authoritarianism," *Political Psychology* 2 (1980): 3–19.

3. Daniel Bell, *The End of Ideology* (Glencoe, Ill.: The Free Press, 1960). Chaim Waxman, ed., *The End of Ideology Debate* (New York: Funk & Wagnalls, 1968).

4. Francis Fukuyama, "The End of History?" *National Interest* 16 (1989): 3–18.

5. Erik Olin Wright, "Explanation and Emancipation in Marxism and Feminism," paper presented at the 1990 Annual Meeting of the American Sociological Association.

6. Robert Heilbroner, "Reflections: After Communism," *New Yorker,* 10 September 1990, 91–100.

7. *See* Ted Goertzel, "Social Movements and Social Change: The Dynamics of Social Transformation" in *Critical Perspectives in Sociology,* ed. Berch Berberoglu (Dubuque, Iowa: Kendall Hunt, 1991).

Index

Bolshevism, 72-73, 74, 89; and commitment script, 87; Harry Guntrip on, 76-77; on Hitler, 74; Sidney Hook on, 75; and International War Crimes Tribunal, 75; as logician, 71; on marriage, 75-76, 87; on Margaret Mead, 155; as moral reformer, 71; pacificism of, 72, 74, 87; parents of, 72, 76, 87; *Practice and Theory of Bolshevism,* 73; *Principia Mathematica,* 76; and protest script, 72, 75, 87, 88; *Sceptical Essays,* 13; and scientific script, 87; and skeptical script, 72, 87; socialism of, 89; and survivor script, 72, 87; and utopian script, 73; on Vietnam War, 75

Sagan, Carl, 157
Saint-Simon, Henri de, 91, 93, 143
Sartre, Jean-Paul, 37
Schlafly, Phyllis, 36, 266, 267; as authoritarian, 55-56; *A Choice Not an Echo,* 287; early years of, 285-86; on feminism's weaknesses, 288-89; and Barry Goldwater, 288; *Kissinger on the Couch,* 287; and National Federation of Republican Women, 288; runs for Congress, 287
Schwarzkopf, Norman, 363
Scientology, 102
Scripts, 86-87; defined, 38; and ideological maturity, 50; ideologies as, 35, 36, 38-71; in life cycle, 48-50; left-right dichotomy outdated, 38; risks and benefits of ideological analysis, 68-71; typology of, 39-47, 64-68. *See also* Authoritarian, the; Committed, the; Dove, the; Hawk, the; Pragmatist, the; Protester, the; Skeptic, the; Survivor, the; Utopian-Dystopian, the

SDS. *See* Students for a Democratic Society
Seale, Bobby, 257, 258
Selma to Montgomery civil rights march, 24
Shachtman, Max, 224, 227, 248
Shaw, Ezel, 309
Shaw, Stanford, 309
Shearer, Derek, 244
Sheehy, Gail, 352-53, 362, 363
Shils, Edward, 51
Silone, Ignazio, 230
Sinclair, Upton, 227
Silverman, Al, 234
Skeptic, The, as "anti-ideological," 66; defined, 40, 47; examples given, 40; and Protesters, 46; Peter Rossi on, 46; and Utopians, 46. *See also* Auguste Comte, Max Eastman, Jeffrey Masson, John Stuart Mill, Bertrand Russell, Revisionism
skepticism, misuses of, 67, as denial, 305-325
Smith, Bradley R., 321-23; *Confessions of a Holocaust Revisionist,* 321; and feelings of persecution, 323; and populist anti-elitism, 322
Smith, George, 68, 143
Smith, Gibbs M., 126
Social Democratic Federation, 160
Socialism, 58; redefined by Sidney Hook, 58; socialism today, 161-62; Swedish model, 162. *See also* The Protestor
Socialist Party, 22
Socialist Workers' Party, 225-26